PRAISE FOR BA.

Do not be deceived: *Baptized in the Spirit* is not mere Pentecostal Theology; rather it is a creative rearticulation of Christian systematic theology illuminated from the perspective of the central experience and distinctive doctrine of Pentecostalism. Macchia sheds new light on all aspects of the traditional theological loci, including theological anthropology, soteriology, and eschatology, as well as on difficult ecumenical topics like ecclesiology, the sacraments, and the role of the papacy! *Baptized in the Spirit* signals the maturation of Pentecostalism wherein it takes Pentecostal theological reflection to the next level precisely by renewing and advancing the wider theological conversation.

—Amos Yong, Ph.D.
Associate Research Professor of Theology
Regent University School of Divinity

Baptized in the Spirit is an extraordinary work. I expect the book quickly to become a standard for understanding global Pentecostal identity. At the same time it is opening up exciting new avenues for ecumenical reflection on the Holy Spirit, the church, and Christian life in the world today. Through the lens of Spirit baptism, Macchia has shown the way beyond a number of theological impasses, enriching the multitude of Christian traditions while pointing us toward the God who overflows with life and love in the Spirit.

—Dale T. Irvin
Acting President and Professor of World Christianity
New York Theological Seminary

Current trends in Pentecostal studies have tended to marginalize the Pentecostal doctrine of Spirit baptism. Frank Macchia, however, contends that Spirit baptism should be the unifying center, the "crown jewel" of Pentecostal theology. Macchia shows how the metaphor functions as the lens through which we gain deeper insights into various theological themes unified around the concept of the kingdom of God, of which the Spirit is the substance. What Macchia has achieved is a theology worthy of the name Pentecostal!

—Simon Chan
Trinity Theological College

Baptized in the Spirit is a fascinating book of outstanding importance. It is rich and rewarding in its efforts to use an increasingly neglected metaphor of Spirit baptism as the organizing principle in theological discourse that provides a broad pneumatology within which to integrate Pentecostal missiological/charismatic concerns.

Dr. Macchia has masterfully used the biblical text to find an expansive use for this metaphor that is eschatological, ecclesiological, charismatic, missiological, and at the same time open to a global diversity of voices.

The author's deep insight in eschatology still allows for a sound ecclesiology in the process; thus, his novel definition of Spirit baptism in the context of interpersonal *koinonia* is extremely useful in healing some fractures within Classical Pentecostalism.

Frank Macchi not only endeavors to reinstate the Pentecostal doctrine of Spirit baptism to its central place as "the crown of Pentecostal distinctiveness," but also helps to further the understanding of the doctrine as central to Christian orthodoxy in general. This masterpiece is a must for every student of theology, particularly those who have global and ecumenical concerns.

—Dr. Cephas N. Omenyo
Department for the Study of Religions
University of Ghana, Legon, West Africa

BAPTIZED
IN THE
Spirit

BAPTIZED

IN THE *Spirit*

A GLOBAL PENTECOSTAL THEOLOGY

Frank D. MACCHIA

ZONDERVAN™

GRAND RAPIDS, MICHIGAN 49530 USA

ZONDERVAN.COM/
AUTHOR**TRACKER**

ZONDERVAN™

Baptized in the Spirit
Copyright © 2006 by Frank Macchia

Requests for information should be addressed to:

Zondervan, *Grand Rapids, Michigan 49530*

Library of Congress Cataloging-in-Publication Data
   Macchia, Frank D.
      Baptized in the Spirit : a global Pentecostal theology / Frank D. Macchia.
         p. cm.
      Includes bibliographical references and indexes.
      ISBN-13: 978-0-310-25236-8
      ISBN-10: 0-310-25236-9
      1. Baptism in the Holy Spirit. 2. Holy Spirit. 3. Pentecostal churches—Doctrines.
   I. Title.
   BT123.M151 2006
   230'.994—dc22   2005031945

This edition printed on acid-free paper.

Interior design by Nancy Wilson

Printed in the United States of America

For Verena, the love of my life

As to a clarification of my relationship to Schleiermacher, what I have occasionally contemplated for here and now ... would be the possibility of a theology of the third article, in other words, a theology predominantly and decisively of the Holy Spirit. Everything which needs to be said, considered and believed about God the Father and God the Son in an understanding of the first and second articles might be shown and illuminated in its foundations through God the Holy Spirit.

Karl Barth,
*Concluding Unscientific Postscript
on Schleiermacher*

CONTENTS

Acknowledgments   9

1   INTRODUCTION:
    FRAMING THE ISSUE 11

2   SPIRIT BAPTISM AND PENTECOSTAL THEOLOGY:
    RETURNING TO OUR CENTRAL DISTINCTIVE 19

       Is Spirit Baptism the Central Pentecostal Distinctive?   20
       From Sanctification to Spirit Baptism: Early Fragmentation   28
       Spirit Baptism and Doctrinal Diversity: The Developing
         Challenge   33
       From Spirit Baptism to Eschatology: Towards Coherence   38
       From Spirit Baptism to Oral Theology: The Challenge
         of Theological Method   49
       Postscript: The Unfinished Business of Pentecostal Theology   57

3   THE KINGDOM AND THE POWER:
    EXPANDING THE BOUNDARIES OF SPIRIT BAPTISM 61

       Spirit Baptism and Regeneration   64
       Spirit Baptism and Water Baptism   72
       Spirit Baptism and Empowerment   75
       Eschatological Framework   85

4   CHRIST AS THE KING AND THE SPIRIT AS THE KINGDOM:
    SPIRIT BAPTISM IN TRINITARIAN PERSPECTIVE 89

       The Pentecost-Kingdom Connection   91
       Spirit Baptism and the Church's Faith in Jesus 107
       Spirit Baptism as a Trinitarian Act 113
       Spirit Baptism and Elements of Life in the Kingdom 129
         - Spirit-Baptized Justification 129
         - Spirit-Baptized Sanctification 140
         - Spirit-Baptized Witness 145
       In Sum 153

5   SIGNS OF GRACE IN A GRACELESS WORLD:
    TOWARD A SPIRIT-BAPTIZED ECCLESIOLOGY 155
        Spirit Baptism and *Koinonia* 156
        Toward a Spirit-Baptized Anthropology 168
        The Spirit-Baptized Church: The Pluralist Challenge 178
        The Spirit-Baptized Church: Toward a Critical Dialectic 190
        The Spirit-Baptized Church: Biblical Models 199
        - People of God 200
        - Body of Christ 201
        - Temple of the Spirit 203
        The Marks of the Spirit-Baptized Church 204
        - Unity 211
        - Holiness 222
        - Catholicity 224
        - Apostolicity 229
        "Marks" of Preaching, Sacraments, and Charismatic Fullness 241
        - Preaching 244
        - Sacraments 247
        In Sum 256

6   BAPTIZED IN LOVE:
    THE SPIRIT-BAPTIZED LIFE 257
        Importance of Divine Love 259
        Toward a Theology of Love 261
        Faith and Love 265
        Hope and Love 269
        Spirit Baptism as Love's "Second Conversion" 280

Scripture Index 283

Subject Index 291

Author Index 293

ACKNOWLEDGMENTS

THERE ARE MANY PEOPLE WORTHY OF THANKS BEHIND THE WRITING OF this book. Amos Yong has been a fellow traveler with me theologically. His insightful remarks concerning my book and the thoughts expressed within it have been invaluable. Further, I wish to thank Dale Irvin for his conversations with me about the book's contents, which have always been encouraging and challenging. My valued colleague Edmund Rybarczyk has also offered helpful remarks on parts of the book. My good friend and pastor, John Sim, has been a support in more ways than one. Words cannot express how indebted I am to my wife, Verena, for her constant support. The dedication is a small token of my love and appreciation. And, of course, my daughters, Desiree and Jasmine, had to forego time with their daddy for many a day because I was at the computer laboring on this project. I owe them a great debt for their sacrifice. Lastly, I am grateful to the churches that have nourished me in the faith and taught me that the Holy Spirit is worthy of attention and discussion among Christians deeply concerned about the roots and dimensions of the Christian life. Though the Spirit speaks of Christ, we are not prevented from speaking of both the Spirit and Christ in exploring their work inaugurating and fulfilling the redemptive will of the Father on earth.

One

INTRODUCTION:
FRAMING THE ISSUE

I SUPPOSE I WAS A TYPICAL EIGHTEEN-YEAR-OLD, EXCEPT I WAS PERHAPS more confused than most about the direction in which my life was going. It was the year 1970, so my state of mind seemed to be shared by many I knew at the time. I had spent most of my teen years trying to run from God and was attempting to figure out where I might possibly run without meeting God when I arrived. I experimented with drugs and lived as though God were nothing more than a distant thought. There were moments when I felt drawn away from my illusionary existence toward the ultimate reality. But I resisted.

Then came that decisive evening shortly after my high school graduation. I woke my father, an Assemblies of God minister, from a sound sleep at about midnight to let him know that I wanted to leave home to find myself. I had always admired him. He was strict but fair. His down-to-earth humility appealed to me. I especially liked the way the church members affectionately called him "Brother Mike." He seemed to relate to them more as a brother than an authoritative pastor, though many took him without question as a lifelong spiritual father. My mother, Elizabeth, besides her crazy sense of humor, had conveyed her deep faith to me by teaching me church choruses as a child. She persuaded me to sing them in church before the congregation. My tenor voice made me a favored choice for singing solos at our local church, an early experience of ministry that was formative to my early spiritual development.

When I woke my father that night, I was far from the faith of my childhood. But telling my father that I wanted to leave home gave him an opportunity to reach out to me. What followed was an all-night conversation that I will never forget. He spoke to me from the Bible and from many stories of faith from my family's history. I was moved deeply. It made me feel that I could not possibly run from God. To do so would cause me to run from something that was deep inside of me, something I could not deny without denying an essential part of who I was.

Hours passed like minutes, but I held out. I would not yet give my heart to Christ, so we both ended up going to bed exhausted. It was near dawn as I entered my bedroom. I knelt next to my bed and wondered what I should pray. I remember telling God that I did not know what to say. I said something simple like, "I only know that I need you, Lord. I give you my life." With that brief prayer, I lay down to the most peaceful sleep I had enjoyed in a long time.

The following day I told my parents what had happened and that I wanted to leave for a Bible college in order to discover my future in God. Yes, I would get my wish to leave home in order to find myself, but in a way that I had not planned. Their joy was tempered by my felt need to leave the neighborhood as soon as possible. There was a network of friends that was sure to tear away at my fledgling faith. I needed time away with God to be grounded in the faith. My father arranged for me to attend Central Bible College in Springfield, Missouri.

My first day on campus contained all of the anxieties of a new experience. I was not sure I wanted to stay. My father persuaded me to give it a month and left me there with high hopes early in the afternoon of the second day. Moments later I purchased a Bible at the bookstore and sat down to read from it in my sparsely-furnished dorm room. The Bible was a large, plain study Bible that I had bought for my classes. I remember turning to the book of Acts. I began reading. Though I was familiar with several of the stories in that book, they seemed to come alive before my eyes as never before. The text drew me in. I was there when the disciples gathered around the risen Christ, and at Pentecost when the Spirit fell on the disciples as they prayed in tongues surrounded by flames of God's holy presence. I was also there when Peter and John were beaten for their faith but rejoiced at the privilege of suffering for Christ, and when Peter witnessed the Gentiles being filled with the Spirit. I accompanied Paul on his journeys and participated in his numerous adventures.

I read the entire book of Acts without moving from my chair. I was awe struck. I opened the shade covering the window next to me and beheld the sun setting. I saw shades of red and yellow across the sky and I could feel the tears roll off of my cheeks. I remember thinking that I could not possibly be the kind of Christian who merely "played church." That certainly was not how the Christians lived in the book of Acts. *God was so real to them.* They lived daily in the awareness of God's presence and guidance. Life was an adventure in the Lord's service and there were moments when God visited them with undeniable signs of divine favor and power. They had a fire burning in their hearts.

I determined in that moment that I wanted to be a Christian like them. I felt a calling from God grip me—God was calling me to lifelong ministry. My presence at that small Bible college in southwest Missouri was no accident. At that very moment, a few of the new students I had met earlier came to my room and invited me to pray with them at the dorm chapel. What timing! The chapel was located on the third floor of the dorm, a small room with benches along the walls and a plain wooden cross at the center of the wall facing the door. No sooner had I entered the room that I fell to my knees and began to pray. I began to cry and to search for words that I could not find. Meanwhile, my schoolmates began to pray for me. I felt a fountain well up within me. It grew stronger and stronger until it burst forth with great strength. I began to pray in tongues. It was not forced, neither from me nor from God. In fact, it seemed at the moment to be the most natural thing to do. By now I lay there on the floor with my eyes fixed on that cross. I felt God's powerful presence embrace me, and while accepting my calling to the ministry, I made promises to God that have accompanied me throughout my life.

I left that room and ran to the pay phone down the hall. I was still so moved that it took all of my strength to tell my parents what had happened. We cried and rejoiced together over the phone. I was certainly going to stay at the college, I explained. I needed to prepare for the ministry that God had for me. They no longer needed to worry about me. I was on a journey with God that would last forever. I had found myself much sooner than I had anticipated. I found myself overwhelmed by the love of God and committed to a life of Christian service.

My testimony may be different in detail but not in spirit from countless others throughout the world. I came to cherish most from my Pentecostal heritage its strong sense of calling from God toward some form of gifted ministry, not just for ordained ministry but for Christian service in general. I came to cherish the awareness of God's presence, on occasion to change us, fill us with the divine presence anew, and move us toward meaningful experiences of self-giving and ministry in the power of the Spirit.

That such testimonies bear witness to genuine experiences of "Spirit baptism" is for me a given. I find that such language is justifiably taken from the book of Acts. Luke makes Spirit baptism a "clothing" with power by which we bear witness to Christ and further the work of the kingdom of God in the world: "Stay in the city," Jesus said to his disciples before ascending, "until you have been clothed with power from on high" (Luke 24:49). They were also told that they would receive power when the Holy Spirit came upon them (Acts 1:8). This clothing with power is used as a functional equivalent by Luke of Spirit baptism.

Though a divine act not dependent on human standards of experience, this clothing with power certainly involves experience. Both Luke and Paul liken the state of someone gripped by the Spirit in this way to a kind of "God intoxication" (Acts 2:13; Eph. 5:18). I do not refer here to a drunken state but rather a consciousness wholly taken up with God so that one feels especially inspired to give of oneself to others in whatever gifting God has created within. It is essentially an experience of self-transcendence motivated by the love of God. Experience is certainly culturally mediated and will vary in nature from person to person, from context to context. But I simply cannot imagine this clothing with power unless some kind of powerful experience of the divine presence, love, and calling is involved, one that loosens our tongues and our hands to function under the inspiration of the Spirit.

On the other hand, in the broader context of the New Testament, Spirit baptism is a fluid metaphor surrounded by ambiguous imagery that suggests broader boundaries pneumatologically than Spirit empowerment. In general, it seems fair to say that Luke's theology of Spirit baptism has a certain "charismatic" and missiological focus (empowerment for gifted service). Indeed, Luke is also concerned with reconciliation between peoples and the quality of community life through Spirit baptism. In all of these effects of life in the Spirit, Luke is concerned with *power for witness* (Acts 1:8). The church is empowered for living witness in its community life, its inspired proclamation, and its multiple ministries in the Spirit. For Luke, the accent is not on *being* in Christ as it is in Paul, but rather *functioning* in Christ in the power of the Spirit.

14

Broadly conceived, one may use the term "charismatic" to describe Luke's understanding of Spirit baptism. Life in the kingdom as a sanctified people is certainly in the background for Luke (Acts 1:3–8; 15:9), but it is the arrival of the kingdom *in power* through the living witness of the church that grabs Luke in his effort to describe Spirit baptism. Luke does not explicitly integrate for us how the arrivals of the Spirit in power to inspire the living witness of the church in its communal life, speech, and deeds, relate to the church's deeper existence by faith and baptism in the life of the kingdom. The relationship between the life of the Spirit and faith/baptism seems fluid and loose in Acts—connected for sure (Acts 2:38), but one is not entirely certain how. One needs help from Paul and other canonical voices to negotiate a broader and more integrated conception of Spirit baptism as an eschatological event that is complex in nature.

Paul is also charismatic in his pneumatology, but his understanding of Spirit baptism is more intimately connected to faith, confession, and sealing through water baptism. Paul is prominently concerned with incorporation into Christ, by which believers become members of Christ's body and of one another (e.g., 1 Cor. 12:13). Moreover, the outpouring of the Spirit has vast ecclesiological and even cosmic significance for Paul. As we will note, it has to do with all aspects of life in the Spirit, including the new creation to come. It has its essence in divine love (Rom. 5:5). Luke's Spirit baptism doctrine is "charismatic," having to do with the divine empowerment of the church as a living witness, while Paul's is primarily soteriological, having fundamentally to do with being in Christ.

Noting this difference between Luke and Paul is not a novel idea for Pentecostals but one affirmed at least similarly by some of the most effective defenders today of the classical Pentecostal doctrine of Spirit baptism as distinct from regeneration or Christian initiation. Roger Stronstad's *The Charismatic Theology of St. Luke* notes that Paul's understanding of Spirit baptism in the context of his pneumatology is "always initiatory and incorporative,"[1] being different from Luke's charismatic use of the metaphor. Stronstad does not deny that Paul's theology of Spirit baptism is soteriological, he only wishes to avoid reading this Pauline meaning into Luke. Similarly, Robert Menzies notes that Paul in his pneumatology (presumably including texts like 1 Cor.

---

1. Roger Stronstad, *Charismatic Theology of St. Luke* (Peabody, MA: Hendrickson, 1984), 10.

12:13) "does not explicitly speak of a gateway experience distinct from conversion."[2] Menzies thus seeks to base the Pentecostal theology of Spirit baptism as a charismatic experience distinct from Christian initiation solely on Luke.

I essentially agree with Stronstad's and Menzies' characterizations of Luke's and Paul's understandings of Spirit baptism, although I think Paul's broader soteriological understanding is implied in Acts, functioning at least as a background to Spirit baptism as empowerment for living witness. I would also define Luke's empowerment for witness more broadly and deeply than mere prophetic speech (Menzies) or charismatic gifting (Stronstad). I think power for witness also involves for Luke a certain quality of communal life that is reconciling and rich in praise and acts of self-giving. But this is a technical point. I really want to ask a further question here: How does one integrate Luke's "charismatic" and Paul's broadly soteriological understandings of Spirit baptism, and how may other canonical voices, such as Matthew and John, be used to enhance the conversation?

Perhaps we should speak of a theology of Spirit baptism that is soteriologically and charismatically defined, an event that has more than one dimension because it is eschatological in nature and not wholly defined by notions of Christian initiation.

Since Luke's definition of Spirit baptism is so profoundly functional and experiential, I have also found helpful the popular charismatic distinction between Spirit baptism theologically defined as a divine act of redemption and initiation into the life of the kingdom involving faith and baptismal sealing, and Spirit baptism as empowerment for Christian life and service that involves an experience (and experiences) of Spirit baptism and filling in life. This distinction between Spirit baptism *theologically* and *experientially* defined should not imply that the latter is not essential to the church. I would never say that Luke's depiction of the winds of the Spirit that set the church aflame with the love of God and propelled them outward are a *super additum* or a luxury item with regard to the nature of the church. The church without this clothing with power, without this enrichment of life in the Spirit that enhances the living witness of the church to the kingdom of God, is somewhat defective (and we are all to some extent defective!).

---

2. Robert Menzies, "The Spirit of Prophecy, Luke-Acts and Pentecostal Theology: A Response to Max Turner," *Journal of Pentecostal Theology* 15 (1999): 72.

This distinction, however, still begs a number of questions. For one thing, we still lack a broader framework in which to integrate these dimensions of Spirit baptism. The church helps to provide this. But that context, as helpful as it is, tends to entangle us in competing notions of Christian initiation and of the church in general. Though there is no way of escaping these issues, a broader eschatological framework for Spirit baptism as a Trinitarian act can open up some interesting possibilities for fresh insights and newly discovered common ground. It is a framework suggested by early Pentecostalism's vision of a "latter-day rain" of the Spirit to prepare the world for Christ's coming.

An eschatological interpretation of Spirit baptism can help us to mend the rift between Spirit baptism as a soteriological and as a charismatic category. Yet, even here, more is needed. We need to explore the nature of God's reign. I am assuming throughout this book a Pentecost/kingdom of God correlation. As a pneumatological concept, the kingdom is inaugurated and fulfilled as a "Spirit baptism." God's kingdom is not an oppressive rule but the reign of divine love. Paul thus calls Pentecost an outpouring of divine love (Rom. 5:5). Before the book is finished, I will be saying that the highest description possible of the substance of Spirit baptism as an eschatological gift is that it functions as an outpouring of divine love. This is the final integration of the soteriological and the charismatic. No higher or deeper integration is possible.

I want to explore from this broad eschatological framework how Spirit baptism might function as an organizing principle of a Pentecostal theology. It may thus be possible to heal the fractures of Pentecostal theology and to contribute to the global Pentecostal conversation about the significance of life in the Spirit for theological reflection. I speak as only one voice from a given context. The use of the word "global" in the subtitle is meant as an invitation for others to converse with me from contexts very different from my own. The indefinite article ("A" Global Pentecostal Theology) is to be accented. Moreover, this is not a systematic theology but rather a description of its organizing principle and a testing of the waters as to how this might relate to certain prominent theological loci. A systematic theology must have a number of other components lacking here and would be organized differently.

Here is how I want to proceed. In the next chapter, I engage the shifts in Pentecostal theology over the past few decades from the lens of Spirit baptism as the chief Pentecostal distinctive. This part of the book will provoke the most interest among specialists in Pentecostal theology. The third chapter contains a critical discussion of issues surrounding the major understandings of Spirit baptism: regeneration, sacramental initiation, and charismatic empowerment. This chapter concludes with a suggestion concerning how we might transcend the current impasse of competing notions of Christian initiation and corresponding understandings of the church. I will use an eschatological view of Spirit baptism to get us beyond a discussion still too bound by differences among competing ecclesiologies. Chapter four engages the significance of Spirit baptism in relation to Christology (Jesus as the Spirit Baptizer). I will also explore the Trinitarian structure of Spirit baptism and end the chapter with a reflection on the different elements of life in the Spirit. Chapter five explores the significance of Spirit baptism for the life of the church. In the final chapter, I discuss Spirit baptism as a baptism in divine love as the ultimate point of integration between the Spirit baptism theologies of Luke and Paul.

I am always called back to my early commitment to Christ and experience of Spirit baptism when I think of those memories that nourish me as a theologian. Especially in response to the Pentecostal view of Spirit baptism I am made to ask: What is this power with which we are clothed to witness for Christ? Is it a raw power without content or guidance other than pragmatic needs and considerations? Is it not the power of divine love poured out upon us from the crucified and risen Christ (Rom. 5:5) and yet to be fulfilled in the transformation of creation into a temple of God's indwelling? Is the essence of the Spirit not, therefore, holy love, or love that does not compromise with evil? Does not God's love confront evil with great power because it is a holy and all-consuming fire? How can we possibly separate Spirit baptism as empowerment from the work of the saving or sanctifying Spirit at the substance of the inauguration and fulfillment of the kingdom of God in power?

The work of the Holy Spirit cannot be compartmentalized or separated out into neat theological categories. The Spirit is a person, not a fragmented set of works or experiences. Formal distinctions can be made in principle, but in reality they exist as an integrated whole. *For all of their talk about the importance of pneumatology, Pentecostals have yet to couch their narrow pneumatological interest in charismatic/missionary empowerment within a broader pneumatological framework.* It is the vision of the whole for which this book reaches. I leave open to my colleagues and friends from near and far as to whether I have in any way achieved my purpose.

Two

SPIRIT BAPTISM AND PENTECOSTAL THEOLOGY:
RETURNING TO OUR CENTRAL DISTINCTIVE

FINNISH PENTECOSTAL THEOLOGIAN VELI-MATTI KÄRKKÄNNEN WROTE correctly that the Pentecostal movement has placed the doctrine of Spirit baptism at the forefront of the theological agenda in modern theology.[1] He also noted rightly that the doctrine is still in the making; "the final word has not yet been said."[2] By the end of this chapter and those following, I will be saying that the final word will not be said of Spirit baptism until the resurrection of the dead and the new heavens and new earth make the entire creation God's dwelling place. To make creation God's dwelling place is to transform it, for new wine cannot inhabit old wineskins. Creation will be changed so that it can enjoy and glorify God forever. God will be the one who speaks this final word. This is because God is the one who has spoken it in creation and, decisively, in Jesus of Nazareth (Heb. 1:1–3).

But until God speaks that final word once and for all, we must speak penultimate words in all humility in a way that is faithful to Christ. This chapter is not so much the story of what Pentecostals have said about Spirit baptism. That summary awaits our next chapter, when we explore

---

1. Veli-Matti Kärkkäinen, *Spiritus ubi vult spirat: Pneumatology in Catholic-Pentecostal Dialogue (1972–1989)* (Helsinki: Luther Agricola Society, 1998), 198.

2. Ibid., 193.

a Pentecostal contribution to an ecumenical pneumatology. Rather, I am interested here in the place that Pentecostals have granted the doctrine of Spirit baptism.

In fact, I believe that examining the place given to Spirit baptism in Pentecostalism is one way of peering into the fascinating discussion that has occurred, especially over the last few decades, over what is really distinctive about Pentecostal theology. The centrality of Spirit baptism to Pentecostal theology is revealed in part by the fact that Pentecostal theological discussion cannot ignore the topic. Pentecostal theology has been shaped as much by a discussion of Spirit baptism as it has by the attempt to decentralize the metaphor as a functional center for theological reflection on God's redemption of the world. Has Spirit baptism lost its place as the central Pentecostal distinctive? Not quite, but there is a definite trend in this direction, especially in Pentecostal scholarship. Allow me to explain.

IS SPIRIT BAPTISM THE CENTRAL PENTECOSTAL DISTINCTIVE?

When one thinks of what is distinctive about Pentecostal theology, usually included is an understanding of Spirit baptism as an empowerment for ministry distinct from regeneration or initiation into Christ. Most Pentecostals view this as a revival or renewal experience in the Christian life and link it to involvement in the extraordinary gifts of the Spirit, especially speaking in tongues and divine healing.

Not all Pentecostals globally have understood Spirit baptism in these ways. For example, most Oneness Pentecostals (known for their Christocentric and "modalistic" understandings of the Trinity) regard Spirit baptism as intimately connected to repentance and baptism in Jesus' name. Chilean and German Pentecostals have had a significant number in their ranks that regard Spirit baptism as regeneration. But enough have understood Spirit baptism as a postconversion charismatic experience to make this view of the doctrine distinctly Pentecostal.

I do not think it is an exaggeration to say that this understanding of Spirit baptism has imprinted itself on the Pentecostal corporate psyche as the crown jewel of Pentecostal distinctives. There is little doubt in my mind that the category has had an enduring influence in Pentecostalism globally. I agree with Simon Chan that Pentecostals are not in agreement over all of their distinctives but that "what comes through over and over again in their discussions and writings is a certain kind of spiritual experience of an intense, direct, and overwhelming nature centering on the person of Christ which they schematize as 'baptism in the Holy Spirit.'"[3]

A number of Pentecostal authors globally can be cited in agreement with Chan concerning the central significance of Spirit baptism to Pentecostal experience and theology. Allan Anderson has stated, for example, that a "fundamental presupposition of all Pentecostal theology is the central emphasis on the experience of the baptism in the Holy Spirit," adding that "all Pentecostal churches throughout the world attach great importance" to this doctrine.[4] Similarly, Korean theologian Koo Dong Yun notes that "out of a number of intriguing characteristics of the Pentecostal-Charismatic movement, 'Baptism in the Holy Spirit' . . . represents the most distinctive doctrine."[5] Sang-Whan Lee agrees that Spirit baptism is a major emphasis of Pentecostalism, adding that the doctrine plays a hermeneutical role in which major Christian beliefs are "interpreted and explored."[6] Miguel Alvarez echoes this view, noting that most Latin American Pentecostals as well "accept the baptism in the Holy Spirit as an event that unveils a new reality," radically reorienting one's relationship to God and opening one up to extraordinary gifts of the Spirit.[7]

This global Pentecostal affirmation of Spirit baptism as a central theological concern is shared by many within the charismatic movement among the mainline churches also. As Henry Lederle wrote: "The major distinctive doctrines of the charismatic movement certainly are Spirit baptism and the charisms of the Holy Spirit."[8] Though most Oneness Pentecostals connect

---

3. Simon Chan, "Evidential Glossolalia and the Doctrine of Subsequence," *Asian Journal of Pentecostal Studies* 2 (1999): 195–211.

4. Allan Anderson, *Zion and Pentecost: The Spirituality and Experience of Pentecostal and Zionist/Apostolic Churches in South Africa* (Pretoria: Univ. of South Africa Press, 2000), 244.

5. Koo Dong Yun, *Baptism in the Holy Spirit: An Ecumenical Theology of Spirit Baptism* (Lanham, MD: Univ. Press of America, 2003), 23–44; Yun's constructive chapter at the end of the book does not take up the classical Pentecostal view, 147–62.

6. Sang-Whan Lee, "Pentecostal Prophecy," *Spirit and Church* 3 (May 2001): 148–49.

7. Miguel Alvarez, "The South and the Latin American Paradigm of the Pentecostal Movement," *Asian Journal of Pentecostal Studies* 5 (2002): 141.

8. Henry Lederle, *Treasures Old and New: Interpretations of Spirit Baptism in the Charismatic Renewal Movement* (Peabody, MA: Hendrickson, 1988), xi.

Spirit baptism to water baptism in Jesus' name and regeneration more intimately than most Pentecostals do, Thomas Fudge states rightly that Spirit baptism for them is the "quintessential Pentecostal experience in which the individual is empowered by God."[9] I believe that the enduring significance of Spirit baptism for Pentecostals is due to a complexity of reasons, one of which is that it provides them with a way of leveling a critique toward the church of what they perceive as a lack of charismatic awareness and conscious participation in the diverse and vibrant witness of the Spirit.

The importance of Spirit baptism among Pentecostal churches is significant, since among all of Pentecostalism's theological distinctives, Spirit baptism has the greatest potential for connecting to other traditions toward the formation of an ecumenical pneumatology. Though Spirit baptism has not received much attention in major tomes of theology, all Christian communions accept the category and have interpreted it in a way consistent with their understanding of the church and Christian initiation. In fact, I will argue in the next chapter that the doctrine of Spirit baptism can function as a lens through which to discuss different ecclesiologies and how they compare with each other.

The ecumenical challenge for Pentecostals, therefore, will be to develop their central distinctive in a way that cherishes what is most important to their understanding of the Christian life and the church while contributing to a broader ecumenical pneumatology. Such a task cannot be confined to North American Pentecostal voices. The need is for Pentecostals globally to reflect on the ecumenical challenge behind their understandings of Spirit baptism as focused on a vocational or charismatic empowerment, as well as on how that notion relates to the greater breadth of the Spirit's work in the Scriptures and among other world Christian communions.

This task is important not only because of the ecumenical challenge facing global Pentecostalism. Though Spirit baptism still has widespread support on a more popular level among Pentecostals, the doctrine is losing its appeal among those involved in Pentecostal theological reflection. Part of the reason for this gradual loss of appeal has been the lack of constructive theological reflection on the charismatic understanding of Spirit baptism shared among Pentecostals. It seems that deeper thinking is needed on why "subsequence"

---

9. Thomas A. Fudge, *Christianity without the Cross: A History of Salvation in One-ness Pentecostalism* (Parkland, FL: Universal Publishers, 2003), 117.

(Spirit baptism as subsequent to regeneration) has been important theologically for most Pentecostals and how this relates to other understandings of Spirit baptism. In the absence of such constructive work, the doctrine will seem to lack ecumenical relevance on a global scale.

New Testament scholars Roger Stronstad and Robert Menzies have breathed some new life into Pentecostal polemics on Spirit baptism by focusing attention on Luke's charismatic theology. What comes through in their work is the conviction that Pentecostals are exegetically justified in making Spirit baptism a charismatic experience rather than an initiation into Christ by faith or the sacraments of initiation.[10] I find their focus on charismatic empowerment in Luke highly significant for a Pentecostal theology of Sprit baptism, although I also find their focus too narrow to account for all of the nuances of Luke's pneumatology. We will take up their challenge in greater detail later.

Of importance in this chapter is the fact that despite the work of Stronstad and Menzies, the doctrine of Spirit baptism is waning in significance among the most prolific among Pentecostal theologians. Spirit baptism is no longer regarded as the most distinctive Pentecostal doctrine or as having central significance to Pentecostal theology without qualification or even rejection among leading Pentecostal theologians and historians today. Not since Harold Hunter's and Howard Ervin's treatments of the doctrine published nearly two decades ago has there been a similar effort to write a theology of Spirit baptism.[11]

For example, in essential agreement with Singaporan theologian Simon Chan, Australian theologian Shane Jack Clifton finds value in the doctrine but maintains that it must be expanded "in the ecumenically affirming context of the twenty-first century global church" to have a fruitful and enduring role to play in Pentecostal theology.[12] Steven Land's seminal effort at writing a

---

10. Roger Stronstad, *Charismatic Theology of St. Luke* (Peabody, MA: Hendrickson, 1984); Robert Menzies, *Empowered for Witness: The Spirit in Luke-Acts* (Sheffield: Sheffield Academic Press, 1991).

11. H. Hunter, *Spirit Baptism: A Pentecostal Alternative* (Lanham, MD: Univ. Press of America, 1980); H. M. Ervin, *Conversion-Initiation and the Baptism in the Holy Spirit: A Critique of James D. G. Dunn, Baptism in the Holy Spirit* (Peabody, MA: Hendrickson, 1984).

12. Shane Jack Clifton, "An Analysis of the Developing Ecclesiology of the Assemblies of God in Australia" (Ph.D. diss.; Fitzroy, Australia: Australian Catholic University, 2005), 288; note also Simon Chan, *Pentecostal Theology and the Christian Spiritual Tradition* (Sheffield: Sheffield Academic Press, 2003), 12.

Pentecostal theology, *Pentecostal Spirituality*, explicitly takes issue with Dale Bruner's description of Pentecostal theology as "pneumatobaptistocentric" (Spirit baptism centered). Land regards Bruner's description as "missing the point altogether" concerning what is really distinctive about Pentecostal theology, which is in Land's view the sanctification of the affections as part of an eschatological passion for the kingdom of God yet to come.[13] Significantly, Land devotes no more than a few pages to the doctrine in his book, even though sanctification, part of his major concern, was the doctrinal category from which the early Pentecostal doctrine of Spirit baptism was taken and later distinguished. The publication of a major Pentecostal theology that practically ignores Spirit baptism represents a significant shift in the axis of Pentecostal distinctives.

Russell P. Spittler has written insightfully that the most popular understanding of Spirit baptism as "subsequent" to regeneration or Christian initiation is a "non-issue," since Pentecostals were more concerned with spiritual renewal than with creating a new *ordo salutis*.[14] Gordon Fee cherishes the experience of the Spirit implied in the Pentecostal doctrine of Spirit baptism but questions the exegesis used to defend this doctrine as subsequent to regeneration.[15] In the context of historical theology, a recent book written on Spirit baptism by Koo Dong Yun presents the popular classical Pentecostal treatment of this doctrine as little more than a historical curiosity.[16]

Even the significant efforts by Stronstad and Menzies to focus on the unique charismatic pneumatology of Luke in order to open up fresh possibilities for viewing Spirit baptism as prophetic or charismatic inspiration has received no significant response from the most prolific among contemporary Pentecostal theologians. Amos Yong, Veli-Matti Kärkkäinen, Juan Sepulveda, Simon Chan, Steven Land, Terry Cross, Edmund Rybarczyk, and other classical Pentecostals working in the area of systematic or constructive theology have sought mainly to develop Pentecostal distinctives in the form of a broadly global and/or ecumenical theology of the Spirit that moves significantly beyond the older classical Pentecostal doctrine of subsequence and tongues

---

13. Steven J. Land, *Pentecostal Spirituality: A Passion for the Kingdom* (Sheffield: Sheffield Academic Press, 1993), 62–63.

14. Russell P. Spittler, "Suggested Areas for Further Research in Pentecostal Studies," *Pneuma* 5 (1983): 43 (39–57).

15. Gordon Fee, "Baptism in the Holy Spirit: The Issue of Separability and Subsequence," *Pneuma* 7 (1985): 87–99, esp. 88, 96–98.

16. Yun, *Baptism in the Holy Spirit*, 23–44.

as initial evidence. They have been inspired by theologians that are closely related to the Pentecostal movement because of scholarly interests or a Pentecostal background, such as Walter Hollenweger, Donald Dayton, Dale Irvin, Ralph Del Colle, Miroslav Volf, Lyle Dabney, Michael Welker, Harvey Cox, and Clark Pinnock. The Pentecostal theologians influenced by these ecumenical thinkers have fortunately seen that too much stress on that which is distinctively Pentecostal can thwart the ecumenical vision necessary to inspire creative and relevant theological reflection.

I have affirmed the general direction of this trend, especially in my more recent writings, and regard my own scholarship as joining these esteemed colleagues in the important work being done. On the one hand, this broad focus on pneumatology helps to grant Pentecostal theology global and ecumenical significance while tempering a preoccupation with Pentecostal distinctives, which, if overemphasized, could isolate Pentecostal theology from the broader ecumenical discussion. On the other hand, all churches have a more important commitment to the biblical witness and may feel compelled to stress something from that witness that appears to be neglected. Besides, without something distinctive, Pentecostalism will not have much to offer others in the ecumenical conversation. Terry Cross has asked the important question here: Can Pentecostals contribute to the major course of the ecumenical meal or are we only expected to bring the relish?[17]

Pentecostal distinctives are valuable if we are to speak at the global and ecumenical table from the vantage point of our unique gifting as a movement of Christian affirmation. I draw here from Oscar Cullmann's insightful analogy between the unique theological and spiritual accents of the world Christian families and the Pauline doctrine of the *charismata*.[18] Pentecostalism has been blessed and gifted by God with certain theological and spiritual accents. We do other Christian families a disservice if we do not preserve and cherish these and seek to bless others with them. Thus, ideal would be a reworking of our distinctives in a way that cherishes our unique accents but expands them in response to the broader contours of the biblical witness and the diversity of voices at the ecumenical table.

---

17. Terry L. Cross, "The Rich Feast of Theology: Can Pentecostals Bring the Main Course or Only the Relish?" *Journal of Pentecostal Theology* 16 (2000): 27–47.

18. Oscar Cullmann, *Unity through Diversity: Its Foundation and a Contribution to the Discussion concerning the Possibilities of Its Actualization* (Minneapolis: Augsburg Fortress, 1988), 55–56.

I have thus come to wonder if the relative neglect of the doctrine of Spirit baptism among Pentecostal theologians might not need to be reconsidered. There can be no doubt that Spirit baptism will need to be defined more broadly than it has among most classical Pentecostals if it is to continue to function as central to Pentecostal theology. The challenge in this broader reworking of the doctrine of Spirit baptism will be to remain true at the same time to Pentecostal experience and distinctive theological accents. I find that Simon Chan has begun to reach for something similar in his seminal reflections on Spirit baptism.[19]

There is still much constructive work to be done in this direction with this creative tension in mind. For example, there is no question but that Menzies and Stronstad have shown Luke's understanding of Spirit baptism to be charismatic. This focus is vital to a global Pentecostal contribution to an ecumenical pneumatology. But it would be fruitful to ask the theological question as to why Luke connects Spirit baptism with charismatic empowerment and gifts such as prophecy, healing, and tongues. In my view, a development of Luke's eschatological understanding of Spirit baptism would have uncovered the theological context for his linkage of Spirit baptism and charismatic signs and would have shown that a charismatic understanding of Spirit baptism developed apart from regeneration, sanctification, and resurrection is an impossibility, even within the context of Luke's unique charismatic and missionary emphases. Yet I also regard the Pentecostal focus on charismatic empowerment to be highly significant ecumenically for uncovering unique features of how we as Pentecostals understand the spiritual life and the nature and purpose of the church.

I have come, therefore, to hold that a Pentecostal theology can benefit from a thorough reexamination of the crown jewel of our theological distinctives, both in terms of its distinct focus and its broader boundaries. Before we launch in this direction, we need to pause in order to locate Spirit baptism in greater detail within the recent trends in Pentecostal theology. More specifically, we need first to explore the reasons for the relative neglect among Pentecostal theologians of Spirit baptism as a metaphor or a theological distinctive.

There are in my view four important reasons for the displacement of Spirit baptism recently as the chief theological distinctive. I will explore each

---

19. Chan, *Pentecostal Theology*, 33–67; see also Amos Yong's reflection on a pneumatological soteriology in *The Spirit Poured Out on All Flesh: The Possibility of Global Theology* (Grand Rapids: Baker, 2005), 104–8.

in greater detail below; here I only briefly mention them. The first reason for the shift away from Spirit baptism as the central Pentecostal distinctive is the early Pentecostal isolation of Christian initiation from charismatic empowerment occasioned by the shift historically from sanctification to Spirit baptism. A fragmented twofold or threefold initiation into the life of the Spirit is difficult to justify in Scripture. Furthermore, fragmented from God's salvific work in Christ, Spirit baptism can appear as an otherworldly experience detached from Christological guidance. It could even appear as elitist. These exegetical and ecumenical difficulties have tended to discourage more recent Pentecostal theologians from centering on the doctrine.

The second reason for the shift away from Spirit baptism is the developing challenge of the diversity of Pentecostal theology discovered in the early history and the current global expanse of Pentecostal beliefs. This discovery tends to relativize for many the significance of Spirit baptism. There is a growing awareness of the fact that early and later Pentecostal theology is not just about Spirit baptism and tongues. We have also become aware of the diversity of viewpoints possible on these distinctives within Pentecostalism globally.

Yet, some refuse to conclude from this diversity that Pentecostal theology is a disconnected cafeteria of ideas. They still assume that Pentecostal theology has always been coherent in some sense. Interestingly, it is not Spirit baptism but eschatology (especially in relation to a passion for mission) that has been most used among Pentecostal theologians of recent to achieve coherence for that which is distinctive about Pentecostal theology. Spirit baptism tends to be seen as relatively insignificant next to the dominance of eschatology for defining Pentecostal theology. Thus, the third reason for the relative neglect of Spirit baptism is the shift in doctrinal focus among the most prolific Pentecostal theologians from Spirit baptism to eschatology.

The deeper question that some are asking, however, is whether or not that which is most distinctive about Pentecostal theology is doctrinal after all. As we will note below, Walter J. Hollenweger has argued that the Pentecostal distinctive is more about how Pentecostals conceive the theological task. Oral, narrative, or dramatic theology allegedly characterizes the global and ecumenical challenge of Pentecostal theology. Those following Hollenweger in this shift from doctrine to theological method have tended to see Spirit baptism as an accident of history, a holdover from the Holiness movement that is not fruitful for an ecumenical pneumatology. The fourth reason, therefore, is the shift under Hollenweger from doctrinal distinctives to theological method in the effort to describe what is most distinctive to Pentecostal theology.

We will discuss each of the above issues in turn with an eye toward cautioning against the displacement of Spirit baptism as the central distinctive of a Christian theology nourished by Pentecostal experience. The reader will need to determine whether or not I am successful in making my case.

FROM SANCTIFICATION TO SPIRIT BAPTISM: EARLY FRAGMENTATION

Our Holiness legacy has been a mixed blessing for us as Pentecostals, and this includes the revision of the Holiness Spirit baptism theology handed down from the earliest Pentecostals. To understand the nature of this mixed blessing, we should understand that Holiness theology was born in revivalism. Its hallmark was a crisis experience following regeneration called a baptism in the Holy Spirit. Pentecostals were born in the same revivalist ethos and borrowed from the Holiness logic of dividing initiation to the life of the Spirit into separate crisis moments. This logic also involved Pentecostals, who, under the influence of William Durham, advocated a "finished work" understanding of the atonement and, therefore, viewed sanctification and other blessings associated with salvation as received through initial conversion to Christ.

Though these "Baptistic" Pentecostals integrated regeneration and sanctification into one event, they followed the Holiness understanding of initiation to the life of the Spirit by positing the charismatic experience as the second blessing. All Pentecostals, Holiness and "Baptistic," ended up shifting their spiritual emphasis from sanctification to Spirit baptism as a charismatic moment.[20] Pentecostals were not consistent in this narrow definition of Spirit baptism as a charismatic empowerment (as we will note in our next chapter), but charismatic empowerment remained the hallmark of the Pentecostal blessing for most Pentecostals. The challenge of how to integrate this charismatic empowerment with sanctification remains to this day.

Exegetically, Pentecostals faced the difficulty of advocating two or three separate receptions of the Spirit in one's entry into the life of the Spirit. The

---

20. Note, e.g., D. William Faupel, *The Everlasting Gospel: The Significance of Eschatology in the Development of Pentecostal Thought* (Sheffield: Sheffield Academic Press, 1996), 13–18.

work of Menzies and Stronstad mentioned above sought at least implicitly to avoid this problem by using the insight of biblical theology into the different theologies of the Spirit taught in the New Testament. Lukan pneumatology was portrayed as narrowly charismatic in nature while Paul's pneumatology (and John's after him) as advocating a soteriological pneumatology.[21] The possibility of a charismatic experience distinct from God's saving grace was formed through a Pentecostal integration of the very different pneumatologies of Luke and Paul. Even if one agrees with Menzies and Stronstad on Luke's narrow charismatic focus, it is still possible to integrate his pneumatology with Paul's in a way that involves an integral understanding of Spirit baptism. One can seek to integrate Luke's pneumatology with Paul's and John's along the lines of a pneumatological soteriology that views the Spirit as the very substance of the Christ life.

Despite points at which we may want to quarrel with James Dunn's early classic, *Baptism in the Holy Spirit*, his effort to note a basic continuity of emphasis throughout the New Testament on the Spirit as the hallmark of Christian identity (the "nerve center" of the Christian life) seems compelling and potentially relevant to the task of granting Spirit baptism a major place in Christian theology.[22] Not as compelling in my view is a rigid separation between regeneration (Paul) and charismatic empowerment (Luke) in support of compartmentalizing the work of the Spirit in the Christian life.

The recent neglect of the doctrine of Spirit baptism in a discussion of what is most distinctive about Pentecostal theology arises also from aspects of this doctrine that proved to be problematic pastorally. The cause of these difficulties relates to the shortcomings of revivalism as a model for the spiritual life. Regeneration as a crisis "new birth" experience became popular in Pietism as a way of understanding the Christian life as a felt experience that moves one to ever-deeper levels of devotion to God in heart and life. The entire Christian life tended to be viewed as a series of crisis moments of renewal in which the born-again experience can be recaptured and affirmed.

---

21. In addition to the sources referenced in footnote 10, see Robert Menzies, "Luke and the Spirit: A Reply to James Dunn," *Journal of Pentecostal Theology* 4 (1994): 115–38.

22. James D. G. Dunn, *The Baptism in the Holy Spirit: A Re-examination on the New Testament Teaching on the Gift of the Spirit in Relation to Pentecostalism Today* (London: SCM, 1970).

Wolfhart Pannenberg has noted insightfully that an isolation of the Christian life into moments of renewal can eclipse its continuity.[23] Believers can end up living between moments of renewal in fear, not knowing the precise nature of their status in between the altar experiences by which they make things right once more with God. Altar experiences themselves can become heart-wrenching struggles toward repentance in which one seeks to eventually warrant approval from God. Anyone who doubts this characterization of revivalism should read the Pietistic literature concerning the *Busskampf* (repentance battle). Battles for repentance according to such literature can take hours and even days to accomplish.[24] Friedrich Nietzsche appropriately referred to such spirituality as potentially masochistic.[25] To ward off this danger, Pentecostals held out assurance to believers that Spirit baptism will grant them a triumphant life above the threat of such ongoing terror.[26]

These misgivings about revivalism aside, I find great value in revivalism in its stress on the Christian life as a lived experience of the Spirit that must be renewed time and again. But there is a broader spirituality that accents the grace of God sustaining all of life within which revivalism must be housed if it is to function as a fruitful model of Christian spirituality. A mining of the Wesleyan roots and eschatological horizon of Pentecostal theology can help in providing this broader context for understanding the revival fires of the Spirit.

The problem is that the revivalistic influence on the Holiness movement caused it to transform John Wesley's more process-oriented understanding of sanctification into a high-voltage crisis experience.[27] Understanding sanctification as a revival experience or a conscious commitment achieved by "laying all on the altar" had the theological and practical value of functioning as an ongoing challenge to a church understood to be too casual about sanctifica-

---

23. Wolfhart Pannenberg, *Christian Spirituality* (Philadelphia: Westminster, 1983), 17ff.

24. See my discussion of this problem in Frank D. Macchia, *Spirituality and Social Liberation: The Message of the Blumhardts in the Light of Wuertemberg Pietism* (Metuchen, NJ: Scarecrow, 1993), 169–70.

25. Friedrich Nietzsche, *Genealogy of Morals* (New York: Vintage Books, 1989), esp. 21.

26. I am grateful to Grant Wacker for bringing to my awareness the significance of the triumphalism of early Pentecostal spirituality in personal conversation.

27. This is the central thesis of Melvin Dieter's insightful work, *Nineteenth-Century Holiness Revival* (Kansas City: Beacon Hill, 1998).

tion. This sanctification moment was turned upon the church as a challenge. To present this challenge effectively, the experience was promoted as fundamentally a renewal for worldly or lazy Christians. The result was a fracturing of one's entrance into the Christian life into dramatic moments of regeneration (for sinners) and sanctification (for Christians).

This development found initial expression in the work of Wesley's younger associate, John Fletcher. Fletcher's work should not be viewed in isolation. We should not forget that a theology of confirmation in the West had distinguished between faith/water baptism and the gift of the Holy Spirit. Laurence Wood has argued that this distinction reappears from Anglicanism via Wesley in John Fletcher's theological distinction between regeneration/baptism and sanctification.[28] Whether or not Wesley himself advocated such a distinction is hotly debated among Wesleyan scholars. One may assume, however, that an analogous relationship between the theology of confirmation and the Holiness and Pentecostal Spirit baptism theology exists. Whatever else may be said of this Spirit baptism theology, it does have an ancient heritage.

In the Holiness theology begun by Fletcher, these moments of regeneration and sanctification were appropriated to persons of the Trinity: the Father creates, the Son redeems, and the Spirit sanctifies. A recent expression of this Holiness theology can be found in Laurence Wood's *Pentecostal Grace*.[29] An appropriation doctrine intended originally to depict the salvation-historical work of the Son (in cooperation with the Spirit) in redemption, and the work of the Spirit (in witness to the Son) in sanctification, becomes internalized as separate stages in an *ordo salutis*. But there are potential problems with this fragmentation. This internalization can eclipse the mutual working of Christ and the Spirit in salvation history, while it overlooks the overlapping nature of soteriological categories in the New Testament.

The separation of Spirit baptism from God's redemptive work in Christ can also end up detaching the spiritual life from Christological guidance, as Donald Dayton has shown.[30] The result can be an otherworldly spirituality that latches onto pragmatic strategies for success to guide the outworking of the spiritual

---

28. See Laurence W. Wood, *The Meaning of Pentecost in Early Methodism: Rediscovering John Fletcher as John Wesley's Vindicator and Designated Successor* (Lanham, MD: Scarecrow, 2002).

29. Laurence W. Wood, *Pentecostal Grace* (Grand Rapids: Zondervan, 1980).

30. Donald W. Dayton, *Theological Roots of Pentecostalism* (Grand Rapids: Zondervan, 1988), 48–54.

life in the concrete worlds of business, politics, and so on. One is left with the dark side of Grant Wacker's insightful characterization of the Pentecostal ethos as a wedding of otherworldly spirituality and a this-worldly pragmatism.[31]

Moreover, the idea of sanctification and Spirit baptism as a higher-life experience can lead those who claim to have had it into thinking that they occupy a superior position in the body of Christ. If one adds to Spirit baptism the necessity of speaking in tongues, the elitism implied in the revivalist understanding of one's entry into the life of the Spirit grows more intense. Of course, revivalism is by no means the only Christian soteriology that implies elitism! Moreover, there are positive features theologically about a soteriology that stresses personal experience, the transformation of a person's life, and the need for dramatic moments of spiritual renewal.

Some may ask at this point, "In light of the numerous problems exegetically and ecumenically with the dominant Pentecostal doctrine of Spirit baptism, why bother with it any longer?" Well, for one thing, Spirit baptism implies a "baptism" in or with the very breath or Spirit of God, indicating a participatory metaphor of our relationship with God that is to have a significant experiential effect. This experiential dimension of Spirit baptism tends to be lacking in the formal definitions of the metaphor among other Christian families in the world. Furthermore, the Pentecostal connection of Spirit baptism with charismatic experience says something profound about the diverse and polyphonic way the Spirit makes Christ present in and through the church. The role of the Spirit in creating an expansively diverse body of Christ in the world can also add much to a global and ecumenically relevant Christian pneumatology. The connection between Spirit baptism and an expansive array of spiritual gifts helps us focus on the relatively neglected vocational dimension of the Christian life and the polyphonic and diverse charismatic structure of the church.[32]

Why abandon or subordinate such a fruitful metaphor for an ecumenical and global theology of the Spirit just because there are technical problems in how Pentecostals have explained the metaphor historically? The difficulties of the particular form of Spirit baptism adopted from the Holiness movement need not hinder us from exploring again the deeper relevance of Spirit baptism against

---

31. Grant Wacker, *Heaven Below: Early Pentecostals and American Culture* (Cambridge, MA: Harvard Univ. Press, 2003).

32. Michael Welker, *God the Spirit* (Philadelphia: Fortress, 1998), esp. 51–66.

the background of a more expansive form of the metaphor taken from the Scriptures and useful in the pollination of pneumatologies across confessional lines.

The ecumenical challenge also involves due consideration of the diversity of Pentecostal belief globally as well as the distinct ways in which theology is conceived among Pentecostals. The waning of Spirit baptism as the crown jewel of a viable Pentecostal contribution to a global and ecumenical pneumatology relates to these issues as well, the topic of our next section.

SPIRIT BAPTISM AND DOCTRINAL DIVERSITY: THE DEVELOPING CHALLENGE

It is also important to note that the exegetical and ecumenical difficulties attached historically to the Pentecostal understandings of Spirit baptism are not the only reasons behind the relative neglect of the doctrine among Pentecostal systematic theologians. The recent lack of interest in Spirit baptism among Pentecostal theologians is due also to the fact that the historical research into Pentecostal theology has shifted the axis of our distinctives to other points of interest. Pentecostal distinctives are now widely recognized among Pentecostal theologians and historians as complex.

Of relevance here is the fact that the challenge of diversity of Pentecostal theological expression arose in reference to Pentecostalism as a global movement. Douglas Peterson took notice of the "globalization" of Pentecostalism before the term was in vogue among Pentecostals and organized a conference along with Murray W. Dempster and Byron D. Klaus in 1997 at Costa Rica under this theme. A volume was published containing the papers from this conference.[33] One of the speakers at the conference was Harvey Cox, who had just published a book in which he argued that the global Pentecostal movement has highlighted "primal" religious experience and expressions in a way that has allowed them to adapt creatively to various cultural settings and take on a colorful global diversity. Pentecostalism potentially offers an alternative ecumenical challenge to those that are more rational, doctrinaire, or literate in nature.[34] A discussion of the Pentecostal belief in Spirit baptism as "subsequent" to regeneration was not given the time of day in Cox's extremely insightful book.

---

33. Murray W. Dempster, Byron D. Klaus, Douglas Petersen, ed., *The Globalization of Pentecostalism: A Religion Made to Travel* (Irvine, CA: Regnum, 1999).

34. Harvey Cox, *Fire from Heaven: The Rise of Pentecostal Spirituality and the Reshaping of Religion in the Twenty-First Century* (New York: Addison-Wesley, 1995).

Decades before these developments, Walter Hollenweger raised issues about the global diversity of Pentecostalism, bringing Pentecostal research to another level. Hollenweger's research revealed a vast doctrinal diversity among Pentecostals worldwide and even within the United States, both now and from the beginning of the movement. Hollenweger's classic, *The Pentecostals*, fell like a bombshell in the late 1960s and early 1970s on geographically sheltered Pentecostal groups surprised by the doctrinal diversity of the movement globally.[35] Hollenweger notes in an interesting postscript to that book:

> There is . . . a broad spectrum of opinion in . . . the definition of baptism in the Spirit, social and individual ethics, the question of biblical hermeneutics, the doctrine of the Trinity and christology. Therefore, talk of "the doctrine" of the Pentecostal churches is highly problematical. What unites the Pentecostal churches is not a doctrine but a religious experience, and this can be interpreted and substantiated in many different ways.[36]

There is no question but that Pentecostal distinctives globally are diverse and variously interpreted. In his study of the variety of theologies among Pentecostal thinkers in the first twenty-five years of the movement, Douglas Jacobsen concluded also that "all the diverse versions of pentecostalism stand to some degree on their own, mutually criticizing each other in complex ways."[37] In particular, the early diversity concerning Spirit baptism noted above continued to characterize the Pentecostal movement. Basic disagreements exist among Pentecostal groups over issues of the relationship of Spirit baptism to initial faith in Christ, water baptism, and speaking in tongues.

There is no universal agreement among Pentecostals worldwide on such questions. The so-called doctrine of "subsequence" (Spirit baptism as distinct from regeneration) has indeed gathered sufficient strength among Pentecostal groups historically so as to be regarded as most distinctively "Pentecostal." Most Pentecostals have viewed Spirit baptism as analogous to a rite of passage among Christians to an intense awareness of the presence of God and an experience of the kingdom of God in power. Such an experience is regarded

---

35. Walter J. Hollenweger, *The Pentecostals*, 2nd ed. (Peabody, MA: Hendrickson, 1988).

36. Walter J. Hollenweger, "From Azusa Street to the Toronto Phenomenon," in *Pentecostal Movements as an Ecumenical Challenge*, ed. Jürgen Moltmann and Karl-Josef Kuschel (Concilium 3; London: SCM, 1996), 7.

37. Douglas Jacobsen, *Thinking in the Spirit: Theologies of the Early Pentecostal Movement* (Bloomington, IN: Indiana Univ. Press, 2003), 12.

among a majority of Pentecostals as an empowerment of Christians for vibrant praise and dynamic witness, both of which are thought to involve signs and wonders of the kingdom that should be experienced to some degree in the everyday lives of ordinary Christians.

Yet, as noted above, not all Pentecostals worldwide advocate the doctrine of subsequence. Nor did all early Pentecostals who distinguished Spirit baptism from sanctification do so consistently (as we will note in the next chapter). Most charismatics from the mainline churches have identified Spirit baptism with the reception of the Spirit at water baptism or the rites of initiation, though they do leave "breathing room" for the *experience* of Spirit baptism to occur later in the Christian life with the kind of spiritual gifting cherished among Pentecostals. Others would identify Spirit baptism as an experience of sacramental grace. Paul Lee's exaggerated statement that there appears an almost "infinite variety" of views within and outside Pentecostalism on the nature of Spirit baptism certainly contains an element of truth.[38]

Many Pentecostals, especially in the United States, consider speaking in tongues as evidence of the experience. Not all Pentecostals globally hold to the doctrine of speaking in tongues as the initial evidence of Spirit baptism, however, though the *experience* of glossolalia is arguably still fairly widespread in the movement. And even among those who hold this initial-evidence doctrine, the relationship between tongues and Spirit baptism varies. Seymour regarded tongues as a sign of the empowerment of the church to reach out to all nations, implying a boundary-crossing experience that produces a diverse church. He noted, "God makes no difference in nationality, Ethiopians, Chinese, Indians, Mexicans, and other nationalities worship together."[39] He later regarded love as the primary sign of Spirit baptism.[40]

---

38. Paul D. Lee, *Pneumatological Ecclesiology in the Catholic-Pentecostal Dialogue: A Catholic Reading of the Third Quinnquennium (1985–1989)* (Dissertatio ad lauream in facultate S. theologiae apud pontificiam universitatem S. Thomae in urbe; Rome), 171. Quoted from Veli-Matti Kärkkäinen, *Spiritus ubi vult spirat*, 184. A significant variety of views on Spirit baptism among Pentecostals and Charismatics are discussed by Henry Lederle's significant *Treasures Old and New.*

39. William J. Seymour, "The Same Old Way," *Apostolic Faith* (Sept. 1906), 3.

40. William J. Seymour, "Questions Answered," *Apostolic Faith* (June-September 1907), 2. I am grateful to Cecil M. Robeck Jr. for directing me to Seymour's emphasis on love as the chief sign of Spirit baptism: "William J. Seymour and the 'Bible Evidence,'" in *Initial Evidence: Historical and Biblical Perspectives on the Pentecostal Doctrine of Spirit Baptism,* ed. Gary B. McGee (Peabody, MA: Hendrickson, 1991), 81.

Tongues were understood by many Pentecostals early on as xenolalia, that is, the capacity to proclaim the good news in the languages of the nations. Others were not so sure that tongues were xenolalia. W. F. Carothers claimed that tongues reveal Spirit baptism to be "a baptism of praise, coming over the balconies of heaven from the glorified presence of our Savior . . . striking up chords of praise we never dreamed existed in our souls and finding adequate expression only in tongues."[41] Unfortunately, after the view of tongues as a xenolalic evangelistic tool understandably waned among Pentecostals, the doctrine of tongues as evidence of Spirit baptism lost much of its global and ecumenical significance as a boundary-crossing experience.

Tongues as evidence became for many Pentecostals proof that we have a more powerful or miraculous experience of the Sprit than nontongue speakers. This individualistic and theologically bankrupt trend lost touch with the rich Lukan understanding of tongues as an ecumenical language that resists making any single language or idiom absolute in significance but rather embraces and transcends eschatologically all human languages and idioms. In my work on glossolalia, I have suggested shifting to the language of "sign" (rather than "evidence," which is not a biblical term) concerning tongues and focusing on the theological rather than a legalistic connection between them.[42] Other extraordinary gifts of the Spirit, such as prophecy, word of knowledge, and especially divine healing, are widely thought to accompany Spirit baptism among Pentecostals as well.

At this point, it is worth noting that the rigidity with which one holds to tongues as evidence of Spirit baptism has varied historically. Especially in the United States, some held to a rigid connection, arguing that one cannot claim to be baptized in the Spirit without tongues. Others recognized that tongues might not immediately follow the experience of Spirit baptism. Early Assemblies of God leader Joseph Roswell Flower believed that tongues should come at some time after Spirit baptism to confirm or culminate the experience but obviously felt that the experience itself did not need tongues to be legiti-

---

41. W. F. Carothers, *The Baptism with the Holy Ghost: The Speaking in Tongues* (Zion City, NY: published by author, 1906), 24.

42. Frank D. Macchia, "Sighs Too Deep for Words: Towards a Theology of Glossolalia," *Journal of Pentecostal Theology* 1 (Oct. 1992): 47–73; idem, "Tongues as a Sign: Towards a Sacramental Understanding of Pentecostal Experience," *Pneuma* 15:1 (Spring, 1993): 61–76.

mate.[43] Actually, initial evidence tends to be most rigidly adhered to among white Pentecostal denominations in the United States. Outside of these boundaries, attitudes toward it vary.

Henry Lederle wrote of a "sliding scale" among Pentecostals and charismatics on the relationship of tongues to Spirit baptism involving different degrees of rigidity.[44] Mainstream charismatics tend not to hold to the doctrine, with notable exceptions such as Presbyterian charismatic theologian J. Rodman Williams, who has been supportive of it.[45] Prominent Pentecostal leader Jack Hayford recently swam against the dominant U.S. Pentecostal stream by writing that one must not establish a "law" of tongues as necessary to Spirit baptism. Spirit baptism opens up the privilege or capacity to pray in tongues but one may not for various reasons choose to exercise it.[46] Pentecostals in the United States are divided over Hayford's proposal. Such diversity globally has caused some Pentecostals to wonder what meaning there is in having a distinctive doctrine in common if there is no universal agreement over most of the issues related to it.

Despite the diversity of distinctive doctrines among Pentecostals, a survey of Pentecostal literature especially in the early years of the movement (but even beyond) reveals that the favored doctrine is definitely the baptism in the Holy Spirit. And despite the diversity of viewpoints concerning the specifics of the doctrine, the vast majority of Pentecostals agree that it is profoundly charismatic, especially with regard to the extraordinary gifts of the Spirit, and is centered on the person of Christ as victor over all that opposes the accomplishment of God's will in the world. The vocational and charismatic dimensions to the experience need to be developed in terms of their

---

43. J. Roswell Flower, "How I Received the Baptism in the Holy Spirit (Pt. 1)," *The Pentecostal Evangel* (Jan. 21, 1933), 1–7; idem, "How I Received the Baptism in the Holy Spirit (Pt. 2)," *The Pentecostal Evangel* (Jan. 28, 1933), 2–13. Note Cecil M. Robeck's insightful discussion of this entire issue, "An Emerging Magisterium: The Case of the Assemblies of God," *Pneuma* 25 (Fall 2003): 164–215.

44. Henry I. Lederle, "Initial Evidence and the Charismatic Movement: An Ecumenical Appraisal," in *Initial Evidence: Historical and Biblical Perspectives on the Pentecostal Doctrine of Spirit Baptism*, ed. Gary B. McGee (Peabody, MA: Hendrickson, 1991), 131–41, esp. 137.

45. J. Rodman Williams, "Tongues as Initial Evidence," unpublished paper, given at Symposium on Tongues as Initial Evidence, Springfield, MO (May 23–25, 1998).

46. Jack Hayford, *The Beauty of Spiritual Language: My Journey Toward the Heart of God* (Dallas: Word, 1992), 89–107.

ecumenical significance and then couched in a more expansive pneumatological context so as to grant the doctrine a vital place in an ecumenical pneumatology. Neglecting the doctrine as merely one minor component of a
plethora of Pentecostal ideas is neither convincing as a historical thesis nor to
my mind fruitful as a theological option at the ecumenical table.

One question that does arise from the above discussion is whether or not
there was and is any continuity to Pentecostal theology. If Spirit baptism is not
adequate to provide such continuity, is Pentecostal theology an experience of
God that attaches itself to a mere cafeteria of theological ideas? Is there no
Pentecostalism but only separate Pentecostalisms? The research into the early
development of Pentecostal theology, especially by Donald W. Dayton[47] and
D. William Faupel,[48] was significant in that it provided a sense of coherence
to what was most distinctive to Pentecostal theology doctrinally. Especially
significant is Dayton and Faupel's turn to a Christ-centered spirituality as
enormously important and Faupel's turn to eschatology as the defining distinctive of the movement that offers a sense of coherence theologically. It is
to this discussion that we now turn.

FROM SPIRIT BAPTISM TO ESCHATOLOGY: TOWARDS COHERENCE

An important development in the research has occurred over the past few
decades that shifts the point of continuity or our chief theological distinctive
from Spirit baptism to eschatology. Donald Dayton maintained that Pentecostal theology, though more diverse than Spirit baptism and tongues, consisted of a coherent devotion to Jesus as Savior, Spirit Baptizer, Healer, and
Coming King. Though these themes were taken individually from the Holiness movement, Pentecostalism found its unique theological distinctive in the
formation of a fourfold *Gestalt* of devotion to Jesus. Interestingly, Dayton
notes that eschatology played a unique role in the influence of Pentecostalism
globally, writing that eschatology

> permeated the early literature of the movement, has resurfaced in key
> periods like the Latter Rain revival of the 1940's, appears even in the
> Catholic Charismatic Movement where the themes of classical Pente-
> costalism have been most transformed by a new theological context, and

---

47. Dayton, *Theological Roots of Pentecostalism*.
48. Faupel, *The Everlasting Gospel*.

characterizes the more distant cousins of Pentecostalism in the African Independent Churches.[49]

Add tongues and Pentecostal theology is born.

In a sense, the shift in focus to eschatology was anticipated also in Hollenweger's attention to narrative as that which is distinctive to Pentecostal theology (discussed below). This is so because narrative shifts the attention from the individual experience of Spirit baptism to the redemptive drama in history. The important shift to eschatology, however, gained its impetus in D. William Faupel's focus on the fourth element of the fourfold gospel, namely, eschatology, especially the latter rain of the Spirit as a charismatic and missionary empowerment given in preparation for Christ's imminent return. Faupel also regarded early Pentecostal theology as Jesus centered but made eschatology the chief theological framework in which Christ's redemptive and charismatic work comes to ultimately conquer all resistance and make all things new. The continuity now becomes eschatology as the overarching category in a theology of history or of the Christian life, not Spirit baptism as a pneumatological doctrine depicting personal charismatic empowerment.

Faupel even quoted an early Pentecostal source as stating that "we are not, as many suppose, wholly taken up with the mere matter of individual experience, solely with reference to the baptism in the Holy Spirit."[50] Most significant to the fourfold gospel, Faupel quotes one of the early Pentecostal voices approvingly: "Salvation, the Baptism in the Holy Spirit, Divine Healing, the ministrations of the Holy Spirit among us are features of a program.... The Second Coming of Lord Jesus Christ is not a feature of the program ... it is THE program. The ... others ... are features of this program leading up to the grand and glorious fulfillment."[51] Faupel portrayed Pentecostalism as an end-time missionary fellowship empowered by the latter-day outpouring of the Spirit and enjoying the full recovery of extraordinary gifts of the Spirit to missionize the world quickly before Christ returns.

How do we respond to Faupel's work as Pentecostal theologians? First, a case can be made that he and Dayton downplay the dominant concern with

---

49. Dayton, *Theological Roots of Pentecostalism*, 143. See also A. B. Simpson, *The Gospel of the Kingdom* (New York: Christian Alliance, 1890), 9.

50. M. W. Plummer, "The Latter Rain Reformation-Revival," *Word and Work* 32 (February 1910), 37, quoted in Faupel, *The Everlasting Gospel*, 41.

51. D. H. Mcdowell, "The Purpose for the Second Coming of the Lord," *The Pentecostal Evangel* (May 2, 1925), 2, quoted in Faupel, *The Everlasting Gospel*, 43.

Spirit baptism in early Pentecostal literature. It is my view that the doctrine dominates early Pentecostal theological concerns more than is generally admitted. There is still value, however, in Dayton's and Faupel's work in noting a broader coherence to Pentecostal theology, although there is some debate between them as to the precise nature of it. In fact, I find Faupel's reference to an eschatological narrative of the outpouring of the Spirit at the heart of Pentecostal distinctives rather compelling as a historical thesis. But Spirit baptism for Pentecostals is the experience that brings to realization personally what the eschatological latter rain of the Spirit brings corporately to an era of time.

In other words, the latter rain of the Spirit assures that Spirit baptism is not just an individual experience but has implications for how we view the entire church and its mission in the world. By contrast, the narrow Pentecostal understanding of Spirit baptism assures us that the belief in the latter rain of the Spirit has implications for personal spirituality. Rather than subordinate Spirit baptism to the latter rain, it would seem truer to Pentecostal theology to view the latter rain of the Spirit as the setting against which the broader implications of Spirit baptism should be understood and even further developed theologically.

Second, we can thus propose, beyond Faupel's intentions, that Spirit baptism should be expanded and reinvigorated by the eschatological nature of the Pentecostal vision of the latter rain rather than subordinated to it. Since eschatological passion for the return of Christ is an important Pentecostal distinctive, it is my view that part of the task facing us is to expand the Spirit baptism metaphor so as to integrate the latter rain with Christ's sanctifying grace or purity with power. This integration cannot proceed on the level of abstract categories such as "purity," "power," or whatever. Such terms function as references to something real and life-changing, namely, the presence of God to save, heal, and empower.

We are not speaking here about just any God but the God who is defined in covenant relation with Israel, as the one who sets the captives free, is the source of all life, and is revealed decisively in the liberating story of Jesus. As the Spirit of Jesus, this is the God revealed in the ever-expansive life of the Spirit poured out at Pentecost for the nations and present in the world through Word, sacrament, and powerful gifts or signs of the presence of Christ and the fullness of redemption to come. Finally, this is the God whose supreme quality is self-giving and redemptive love. In this light, "purity" and "power" cannot be played off against one another or synthesized abstractly but viewed as attributes and works of the God revealed in Scripture, especially in Christ as redemptive love, who is present polyphonically in ever-expansive and gifted relationships of love and faithfulness. It is divine love that is both pure and powerful.

Moreover, we cannot deny that this divine self-giving has a story and a plot, a history and an enfolding, that it comes to us though it also abides in and emerges from us. It is yet to come but already at work. Thus, eschatology is at its heart. I find Spirit baptism to be a useful metaphor for getting at the pneumatological substance of eschatology. Eschatology is helpful for showing the expansive reach of pneumatology, because eschatology implies a participation in God that is both purifying and empowering, presently at work and still unfulfilled, and life-transforming and demanding in terms of how we will respond to the reign of God in our times. This expansive reach is also aided by conscious recognition of the first article of the Creed concerning "God the Father, Creator of heaven and earth." Eschatology can only involve all of creation in its implicit yearning for the kingdom to come if the Spirit is seen as involved in the reach of life toward renewal in all things.

This question of the reinvigoration of Spirit baptism through eschatology, especially as it relates also to sanctification, requires further discussion. Though revitalizing or expanding the doctrine of Spirit baptism was not his goal, Steven J. Land helped to guide us in the initial step of integrating sanctification and eschatology in his significant book *Pentecostal Spirituality*, where he defines sanctification as the transformation of the affections into passions for the kingdom of God to come.[52] Similarly, under Land's influence, Samuel Solivan sought to wed Pentecostal spirituality and social concern with an understanding of Pentecostal pathos as a groaning for the redemption to come in solidarity with the suffering creation.[53]

Focusing spirituality on pathos and as a passionate yearning and sighing for the kingdom of God to come helps to connect personal sanctification with the eschatological latter rain. As I have shown elsewhere, the Blumhardts (Johann and his son Christoph), nineteenth-century southern German Pietists, had a profound influence on European Pentecostalism (and other Pietist

---

52. See Land, *Pentecostal Spirituality*.

53. Samuel Solivan, *The Spirit, Pathos and Liberation: Towards a Hispanic Pentecostal Theology* (Sheffield: Sheffield Academic Press, 1998).

churches) through their emphasis on divine healing as a sign of the kingdom of God dawning in the latter days, setting up a latter-day outpouring of the Spirit. Interestingly, they also connected this eschatological hope to personal piety through a spirituality shaped by a yearning and groaning for the kingdom of God in power to make all things new. Under the influence of his father's accent on healing, Christoph even came to view the latter-day outpouring of the Spirit as involving global social justice.[54]

My work on the Blumhardts paralleled the work of Land and Solivan not only in time but also theme. We all used the kingdom of God motif as an integrating concept to bring together personal piety, communal worship, and social praxis. We were not in this earlier work concerned particularly with the narrow Pentecostal understanding of Spirit baptism, despite its importance. Eschatology was the new frontier for us that gave us entry into both an aspect of our own tradition and the broader renewal of theology in the twentieth century that utilized apocalyptic eschatology as a way of applying prophetic criticism to both the church and the world.

The kingdom of God is indeed a powerful Protestant distinctive that arose with great force in Pietistic movements in order to fuel the surge toward missions and to stress the important but relative place of the church vis-à-vis the outworking of God's redemptive love in the world. When I first read Land's book, I was not particularly surprised that he did not use his integration of sanctification and eschatology as a context for rethinking the Pentecostal doctrine of Spirit baptism. I even recall noting as promising the fact that Spirit baptism received little attention in his book. The near absence of Spirit baptism in his book represented a significant shift away from Spirit baptism as a dominant concern among Pentecostal theologians.

I have come in recent years, however, to explore another alternative, namely, redefining Spirit baptism in the light of sanctification and eschatology. In doing so, I intend to augment the kingdom of God motif with the sanctification theme of participation in, and union with, God. Spirit baptism is well suited as a point of integration between sanctification and eschatology, since it is a metaphor that implies a participation in the life-transforming presence of God.

Before I get too far ahead of myself, let me say that Land's neglect of Spirit baptism is understandable, despite the fact that the ecumenical signif-

---

54. See Macchia, *Spirituality and Social Liberation*.

icance of the central Pentecostal distinctive was left relatively undeveloped in the process. Given the narrow definition Pentecostals have granted the term, it is not surprising that Land would want to shift the focus to eschatology in his effort to integrate purity and power. He remarked that those who see Pentecostalism as fundamentalist Christianity with Spirit baptism and spiritual gifts "tacked on" will be disappointed with his book.[55] Land found in eschatology a more encompassing distinctive than debates over subsequence or initial evidence. Moreover, Land responded to the historical scholarship that has over the past few decades broadened and diversified Pentecostal distinctives beyond Spirit baptism as a charismatic experience evidenced by tongues. As noted above, there is little question but that work in the early history of Pentecostal theology has tended, I think not entirely accurately, to relativize Spirit baptism as only one distinctive among others.

Land agrees, however, with relativizing Spirit baptism in this way. In agreement with Faupel, he contested in response to Dale Bruner's charge that Pentecostals are Spirit-baptism centered:

> To locate the theological center of Pentecostalism in Spirit baptism as Bruner does, or to see tongues as the only thing that distinguishes the spirituality from that of the Holiness or evangelical movements is to miss the point altogether. It is the eschatological shift within the Holiness movement toward premillennialism that signals what is decisive.[56]

Land recognizes the problem in Pentecostalism with regard to the fracture between purity and power, but he does not confront it directly and specifically as an enduring problem connected to the Pentecostal understanding of Spirit baptism. His strategy, rather, is to note an underlying integrationist tendency in Pentecostal spirituality, maintaining that sanctification and empowerment in reality among Pentecostals are "more fused together than split apart or even prioritized."[57] He explains that in Pentecostal spirituality we have among these distinct elements of purity and power "an infusion—because of the Spirit's effusion—of apocalyptic vision and power, which alters the way in which Christ, church, the Christian life and change are seen."[58]

---

55. Land, *Pentecostal Spirituality*, 29.
56. Ibid., 63.
57. Ibid.
58. Ibid.

Land's emphasis on the integrationist tendencies in the Pentecostal understanding of purity and power may cause some to understand his discussion as slanting more in the direction of what he wants Pentecostal spirituality to be than what it actually is.[59] Land rightly notes that he intended to do both.[60] I would maintain that his effort to integrate purity and power is present in seed form in Pentecostal theology but that the counter tendencies are just as pronounced, a point not given equal attention by Land.

In short, Land used eschatology to reconnect purity and power in the following three ways. First, he implies that apocalypticism is as ancient as the New Testament itself and can thus represent the recovery of something vital to ancient Christian faith. Land agrees with Käsemann that apocalyptic eschatology was the mother that cradled early Christianity, remarking that "Pentecostals were adopted by and adopted this 'mother 'and became sons and daughters, prophets and prophetesses of the new order of the Latter Rain of the Spirit."[61]

Second, as noted above, Land seeks to reconnect the Pentecostal emphasis on charismatic power in the latter rain of the Spirit with a sanctification doctrine. This connection is forged by an understanding of sanctified affections as passions for the kingdom of God.

Lastly, Land borrows from Moltmann to suggest a Trinitarian understanding of the eschatological realization of the kingdom of God in history so as to keep the continuity of Christ and the Spirit in one's understanding of the *ordo salutis* (Land prefers *via salutis* ["way of salvation"] in order to preserve his robustly eschatological emphasis).[62] Though this latter point received little development in his book, he rightly implies that a healing of the fractures in Pentecostal soteriology will require a rethinking of the Trinitarian context for salvation history.

I agree with Land's insight into the implicit integration of purity and power in Pentecostal spirituality and with his important insight into the role that eschatology can play in theologically understanding and developing it. As I will note in the next chapter, there is in early Pentecostal language a Wes-

---

59. Harvey Cox, "A Review of *Pentecostal Spirituality: A Passion for the Kingdom* by Steven J. Land," *Journal of Pentecostal Theology* 5 (1994): 5 (3–12).

60. Steven J. Land, "Response to Professor Harvey Cox," *Journal of Pentecostal Theology* 5 (1994): 14.

61. Land, *Pentecostal Spirituality*, 63.

62. Ibid., 75.

leyan understanding of Spirit filling and empowerment as a filling and transformation by the love of God, despite the dominant emphasis on charismatic
empowerment. But the formal doctrinal distinctions among most early Pentecostals between sanctification and Spirit empowerment also imply some
theological confusion and problems that require resolution. I would thus
regard Land's vision of Pentecostal spirituality as enormously insightful and
helpful as far as it goes but not penetrating enough into the potential problems to be faced in theologically reflecting on the role, if any, of Pentecostal
Spirit baptism in the sanctification of the affections. Land recognizes the problems by making the bridging of purity and power his major concern, but he
does not explore sufficiently the doctrinal location (Spirit baptism) where the
fracture between purity and power originally developed most explicitly.

Furthermore, Land's use of the kingdom of God as a dominant theological category is promising, since the kingdom has mainly to do with divine sovereignty and authority, especially in the form of an ultimate claim and an
ethical imperative. Land exploits this concept in order to integrate truth with
both the affections and the praxis, an integration for which the kingdom concept is well suited. It is especially well-suited for developing the integration
of spirituality and social concern. The kingdom also fits well with the Pentecostal penchant for power encounters and divine victories over the powers of
darkness, especially through spiritual gifts.

Interestingly, while the "kingdom of God" has been a dominant Protestant
and Pietistic theme, the Catholic emphasis has been on union with God, even
(in Augustine and Aquinas) on participation in God (an Eastern Orthodox
theme as well). Spirit baptism as an implicitly participatory metaphor of our
relationship with God may be useful in connecting with both "kingdom of
God" and personal "participation in God" as soteriological concepts. We
should also recognize that by itself, "kingdom" can be an alienating concept
for some, especially for those seeking less hierarchical or male-dominated
images for the polyphonic presence of Christ through the Spirit among the
people of God.

I find the category of the kingdom of God helpful, especially since I have
used it myself in my work on the Blumhardts and will use it here as well. I
have come, however, to view this category as subordinate to the notion of
participation in the ever-expanding fullness of divine love through the presence of Christ. The kingdom of God gains its substance as a historical dynamic
from the expanding presence and victory of God's love in both purity and

power especially in the church but also throughout the world, both implicitly and explicitly through the church's missionary arm. Later, I will develop the implications of Spirit baptism as a participatory metaphor for the *koinonia* that is central to our relationship with God and the nature of the church.

Divine authority and reign need not be alienating notions, since they have to do with the liberating reign of mutually edifying love. The Christ who returns victoriously to reign on earth has his robes baptized in blood as a symbol of the baptism of his death in his self-giving in divine love for the salvation of the world (Rev. 19:13). It is love that conquers in Christ and not hate, self-giving and not self-serving. That this love has a judgmental side for those who oppose it cannot be denied. But this judgment is not its divine intention. Indeed, in love, the Son was "delivered up" for our transgressions, just as the sinners are delivered up to their sinful passions (Rom. 1:26–27) in order that in his resurrection by the Spirit of holiness they might be justified (1:4; 4:25). Baptism in the Spirit implies a baptism into Christ and into God, a participation in the divine life by which we place on God our death, sin, suffering, and isolation in order to partake of his life everlasting, righteousness, healing, and fellowship.

Land is correct in noting that the "unfinished theological task of Pentecostalism is to integrate the language of holiness and the language of power."[63] This integration in part is precisely what is needed in our renewed discussion of Spirit baptism as a point of departure for a Pentecostal theology of the third article. Significantly, a somewhat different, though similar, response to Faupel's work was made by Catholic charismatic theologian Peter Hocken. The significance of Hocken's response was in the fact that he did not use eschatology to relativize Spirit baptism as Land did, but rather to expand and redefine the concept so that it might more fruitfully serve as the chief Pentecostal distinctive.

At a Society for Pentecostal Studies conference in 1992, Hocken suggested that the metaphor of the baptism in the Holy Spirit as used by John the Baptist was "predictive" in nature or focused on the eschatological event of final salvation and judgment. Hocken contrasted this with the narrower use of the metaphor in Pentecostal theology to refer to a stage in the individual Christian's experience of the Spirit. Though he found this formal Pentecostal definition of Spirit baptism too narrow to capture the breadth of the

---

63. Ibid., 23.

biblical notion, he also noted that the broader view was implicit in early Pentecostal testimonies that tied Spirit baptism to "signs that are classic indications of the Spirit's work: deep conviction of sin, awareness of the preciousness of the blood of the Savior and exaltation of the glorified Christ."[64]

What was significant about experiences of Spirit baptism among Pentecostals for Hocken was the fact that these events renewed the power of Pentecost in the experience of believers. The doctrine of the second and third blessings were incidental: "They were historical accidents reflecting the particular historical currents and experiences of the Pentecostal precursors."[65] Hocken concludes that "the terminology of the latter rain is much more central to the meaning of this work of the Spirit than the frameworks of second and third blessing."[66] He agrees with Faupel that the latter rain is more significant to Pentecostal distinctives than Spirit baptism as merely a step in one's personal *ordo salutis*. But, significantly, Hocken goes back to the biblical witness to suggest a more expansive definition of Spirit baptism in the light of the Pentecostal latter rain. I am convinced that he can help us move forward toward a renewal of the Spirit baptismal metaphor, even though I think Spirit baptism as a "second blessing" was more significant to early Pentecostals than Hocken admits and can still be significant for Pentecostals globally and ecumenically.

As we will see, resources for this redefinition of Spirit baptism can be found in what Donald Gelpi elaborates as a baptism in God's "breath" as an eschatological gift.[67] There are other Pentecostal voices globally that have called for an eschatological redefinition of the baptism in the Holy Spirit, such as Tak Ming Cheung.[68] Narciso C. Dionson has done so as well, noting that accepting Spirit baptism as fulfilled eschatologically means that "we no longer have to be drawn into the debate whether the purpose of Spirit baptism is soteriological or missiological, whether it is conversion initiation or second

---

64. Peter Hocken, "Baptism in the Spirit as Prophetic Statement: A Reflection on the New Testament and on Pentecostal Origins," paper delivered at the Society for Pentecostal Studies, Springfield, MO (Nov. 12–14, 1992), 16–17.

65. Ibid., 18.

66. Ibid.

67. Donald Gelpi, "Breath Baptism in the Synoptics," paper delivered at the Society for Pentecostal Studies, Pasadena, CA (Nov. 20, 1982).

68. Tak-Ming Cheung, "Understandings of Spirit Baptism," *Journal of Pentecostal Theology* 8 (1996): 115–28.

stage blessing."[69] Though Dionson does not develop why an eschatological understanding of Spirit baptism delivers us from the debates raised by the subsequence doctrine, he has certainly pointed in the direction of a fruitful attempt to do so. Last, Lyle Dabney has sought to define Spirit baptism as the eschatological gift of new creation in order to suggest a pneumatologically rich point of departure for soteriology.[70]

There is a mounting chorus of voices implying that eschatology is a way of revitalizing the Pentecostal doctrine of Spirit baptism and taking us further in the current discussion of Pentecostal theology. Implied in these voices is the fact that an eschatological interpretation of Spirit baptism not only revitalizes Spirit baptism by expanding it theologically, but there is also the possibility of revitalizing eschatology as a richly pneumatological concept.

If the Spirit is anything in the Bible, it is an eschatological gift (e.g., Ezek. 39:10; Matt. 12:28; Eph. 1:13–14; Heb. 6:5). Recognizing that eschatology is richly pneumatological opens the door to seeing the flames that ignite eschatological passion as the flame of divine love through the rich and diverse presence of Christ among us and the future culmination of that redemptive love at Christ's coming. Participation in God is participation in the eschatological freedom of the divine life in history to move all things toward new creation. Under the banner of love, eschatology can be seen as a healing as well as conquering concept, helping to fill out the dominant Pentecostal concern with the triumph of faith. There would exist through this eschatological reinvigoration of Spirit baptism a way of defining the substance of eschatology meaningfully for the spiritual life and the sanctified walk.

Despite the need for qualification, the shift to the latter rain of the Spirit as the most distinctive Pentecostal emphasis in the work of Faupel and Land has provided the impetus for many to break free from the concept of "stages

---

69. Narciso C. Dionson, "The Doctrine of the Baptism in the Holy Spirit: From a Pentecostal Pastor's Uneasy Chair," *Asian Journal of Pentecostal Studies* 2 (1999): 238. While this manuscript was in the initial stages of editing, I discovered a similar proposal by Larry Hart, who finds Spirit baptism to be "multidimensional" because it is eschatological: "Spirit Baptism: A Dimensional Charismatic Perspective," in *Spirit Baptism: Five Views*, ed. Chad Brand (Nashville: Broadman & Holman, 2004), 105–80.

70. D. Lyle Dabney, "'He Will Baptize You in the Holy Spirit': Recovering a Metaphor for a Pneumatological Soteriology," paper delivered at the Society for Pentecostal Studies, Tulsa OK (March 8–10, 2001).

of initiation" promoted by the doctrine of Spirit baptism as inherited by Pentecostals from the Holiness movement. This shift away from fragmentation is not to deny a distinction between regeneration, baptism, and Spirit filling as a prophetic call. But these aspects of initiation to the life of the Spirit must be seen as integrated within the one work of the same Spirit.

Since eschatology has become a powerful force in the renewal of systematic theology in the twentieth century, the shift from Spirit baptism to the latter rain of the Spirit seemed natural for many Pentecostals within the contemporary theological climate. It is quite telling that Jürgen Moltmann (next to Wesley and Barth) was Land's major source of inspiration in writing his *Pentecostal Spirituality*. This shift to eschatology as the central Pentecostal distinctive is by no means the only development in Pentecostal theology worthy of note (as we will see), but it is to me most interesting and helpful in rethinking Pentecostal theology for the twenty-first century.

As the reader can tell by now, I will suggest a doctrine of Spirit baptism that is Trinitarian and eschatological. The terms *eschatology* and *Spirit baptism* are naturally ambiguous and require definition, which the following chapters will attempt to give. The ambiguity of the two metaphors is related, since both point to realities hidden with Christ in God and only signified in the promise of new creation through the Spirit in the here and now. We stammer to give voice to this reality but realize that we struggle to express that which is too deep for words (Rom. 8:26).

Spirit baptism in the context of eschatology will be explored in future chapters. But before we embark on this reflection, we need to consider one more challenge facing our task, namely, the question as to whether what is most distinctive to Pentecostal theology can be focused on a point of doctrine. The waning significance of Spirit baptism in current Pentecostal theology is due in part to the conviction that how Pentecostal theology is conceived is what is most distinctive to Pentecostal theology and not any particular doctrinal construction. We turn once more to Walter Hollenweger to explore this conviction.

FROM SPIRIT BAPTISM TO ORAL THEOLOGY:
THE CHALLENGE OF THEOLOGICAL METHOD

Hollenweger not only diversified the doctrinal distinctives of Pentecostal theology, he shifted what was most distinctive about Pentecostal theology from doctrinal points to how theology itself was conceived. He wrote:

A description of these theologies cannot begin with their concepts. I have rather to choose another way and describe how they are conceived, carried and might finally be born. I am not sure whether the moment of birth has come yet, but that something is growing, is in travail and will finally break forth with elemental strength, is all too clear.[71]

Hollenweger did not focus on doctrinal issues but on the oral and dramatic nature of how theology is conceived among Pentecostals. Largely following his lead, some have come to regard any doctrinal construal of what is most distinctive about Pentecostal theology as of secondary importance to the way in which "theology" is actually conceived among Pentecostals.

This shift in focus from doctrinal points to what may be regarded as theological method made the centrality of Spirit baptism to Pentecostalism seem like an accident of history, a doctrinal holdover from the Holiness Movement that is not at all significant to what is most distinctive about Pentecostal theology. The narrow and ecumenically irrelevant understanding of Pentecostalism as a revivalistic "tongues movement" was replaced in Hollenweger's work with a Pentecostalism that seemed ecumenically relevant, at the forefront of a way of doing theology that is not burdened with post-Enlightenment standards of rational discourse.

Because of the work of Hollenweger and others, it became increasingly difficult to publish a book on Spirit baptism as subsequent to conversion and necessarily evidenced by tongues without appearing provincial in one's theology and completely off the mark in terms of what is really ecumenically significant about global Pentecostalism. His research spawned a generation of Pentecostal theologians convinced that Pentecostal distinctives are far broader and ecumenically relevant than the doctrines of Spirit baptism as subsequent to conversion or speaking in tongues as evidence of Spirit baptism.

Hollenweger has made many consider whether or not a doctrinal distinctive such as Spirit baptism can function fruitfully in a Pentecostal contribution to an ecumenical pneumatology. The obvious implication of his work is that doctrinal conceptions among Pentecostals are too diverse to provide us with that which is theologically distinctive to the movement. That which is really distinctive or most significant about Pentecostal theology for Hollenweger consists of forms of expression that lie close to the heartthrob

---

71. Walter J. Hollenweger, "Theology of the New World," *Expository Times* 87 (May 1976): 228.

of human experience of the divine. We refer here again to Harvey Cox's "primal" experience.

From this kind of concern, Hollenweger almost single-handedly shifted the direction of thinking about Pentecostal distinctives toward such a direction at a time when Pentecostals outside of Western contexts were beginning to grab the attention of the West and questions were beginning to be raised (especially in relation to the charismatic movement and the entry of Pentecostals into ecumenical dialogue) about the ecumenical relevance of dominant Pentecostal views of the doctrines of Spirit baptism and speaking in tongues. Hollenweger shifted the attention at this time to what seemed for many to be the more ecumenically relevant orality of liturgy, narrativity of theology and witness, maximum participation in reflection, prayer, and decision making within reconciling communities, inclusion of dreams and visions into personal and public forms of worship, and a correspondence of mind and body through healing and the dance.[72]

Of course, Pentecostals were not the only Christians outside of the West or in the southern hemisphere who approached theology through oral discourse and the dance, but Pentecostals were emerging in that part of the world as a major voice and an outstanding example of such experiential and oral theologizing. Furthermore, Hollenweger became fascinated by what he saw as a unique merging of Western Catholic perfectionistic spirituality channeled through Wesley and a non-Western narrative and oral approach to doing theology. Such integration uniquely gave Pentecostalism its vast global, ecumenical appeal and accounted in part for its rapid spread in the world.[73]

There is no question but that Pentecostalism worldwide has more or less favored less rational forms of theological discourse, especially on the grassroots level and when not straining to mimic their fundamentalist critics. Allan Anderson, who followed Hollenweger at the University of Birmingham in England, insightfully called Pentecostal theology in Africa "enacting theology," because it is dramatically produced in story, song, dance, and other movements.[74] Such a Hollenwegerian turn to how theology is done among Pentecostals has opened up fresh insights into the significance of the prevalence of narrative, oral, and

---

72. Note, e.g., Walter J. Hollenweger, "Priorities in Pentecostal Research: Historiography, Missiology, Hermeneutics, and Pneumatology," in *Experiences in the Spirit*, ed. J. A. B. Jongeneel (Bern: Peter Lang, 1989), 9–10.

73. Ibid.

74. Allan Anderson, *Zion and Pentecost*, e.g., 253.

dramatic forms of theology among Pentecostals worldwide. A theology deeply committed to the life of the Spirit cannot neglect aspects of experience in Christ that lie outside the limits of rational discourse. As Simon Chan notes, expanding theology to include prayer and other forms of worship and spirituality has ancient roots and needs to be respected in theological discourse today.[75]

Such insights into how Pentecostals do theology can also help us distinguish ourselves from the dominant fundamentalist hermeneutic shared among our most severe critics. Gerald Sheppard has shown that the fundamentalists were preoccupied with the modernist quest for scientific objectivity and the proper use of historical method in getting at the true meaning of Scripture and understanding its authority in governing Christian truth. The Pentecostals, however, were not originally part of this modernist debate. They were more interested in discerning the truth and authority of Scripture spiritually.[76] The hermeneutical gap for them was not primarily historical but spiritual. They did not advocate an objective and scientific analysis of the text that alienated the reader from the Scripture. They advocated a participation in the text that defined one's life and calling as a Christian and a church.

I was nourished in this participatory form of biblical interpretation growing up in a Pentecostal church. I still recall how struck I was as a seminary student by Hans Frei's masterpiece, *The Eclipse of Biblical Narrative*.[77] Frei gave me the academic language and concepts to understand how my community of faith relates to the biblical text in the context of the historical-critical methods of investigation. Frei noted how the historical-critical interpretation of the Bible has eclipsed the narrative function of the biblical text. Rather than entering the world of the biblical text in order to have one's own life context illuminated, the historical critic stood outside of the text, armed with tools that sought to locate the world of the text into a hypothetical understanding of real history.

Pentecostals telling stories and dancing within the world of the larger narrative of Scripture is one way in which the narrative function of Scripture can

---

75. Simon Chan, *Spiritual Theology* (Downers Grove, IL: InterVarsity Press, 1998), 45–46.

76. Gerald T. Sheppard, "Word and Spirit: Scripture in the Pentecostal Tradition (Part 1)," *Agora* (Spring 1978), 4–5, 17–22, esp. 4–5.

77. Hans Frei, *The Eclipse of Biblical Narrative: A Study in Eighteenth and Nineteenth Century Hermeneutics* (New Haven, CT: Yale Univ. Press, 1980).

emerge once more as prominent in the life of the church. As Jerry Camery-Hoggatt has reminded us, narrative interpretation provides the groundwork for a more participatory understanding of biblical interpretation that is shared by many Christian groups globally.[78] Pentecostals can also enter into discussion with a broad range of postmodern approaches to the biblical text built on what Leo Perdue has called the "collapse of history" in biblical exegesis today.[79]

Nevertheless, historical-critical tools of investigation are not to be dismissed, only qualified. Barth called them a valuable preparation (*Vorbereitung*) for a hearing of the Word of God in Scripture in a way that involves us wholly in this text.[80] Though there are other contexts for understanding the semantic thrust of the text besides ancient historical settings, such as the canonical context of the transformation of pre-biblical traditions into Scripture, historical-critical investigation into the biblical text can grant us important insights into the theological tensions that existed in the formation historically of prebiblical traditions and the biblical canon. Such tools have yielded much fruit, especially for ecumenical agreement on the biblical roots of the doctrines of the faith. One cannot deny their value. Within a participatory exegesis, there are critical issues that require exploration utilizing all of the tools at the disposal of academic discussion. There are also contextual issues that cannot be ignored, which are informed by the differences between what can be known about the ancient contexts involved in the formation of Scripture and contemporary situations.

Furthermore, systematic theological discourse urges one to reflect on the coherence of truth across a broad diversity of theological expressions possible through contextually inspired narratives and dances. Systematic theologians are needed to reflect on this coherence within Scripture and across the spectrum of the dogmatic loci that have emerged historically as most important to what George Lindbeck would call the doctrinal grammar of faith.[81] Systematic

---

78. Jerry Camery-Hoggatt, *Speaking of God: Reading and Preaching the Word of God* (Peabody, MA: Hendrickson, 1995).

79. Leo Perdue, *The Collapse of History: Reconstructing Old Testament Theology* (Minneapolis: Augsburg Fortress, 2005).

80. See Barth's "Preface to the Second Edition," in *The Epistle to the Romans*, trans. Edwyn C. Hoskyns (New York: Oxford Univ. Press, 1977), 6–7.

81. George Lindbeck, *The Nature of Doctrine: Religion and Theology in a Postliberal Age* (Philadelphia: Westminster, 1984), 24.

reflection on this doctrinal framework that focuses on the coherence of truth across the spectrum of doctrinal loci can offer a valuable service to Pentecostal communities that utilize forms of theological expression close to the heart-throb of prayer and Christian experience of God.

Geoffrey Wainwright's *Doxology: The Praise of God in Worship, Doctrine, and Life,* opened up for many of us a fresh way of discerning the ecumenical significance of worship for writing a systematic theology. *Lex orandi, lex credendi* ("rule of prayer, rule of faith") can be construed so as to make doctrine determinative for worship or worship determinative for doctrine. Wainwright noted that Protestant theology has favored the former while Catholic theology the latter.[82] Either way, Christian truth and identity comes to expression first in worship—enacted in worship, if you will—only to find both guidance from the doctrinal loci as well as serving to shape that doctrine historically. As Paul Tillich noted so well in his *Dynamics of Faith*, faith is complex and has experiential, practical, and rational dimensions. None of these can be completely neglected in any form of theological discourse.[83]

Wainwright's theological method helps us to understand how theology that emerges first in more experiential forms of expression such as prayers, songs, stories, and dances is both shaped by and shapes the more systematically and intellectually conceived doctrinal symbols. There is no question but that the significant hermeneutical discussion provoked by George Lindbeck's *The Nature of Doctrine* has made it difficult to conceive of a religious experience apart from a symbolic framework that includes deeply and corporately held doctrinal concepts, which function not only to express but also to cradle such experience. Lindbeck attempts to account for changes caused by Christian experience among symbols of the faith including doctrine by rightly regarding Christian experience as practical. He concludes that anomalies can develop among the symbols of the Christian faith as the experience of faith enters new contexts. Such doctrinal anomalies can develop through the ongoing contextualization of the faith.[84]

---

82. Geoffrey Wainwright, *Doxology: The Praise of God in Worship, Doctrine, and Life* (New York: Oxford Univ. Press, 1980), esp. 218–50.

83. Paul Tillich, *Dynamics of Faith* (New York: Harper & Row, 1972).

84. George Lindbeck, *Nature of Doctrine,* 89; see Frank D. Macchia, "Christian Experience and Authority in the World: A Pentecostal Viewpoint," *Ecumenical Trends* 31:8 (December 2002), 122–26.

Though Pentecostals welcome this praxis-oriented understanding of Christian experience, we also want to center Christian experience in the impact of the Holy Spirit on our worship as well. One cannot deny that worship can play a revolutionary role in the transformation of our symbols, including our doctrinal formulations. Anomalies do not occur in doctrinal formulations solely from the practical demands of contextualization, as Lindbeck maintains. At any rate, the point to be made here in relation to Hollenweger is that there is more of a reciprocal relationship between experience and doctrinal concepts among Pentecostals than he has recognized. One cannot in my view distinguish as sharply as Hollenweger does between early Pentecostal experience and the doctrinal symbol of Spirit baptism.

Hollenweger's scholarship does remind us, as Emil Brunner pointed out, that in addition to the issue of the continuity of sound doctrine, there is also the continuity in the church of new life in the Holy Spirit.[85] In eschatological freedom, the Spirit works in the expansion and continuity of both doctrine and life (as we have implied, the two are inseparable, though distinct). The Word of God comes to us not only in words but in power (1 Cor. 2:4; 4:20), which Paul defines as the power of love (1 Cor. 13). Brunner notes that in the *pneuma*, of which the church was conscious, existed extraordinary powers "that are lacking today."[86] The Spirit is the "stepchild" of theology today because theologians are accustomed to developing the logic of faith to the neglect of its dynamism and power.[87] Gary D. Badcock notes in addition that there is no lack of theological treatises on the Spirit, but that even here there is a lack of willingness to integrate into the discussion "the somewhat a-logical, unpredictable, indefinable work of the Spirit in the world."[88] To be rightly pneumatological (and rightly *theo*logical), theology needs to develop an idiom that seeks to "glorify God and enjoy him forever."

To use a secular analogy, reading certain theologies today can seem like reading manuals on love as a psychological and sociological phenomenon that never touch on the power that it exercises in life to change us and to move us aesthetically, spiritually, morally, and so on. Such manuals have an important

---

85. Emil Brunner, *Das Missverständnis der Kirche* (Zürich: Theologischer Verlag Zürich, 1988), 53–54.

86. Ibid.

87. Ibid.

88. Gary B. Badcock, *Light of Truth and Fire of Love: A Theology of the Holy Spirit* (Grand Rapids: Eerdmans, 1997), 6.

role to play in understanding love, but alone they are potentially reductionistic and uninspiring. Hollenweger wants to direct our attention to a theological language that lies closer to the experience of the love of God than many expressions of academic theology today. Oral and dramatic theology does this, though such is not the only idiom available and cannot be if theology is also to be an intellectual discipline, which it must be.

The point I wish to stress at this juncture is that Hollenweger's shift to oral and dramatic theology need not leave Spirit baptism behind. The church has lived for centuries with both narrative and doctrinal expressions of the faith, and Spirit baptism as a biblical metaphor can function well as our chief distinctive on both levels. The difficulty that I have with Hollenweger's discussion of Spirit baptism is his categorization of it solely on the side of doctrinal symbols conceptually formulated and defined.[89] Spirit baptism is also a metaphor in the biblical material and in much Pentecostal preaching that expresses in various ways a particular "twist" on the Christian story, which the vast majority of Pentecostals globally would embrace.[90] This take on the Christian story sees the victory of God in Christ as pneumatological in emphasis. It is also eschatological, charismatic, and deeply experiential. In Spirit baptism, the divine-human interaction is not just an abstract issue to be debated but an overwhelming participation in God that is sanctifying and ever more expansive and diversifying charismatically.

Whether experiential or doctrinal, Spirit baptism can function in multiple ways to guide the Pentecostal movement towards a Trinitarian, Christoformistic, pneumatologically rich and diverse, and eschatologically robust version of Christian life and thought. This is because Spirit baptism draws one into the field of God's presence and transforms one's life with the love of God. Everything we do and say, from Scripture reading to action in the world, takes place as a functional component of this baptism. This baptism implies that we do not relate to God as an object of reflection; rather, we are baptized into God as a powerful field of experience, which opens up wonders and joys as a daily experience.

That this presence is also experienced in anguish and suffering is testified and preached about in Pentecostal churches as well, though, admittedly, not

---

89. Hollenweger does this in "Priorities in Pentecostal Research," 15–17.
90. See Kenneth J. Archer, "Pentecostal Story: The Hermeneutical Filter for the Making of Meaning," *Pneuma* 26:1 (Fall 2004), 36–59.

nearly as often (or often enough). Spirit baptism means that from both bliss and sorrow, prayer becomes central to how we think and act in relation to God. One is called to lose oneself in the loving presence of God like a bird soars on the wind and a fish swims in water. One loses oneself in this love only to find oneself again.

POSTSCRIPT: THE UNFINISHED BUSINESS OF PENTECOSTAL THEOLOGY

In short, what is the unfinished business of Pentecostal theology? It is not just narrative theology as a Pentecostal distinctive but the narrative theology of Spirit baptism in Acts in relation to other voices in the biblical canon. As we have mentioned and will discuss in future chapters, Roger Stronstad and Robert Menzies have argued for a distinctive understanding of Spirit baptism in Acts that is not soteriological in function but rather charismatic. Menzies restricts Spirit baptism in Luke further to the power to engage in prophetic gifts, including speaking in tongues, in order to affirm that all Christians are charismatic by virtue of conversion to Christ.[91] Their broader purpose is to secure the exegetical basis for the Pentecostal experience of Spirit baptism as empowerment for charismatic, especially, prophetic service. As they see it, such a distinct experience can be lost to the church if we read a Pauline soteriological understanding of Spirit baptism and the Spirit's work into Luke and fail to recognize Luke's exclusively charismatic understanding of the Spirit baptismal metaphor.

Their arguments have gained a hearing in the Pentecostal churches and academy. The Assemblies of God position paper on Spirit baptism even recommends Stronstad's book, *The Charismatic Theology of St. Luke*, for further reading.[92] What many fail to note about Stronstad's and Menzies' exegetical conclusions, however, is their recognition of the fact that *Spirit baptism in the context of Paul's pneumatology is soteriological*. Stronstad notes that Paul's theology of Spirit baptism (1 Cor. 12:13) and related pneumatology "is always initiatory and incorporative" into Christ and the life of the church.[93] Similarly, Menzies notes that Paul "does not explicitly speak of a gateway experience

---

91. Robert Menzies, "The Spirit of Prophecy, Luke-Acts and Pentecostal Theology: A Response to Max Turner," *Journal of Pentecostal Theology* 15 (1999): 73.

92. See the box, "Q&A on the Holy Spirit," in Roger Stronstad, "They Spoke in Tongues and Prophesied," *Enrichment Journal* 10:1 (2005): 82.

93. Stronstad, *Charismatic Theology of St. Luke*, 10.

distinct from conversion."[94] Pentecostal scholar of Spirit baptism Harold Hunter had also earlier concluded that Paul's understanding of Spirit baptism, unlike Luke's, is integral to salvation.[95] These scholars obviously do not want to commit the error of reading a Lukan understanding of Spirit baptism into Paul. But this worthy goal leaves wide open the broader task of constructing a Pentecostal doctrine of Spirit baptism that integrates the soteriological and the charismatic.

Stronstad's and Menzies' conclusions seem to indicate that Spirit baptism is a fluid metaphor in the narrative witness of Scripture, taking on different nuances of meaning. But they do not dwell on this point. They are focused on distinguishing Luke's Spirit baptism theology from Paul's, so they fail to raise the broader question as to how to integrate Luke's charismatic and Paul's soteriological understandings of the metaphor. Menzies states that the two views "complement one another," but more is needed to unpack what this might mean theologically or what all-encompassing framework pneumatologically might be useful in couching the complementary relationship between them.[96] Perhaps this task is more in the domain of systematic theology than New Testament studies. This is the task I wish to initiate in the following discussion.

In going about this task, we will need to raise the question as to whether or not Luke's understanding of Spirit baptism is indeed *only* charismatic or prophetic, or whether Luke had something broader in mind than the revival experiences or missionary empowerment of individual Christians. Luke does couch Spirit baptism within the inauguration and fulfillment of the kingdom of God (Acts 1:2–8; 2:17–21), and he seems more taken with the reconciliation of different cultural groups within the church than with the quality of experience among individual Christians.

Korean theologian Youngmo Cho, following Menzies' exegetical conclusions, maintains that Luke only relates the inauguration of the kingdom of God indirectly to Spirit baptism. Spirit baptism for Luke does not inaugurate the kingdom of God but is rather the "power to proclaim the Kingdom."[97] Again, in Cho's analysis, Luke's pneumatology is distinguished from Paul's, for Luke regards Spirit baptism as empowerment for witness while Paul identi-

---

94. Menzies, "The Spirit of Prophecy," 72.
95. Hunter, *Spirit Baptism*, 53.
96. Menzies, *Empowered for Witness*, 242.
97. Youngmo Cho, "Spirit and Kingdom in Luke-Acts: Proclamation as the Primary Role of the Spirit in Relation to the Kingdom of God in Luke-Acts," *Asian Journal of Pentecostal Studies* 6:2 (July 2003): 197.

fies the Spirit as the source of the kingdom of God. Yet, does not the proclamation of the kingdom of the Spirit participate in the inauguration of the kingdom? At the very least, he does suggest some kind of relationship between them. However, Matthew clearly does relate them directly. According to Matthew, John the Baptist predicts the coming of the Spirit Baptizer in the context of John's proclamation of the kingdom of God (Matt. 3:1–12) and has Jesus speak of the Spirit as functioning to bring the kingdom of God to people in acts of deliverance: "But if I drive out demons by the Spirit of God, then the kingdom of God has come upon you" (12:28).

The bottom line is this: If we grant that Luke's conception of Spirit baptism is at least prominently charismatic, calling for an experience of prophetic and charismatic empowerment among Christians, what might a systematic doctrine of Spirit baptism look like in the light of Paul and other New Testament voices? It is a question that many who follow Stronstad's and Menzies' exegetical conclusions have not yet asked. It is a question that I am asking in this discussion, and my suggestion for answering it follows.

Suffice it to say here that the Spirit baptismal metaphor can be descriptive of both God's action in inaugurating the kingdom of God and our empowered witness to this kingdom in the world. The Pentecostal experience of Spirit baptism fashioned from the book of Acts can be couched within a broader pneumatological framework of God's sanctifying grace and the inauguration of the kingdom of God in power, a broader framework implied by Luke but explicitly provided by Matthew and Paul (not to mention John). This effort requires taking a broad range of Scripture into consideration.

Such a task is urgent, since a compartmentalization of the Pentecostal understanding of Spirit baptism as a post-conversion charismatic empowerment will fail to enrich our understanding of the soteriological functions of the Spirit and vice versa. For example, on the one hand, does not the charismatic and missionary empowerment of the Spirit grant the church's kingdom life an outward-moving orientation toward the "other"? On the other hand, without the kingdom life of the Spirit, what is this "power" that inspires the charismatic or prophetic involvement of Christians—mere raw energy? A Spirit baptism doctrine that integrates soteriological and charismatic functions will enhance both in Pentecostal theology.

In the discussion that follows, I will ask the question suggested by the themes that have emerged over the last several decades of Pentecostal scholarship, namely: What unites sanctification, charismatic empowerment, and the inauguration of the kingdom of God in power in the life of the church and throughout the creation? What is the greatest gift of all that purifies, inspires all spiritual gifts, and reaches for the fulfillment of the kingdom of God throughout creation until we see the Lord "face to face" (1 Cor. 13:12)?

Paul notes concerning both the power behind his mission and the source of salvation: "For Christ's love compels us, because we are convinced that one died for all, and therefore all died. And he died for all, that those who live should no longer live for themselves but for him who died for them and was raised again" (2 Cor. 5:14–15). This love has been poured out upon us by the Spirit of God (Rom. 5:5), the Spirit who proceeds from the Father and is mediated to us by the crucified and risen Christ. It is this supreme gift of the Spirit as the gift of divine love that can ultimately serve as the point of integration. Our final conclusion will be that Spirit baptism is a baptism into the love of God that sanctifies, renews, and empowers until Spirit baptism turns all of creation into the final dwelling place of God. Along the way, Pentecostals will be justified in calling Christians to a Spirit baptism as a fresh experience of power for witness with charismatic signs following.

THE KINGDOM AND THE POWER:
EXPANDING THE BOUNDARIES OF SPIRIT BAPTISM

WHERE DO WE GO FROM HERE? THE CENTRALITY OF SPIRIT BAPTISM in the Pentecostal and charismatic movements stands in stark contrast to the neglect of the metaphor in other traditions. If treated at all outside of Holiness, Pentecostal, and charismatic churches, the topic tended to be discussed within the meaning of Christian baptism. Even under baptism one will usually not find an explicit discussion of Spirit baptism in its own right. The neglect is puzzling in the light of the fact that all four gospels introduce the ministry of the Messiah with the Spirit baptism metaphor in a way that does not merely predict the effects of Christian baptism but, more broadly, explains what will usher in the kingdom of God (e.g., Matt. 3:2–12; cf. Acts 1:2–8).

Furthermore, the fact that Spirit baptism is the major theological accent of most Pentecostal and charismatic churches, one of the largest Christian movements in the world, should attract some ecumenical attention. But not much attention has been paid ecumenically to the topic, due in part no doubt to the relative lack of Pentecostal involvement in ecumenical conversations. For example, Emmanuel Lanne's lengthy treatment of baptism from a global, ecumenical perspective in the *Dictionary of the Ecumenical Movement* devotes one sentence to Spirit baptism, only to dismiss it with the remark that the Pentecostal focus on this topic "poses problems for other Christian communions."[1] This isolated remark

---

1. Emmanuel Lanne, "Baptism," *Dictionary of the Ecumenical Movement*, ed. Nicholas Lossky et. al. (Grand Rapids: Eerdmans, 1991), 79.

stands unexplained. No entry on Spirit baptism exists anywhere else in this dictionary. The casual way in which the Pentecostal focus on Spirit baptism is raised and dismissed, if it is raised at all, has not been unusual in ecumenical or theological discussions on pneumatology or baptism.[2]

As we have seen, the Pentecostal isolation of Spirit baptism from Christian initiation is indeed problematic. But, then again, so is the failure to imagine any meaning to Spirit baptism as a distinct category worthy of focused theological reflection. The recent monographs on the subject have been provoked in large measure by the Pentecostal challenge. We should all be grateful to scholars such as Kilian McDonnell, George Montague, and James Dunn for the service they have granted us by reflecting on Spirit baptism from the vantage point of sacramental and nonsacramental traditions. The Pentecostal responses from scholars such as Harold Hunter, Howard Ervin, Roger Stronstad, and Robert Menzies have done much to stimulate theological discussion of this important biblical metaphor. So, where do we go from here?

We start by recognizing some of the critical issues involved in the dominant approaches to the Pentecostal doctrine of Spirit baptism so as to suggest a way forward. I will share from the start my conviction that the boundaries of the discussion need to be expanded. The overarching debate with Pentecostals over the issue of Spirit baptism has tended to focus the discussion on the issue of Christian initiation. Though this focus has value, especially for Pentecostals who have qualified their understanding of Spirit baptism in its light, it has exhausted its usefulness.

This is so because the focus on Christian initiation tends to bind the discussion to the larger impasse of competing ecclesiologies. Word ecclesiologies tend to interpret Spirit baptism in relation to the adequacy of the Word of God and faith to constitute the church and to initiate one into all of the spiritual blessings found in Christ (Eph. 1:3). Sacramental ecclesiologies are prone to interpret Spirit baptism in relation to the church as the sacrament of grace and to one's incorporation into the body of Christ through the sacraments of initiation. The Pentecostals see the church as the empowered and charismatic community. Spirit baptism is thus viewed as the personal renewal

---

2. For example, G. C. Berkouwer's fine volume on the sacraments devotes two pages to Spirit baptism (*The Sacraments* [Grand Rapids: Eerdmans, 1969], 95–96), but he limits his discussion to the narrow issue of the relationship between John's baptism and Christian baptism. Spirit baptism warrants in his lengthy discussion of baptism no theological reflection in its own right.

needed to bring the church back to the rich and powerful charismatic life evident in the book of Acts. Can we get beyond this impasse?

We can possibly break free from the limitations of past debates if we shift the context of the discussion to that which involves but transcends the church, namely, the inauguration and fulfillment of the kingdom of God. As we will have occasion to note, Spirit baptism has profound implications for the constitution and *koinonia* of the church. But it is my conviction that not even the ecclesiological interest, though valuable in lifting Spirit baptism beyond the boundaries of individual renewal experiences, is adequate to break us out of the current impasse in the discussion or to capture the full breadth of the metaphor as used in the New Testament. The love of God poured out upon us in the gift of the Spirit (Rom. 5:5) cannot be exhausted by the *koinonia* of the church. The Pentecostal attention to eschatology and the missionary outreach of the church implies as much.

The need to expand the discussion to see Spirit baptism in the light of the kingdom of God has implications for personal spirituality as well. On an individual level, the debate over competing ecclesiologies translates into the nature of Christian initiation and whether or not there is a Spirit baptismal experience to be had for people of faith that will open them to the kind of charismatic ministry evident in Acts but lacking to a significant degree in many churches. There are charismatics who have advocated mediating positions that seek to incorporate the Pentecostal desire for a Spirit baptismal experience within an otherwise word or sacramental ecclesiology. Many have distinguished between Spirit baptism *theologically defined* as Christian initiation and Spirit baptism as an *experience* of renewal to be had by all believers. This train of thought is in the right direction, I believe, but it makes an unfortunate distinction between theology and experience. If the fulfillment of the kingdom of God and not the narrow concern for Christian initiation is in view, a theology and an experience of Spirit baptism can be integrated on a higher level within a theology of the kingdom of God that has both incorporative and experiential dimensions. This option should become clearer throughout the discussion of this and the next two chapters.

In this chapter, we will lay the ground work for expanding the boundaries of Spirit baptism in preparation for the chapters that follow, which will discuss Spirit baptism in various aspects of the doctrine (Trinitarian/soteriological and ecclesiological) and the essence of Spirit baptism as a baptism in divine love. We will survey here the major understandings of the metaphor, regeneration, sacramental initiation, and empowerment for witness, only to conclude with a brief reflection on the kingdom of God as the means for expanding our discussion of Spirit baptism.

SPIRIT BAPTISM AND REGENERATION

At the base of Spirit baptism is a proclaimed promise of new life in Christ: "For the promise is for you, for your children, and for all who are far away, everyone whom the Lord our God calls to him" (Acts 2:39, NRSV). This promise was preached and received through repentance and faith. It comes to us, therefore, as a gospel of what God has done for us to give us new life in Christ. This gospel is the presupposition of all human reception and experience of the gift of the Spirit. Spirit baptism in the evangelical traditions influenced by Reformed theology has thus been defined according to this presupposition, namely, as regeneration by faith in Christ as proclaimed in the gospel.

The connection of Spirit baptism to the gospel implies an accent on the divine action in Spirit baptism and the necessary response of trusting the promises of God. The influence of Reformed theology can be seen from emphases on the preached Word of God, the sovereignty and freedom of the divine action in bestowing the Spirit on those who accept Christ, and the sufficiency of Christ as embraced in faith for the spiritual life. Talk of sacramental "means of grace" as efficacious in baptizing believers in the Spirit can within this evangelical concern be regarded with suspicion that the grace of God is somehow being placed at the disposal of the church as an inherent capacity of sacramental forms. Water baptism would thus tend to be viewed as the human response or witness to what God has done in Spirit baptism. Furthermore, talk of a Pentecostal "second blessing" distinct from regeneration seems to call into question the sufficiency of Christ for salvation.

Reformed theology is, of course, more complex than the description of Spirit baptism given above. As we will note in a later chapter, John Calvin did not hesitate to speak of the sacraments as efficacious or as the *instrumentum* of grace. The view of Spirit baptism described above is typically held among many within "evangelical" or "Free Church" traditions. Yet, a number of Baptist theologians have also moved in the direction of a sacramental understanding of baptism as in some sense instrumental in God's effecting a relationship with Christ through the Spirit.[3] More recently, even the concept of a sacramental symbol tends to imply the capacity of symbol to bring to realization that to which the symbol points.[4]

With regard to the Pentecostal challenge, there are also Reformed theologians, such as Karl Barth and Hendrikus Berkhof, who have placed a heavy emphasis on the vocational dimension of faith, beyond the implications of justification and even sanctification as they have been traditionally defined. In both issues of sacrament and empowerment, the accent among Reformed theological giants has been on the primacy of the Word of God and of our faith in the gospel for occasioning Spirit baptism and for providing us with an understanding of water baptism as the "sign and seal" of salvation. Thus, the distinctness of Spirit baptism as the divine act of freely binding us to Christ through our faith in the gospel shows all of the marks of a Reformed theological influence.

In short, Spirit baptism from the perspective described above is essentially the possibility of "repentance unto life" (Acts 11:18). It is God's act by which Christian identity is established by grace and the gift of the Spirit in the context of faith in Christ. Implicit in this doctrine is the fact that faithfulness to Christ is a miracle that has at its base the power of the Word of God as a river of new life, a life that is free but also costly in terms of the journey that it requires of those swept up in its current.

For example, Karl Barth viewed Spirit baptism as a fundamental alteration in one's loyalty from darkness to light. He called it a liberation and a radical change in a person, a passage from death to life.[5] As miraculous, Spirit baptism implied for Barth an accent on the divine possibility of faithfulness to God on behalf of the creature. It is first and foremost not an enhancement of our moral or religious possibilities or something that we do with the aid of divine grace. Though involving faith in Christ, Spirit baptism is first God's act before it ever involves the faithful response that it makes possible.[6] Hence,

---

3. See Geoffrey Wainwright, *Christian Initiation* (Richmond, VA: John Knox, 1969), 50ff.

4. See Karl Rahner, "Theology of the Symbol," *Theological Investigations*, vol. 4, *More Recent Writings*, trans. Kevin Smyth (New York: Crossroad, 1982), 221–52.

5. Karl Barth, *Church Dogmatics*, vol. 4, part 4, trans. G. W. Bromiley and T. F. Torrance (Edinburgh: T&T Clark, 1969), 6–9.

6. Ibid., 3.

we cannot begin to understand this baptism unless we stand before it with "helpless astonishment."[7]

Barth knew that a focus on the miraculous nature of Spirit baptism would raise questions about the possibility of human freedom and cooperation with God in the context of God's sovereign act of redemption. Barth did not want to deal with such issues in the abstract. Thus, the divine possibility of human faithfulness implied in Spirit baptism became for Barth the Christological possibility.[8] The Christological possibility of our faithfulness to God grounds the theological discussion in the specific and concrete divine action in history and not on abstract theological prolegomenon.

The key question involved in Spirit baptism thus becomes how the story of divine and human faithfulness played out in the life, death, and resurrection of Jesus comes to involve us. How does Jesus' story become our story? Interestingly, Barth (à la Oscar Cullmann) came to see Jesus' entire life story as a general "baptism" from death to life that is done on behalf of humanity as a whole.[9] How divine sovereignty and human freedom relate is thus dramatized for us in the story of Jesus and made real in us through the Spirit. Barth sought to avoid a "christomonism" that defines anthropology and all other theological loci only according to Christology and an "anthropomonism" that defines Christology according to the realization of an abstract, anthropological ideal. Christology is fundamentally determinative for human freedom in relation to God, but human freedom still brings with it all that is distinctly human in a particular person's life.[10]

As a Reformed theologian (and under the influence of the book on baptism written by his son Markus), Barth defended the freedom and sovereignty of the Spirit in Spirit baptism. Spirit baptism is not formalized in water baptism nor mediated by the church. The church "is neither author, dispenser, nor mediator of grace and its revelation."[11] The church can at best "participate as assistant and minister" in the "self-attestation or self-impartation of Jesus Christ himself" in the gospel.[12] But the granting of Spirit baptism in one's acceptance of the gospel by faith does call for water baptism as the church's

---

7. Ibid.
8. Ibid., 11–13.
9. Ibid., 23.
10. Ibid., 19–20.
11. Ibid., 32.
12. Ibid.

fitting, obedient response to God's gracious self-giving. As such, water baptism also witnesses to the grace of God given fundamentally in the proclaimed Word. Spirit baptism is God's free act mediated only by God in that Word from which the sacraments draw their power and significance.

According to a widely-discussed treatment of Spirit baptism from a similar perspective by James Dunn, Spirit baptism is the bestowal of the Spirit that functions as God's decisive act of establishing Christian identity. In his classic, *Baptism in the Holy Spirit*, Dunn's accent is much more on the pneumatological sphere of Christian identity than on the Christological possibility of our faithfulness to God.[13] The Holy Spirit is the nerve center of the Christian life that marks one essentially as a Christian. Dunn deals with the Christological basis of pneumatological experience elsewhere in his highly significant *Jesus and the Spirit*, especially with regard to Jesus' sonship and charismatic ministry.[14]

With his accent in his Spirit baptism book on the pneumatological sphere of Christian identity, however, Dunn involves Spirit baptism more richly than Barth does in the unique Christian experiences and giftings of the Spirit. Barth does not exclude this consequence of Spirit baptism, noting quite broadly that Spirit baptism has to do with faithfulness in "thought, speech and action in responsibility to God, in living hope in him, in service to the world, in free confession, in unceasing prayer."[15] But Barth's accent in discussing Spirit baptism is on the divine possibility in Christ for such consequences and not on that which is graspable in human experience.

Dunn, on the other hand, significantly stresses the realm of the Spirit as the locus of Christian identity and is not hesitant to note that the gift of the Spirit is dramatically experiential in the New Testament. He points out that in the New Testament "the reception of the Spirit was a very definite and often dramatic *experience*."[16] Dunn establishes this insight not only on the basis of Lukan texts but on others as well, including Paul. Dunn's conclusion that

---

13. James D. G. Dunn, *The Baptism in the Holy Spirit: A Re-examination of the New Testament Teaching on the Gift of the Spirit in Relation to Pentecostalism Today* (London: SCM, 1970).

14. James D. G. Dunn, *Jesus and the Spirit: A Study of the Religious and Charismatic Experience of Jesus and the First Christians as Reflected in the New Testament* (Philadelphia: Westminster, 1975).

15. Barth, *Church Dogmatics*, vol. 4, part 4, x.

16. Dunn, *Baptism in the Holy Spirit*, 105, 113.

Spirit baptism involves an experience is a significant turn in the direction of a distinctly Pentecostal understanding of Spirit baptism (as we will have occasion to elaborate upon below).

Though critical of Pentecostal theology, Dunn gives some credence to it by emphasizing that Spirit baptism has at least experiential and charismatic implications for the Christian life and criticizes the mainline churches for reducing the discussion of the Christian's experience of the Spirit to sacramental or psychological categories.[17] Dunn's criticism of Pentecostal theology is found in his conviction that the Spirit is given in connection with repentance and faith in the gospel. Water baptism bears an indirect relationship to Spirit baptism in the sense that water baptism functions as the fulfillment of one's act of repentance and faith. There are Pentecostal scholars, such as Gordon Fee, who have embraced Dunn's view of Spirit baptism and, like Dunn, find value in the charismatic experience of the Spirit cherished by the Pentecostal heritage.[18]

There is little question but that the accent of this general understanding of Spirit baptism is on faith in Christ as the moment of the Spirit's reception. How else is one to explain Dunn's strenuous efforts to show that the Samaritans' faith was defective in Acts 8 prior to their reception of the Spirit? It is unlikely that Luke fashioned his narrative to highlight this point. But Dunn's major point concerning Acts 8 is that for Luke, the giving of the Spirit is most decisive to Christian identity. Not even faith and baptism are adequate without the chief sign of Christian identity, namely, the Holy Spirit's presence.[19]

Dunn is quite right about this aspect of Luke's theology. Yet, is not Luke's point that Christian identity is signified and fulfilled in the Spirit that comes with power to renew the people of God charismatically and to propel them into the world? There is no question but that Luke connects Spirit baptism inseparably to repentance and faith. Severing Spirit baptism from these would be to sever it from John the Baptist's ministry, something Luke is careful not to do despite his emphasis on Christ's work as its fulfillment (Acts 1:5). Spirit baptism is thus "repentance unto life" (11:18). But, for Luke, Spirit baptism also catches believers up in a prophetic calling and empowerment for service.

---

17. Ibid., 225.

18. See Gordon Fee, "Hermeneutics and Historical Precedent—A Major Problem in Pentecostal Hermeneutics," in *Perspectives on the New Pentecostalism*, ed. Russell P. Spittler (Grand Rapids: Baker, 1976), 119–32.

19. Dunn, *Baptism in the Holy Spirit*, 67.

How else is one to explain Luke's strenuous efforts to show that the endowment of the Spirit was a public event manifested in signs of prophetic inspiration and power?

What needs to be explored, therefore, from Barth's and Dunn's perspectives is in what sense Spirit baptism involves our empowerment for gifted service in the world. Hendrikus Berkhof has noted correctly that Barth's general soteriology highlights the vocational element of the Christian life, because faith for Barth is the first step of Christian obedience. This understanding of faith explains why Barth cannot separate dogmatics from witness or ethics. Berkhof also notes that Pentecostals have done much to accent the vocational dimension of faith through its doctrine of Spirit baptism. He rejects, however, the typical Pentecostal separation of the vocational from the other elements of the life of faith and desires to define Spirit baptism as involving justification, sanctification, and vocation.[20]

It is important to note that, though Barth's *soteriology* contains an important place for vocation, his discussion of *Spirit baptism* does not highlight the vocational dimension, though such is by Barth's own admission clearly part of the doctrine's broad consequences for life. Barth notes that this vocational element is the accent of most of the New Testament texts concerning Spirit baptism, but he chooses instead to focus his essay concerning the doctrine on what he terms the "assumption" of preparation for ministry in the gift of new existence in Christ.[21]

Dunn's earlier classic treatment of Spirit baptism focuses on the same divine presupposition isolated by Barth, though with a more robust accent on the pneumatological sphere of Christian identity. Though the presupposition of vocational empowerment and gifting in the divine act of establishing our new existence in Christ is important to the doctrine of Spirit baptism (even for Luke), should not that which proceeds from this presupposition receive at least equal attention in our understanding of the metaphor if we are to be faithful to the New Testament? After all, Luke clearly stresses power for inspired witness in his narrative theology of Spirit baptism (e.g., Acts 1:8). Can we discuss this doctrine without making it something profoundly experiential and practical in implication for the Christian life?

---

20. Hendrikus Berkhof, *Doctrine of the Holy Spirit* (Louisville: Westminster John Knox, 1976), 46–56.

21. Barth, *Church Dogmatics*, vol. 4, part 4, 31.

Interestingly, we can note a tension in Dunn's discussion of Spirit baptism between his dual assumptions that Spirit baptism normally establishes Christian identity at the moment of faith and the fact that the gift of the Spirit was also something normally *experienced* in the New Testament. This tension is due to the fact that Dunn limits Spirit baptism to the notion of Christian initiation to the life of the Spirit and does not recognize the more expansive eschatological fulfillment of the metaphor in Acts and elsewhere in the New Testament. Initiation to the life of the Spirit is not dependent on human experience, but the experience of the kingdom of God in power is certainly involved in Spirit baptism as an eschatological gift of ever-new participation in the life and mission of God. This recognition would have helped Dunn to see how Spirit baptism can be received by faith alone and yet be experienced in a way that is integral to the fulfillment of the metaphor's meaning to the life of the church. Spirit baptism assumes initiation to the life of the Spirit and incorporation into the people of God by faith in Christ, but it is also in its more expansive eschatological fulfillment an experience of power among other things to be sought after and enjoyed among the people of God.

What also requires exploration in Barth's and Dunn's understandings of Spirit baptism is how it involves participation in the sacraments. Is water baptism merely *indirectly* connected to Spirit baptism through the role of the former in fulfilling repentance and faith in Christ? Does not water baptism have sacramental significance as a divine act as well as a human one? An affirmative answer is implied by the theological complexity of the sacraments in Reformed theology, especially in the context of Calvin's rich discussion of it. Romans 6:4 states that we are "buried with Christ *through baptism*." Dunn concedes that this text at face value seems to grant water baptism a role in *effecting* the establishment of our identification with Christ. But "not without some hesitation," Dunn felt compelled by what Paul said elsewhere on the matter to regard the "through baptism" of Romans 6:4 as a reference to the submission of the believer by faith and repentance "to the action of God" in Spirit baptism.[22]

Dunn's hesitation in placing water baptism solely on the side of human repentance and faith is warranted. Romans 6:3 and Colossians 2:12 identify water baptism as a being "buried" and "raised" with Christ *by God*. Through baptism we are "buried," "raised," and "clothed." These terms are in the pas-

---

22. Dunn, *Baptism in the Holy Spirit*, 145.

sive voice, implying a divine action. Baptismal texts in the New Testament imply that water baptism participates in some way in the divine action of Spirit baptism and not only in the prior human faith and repentance by which Spirit baptism is received as a life-transforming event.

A view of water baptism as "symbolic" of the divine action thus falls short of the richness of Reformed theology if a simplistic understanding of "symbol" is embraced that denies participation of the symbol in the saving power of Christ through the Word. A metaphysic of participation in the action of God by God's grace can be brought to bear on the sacraments, in which their symbolic function is understood in the complex sense of facilitating the divine act of bringing the reality signified to the life of the recipient. Like an embrace brings the love signified in it to the experience of the recipient, so baptism and the Eucharist bring the divine embrace to the life of the believers present to receive it. The same can be said of the relationship between Spirit and water baptism.

Pentecostals are beginning to reconsider the significance of water baptism for Christian initiation and the gift of the Spirit. In the 1989 Final Report of the international Catholic/Pentecostal Dialogue, the Pentecostals noted:

> All Pentecostals would consider baptism to be an integral part of the whole experience of becoming Christian.... Pentecostals do feel the need to investigate further the relationship between baptism and salvation in light of specific passages which appear to make a direct link between baptism and salvation (e.g. John 3:5; Mark 16:16; Acts 22:16; 1 Pet 3:21). (#50–51).

This statement, however, is followed by one that has most Pentecostals regarding baptism more as a witness to a personal identification with Christ than the decisive act of that identification (#52). And a following statement notes, "Pentecostals do not see the unity between Christians as being based in a common water baptism, mainly because they believe that the New Testament does not base it in baptism. Instead, the foundation of unity is a common faith and experience of Jesus Christ as Lord and Savior through the Holy Spirit" (#55).[23]

---

23. *Perspectives on Koinonia: Report from the Third Quinquennium of the Dialogue between the Pontifical Council for Promoting Christian Unity and Some Classical Pentecostal Churches and Leaders 1985–1989.* Available at http://www.prounione.urbe.it/dia-int/pe-rc/doc/i_pe-rc_pent03.html.

The bottom line is that water and Spirit baptism seem more intimately connected than Barth or Dunn have assumed. In other words, the New Testament implies that water baptism is taken up by God so that it participates in the divine agency that incorporates us into Christ. The value of Barth's and Dunn's understanding of Spirit baptism is that it properly corrects any assumption that the grace of God is at the church's disposal in its sacramental life or that personal faith is not essential to their effectiveness. The divine action is never to be taken for granted in anything we do, even as the church of Jesus Christ. But there is also the promise given in God's Word and assumed in the gospel that sacramental actions received in faith are granted participation by God in the bestowal of grace. Baptism is our next concern.

SPIRIT BAPTISM AND WATER BAPTISM

The Spirit not only binds us to Christ through the proclaimed gospel but also in "signs following." These signs are primarily the sacraments as the universally valid means instituted by Christ through which Christ is present in the church. "Repent, and be baptized every one of you in the name of Jesus Christ so that your sins may be forgiven; and you will receive the gift of the Holy Spirit" (Acts 2:38, NRSV). Those from sacramental traditions, such as Kilian McDonnell and George Montague, have sought to understand Spirit baptism as universally experienced among Christians through water baptism (essentially) but also, more broadly for many, the sacramental rites of initiation (baptism/confirmation and Eucharist).[24]

The often lengthy separation of confirmation from infant baptism in the West created a controversy concerning when the Spirit is bestowed. Is the Spirit bestowed at baptism, in confirmation, or in the complex of sacraments of initiation? Interestingly, some sacramental theologians in the West have pointed to texts like Acts 8 to justify a distinction between baptismal initiation and the reception of the Spirit (understood normally as the prototype of confirmation).[25]

There is an obvious similarity here with Pentecostal exegesis of Acts 8 that distinguishes faith in Christ from the reception of the charismatic Spirit.

---

24. Kilian McDonnell and George T. Montague, *Christian Initiation and Baptism in the Holy Spirit: Evidence from the First Eight Centuries* (Collegeville, MN: Liturgical, 1991).

25. See Wainwright, *Christian Initiation*, 34–35.

Both views distinguish baptismal initiation and the reception of the charismatic Spirit for Christian vocation. Despite this similarity, the gift of the Spirit is connected with sacramental initiation in Catholic tradition, whereas most Pentecostals (the Oneness Pentecostals being the outstanding exception) would see Spirit baptism as post-initiation. Pentecostals would also find sacramental initiation among children as falling short of the need to lead young people to a born-again experience and a conscious experience of empowerment for life witness.

This problem is especially acute in countries where a good part of the population may be infant baptized but absent from the life of the church or active faith in Christ. The Pentecostal message of personal regeneration and empowerment for prophetic witness in such contexts is sorely needed and should not be resented. Nevertheless, the Pentecostals in such contexts should be cognizant of the fact that such infant-baptized persons not currently active in the church have already in a profound sense been laid claim to by God in the bosom of the historic church. Evangelism should not proceed without recognition of this fact.

The challenge posed by the sacramental view of Spirit baptism is based in the observation that Jesus' reception of the Spirit at his baptism was paradigmatic of the connection between baptism and the reception of the Spirit among Christians (Acts 2:38; 19:5–6; 1 Cor. 12:13, which is understood literally as water baptism). Incidentally, the recognition of the paradigmatic nature of Christ's baptism for understanding Christian water baptism has had broad ecumenical significance for a more sacramental appreciation of water baptism, including some among leading Free Church theologians.[26] There is but "one baptism" in water and Spirit (Eph. 4:5). As we have noted, we are buried and raised with Christ "through baptism," implying an intimate relationship between water baptism and Spirit baptism (Rom 6:4; Col. 2:12).

Interestingly, like Dunn, McDonnell and Montague grant validity to the Pentecostal movement by regarding Spirit baptism as linked in the New Testament and the writings of the church fathers to charismatic experience. In the view of McDonnell and Montague, sacramental grace given in Christian initiation will eventually (either at the moment of initiation or later) burst forth in experiences of charismatic power. Though in their view Pentecostals have

---

26. Ibid., 50–51.

a faulty *theology* of Spirit baptism by detaching it wrongly from sacramental initiation, Pentecostals do validly call the church to the *experience* of Spirit baptism in life.[27] This view of Pentecostal theology became popular among charismatics in the mainstream churches who preferred to speak of Spirit baptism as a "release of the Spirit" in the Christian life.

There are Pentecostals, such as Simon Chan, who have been attracted to this doctrine of Spirit baptism as given sacramentally but released in life experience later.[28] Other Pentecostals fear that this view of Spirit baptism as given in Christian initiation but released in life precludes the need to seek a definite reception of the Spirit for empowered witness. Catholic theologian Francis Sullivan supports this concern and has quoted persuasively from Thomas Aquinas in favor of a new endowment of the Spirit that is subsequent to sacramental initiation and is not to be viewed as merely the outworking of sacramental grace. Pentecostals and charismatics who desire to view Spirit baptism as a genuinely new beginning in the Christian life find Sullivan's arguments attractive. However, unlike the Pentecostal view of Spirit baptism as a one-time event after conversion to Christ, Sullivan views every breakthrough or filling of the Spirit as a fresh Spirit baptism.[29]

Comparing McDonnell's position with Sullivan's tempts one to seek an integrated position that embraces both as two sides of how one understands the ongoing reception of the Spirit in life. Can grace both emerge from what is granted in Christian initiation *and* confront us from beyond with something genuinely new? Are we not talking here about two sides of the same coin, since what is granted in initiation is a living relationship with God and not a "material" deposit of grace that can somehow burst forth in life? Are we not talking about the gift of the living, eschatological Spirit, who constantly calls us to new frontiers of spiritual renewal? Can not the Spirit who indwells us still come to us in a way unprecedented since the new birth in Christ is itself unprecedented and continues to be such? I believe so. In the context of a sacramental ecclesiology, Pentecostal theologian Simon Chan appeals to the invocation of the Holy Spirit in the celebration of the Eucharist as a way of

---

27. McDonnell and Montague, *Christian Initiation and Baptism in the Holy Spirit*, 376ff.

28. Simon Chan, "Evidential Glossolalia and the Doctrine of Subsequence," *Asian Journal of Pentecostal Studies* 2 (1999): 195–211.

29. Francis A. Sullivan, *Charisms and Charismatic Renewal: A Biblical and Theological Study* (Ann Arbor, MI: Servant, 1982).

connecting an ongoing, fresh reception of the Spirit to baptism as the rite of initiation.[30]

Chan's position can be useful to Pentecostals as a way of discovering the significance of the sacramental life of the church for our life in the Spirit. While not denying the significance of the sacraments in the Christian's experience of the Spirit, there are Charismatic theologians who would want to define Spirit baptism theologically as a gift of grace received as an immediate experience of the Spirit. Morton Kelsey has noted, for example, that glossolalia implies a reality nearly lost to modern theology, namely, that one can have direct contact with the divine Spirit in a way that penetrates deeply into the core of one's being.[31] But, as Donald Gelpi has noted, such experiences are also ecclesial and sacramental. As Gelpi stated, "The Christian encounters his God not simply by delving into his own human psyche but by acknowledging God's saving presence in the historical Christian community of which he is a member."[32]

Furthermore, baptism and Eucharist remind us that personal redemption is connected to the renewal of creation, for the creation awaits the resurrection of the children of God as the firstfruits of its own renewal (Rom. 8:19–21). We will elaborate on this cluster of issues in and after our discussion of the Pentecostal understanding of Spirit baptism.

SPIRIT BAPTISM AND EMPOWERMENT

The baptism in the Holy Spirit not only assumes a divine promise of new life through faith in Christ with sacramental signs following, it is a promise of power for witness with charismatic signs following: "But you will receive power when the Holy Spirit has come upon you; and you will be my witnesses" (Acts 1:8). "All of them were filled with the Holy Spirit and began to speak in tongues as the Spirit gave them the ability" (2:4). There is no question but that the witness of Acts is not just about how the Spirit brings one to faith in Christ or seals that commitment in baptism. There is something more than a hidden mystery to be affirmed by faith at work in this narrative, but also the fulfillment of faith through inspired witness and the confirmation of faith in signs of the new creation in Christ.

---

30. Chan, "Evidential Glossolalia and the Doctrine of Subsequence," 211.

31. Morton Kelsey, *Tongue Speaking: The History and Meaning of Charismatic Experience* (New York: Crossroad, 1981).

32. Donald L. Gelpi, *Pentecostalism: A Theological Viewpoint* (New York: Paulist, 1971), 145.

The narrative of Acts has Christian communities caught up at decisive moments in the powerful presence of the Spirit in a way that moves them to vibrant praise, inspired witness with signs and wonders following, and bold acts of reconciliation. The presence of the Spirit was not just assumed by virtue of affirming a gospel message or performing a sacramental rite. The church knew full well when the Spirit visited, because it was a reality that was felt and that produced tangible results. Spirit events caused even unbelieving audiences to ask in astonishment, "What does this mean?" (Acts 2:12). The Lukan Spirit in Spirit baptism is the Spirit of *witness*.

I agree with Stronstad and Menzies that the Spirit in Acts is the *Charismageist* ("the charismatic Spirit") that inspires bold proclamation and other signs of the presence of Jesus' charismatic and prophetic ministry in the church. The story of Jesus' inauguration of the kingdom of God for Luke is characteristically about "how God anointed Jesus of Nazareth with the Holy Spirit and power and how he went around doing good and healing all who were under the power of the devil, because God was with him" (Acts 10:38). Luke highlights this point that God was powerfully with Jesus in his mission, because he was convinced that God is with the church of Jesus Christ in much the same way. In summarizing Peter's message to the Gentiles, Luke focuses on Jesus' anointing "with the Holy Spirit and power" to heal the sick and otherwise deliver those oppressed of the devil because Luke sees Pentecost as the empowerment of God's people for analogous ministry in their time. Pentecostals are convinced that the same is true today.

Pentecostals do well to highlight the empowerment for prophetic witness in their understanding of Spirit baptism. They focus not on one's initial conversion to Christ but on becoming the church for the world. The nineteenth-century Pietist and social activist Christoph Blumhardt once wrote that one must convert twice: from the world to God and from God to the world. Pentecostals see Spirit baptism as a prophetic call that draws one close to the heart of God in praise and prophetic empathy for the world but which accents the "second conversion" by empowering one for witness in the world.[33] One is reminded here of Moltmann's divine inhale that draws people together in communion and praise and the exhale of the divine Spirit

---

33. Quoted by J. Harder in the introduction to Christoph Blumhardt, *Ansprachen, Predigten, Andachten, und Schriften*, hrsg. J. Harder (Neukirchen: Neukirchen-Vluyn, 1978), 1:12.

that drives one vocationally and charismatically into the world.[34] The accent on spiritual gifts highlights the freedom of the Spirit eschatologically in driving God's people toward a more expansive witness. As Moltmann notes, through the gifts of the Spirit, the Spirit exercises eschatological freedom to expand, diversify, and proliferate the many expressions of divine grace in the world.[35]

Pentecostals are not at all agreed on how to relate the first and second "conversions." The older tendency was to see Spirit baptism as a separate reception of the Spirit that functioned as a rite of passage to spiritual fullness and spiritual gifts. What I regard to be a more helpful trend, the tendency now among many Pentecostals is to accent the gift of the Spirit given in regeneration and to view the Pentecostal experience of Spirit baptism as empowerment for witness as a "release" of an already-indwelling Spirit in life. Under the influence of the charismatic movement, the language of fullness tends to be replaced with "release of the Spirit" as an "enhancement" or "renewal" of one's charismatic life.[36] Anthony Palma notes tellingly:

> The Spirit works internally in a repentant and believing person to effect the new birth. He does not then depart from the believer, to come back again at the time of infilling. Some are confused because of Spirit baptism imagery that the New Testament uses, such as "baptized in," "poured out," "falling upon," "coming upon." But these are only figurative and graphic ways of portraying an overwhelming experience of the already indwelling Spirit. This is why some call it a "release" of the already indwelling Spirit.[37]

Implied is that all Christians are charismatic.[38] Christians at whatever level of spiritual maturity find their ministries enhanced with greater power and effectiveness through an experience of Spirit baptism.

---

34. Jürgen Moltmann, *The Spirit of Life: A Universal Affirmation* (Minneapolis: Augsburg Fortress, 2001), 45.

35. Ibid.

36. See, e.g., a recent issue of *Enrichment Journal* (Assemblies of God) on Spirit baptism in which such notions dominate: Gordon Anderson, "Baptism in the Holy Spirit, Initial Evidence, and a New Model," *Enrichment Journal* 10:1 (2005): 70–78.

37. Anthony Palma, "Spirit Baptism: Before and After," *Enrichment Journal* 10:1 (2005): 94.

38. Robert Menzies, "The Spirit of Prophecy, Luke-Acts and Pentecostal Theology: A Response to Max Turner," *Journal of Pentecostal Theology* 15 (1999): 72.

Pentecostals, however, still want to preserve the need for Christians to seek a definite work of the Spirit in their lives that will give them experiences analogous to those described in the book of Acts. They feel that without a "Spirit baptism" to be sought among Christians, the Lukan experience of empowered witness accompanied by a proliferation of extraordinary spiritual gifts could be significantly lost to the churches. To hold that Spirit baptism has occurred through regeneration by faith in Christ or the sacraments of initiation seems for many classical Pentecostals to doom the endurance of Pentecostal experience in the churches.

The growing body of Third Wave churches that advocate something close to Pentecostal spirituality without a doctrine of Spirit baptism as distinct from conversion does seem to call this Pentecostal assumption into question. Nevertheless, even these churches owe something to the historic rise of the Pentecostal movement, whether they choose to recognize this or not. A case can be made that early Pentecostals effectively used the category of "Spirit baptism" from Acts to describe the need to seek and yearn for charismatic renewal and empowerment. In so doing, they spawned a global revival that has arguably influenced Christian spirituality favorably throughout the global church toward the end of the twentieth century and into the twenty-first.

The Pentecostals viewed this Spirit baptism as distinct from initial Christian conversion or the sacraments of initiation in order to present it to the church as an ongoing challenge to its life in the world. They were revivalists, as much concerned with reviving the saints as with converting the sinners. Pentecostals would thus have approved of the challenge posed to Christians by Martyn Lloyd-Jones concerning the assumption that one "has it all" at the moment of Christian faith:

> Got it all? Well, if you have "got it all" I simply ask in the name of God, why are you as you are? If you have got it all, why are you so unlike the New Testament Christians? Got it all! Got it at your conversion! Well, where is it I ask?[39]

At its worst, such a challenge can be arrogant and elitist. At its best this challenge can be seen as advocating a kind of "second conversion," an awakening to one's vocation in the world and gifting to serve as a witness to Christ.

---

39. As quoted in Henry I. Lederle, *Treasures Old and New: Interpretations of Spirit Baptism in the Charismatic Renewal Movement* (Peabody, MA: Hendrickson, 1988), 152.

As Roger Stronstad noted, Pentecostals advocate a "prophethood of believers," since everyone is a bearer of the Spirit to dream dreams, have visions, and speak under the inspiration of the Spirit in praise to God and in witness to Christ.[40] Pentecostals rightly look at the prevalence of bench-warmers in the churches (including Pentecostal churches) and would encourage them to be baptized in the Spirit in dynamic praise and charismatic power for service toward others. Spirit baptism for Pentecostals is not just a component of a theological discussion of the relationship between Spirit and water baptism in the New Testament. It is an empowering calling and gifting for a living witness to Jesus that is the birthright of every Christian as a bearer of the Spirit. It is also an ongoing challenge to every lifeless church.

The desire to preserve the experience of empowerment for mission as a force for renewal in the church, however, should not neglect the broader pneumatological themes (even in Luke) that are needed to grant this spiritual power its deeper meaning. The issue important to confront here is whether or not the Spirit is exclusively empowerment for prophetic mission in Acts. Luke confronts the reader at the start of his Acts with the fact that before Jesus' ascension, he spoke to the disciples "about the kingdom of God" (Acts 1:3). The disciples are gathered in Jerusalem, the significant city to the kingdom's fulfillment. It is in answer to their question about the fulfillment of the kingdom that Jesus directs them to the coming empowerment of the Spirit for witness (1:8). The powerful presence of the Spirit in Spirit baptism was not only felt in proclamation and spiritual gifts. In Acts, powerful moments in the Spirit enriched praise and *koinonia*, created devotion to the teaching of the apostles, inspired the common meal, and broke down barriers between estranged people (cf. 2:42).

The outpouring of the Spirit at Pentecost has broad boundaries, though empowerment for witness seems to represent the overall goal of the effects of Spirit baptism for Luke. Of significance to Pentecostalism's Wesleyan roots, those anointed for prophetic service in Acts are also considered as cleansed and consecrated for the master's use (Acts 15:8–9). The powers of the kingdom surrounding Pentecost are sanctifying and should not be separated from the Pentecostal blessing.

---

40. Roger Stronstad, "The Prophethood of Believers," in *Pentecostalism in Context: Essays in Honor of William W. Menzies*, ed. Wonsuk Ma and Robert P. Menzies (Sheffield: Sheffield Academic Press, 1997), 60–77.

The focus on prophetic calling and vocation overlaps with the doctrine of sanctification, since the prophet in the Scriptures was separated from sin and consecrated for a holy task. Since all Christians share, in some sense, the prophetic calling as bearers of the Spirit, sanctification as consecration for a holy prophetic task applies to the church as a whole. As noted in our last chapter, the formal way that most early Pentecostals related Spirit baptism to sanctification was to sharply distinguish between them as stages of initiation to the life of the Spirit, even appropriating them to persons of the Trinity. The Pentecostals following this approach shifted pneumatology from sanctification to Spirit baptism as a charismatic experience. Sanctification was then placed under the work of Christ, whether formally viewed as distinct from regeneration or not.

In a brief essay entitled "The Spirit Follows the Blood," one Pentecostal author even denied that the Spirit sanctifies, "for he is not our Savior." It is the blood of Christ that cleanses from sin and purifies in preparation for the gift of power by the Spirit.[41] Indeed, how Christ can be said to do anything in the life of the believer without the agency of the Spirit is baffling. Furthermore, it did not occur to the early Pentecostals who followed this train of thought that this rigid relegation of sanctification to Christ alone contradicts 1 Peter 1:2 as well as the biblical portrayal of the inseparable workings of Word and Spirit. It also neglects the overlapping nature of soteriological categories in the New Testament.

Fortunately, the "fourfold gospel" of Pentecostal theology implied that Christ is the one who both saves and Spirit-baptizes through the agency of the Spirit. But this Christological focal point still did not prevent many Pentecostals from fracturing Christ's saving work from his role as Spirit baptizer. In fact, one could say that Pentecostals parted from their Holiness forebears by defining sanctification as a Christological category. They splintered Christ's sanctifying from his Spirit baptismal ministry for ecclesiological reasons. They wanted to preserve their uniqueness as an empowered and charismatically endowed community as well as their use of Spirit baptism as a critical challenge to a divided and spiritually slothful church. They ended up, however, with a weakened Christological criterion for the higher life.

This formal distinction between Christ's sanctifying and Spirit baptismal work, however, is not the whole story. William Seymour implied a more inte-

---

41. "The Spirit Follows the Blood," *The Apostolic Faith* (April 1907), 3 (author unknown).

gral connection between sanctification and Spirit baptism by stating that Spirit baptism is the gift of power "upon the sanctified, cleansed life."[42] Implied here is that Spirit baptism empowers, renews, or releases the sanctified life toward outward expression and visible signs of renewal. I have also found numerous references in early Pentecostal literature to Spirit baptism as a baptism in the love of God. This description of Spirit baptism is made especially in reference to Romans 5:5, which refers to the love of God "shed abroad" (KJV) in our hearts, a "Pentecostal" image that did not escape the attention of a number of early Pentecostal pioneers.

The Pentecostal image of a divine outpouring is connected here to Wesley's understanding of sanctification as a transformation by the love of God. Seymour wrote in 1908 an answer to a question about what the evidence of Spirit baptism is: "Divine love, which is charity. Charity is the Spirit of Jesus."[43] Seymour's *Apostolic Faith* paper would say more than once concerning the baptism in the Holy Spirit: "This baptism fills us with divine love."[44] This paper also gives a testimony from a "Nazarene brother" who called his Spirit baptism a "baptism of love."[45]

[handwritten margin note: ✱ THIS IS GOOD]

These were not the only voices among the early Pentecostals to write about Spirit baptism as a filling with divine love. Assemblies of God pioneer E. N. Bell, for example, referred to Romans 5:5 to describe Spirit baptism as a baptism in the love of God: "not a scanty sprinkling but a regular 'outpour.'"[46] In an implicit allusion to Romans 5:5, a brother Will Trotter wrote an article entitled "A Revival of Love Needed," in which he wrote, "I tell you that this entire 'tongues movement,' independent of works of grace positions held, needs . . . to get down and get the thing that loves in their hearts, that

---

42. William J. Seymour, "The Way into the Holiness," *The Apostolic Faith* (October 1906), 4.

43. "Questions Answered," *The Apostolic Faith* (June–September 1907), 2.1. I am grateful to Cecil M. Robeck Jr. for directing me to this quote: "William J. Seymour and the 'Bible Evidence,'" in *Initial Evidence: Historical and Biblical Perspectives on the Pentecostal Doctrine of Spirit Baptism*, ed. Gary B. McGee (Peabody, MA: Hendrickson, 1991), 81.

44. "The Old Time Pentecost," *The Apostolic Faith* (September 1906), 1; note also, "Tongues as a Sign," *The Apostolic Faith* (September 1906), 2 (authors unknown).

45. "The Old Time Pentecost," *The Apostolic Faith* (September 1906), 1 (author unknown).

46. E. N. Bell, "Believers in Sanctification," *Christian Evangel* (September 19, 1914), 3.

divine flame shed abroad by the Holy Ghost." He concludes, "Get the flame, the pentecostal flame, if you like the term better—but get it."[47]

As yet another example of an identification of Spirit baptism with an "infusion" of divine love is the Oneness Pentecostal pioneer Frank Ewart, describing Spirit baptism this way: "Calvary unlocked the flow of God's love, which is God's very nature, into the hearts of his creatures."[48] Stanley Frodsham made both tongues and love consequences of Pentecost: "Therein we see in their brightest luster the union of gifts and graces in believers."[49]

Of course, this language is revivalistic and not process oriented. But growth in love does have its dramatic moments of filling, ecstasy, and power, does it not? As noted in our previous chapter, there is no question but that Spirit baptism has often been interpreted throughout Pentecostalism with a heavy emphasis on the Spirit as the *power* of God for enhancing worship and service and overcoming the obstacles to the life of faith, especially with the aid of powerful manifestations and gifts of the Spirit. This is true of Pentecostal and charismatic churches in Asia, Africa, the United States, Europe, and Latin America. The "power encounter" is the byword for global Pentecostal mission.[50] Theologically, this emphasis on spiritual power is tied to the military metaphor for the Christian life favored by Pentecostals. As E. Kingsley Larbi notes with regard to African Pentecostalism, Pentecostalism does not recognize any "demilitarized zone" but rather accents the battle for the victory of the kingdom of God over the forces of sin and darkness.[51]

I do not wish to denigrate this Pentecostal focus on power. The love of God is not sentimental. It is also not reducible to an ethical principle, as valuable as that is. God's love is powerfully redemptive and liberating. It is also not confined to the inner transformation of the individual but propels people outward to bear witness to Christ. In my view, the vocational and charismatic

---

47. Will Trotter, "A Revival of Love Needed," *The Weekly Evangel* (April 3, 1915), 1.

48. Frank Ewart, "The Revelation of Jesus Christ," in *Seven Jesus Only Tracts*, ed. Donald W. Dayton (New York: Garland, 1985), 5.

49. Stanley H. Frodsham, "Back to Pentecost: The Effects of the Pentecostal Baptism," *The Pentecostal Evangel* (October 30, 1920), 2.

50. A representative development of this theme in Pentecostal literature is Anita Chia, "A Biblical Theology of Power Manifestation: A Singaporean Quest," *Asian Journal of Pentecostal Studies* 2 (1999): 19–33.

51. E. Kingsley Larbi, *Pentecostalism: The Eddies of Ghanaian Christianity* (Dansoman, Accra Ghana: Centre for Pentecostal and Charismatic Studies, 2001), 423.

elements highlighted by Pentecostals hold potential for expanding our understanding of sanctification so that it involves a "prophetic call."

Part of the reason why Pentecostals resisted a formal connection between sanctification and Spirit baptism was the connection forged early on between Spirit baptism and speaking in tongues. At times, it seemed in the early literature that the merely "sanctified" are not yet Spirit baptized, simply because they do not speak in tongues. Yet, when describing why tongues uniquely symbolize Spirit baptism, Pentecostals turned usually to a notion of what may be termed the sanctification of human speech. The unruly tongue is said to be tamed and transformed into a source of telling truth, praising God, or bearing witness to Christ. Seymour saw tongues as a sign that God is causing the people of God to cross boundaries: "God makes no difference in nationality, Ethiopians, Chinese, Indians, Mexicans, and other nationalities worship together."[52]

As we will note, such a connection between Spirit baptism and tongues speech (and other forms of inspired speech) can be theologically significant. Catholic theologian Simon Tugwell, for example, sees scriptural support for the notion that inspired speech is "in some way symptomatic of the whole working of the Holy Spirit in our lives, a typical fruit of the incarnation."[53] Further more, Seymour and others referred on occasion to the divine healing of the body, another favored spiritual gift among Pentecostals, as the "sanctification of the body."[54] This language further supports the idea that Pentecostals described Spirit baptism on occasion as an enhancement of sanctification rather than simply an additional work beyond it.

It is my view that early Pentecostals separated sanctification from Spirit baptism only by defining sanctification narrowly and negatively as a cleansing or a separation from sin. Sanctification, however, is also positively a consecration unto God in preparation for a holy task, as it was for the Old Testament prophets and Jesus of Nazareth. As an aspect of the life of discipleship to which we are consecrated and called, sanctification involves a transformation by the Spirit of God into the very image of Christ "from glory to glory" (2 Cor. 3:18).

---

52. William J. Seymour, "The Same Old Way," *Apostolic Faith* (September 1906), 3.

53. Simon Tugwell, "The Speech-Giving Spirit," in *New Heaven? New Earth?* ed. S. Tugwell et al. (Springfield, IL: Templegate, 1976), 128.

54. E.g., William J. Seymour, "The Precious Atonement," *Apostolic Faith* (September 1906), 2.

It is interesting that the distinction between sanctification and Spirit baptism can only be sustained through a reductionistic understanding of sanctification as an inward cleansing and of Spirit baptism as an outward empowerment for a holy task. In a sense, sanctification was fractured for many early Pentecostals along the line of its negative and positive (as well as inward and outward) effects. This point raises the legitimate question as to the degree to which the separation of sanctification from Spirit baptism was more semantic than substantial. Pentecostal pastor and theologian David Lim thus calls Spirit baptism for Pentecostals "vocational sanctification."[55] In this light, I would include both Holiness and Pentecostal movements as advocating a vocational and at least implicitly charismatic understanding of Spirit baptism.

The bottom line is that Spirit baptism as an experience of charismatic power and enrichment cannot be separated from regeneration/sanctification and Christian initiation. The experience of Spirit baptism is inseparable from its broader pneumatological framework in the constitution of the church and the fulfillment of the kingdom of God. Spirit baptism in Pentecostal experience is a "release" of the Spirit in life for concrete experiences of consecration and charismatic enrichment/power. The experience is both sanctifying and empowering, for it arises from the Spirit of the kingdom, the Spirit of God as love. Pentecostals should continue to encourage Christians to experience Spirit baptism after they come to Christ, but should also bear in mind that Spirit baptism as an act of God, as an ecclesial and historic work of the Spirit in inaugurating the Kingdom of God, has broader boundaries.

If Paul's doctrine of Spirit baptism in the context of his ecclesiological and cosmic pneumatology is soteriological, as both Stronstad and Menzies conclude, we are faced with the challenge of how to integrate this with Luke's accent on empowerment for witness. The Spirit's work in inaugurating the kingdom in holiness and power is a way to do it. Spirit baptism is a divine act that changes us and creation into God's dwelling place and an experience of this divine possession and infilling that releases the Spirit as a potent force in the life of the believer.

What justifies our expansive understanding of Spirit baptism as a setting for Pentecostal experience? It is now time to draw some conclusions from a reflection on the biblical text concerning how Pentecostals can begin to de-

---

55. In personal conversation with the author.

velop a globally diverse and ecumenically sensitive understanding of Spirit baptism. My more constructive reflections await future chapters.

ESCHATOLOGICAL FRAMEWORK

What justifies expanding the boundaries of Spirit baptism beyond individual experience or even the life of the church? At this point, I wish to note that those who view Spirit baptism as fundamentally an ecclesial dynamic will understand John the Baptist's use of the metaphor as solely predictive of what occurred at Pentecost. I want to suggest something else, namely, an understanding of the Baptist's use of the metaphor in its own right first, before we bring Pentecost and the essence of the church into the picture. This move allows us to define Spirit baptism first as related to the kingdom of God before it is applied to the church. John's preaching was, "Repent, for the kingdom of heaven is near" (Matt. 3:1–2). Jesus also speaks about Spirit baptism in the context of his teaching on the kingdom (Acts 1:3) and the disciples' question concerning the kingdom's fulfillment (1:6) as they gather in Jerusalem, the location traditionally associated with the fulfillment of the kingdom in Jewish tradition. How Spirit baptism relates to what we regard as most important to the life of the church should be developed after Spirit baptism as the ministry of the Messiah to usher in the kingdom of God is acknowledged.

As Matthew 3:11–17 attests, John the Baptist saw himself as standing on the edge of the end of the world announcing the Messiah's act of "baptizing in the Spirit" (only the verb form is used) as the final act of salvation. The Messiah would give forth the breath of God as the final act of redemption. John knew that his water baptism did not have the power to bring down the Spirit and to end the age. Bringing the Spirit was uniquely the role of the Messiah.

The prophets of old said in effect, "We circumcise the foreskin but God will circumcise the heart." So John uses similar prophetic rhetoric to say in effect, "I can baptize in water unto repentance, but the Messiah will baptize in the Spirit unto judgment and purgation/restoration." John's baptism was preparatory, namely, to gather the repentant together in preparation for the final judgment and restoration. But "apocalyptic transcendence" belongs to the Messiah alone. Only from him will the wind of the Spirit blow away the chaff and store the wheat into barns. That the Messiah will be anointed of the Spirit is foretold. But insight into the Messiah's role to dispense and baptize in the Spirit is unique to John the Baptist's message.

Consistent with our eschatological theme, the opening of the heaven at Jesus' baptism is a typical sign depicting an apocalyptic revelation.[56] The descending of the dove is reminiscent perhaps of the Spirit brooding on the waters of creation and the sign of new creation in the story of Noah.[57] Jesus is being commissioned here to usher in the kingdom of God in power to make all things new: "But if I drive out demons by the Spirit of God, then the kingdom of God has come upon you" (Matt. 12:28).

It seems clear that Spirit baptism in Matthew 3 and parallel Synoptic texts is granted broad eschatological implications that cannot be exhausted in any version of Christian initiation or of the essence of the church. Interestingly, Donald Hagner points out that the church connected to the gospel of Matthew saw parallels between its Christian baptism and Jesus' Jordan experience. But Hagner notes insightfully that this church also recognized the unique eschatological undertones in the complex of events at the Jordan that await fulfillment at the end of salvation history.[58] I believe that Hagner's insight can be applied quite broadly. The vision of Spirit baptism foretold by John the Baptist and depicted in Jesus' Jordan experience pointed to final judgment and to the final sanctification of the entire creation.

Spirit baptism points to redemption through Christ as substantially pneumatological and eschatological. Pentecost certainly baptizes the disciples in the Spirit, but Luke is quick to note as well the final apocalyptic horizon of this event (Acts 2:17–21). The theophany at Pentecost of tongues, fire, and the sound of a wind (2:1–4) are but foreshadows of the final theophany at the great Day of the Lord consisting of "blood and fire and billows of smoke" and cosmic signs as well (2:19–20). Spirit baptism is signaled at Pentecost by an eschatological theophany of the presence of God to restore and to judge. It is given at Pentecost but fulfilled in the final act of salvation at Christ's return.

In Spirit baptism, the church is allowed to participate in, and bear central witness to, the final sanctification of creation. Regeneration by faith in the context of the gospel and the sacraments of initiation do not grant one

56. John Nolland, *Luke 1–9:20* (Word Biblical Commentary 35A; Dallas: Word, 1989), 162.
57. Donald A. Hagner, *Matthew 1–13* (Word Biblical Commentary 33A; Dallas: Word, 1993), 58.
58. Ibid., 60.

grace merely as a deposit that can later burst forth in charismatic experience. Rather, the experience of new life in faith, hope, and love in the context of the gospel, the sacraments, and the Pentecostal experience of prophetic consecration (with charismatic signs following) allows one to participate already in a Spirit baptism that is yet to come. It is always present and coming, emerging and encountering. The Pentecostal belief in the connection between Spirit baptism and sanctification, on the one hand, and between Spirit baptism and the latter rain of the Spirit to end the age, on the other, can nourish an ecumenical doctrine of Spirit baptism in which many voices can have a significant role to play.

Spirit baptism is somewhat ambiguous as a metaphor and fluid in its meaning throughout the New Testament, because it is an eschatological metaphor that depicts the various ways in which we participate through the Spirit in the rich blessings of Christ located in heavenly places (Eph. 1:3, 12). After John's picturesque description of the Messiah's eschatological judgment and restoration, Acts describes the church's participation in this Spirit baptism through repentance, faith, water baptism, the Eucharist, koinonia, and, especially, empowerment for witness (Acts 2:37–47).

Although Luke accents the participation in Spirit baptism that flows from faith, especially as visibly demonstrated, Paul focuses attention on the act of Spirit baptism that leads to the attachment to Christ by faith (1 Cor. 12:13). Paul does not neglect the charismatic dimension of participation in the life of the Spirit. Luke does not omit the importance of faith and baptism in the reception of the missionary Spirit. But Paul's accent is on Spirit baptism as that which initiates us to faith in Christ as members of his body, while Luke highlights the power of the Spirit that proceeds from faith.

Though there is a variety of accents, there is a consistent witness in the New Testament to the centrality of the Spirit to the realization of the kingdom of God in power. In this variety are the raw materials that feed various ecclesiologies. I will explore the implications in Spirit baptism for ecclesiology in a future chapter. The various Trinitarian accents will be addressed in the following chapter on Spirit baptism and the Christian life. Throughout, it will be possible to enhance our understanding of preaching and the sacraments in the light of the experience of the charismatic and prophetic Spirit celebrated in the Pentecostal understanding of Spirit baptism. The kerygma and the sacraments are not directed to the formation of a redemption cult but the fulfillment of God's missionary and eschatological goals for the world.

We will note that the Spirit is uniquely the eschatological gift that brings to us the "powers of the age to come" (Heb. 6:5). Dry bones live again (Ezek. 37), and one is born anew (John 3:1–8). The Spirit that hovered over the waters of the deep and from which all of life draws its sustenance is also the gift of God's coming with new life in the midst of its graceless attrition. This Spirit engulfs life with life. Spirit baptism is a baptism from death to life in which we participate by faith with sacramental and charismatic signs following. It comes by grace alone through the Christ event and the proclamation of the gospel, although it does not omit our participation in the process. It liberates us unto such participation.

As a result, Spirit baptism is not only a divine action but a human experience. It is an experience that touches and involves us but which we cannot fully grasp consciously. Spirit baptism thus produces a variety of giftings and experiences. It proliferates and diversifies life in the direction of the resurrection of the dead and the new heavens and new earth.

Four

CHRIST AS THE KING AND THE SPIRIT AS THE KINGDOM:

SPIRIT BAPTISM IN TRINITARIAN PERSPECTIVE

Let us discuss the broad pneumatological framework in the kingdom of God of the Pentecostal experience of Spirit baptism. Gregory of Nyssa wrote: "The Spirit is a living and a substantial and distinctly subsisting kingdom with which the only begotten Christ is anointed and is king of all that is."[1] If, as Gregory tells us, Christ is the King and the Spirit the kingdom, Spirit baptism is the means by which creation is transformed by this kingdom and made to participate in its reign of life. Spirit baptism brings the reign of the Father, the reign of the crucified and risen Christ, and the reign of divine life to all of creation through the indwelling of the Spirit.

Death reigned over the creation. That reign has still not been removed from creation, although it has been decisively undermined by God. Christ's risen life has already intruded into death's domain and reigns in a sense already so that the days of death's reign are now numbered. The evil dragon of the Apocalypse knows that his time is short (Rev. 12:12). This is because God has acted decisively to make the creation into a holy temple, the very dwelling place of God.

The purpose of this chapter is to unfold this brief statement. It should become clear by its end that none of the theological understandings of

---

1. Gregory, *On the Lord's Prayer* 3; cited in Kilian McDonnell, *The Other Hand of God: The Holy Spirit as the Universal Touch and Goal* (Collegeville, MN: Liturgical, 2003), 226.

Christian initiation to the life of the Spirit discussed in our previous chapter can exhaust the meaning of Spirit baptism. The connection between Spirit baptism and the inauguration of the kingdom of God attributed to John the Baptist (Matt. 3:1–12) and to Jesus himself (Acts 1:2–8) grants this metaphor eschatological expansiveness and transcendence. Even John the Baptist's initial announcement could not exhaust the meaning of the metaphor. This announcement of the coming of Jesus as the Spirit Baptizer would have vast significance for the faith and life of the people of God.

We will start this chapter by developing the connection between Spirit baptism and the fulfillment of the kingdom of God suggested by John the Baptist's messianic expectation and assumed elsewhere in the New Testament. There is a remarkable continuity of thought in the New Testament about the significance of Spirit baptism, despite the ambiguity and fluidity of the metaphor. I say this aware of the fact that the metaphor itself would not play a prominent role among all of the writers of the New Testament. I agree with James Dunn that the metaphor is somewhat ambiguous and fluid in the New Testament. But as Dunn has also shown, the rich horizons of meaning that emerge in the witness of Spirit baptism to Jesus as the one who bestows the Spirit are united by the conviction that the Holy Spirit is the "nerve center" of the Christian life and the decisive element of Christian identity. There is also continuity to this fluid metaphor that I believe links Spirit baptism to the eschatological fulfillment of the kingdom of God, namely, the reign of life through the divine sanctification and indwelling of creation.

It is my conviction further that Spirit baptism is decisive for the identity of Jesus in the New Testament as the Savior and Bestower of life. Spirit baptism is essential to Jesus' identity as the "man for others" obedient to the loving will of the Father for creation as the "God for others." The union of wills between the Father and Jesus is connected to their unity of essence. Spirit baptism is thus also decisive for the early Christian assumption that Jesus bears a unique relationship to God the Father. If Jesus breathes or bestows the very breath of God, he stands on the divine side of the Creator/creation relationship. After we explore more fully the relationship between Spirit baptism and the kingdom of God, therefore, we will turn our attention to the role of Spirit baptism in the early formation of faith in Jesus as Lord and Savior and, eventually, to the church's Trinitarian confession. The Trinitarian structure of Spirit baptism is important to explore for our desire to arrive at a full-orbed soteriology in the light of Spirit baptism.

This entire discussion from the linkage between Spirit baptism and the kingdom of God to the church's faith in Jesus as the source of divine life and to the Trinitarian structure of Spirit baptism will thus provide the background in this chapter for a Trinitarian and eschatological understanding of the elements of life in the Spirit (justification, sanctification, charismatic empowerment). By the time we complete that discussion, my understanding of Spirit baptism as a metaphor of life in the Spirit should be clear. It all starts with the link between Spirit baptism and the kingdom of God. Let us begin.

THE PENTECOST-KINGDOM CONNECTION

John the Baptist announced the coming of Jesus as Spirit Baptizer within the context of the Messiah's role in ushering in the kingdom of God (Matt. 3:1–12). Just before the Spirit would be poured out on the day of Pentecost, Luke has Jesus quoting John the Baptist's announcement of the coming Spirit baptism in the context of Jesus' teachings concerning the kingdom of God (Acts 1:3). Jesus then teaches on Spirit baptism in the light of the kingdom of God and its fulfillment (1:3–6) as the disciples gather in Jerusalem, the city associated with the fulfillment of the kingdom in Jewish tradition, except Jesus directs the disciples' attention away from the details of the future to the present empowerment of the Spirit by which the disciples will bear witness to the kingdom's coming in power. The connection between Spirit baptism and the kingdom of God seems obvious in the New Testament, but the theological nature of this connection is not. What does it mean theologically to say that Jesus will usher in the kingdom of God as the Spirit Baptizer?

I will state from the outset that the kingdom of God provides us with a meaningful theological context for Spirit baptism mainly because the substance of the kingdom in the Scripture is pneumatological: "For the kingdom of God is not food and drink but righteousness and peace and joy in the Holy Spirit" (Rom. 14:17 NRSV). As Gregory of Nyssa noted above, the Son is the King and the Spirit is the kingdom in the fulfillment of the Father's will. Through Christ as the Spirit Baptizer, the Spirit brings creation into the kingdom of the King by indwelling all things with the divine presence so as to deliver creation from the reign of death unto the reign of life. Before we reach this conclusion, however, we need to explore a few preliminary steps.

Let us begin with the issue of lordship, which is essential to the theology of the kingdom of God. As George Eldon Ladd noted, the kingdom is "the divine sovereignty in action."[2] Recognition of God's lordship is not achieved through abstract reflection but is rather discerned among the people of God. As a historical and not a spatial category, God's lordship in the Old Testament was recognized primarily in mighty acts of deliverance and redemption. God's telling Moses that God "will be" what God "will be" (Ex. 3:14) gained substance in what God would later prove to be in fulfillment of the divine promise of salvation. Exodus 6:1–13 thus defines the divine name ("LORD") according to the fulfillment of a promise that God will prove to be the deliverer who fulfills mercy and justice: "You shall know that I am the LORD your God, who has brought you out from the yoke of the Egyptians" (6:7).

These acts of redemptive history form the context for recognizing the sole lordship of God in the Decalogue: "I am the LORD your God, who brought you out of Egypt, out of the land of slavery. You shall have no other gods before me" (Ex. 20:2–3). The capacity to obey the law is rooted in the Lord's prior faithfulness in calling Israel as a people and setting them free from bondage. The law is meant as a signpost of the freedom Israel gained from God's liberating deeds in history. Israel's freedom as a people was dependent on God's liberating reign in the context of history.

The problem is that the freedom of obedience to the law was hindered for Israel in the debilitating conditions of its existence as a nation within the negative effects of sin and oppression. In the course of time, Israel had to wrestle with interpreting God's lordship in history within the brute facts of captivity and the power of evil in the world. As Paul Hanson has shown, the tension implied in this wrestling gave rise to the apocalyptic movement or the "eschatologization" of the belief in divine lordship.[3] The prophetic impulse of historical fulfillment and responsibility was set in tension with the apocalyptic hope for a divine deliverance that would bring final justice and restoration. The hope was spawned that one day the very breath of God would come to inhabit God's people in a way that would allow them to lay hold of freedom to obey the law (Ezek. 36:26).

The Middle Eastern notion of justice had everything to do with deliverance, justice, and restoration. It did not arise from decisions by an impartial judge but rather from acts of mercy and deliverance. We can draw the con-

---

2. George Eldon Ladd, *The Gospel of the Kingdom* (Grand Rapids: Eerdmans, 1959), 24.

3. Paul Hanson, *The Dawn of Apocalyptic: The Historical and Sociological Roots of Jewish Apocalyptic Eschatology* (Philadelphia: Fortress, 1979).

clusion from these insights that the kingdom in the Old Testament is present where God is present to exercise divine lordship redemptively in the world.

The Old Testament connects the coming of God to redeem the world and to establish God's reign as Lord with a final outpouring of the divine breath on all flesh (Joel 2:28). God states that the Spirit will one day reveal God's presence to Israel: "I will no longer hide my face from them, for I will pour out my Spirit on the house of Israel" (Ezek. 39:29). God will cleanse Israel and give them the divine Spirit so that they can follow the law (36:25–27). The lordship of God will be revealed as the Spirit grants new life like the coming up out of the grave of despair: "Then you, my people, will know that I am the LORD, when I open your graves and bring you up from them. I will put my Spirit within you and you will live" (37:13–14a). This divine breath is said to rest on God's chosen messenger (Isa. 61:1–3), a promise that takes on messianic significance.

How does the metaphor of Spirit baptism connect with this hope for the coming presence of God as Lord to cleanse, fill, and redeem? As Oscar Cullmann has noted, John's baptism was most likely taken in large part from the Jewish cleansing rituals, possibly from proselyte baptism for Gentile converts.[4] John makes his baptism a vehicle of repentance for those who wish to be cleansed in preparation for the coming of the divine breath in final judgment and restoration (Matt. 3:8). John most likely poured water over the heads of those who came into the Jordan to be baptized as a symbol of washing and cleansing. Echoes of pouring water in ritual cleansing can be found in Joel's and Luke's descriptions of the Spirit's arrival to end the age and to bring salvation as a great outpouring of the divine Spirit on all flesh (Joel 2:28; Acts 2:17).

Luke also borrows at least analogously from the promise that the Spirit will be given to restore God's people to proper faithfulness. He will use the metaphor of divine filling for those who obey God so that they will function as a holy temple of God's presence (Acts 1:8; 5:32). Spirit baptism as a metaphor carries echoes of divine presence, cleansing, and prophetic witness. It describes how the latter-day revelation of divine lordship will suddenly and dramatically arrive as a great flood of God's living and redeeming presence.

How the anointing of the Messiah relates to the final outpouring of the divine Spirit before the great Day of the Lord is unclear in the Old Testament.

---

4. Oscar Cullmann, *Baptism in the New Testament* (London: SCM, 1950), 62.

How will the arrival of the anointed Messiah occasion the final outpouring of the Spirit? As we will note, John the Baptist will answer this question with his novel announcement of the Messiah as the Baptizer in the Spirit. This pneumatological revision of Jewish messianic expectation is unprecedented and will have far-reaching implications for the early faith in Jesus as both Messiah (Christ) and Lord or as the one who inaugurates the kingdom of God and shares in its reign along with his heavenly Father.

Suffice it to say here that the connection that John the Baptist will forge between Jesus as the Spirit Baptizer and the inauguration of the kingdom of God to establish God's lordship in history is rooted in the Old Testament assumption that the divine presence will make this lordship a reality as a source of freedom and redemption for humanity. In the Old Testament, there is thus a notion of the kingdom of God as arriving when God arrives at some future time to fully restore creation to the divine lordship. As Walter Kasper notes, "In the tradition of the Old Testament and of Judaism the coming of the kingdom of God means the coming of God."[5]

In fulfillment of Old Testament hopes, God's lordship or kingdom is revealed in the Gospels in the conquering of darkness and death through the presence of the Spirit in the liberating acts of Jesus: "But if I drive out demons by the Spirit of God, then the kingdom of God has come upon you" (Matt. 12:28). The will and reign of God are accordingly not external to God as something that God imparts aside from God's own presence. Jesus was convinced that the time of the kingdom was near and, in fact, was already arriving in signs of God's presence in his ministry through the Spirit to set people free (Matt. 12:28; Luke 4:18). To ask for God's sovereign will to be done "on earth as it is in heaven" is to ask for God's very presence to perform it. God is both the giver and the gift of life (Athanasius). The kingdom of God comes in power through God's presence to make all things new (Rev. 21:5).

The kingdom of God was viewed in nineteenth-century liberal Protestant theology as an ethical and communal reality. In the twentieth century, the development from Albert Schweitzer to Johannes Weiss placed a new focus on the apocalyptic and otherworldly nature of the kingdom of God in the New Testament. Both trends are one-sided and distorted. The kingdom of God is God's act and, therefore, out of our grasp. Yet, the kingdom of God also involved human witness, fellowship, and justice in and through

---

5. Walter Kasper, *Jesus the Christ* (Mahwah, NJ: Paulist, 1976), 78.

the church and even outside the context of the church. The kingdom of God involved new creation in the dynamic presence of Christ by the Spirit. Gregory of Nyssa rightly stated that Christ is the King and the Spirit is the kingdom. AMEN

The kingdom of God in the Gospels is primarily a redemptive presence. The transformation of life by the kingdom of God thus implies that new life does not merely emerge from the old. John says we are born from above, "not of natural descent, nor of human decision" (John 1:13). One thus enters the life of the kingdom through rebirth by the Spirit (3:5). Similarly, Paul notes that flesh and blood cannot inherit the kingdom of God, "nor does the perishable inherit the imperishable" (1 Cor. 15:42, 50). Moltmann notes that just as the risen Christ does not evolve out from the crucified Christ, so the new creation does not simply emerge or evolve from the old creation.[6] The path to glory is the cross, and nothing will pass through that door without first being purged and transformed by the refining fire of God's own presence. For us personally this means, "Repent and be baptized, every one of you in the name of Jesus Christ for the forgiveness of your sins. And you will receive the gift of the Holy Spirit" (Acts 2:38).

Moltmann uses the category of divine *advent* or coming as essential to the kingdom of God in order to accent the transcendence of the new and its discontinuity from the old. He is careful not to advocate a radical sense of discontinuity, however, as though God's coming is to be defined as an "interruption," such as the term "in-breaking" might imply. The appropriate category is rather *conversion*. God's coming in power to bring about the kingdom in our midst is felt in the transformation of the creation into new creation or into new possibilities for life.[7] A god who seeks to preserve things as they always were is not the God of the Hebrew or Christian Scriptures. Rather, the present is marked off from the past through hope in the God who embraces but also transcends the historical moment.

I prefer the term *presence* over advent, since in the divine presence one has access to both the continuity of the Christian life and the ongoing renewal

---

6. Jürgen Moltmann, *The Trinity and the Kingdom* (San Francisco: Harper & Row, 1981), 28.

7. Jürgen Moltmann, *The Coming of God: Christian Eschatology* (Minneapolis: Fortress, 1996), 22–23. Concerning the kingdom of God as a new creation concept, note also John Bright, *The Kingdom of God: The Biblical Concept and Its Meaning for the Church* (Nashville: Abingdon, 1957).

that is possible in our living relationship with God. After all, this presence is of a living God who encounters us with newness as well as holds us in grace. Thus, there is continuity between the old and the new created from the divine side. As Moltmann notes further, "What is eschatologically new itself creates its own continuity, since it does not annihilate the old but gathers it up and creates it anew."[8] The term advent is still useful, however, not just because it is biblical ("thy kingdom come") but also because it symbolizes the transcendence and newness of our experience of the God who abides in us and within history.

The miracles that accompany the ministry of Jesus foreshadow the presence of the kingdom as a new creation that does not just abandon the old creation but renews it (Luke 4:18). The same is said of the signs and wonders that can accompany the proclamation of the gospel today (1 Cor. 2:4–5) as well as our acceptance of it by faith (Gal. 5:5). These miracles do not simply "interrupt" the natural order (creating a "gap" in "natural laws"). It is much more the case that the natural order is transformed in extraordinary ways or taken up by the Spirit of God and made to function in extraordinary ways (in ways that transcend "ordinary" capacities) as a deeper sign that all of creation is being graced by the presence of the Spirit, who groans with the creation and facilitates its reaching for the liberty to come (Rom. 8:22).

The line between the ordinary and the extraordinary is fine indeed, not because there is no such thing as signs and wonders, but because all of creation is graced by God's Spirit in ways unknown to us. Thus, the kingdom can be said to be both present in the creation as graced by God as well as "come" in fresh power to bring the "powers of the age to come" (Heb. 6:5) to bear on the present moment. The fact that the new does not annihilate creation but rather transforms it implies continuity of identity in God throughout one's spiritual journey. God both indwells and continues to come in newness. As Moltmann notes, "God already sets present and past in the light of his eschatological arrival, an arrival which means the establishment of his eternal kingdom and his indwelling in the creation renewed for that indwelling."[9]

In other words, in the renewal of creation for the divine indwelling, God can be said to be present already to establish the reign of the divine love and

---

8. Ibid., 29.
9. Ibid., 23.

life, overthrowing the reign of sin and death. This ongoing transformation involves a sense of continuous abiding in God and God in us as God indwells us penultimately as a foretaste of the final indwelling of all things. Decisively inaugurated in the life, death, and resurrection of Jesus, the kingdom of God becomes a dynamic within history through the outpouring of the Spirit that is directed toward the divine indwelling in all of creation so that all things might be conformed to Christ's image.

We may thus say that the kingdom is "now" but also "not yet." As Ladd notes, the kingdom of God represents the sovereign rule of God inaugurated in Christ's redemptive work but yet to be fulfilled in his return in power to make all things new.[10] The parables of the kingdom in Matthew 13, for example, imply both a "now" and a "not yet" of the kingdom in the world. The kingdom is like a seed yet to grow into a tree (Matt. 13:31–32). New creation, however, is not merely future. In eschatology, the future overlaps the present and interprets the past anew (altering its hold on us). In Jesus' proclamation of the kingdom, "the present and the past are inextricably interwoven."[11]

The Spirit liberates creation from within history toward new possibilities for free, eschatological existence. In the words of Jan Lochman, the Spirit is the great "dialectician" that drives historical existence toward freedom and transcendence.[12] It is important to note, therefore, that the relationship between the now and the not-yet is not static but dynamic. This dynamism has its roots in the fact that the kingdom has to do, not with a place, but rather with *life*, the life of the Spirit of God (Matt. 12:28; Rom. 14:17), opening up the creation to new possibilities of renewal and hope.

The life of the kingdom is the life of the Spirit in which God's reign actively conquers the dark forces and liberates lives to new hope (Matt. 12:28). It is thus not only a divine attribute but the participation of the creature by God's grace in the divine nature. Accordingly, it is not primarily about religion but about a life in God, filled with the fruit of the Spirit and dedicated to God's righteousness on earth: "For the kingdom of God is not a matter of eating or drinking [i.e., food laws] but of righteousness, peace and joy in the Holy Spirit" (Rom. 14:17).

---

10. Ladd, *The Gospel of the Kingdom*, 24.

11. Wolfhart Pannenberg, *Theology of the Kingdom of God* (Philadelphia: Westminster, 1969), 53.

12. Jan Milic Lochman, in *Dogmatik im Dialogue*, ed. F. Buri, H. Ott, and J. M. Lochman (Gütersloh: Gütersloher Verlagshaus Gerd Mohn, 1973), 1:135.

Similarly, Jesus extolled the virtues of the kingdom of God, such as justice, mercy, and faithfulness, over the ceremonial laws of Israel, such as tithing (Matt. 23:23). According to Jesus, one lives out the law in a life taken up in the kingdom of God and its righteousness and not primarily through dedication to the outward forms of religion. If Pentecost at the time of Jesus was a celebration of the giving of the law at Sinai, the outpouring of the Spirit at Pentecost became a powerful symbol of the fact that proper devotion to God, to which the law points, can be experienced penultimately in the liberating presence of the Spirit.

The pneumatological substance of the kingdom of God gives us a clue as to why John the Baptist connected the coming Spirit Baptizer with the coming of the kingdom. Implicit in John's announcement is the indication that Spirit baptism inaugurates the kingdom of God because through this baptism the Spirit is bestowed to end the age and to bring about the final transformation of all things. John knew that his water baptism did not have such apocalyptic significance. John did not have the authority to bring the Spirit, bestow the Spirit, and bring about the final judgment and sanctification of creation. He did not bear the winnowing fork; he could not clear the threshing floor. Only the Messiah could baptize with and in the divine breath. Only the Messiah had that right. Only God had that right.

Using prophetic rhetoric, John says something similar to the Old Testament words of Jeremiah that Israel is to circumcise the heart in anticipation of God's turning their hearts from stone to flesh through the Spirit (Jer. 4:4; cf. Ezek. 36:26). Similarly, John could baptize with or in water as a sign of repentance, but only the Messiah could baptize in the divine breath unto judgment, purgation, and new life. It is through this Spirit baptism that the kingdom will come in judgment and purgation. Nothing will be left standing except what God's sovereign reign has established.

I am assuming that John the Baptist had something in mind concerning Spirit baptism other than judgment. It has been argued that John's only reference was to judgment. The breath of God will come through the Messiah's eschatological appearance to blow away the resistance to God's reign as the natural wind blows the chaff from the wheat. Nothing that opposes God's reign will be left standing.[13] The baptism in the Spirit "and fire" (Luke 3:16)

---

13. James D. G. Dunn, "Spirit-and-Fire Baptism," *Novum Testamentum* 14 (1972): 81–92.

would mean the same thing, namely, the eschatological judgment of God through the coming of the kingdom of God: "His winnowing fork is in his hand to clear his threshing floor and to gather the wheat into his granary, but he will burn up the chaff with unquenchable fire" (v. 17).

As Lloyd Neve has pointed out, the divine breath in the Old Testament (especially Isaiah) can refer to the power of God's wrath and judgment.[14] Note the similarity of Isaiah's description of God's wrath against the nations with John the Baptist's imagery: "His breath is like a rushing torrent, rising up to the neck. He shakes the nations in the sieve of destruction" (30:28). The previous verse (30:27) notes that God's tongue is a "consuming fire."

There is no question but that judgment is prominent in John's implicit connection between the Messiah's role as Spirit Baptizer and as Inaugurator of the kingdom of God. This fact may have been involved in John's question from prison concerning whether or not "another" is to be expected to fulfill the establishment of the kingdom of God on earth (Luke 7:18–19). That the Spirit is healing and liberating the sick and oppressed may not have been primarily or mainly what John intended when he foretold the coming of the Spirit Baptizer. The charismatic dimension of the Messiah's ushering in of the kingdom of God became far more prominent to the nature of that kingdom than John may have expected. Obviously, the "functional ambiguity" of this biblical metaphor would take on a richer meaning in its messianic and eschatological fulfillment than John himself had realized.

Yet, there are overtones in John's poetic description of the baptism in the divine Spirit that imply purgation and restoration as well as judgment. After all, the wheat is stored into barns as the chaff is blown away by the mighty breath of God (Luke 3:17). "Spirit and fire" may have functioned for John as overlapping metaphors to imply restoration and judgment. The testimony of John's Gospel, accordingly, interpreted the coming of the Spirit and the kingdom through Jesus as penultimately fulfilled in a "new birth" from above that makes one a participant in the coming reign of God (John 1:13; 3:5). Indeed, the message of the Gospels that the Spirit Baptizer is already bringing the kingdom of God to bear on human experience and life (Matt. 12:28; Luke 4:18) significantly qualifies the apocalyptic hope shared even by John the Baptist that the Messiah will bring the Spirit to end the age with final judgment and purgation.

---

14. Lloyd Neve, *The Spirit of God in the Old Testament* (Tokyo: Sheibunsha, 1972), 45, 51.

Luke also makes the issue of the kingdom of God the context for understanding the fulfillment of Spirit baptism. By his account, Jesus discusses the kingdom with the disciples as the setting for quoting John the Baptist's announcement of the coming Spirit baptism (Acts 1:3). As I noted, Luke's Acts further qualifies the apocalyptic context of Spirit baptism by granting the eschatological breath of God necessary to inaugurate the kingdom of God in power penultimate fulfillment in history through the metaphor of Spirit "filling" (cf. Acts 2:4). Such language implies more than repentance and cleansing. John's announcement of the coming Spirit baptism would be fulfilled in ways he could not have anticipated.

As I will note, the early church focused on Jesus as raised from the dead to be the one who bestows the divine Spirit (John 20:22; 1 Cor. 15:45) for new creation by the indwelling of God. Jesus' role as Spirit Baptizer transcends John's baptism, but it does not abandon it. The repentance and cleansing implied in John's baptism is taken up into Spirit baptism with one very important addition, namely, the people of God are baptized in the Spirit to become a holy temple indwelled by the very breath of God. Spirit baptism encompasses repentance and new life, cleansing and infilling. As members of the Jerusalem church noted in Acts 11:18, the Gentiles' Spirit baptism gave them "repentance unto life."

Thus, Spirit baptism for Luke does not just cleanse as John's baptism did, but it fills the temple with God's holy presence. The entire debate in Acts will relate to whether or not the uncircumcised Gentiles can be regarded as cleansed so that they might join the messianic community and mission. When God's holy breath indwells the Gentiles as living temples, proof positive is offered that they have indeed been cleansed by God. The conclusion of the first great council of the Christian church, the Jerusalem Council, concerning the Gentiles after their Spirit baptism was that in purifying their hearts by faith, God "made no distinction between us and them" (Acts 15:9). The transformation of the heart by the indwelling of the divine Spirit foretold by Ezekiel 36:26 had come to pass. God now reigns in the hearts of both Jew and Gentile by the baptism in the Holy Spirit.

For Luke, Spirit baptism does not just sanctify but also empowers for witness. This empowerment brings believers into the holy presence of God in praise and declarations of God's mighty deeds (Acts 2:4–5) and drives them outward to the corners of the earth in witness to Christ with many extraordinary signs of God's presence to save (1:8; 10:38–39). As Moltmann has noted, the metaphor of breath, like water, is used of the Spirit in the Bible to imply movement and change.[15] The breath of God through Pentecost inhales the people of God into God's holy presence and exhales them outward into all the world to proclaim the good news and to continue Jesus' ministry of deliverance for the sick and oppressed. The penultimate fulfillment of Spirit baptism for Luke is akin to a prophetic call that draws people close to the heart of God in praise and prophetic empathy in order to empower them for witness in the world.

For Luke, Spirit baptism does not only purge and indwell so that the people of God can be a holy temple, it empowers so that they may also function as a living witness. The flame of the Spirit that burns within God's people as a holy temple is a spreading flame. This is what Pentecostals focus on in their definition of Spirit baptism. I will not deny this definition, only set it within a broader theological framework.

It is indeed interesting that Luke does not preserve the baptism in "fire" in his description of the realization of Spirit baptism at Pentecost as a restorative and empowering reality (Acts 1:8). The tongues of fire in Acts 2:4 are probably signs of God's holy presence without the judgmental emphasis of John the Baptist's prediction.[16] Dunn has noted that Luke's omission of the baptism in fire may be due to the fact that Jesus' death was itself a baptism of judgment taken for others (Luke 12:49–50; cf. Matt. 20:22–23), so that believers may only receive the baptism of Spirit as a purging, restorative, and empowering divine presence.[17] Luke, however, does not hesitate to note that judgment is still on the horizon of the outpouring of God's holy breath on all flesh, for there will be signs on the earth and in the heavens of the great Day of the Lord as this outpouring reaches its final fulfillment. Spirit baptism is directed to *all flesh*, not just to all peoples but to everyone who calls on the name of the Lord as the firstfruits of the renewal of creation in the midst of cosmic upheaval ("wonders in the heavens above," etc., Acts 2:17–21). In a sense, the followers of Jesus were "baptized" in the Spirit at Pentecost. But

---

15. Jürgen Moltmann, *The Spirit of Life: A Universal Affirmation* (Minneapolis: Fortress, 1992), 278.

16. Glen Menzies, "Pre-Lukan Occurrences of the Phrase 'Tongue(s) of Fire,'" *Pneuma* 22:1 (Spring 2000): 27–60.

17. James D. G. Dunn, *Baptism in the Holy Spirit: A Re-examination of the New Testament Teaching on the Gift of the Holy Spirit in Relation to Pentecostalism Today* (London: SCM, 1970), 42–43.

Luke still sees Spirit baptism as a final outpouring that culminates with the Day of the Lord. In Acts 2, Spirit baptism is "now" and "not yet."

Many Pentecostals may not be accustomed to such a cosmic, eschatological understanding of Spirit baptism. But Spirit baptism as a kingdom and eschatological concept has this cosmic significance as its theological context in the New Testament. I learned from the great Ernst Käsemann that there is an inseparable connection between personal redemption/empowerment and cosmic renewal in the apocalyptic theological context of the Spirit's work in the New Testament that makes a restriction of our pneumatological categories to personal, existential, and even ecclesial contexts unthinkable (cf. Rom. 8:18–25). This book represents a similar effort in relation to Spirit baptism. If one locates John's announcement of the Spirit Baptizer in the context suggested by Matthew 3 and Acts 1, Spirit baptism will need to be developed in the light of the apocalyptic context of the coming of the kingdom of God in power within all of creation.

Of course, as noted above, the pneumatological experience of the kingdom of God in the here and now, especially in Luke, qualifies the apocalyptic context considerably. What became fascinating to me in my research was the way in which the divine infilling that represented Luke's focus and the cosmic transformation implied in apocalyptic hope came together in Paul under the symbol of Pentecost and Spirit baptism. In this light, take careful note of what Paul says in that passage that may be referred to as Paul's description of Pentecost:

> But to each one of us grace has been given as Christ apportioned it. This is why it says:
>
> "When he ascended on high,
>   he led captives in his train
>   and gave gifts to his people."
>
> (What does "he ascended" mean except that he also descended to the lower, earthly regions? He who descended is the very one who ascended higher than all the heavens, *in order to fill the whole universe*.) (Eph 4:7–10 TNIV, italics added)

Notice that Christ's ascension and bestowal of the Spirit and the Spirit's gifts on the church (the symbol of Pentecost) have as their ultimate goal that Christ "fill the whole universe" with his presence. Seen as an eschatological concept, Pentecost becomes a symbol, not only of the divine breath filling and charismatically empowering God's people, but also indwelling all of creation one day. Not to be neglected is Paul's description of the penultimate fulfillment of Spirit baptism as the experience of the Spirit in one's initiation into the body of Christ (1 Cor. 12:13). But Paul finds in Pentecost as well the symbol of Christ's indwelling *all things* through the Spirit of God. The kingdom thus centrally involves but also transcends the church.

What do Pentecost and the eventual divine indwelling and transformation of all of creation have to do with the kingdom of God for Paul? In Pauline terms, the kingdom of God and the divine indwelling of creation converge in the final deliverance of creation from the dominion of death (bondage to sin and death) unto the liberating dominion of life. The ultimate goal of Spirit baptism is thus also the goal of the kingdom of God: the final dominion of life over death as all of creation becomes the dwelling place of God's Holy Spirit. Notice how Paul connects the fulfillment of the kingdom of God with the final, divine indwelling of all things:

> For as in Adam all die, so in Christ all will be made alive. But in this order: Christ, the firstfruits; then, when he comes, those who belong to him. Then the end will come, when he hands over the kingdom to God the Father after he has destroyed all dominion, authority and power. For he must reign until he has put all his enemies under his feet. The last enemy to be destroyed is death. . . . When he has done this, then the Son himself will be made subject to him who put everything under him, *so that God will be all in all* (1 Cor. 15:22–26, 28 TNIV, italics added; cf., Rom. 8:14–25).

The passage ends with a description of the fulfillment of the kingdom of God: "that God may be all in all" (1 Cor. 15:28), namely, that God's rule is fully manifested throughout creation through the Son as the Bestower of the Spirit to indwell all things. In the fulfillment of the kingdom, God delivers creation from the dominion of death by indwelling all things with eternal life. John the Revelator shares a similar vision of the end. When the kingdom of God is fulfilled as the new Jerusalem descends from heaven, God tabernacles with creation (Rev. 21:3). God proclaims from the throne, "I am making everything new" (21:5). Temple theology is expanded to involve the people of God and, ultimately, all of creation.

God reigns ultimately in the deliverance of creation from death unto life, a deliverance that we foreshadow in "repentance unto life" (Acts 11:18) in our penultimate participation in Spirit baptism. We are filled with the Spirit as a foreshadow of the divine indwelling in all of creation. Though God already pervades all of reality (Acts 17:28; Col. 1:17), the final goal of divine indwelling is redemptive in significance: that all of creation be brought into "eternal life" or the filial relationship between Jesus and his Father (John 17:4) by being transformed into the image of the risen Christ. This is why all of creation is made by and for the Son (Col. 1:15–16). The kingdom of God comes through the divine presence in the transformation of all things by the Spirit into the image of Christ.

These eschatological passages beautifully tie together the kingdom of God and the divine infilling implied in Spirit baptism and the symbol of Pentecost. I do not deny Moltmann's point that the kingdom of God is a historical and political metaphor. He thus sees the need to augment it with a vision of cosmic transformation.[18] In my reading of the New Testament, however, the fulfillment of the kingdom most broadly defined involves cosmic transformation. One could also augment the kingdom metaphor with a more personal notion of union with or participation in God.

It is interesting, as H. Richard Niebuhr has noted, that the kingdom of God has been the chief Protestant distinctive but it has been union with God that has served as the main Catholic emphasis.[19] Similarly, Stanley Grenz has recognized that the dominance of the kingdom of God motif in the twentieth century has an element of ambiguity to it that requires other concepts in one's quest to develop an integrating principle for theology. Grenz wishes to unite both kingdom and communion to form a mutually illuminating principle around which one could discuss other theological loci.[20] Indeed, as we will note, the kingdom of God as a reality established through the divine outpouring of the divine presence implies that the kingdom is driven by love and communion. Especially in the light of the Trinitarian context for the kingdom of God and Spirit baptism, we can develop the life-transforming communion of God's love as the very heart of the reign of God established through Spirit baptism.

---

18. Moltmann, *The Coming of God*, 132.

19. This is part of the central thesis of H. Richard Niebuhr's, *The Kingdom of God in America* (Middletown, CT: Wesleyan Univ. Press, 1988).

20. Stanley J. Grenz, *Revisioning Evangelical Theology: A Fresh Agenda for the 21st Century* (Downers Grove, IL: InterVarsity Press, 1993), 137–62. I am grateful to my Vanguard University colleague Gary Tyra for drawing my attention to this reference.

Such augmentation does not replace the kingdom motif in Scripture but fills it out. Still relevant for our time is K. Blaser's statement that the kingdom of God has been the central theological problem in the twentieth century.[21] With regard to cosmic transformation, Paul stretches the kingdom metaphor to describe just such a vast new creation as we noted above. Sin and death are viewed as alien powers that hold creation under the kingdom of darkness, while the life-transforming reign of God brings creation under the dominion of life. This new dominion is the kingdom of God fulfilled. The kingdom comes in power to overthrow the powers of sin, sickness, and death and to fill the entire creation with the very presence of God's Holy Spirit, which is the ultimate victory of life over death, the reign of life overthrowing the reign of death (cf. Rom. 8:18–25).

Since the kingdom of God is pneumatological in substance, it also has love, the love enjoyed between the Father and the Son and with creation, as its substance. Since the kingdom is manifested through God's loving and redemptive presence, the kingdom involves participation in the very presence of God as well. This establishment of God's reign is Spirit baptism ultimately fulfilled. As beings filled with the Spirit and committed to the Christ life, we are harbingers of the new creation to come and the kingdom of God fulfilled: "If I drive out demons by the Spirit of God, then the kingdom of God has come upon you" (Matt. 12:28).

All of our soteriological and charismatic categories achieve their coherence in this wedding of the kingdom of God and Spirit baptism begun in the message of John the Baptist and fulfilled with different nuances elsewhere in the New Testament. Pentecostals have intuited this wedding by stressing the experience of Spirit baptism as the presence of God to empower us for witness to Christ as the one who conquers sin, sickness, and death. Pentecostals have long connected Spirit baptism to the signs and wonders of the inauguration of the kingdom of God that foreshadow the new creation to come.

Accordingly, a "charismatic" understanding of Spirit baptism resists the reduction of Christianity to an anthropocentric redemption cult such as one had in ancient mystery or gnostic religions. Debates over Christian "initiation" understood as personal redemption or even incorporation into the grace of the church require the Pentecostal understanding of Spirit baptism as an

---

21. K. Blaser, "Mission und Erweckungsbewegung," in *Pietismus und Neuzeit*, ed. M. Brecht et al. (Göttingen: Vandenhoeck & Ruprecht, 1981), 144.

empowering and vocational force to expand the boundaries of the discussion. A secret initiation ritual that distinguishes "us" from "them" is not what Spirit baptism is all about.

Spirit baptism is a liberating force that reorders our lives according to the loving reign of God in the world. It is fulfilled in the renewal of creation with apocalyptic signs in the heavens and the earth. Until then, sons and daughters, rich and poor, young and old are all caught up in the liberating service of God's loving reign in the world to the glory of God (Acts 2:17–21). Spirit baptism constitutes the church and causes the church to missionize for the sake of the kingdom. But Spirit baptism also transcends the church because it inaugurates the kingdom.

Though Spirit baptism implies personal meanings, it is not confined to these. The whole of creation is meant through God's indwelling to glorify God and to enjoy him forever. The kingdom of God is thus presently liberating and transformative in all dimensions of life. By the Spirit, the poor receive hope, the lame walk, and the blind see (Luke 4:18). The holistic thrust of the Spirit's work is personal, relational, and even political. The kingdom is indeed a metaphor drawn in part from politics. It involves the fulfillment of human aspirations for the new Jerusalem on earth and for the spiritual enlightenment, intimacy with God, and universal justice and mercy in human relationships that the new polis of God inspires. The fulfillment of the kingdom of God in the new creation is pictured like a temple of God's indwelling but also like a city or a society governed by life, love, and justice (Rev. 21:1–5).

Toward that eschatological fulfillment, the kingdom of God has a righteousness that reorders life toward the so-called "weightier matters of the law" (Matt. 23:23 NRSV). God's mercy and justice are the values of the kingdom for which we thirst and by which we prioritize our lives. "But seek first his kingdom and his righteousness" and all other things will be provided for life's sustenance (6:33). Spirit baptism calls for such a life in the here-and-now in anticipation of the final victory of life over death, righteousness over unrighteousness.

The kingdom of God is also the kingdom of Christ, because he is the one who is the incarnate Word and the chief bearer of the Spirit. He inaugurates the kingdom of God in his person and work as both the sanctified Son and the charismatic Christ. The transformative power of the kingdom, therefore, has a *Christoformistic* goal and direction. The field of the Spirit and of the kingdom is the field of the risen and ascended Christ's increasingly diverse presence. It is also the field of the crucified Christ, meaning that it is realized among us in the power of the risen Christ as we bear one another's burdens and reach out to others in solidarity with suffering victims everywhere. It thus has its eternal root in the loving relationship between the Father and the Son in the Spirit. Spirit baptism is the will of the Father to indwell the creation through the Spirit in order, by the Spirit, to involve creation in the relationship between the Father and the Son (John 17:20–23).

It is obviously now time to grant Spirit baptism greater Trinitarian specificity. To do this, we need to start with the role of Spirit baptism in the rise of faith in Jesus as the Savior and the source of new life.

SPIRIT BAPTISM AND THE CHURCH'S FAITH IN JESUS

The baptism in the Holy Spirit can be seen as of seminal importance to the development of the church's early confession of faith. Spirit baptism is not only to be seen as the chief distinctive of Pentecostal theology but also implicitly as seminal to the church's confession of Christ as sent from the Father to transform all things through the Spirit. By rediscovering the metaphor of Spirit baptism, Pentecostals globally can help the Western church to appreciate more fully a somewhat neglected feature of the early confession of Jesus as Lord. The significance of Pentecostalism may prove after all to involve a bit more than an experiential invigoration of the Christian life.

Consider this: All four Gospels announce the significance of the Messiah's coming in his role to baptize in the Spirit. The reader from the very beginning of the New Testament canon is struck with an unprecedented Christological claim. Nowhere in the Old Testament or in Jewish messianic expectation is the Messiah anticipated as the agent in the impartation or pouring out of the Spirit. In this light, Acts appropriately begins with Jesus' affirmation of John the Baptist's description of the coming Messiah as the Baptizer in the Spirit (1:5–8). The rest of Acts can be seen as an effort to come to terms theologically with this understanding of Christ, especially in terms of the new unity in the Spirit achieved between Jew and Gentile.

It is not incidental to the message of Acts that the Jerusalem Council met to discuss the implications of Spirit baptism for the inclusion of Gentiles into the messianic community on the basis of the one faith in Christ shared universally by both Jew and Gentile (Acts 15). In describing the road to the Jerusalem Council, Acts 11:16–17 specifically hearkens back to John the Baptist's designation of Jesus as the Spirit Baptizer introduced at the beginning of

Acts in 1:5–8 to justify the inclusion of Gentiles into the blessings of the eschatological Spirit through faith in Christ. The first five books of the New Testament can be seen to function much like the Pentateuch in the Old Testament, namely, to define the gospel to be elaborated upon in the remainder of the New Testament. All of these foundational books highlight Spirit baptism as the central feature of Jesus' identity as Messiah and the Christological foundation for the faith of the church that unites Jew and Gentile.

Spirit baptism for Acts, however, means that the church would find its essence and unity in Christ as the one who bestows the Spirit, not in Jewish law. This insight was seminal to the formation of the early faith of the church. For the earliest Jewish Christians it was nothing short of a major paradigm shift. It is only because we have become so separated from the early debate over the proper conditions for the inclusion of Gentiles into the messianic community that we fail to see how enormously significant Spirit baptism was to the church's initial acceptance of Gentiles within the sole confines of an affirmation in the Spirit of Christ as Lord (1 Cor. 12:1–3).

It seems that the burning issue for the first-century churches had to do with Spirit baptism, or the implications of receiving the Spirit by faith in Christ rather than by obedience to the law. Put another way, the issue had to do with the implications inherent within Jesus' role as Baptizer in the Spirit for the church's expansively diverse identity and mission. In continuity with the Jerusalem Council, Paul isolated the issue of the reception of the Spirit from Christ "by faith alone" as key to understanding the revelation of the gospel given to him and proclaimed by the apostles (Gal. 3:1–5; 1:6–9). Paul gets to the major point of his defense of the gospel in Galatians when he asks, "I would like to learn just one thing from you: Did you receive the Spirit by observing the law, or by believing what you heard?" (3:2).

As Charles Cosgrove has shown, it is the reception of the Spirit by faith that represents the key issue in Paul's struggle to define the gospel in Galatians.[22] The main issue for Paul is not circumcision but new creation (Gal. 6:15), because how one enters the realm of the Spirit, of God's favor, was the burning issue for Paul's letter. For Paul, Jesus redeemed us from the curse of the law "in order that the blessing given to Abraham might come to the Gentiles through Christ Jesus, so that by faith we might receive the promise of the Spirit"

---

22. Charles Cosgrove, *The Cross and the Spirit: A Study in the Argument and Theology of Galatians* (Macon, GA: Mercer Univ. Press, 1989), 40–45.

(3:13–14). Indeed, the life of the Spirit received by faith in Christ is the key characteristic of the church's participation in the kingdom of God for Paul (Rom. 14:17). By all counts, the Jerusalem Council essentially agreed. Jew and Gentile were originally united by their faith in Jesus as the Spirit Baptizer.

I would like to highlight the fact that the reign of God was present in Christ and his proclamation through the Spirit (Matt. 12:28), who was also the agent in his resurrection (Rom. 1:4). He is risen to break the bonds of sin and death and to impart the Spirit of new life. These facts lead to the New Testament conviction that it is mainly Jesus as the Imparter of new life that gave rise to the church's focus on *him* as the object of worship and the means by which God redeems creation. As Kilian McDonnell noted, "The universal mediation of the Spirit makes it possible for Christ to be the center of the gospel."[23] Unfortunately, a gradual neglect of the significance of the Spirit in Christ's identity as Lord of salvation occurred in the second century and beyond as a result of the church's reaction to the adoptionists, who viewed Jesus as merely a Spirit-inspired man. The gradual eclipse of Spirit Christology by Logos Christology is widely known.

Such is ironic, especially since John, the major New Testament voice behind the development of Logos Christology, implicitly connects Jesus as the Logos of the Father (John 1:1–14) with his being the source of life (1:13; 3:16; 10:10; 11:25–26) or the one who breathes the Spirit of God for redemption (20:22) as God breathed forth the breath of life at the creation of humanity (Gen. 2:7). Deep within Israel's memory is the characterization of the breathing or pouring forth of the divine Spirit as a divine activity (e.g., Gen. 2:7; Joel 2:28). This is why there was no Jewish messianic expectation that involved the Messiah's imparting the Spirit of God. Although the Jews expected the Messiah to be anointed of the Spirit (e.g., Isa. 61:1–3), the idea that the Messiah would impart or baptize in the Spirit is unprecedented in Judaism. Such was a divine activity for ancient Jewish writings.

Pannenberg has convincingly noted that later Christological statements about the Son's preexistence with the Father evolved from the early proclamation of Jesus as raised from the dead.[24] I wish to stress that this emphasis on the resurrection of Jesus involves Jesus as the one raised from the dead *to*

---

23. McDonnell, *The Other Hand of God*, 206–7.
24. Wolfhart Pannenberg, *Systematic Theology*, 3 vols. (Grand Rapids: Eerdmans, 1998–), 1:265.

bestow the Spirit: "So it is written, 'The first man Adam became a living being'; the last Adam, a life-giving spirit" (1 Cor. 15:45). The announcements of the coming of the Messiah as Baptizer in the Spirit in the Gospels represent a shadow cast from the significance of the resurrection. Indeed, one could say that Jesus as the Spirit baptizer is the unique Christological privilege in the Gospels, because it foreshadows and fulfills the chief purpose of the resurrection, namely, that Jesus become a "life-giving Spirit" (15:45).

Spirit baptism thus plays a fundamental role in defining the pneumatological substance of Christ's work in ushering in the kingdom of God, setting the stage for the church's conclusion that the God of the kingdom is Father, Son, and Spirit. After all, God as Father was not totally alien to Judaism, neither was the idea of a divine presence through God's mighty breath. It is God the Son as the Spirit Baptizer that became the unique link between the Father and the Spirit and, indirectly, to the doctrine of the Trinity.[25]

Thus, in a sense, Christ's deity can be said to have been deduced in significant part from his resurrection from the dead as a "life-giving spirit" (1 Cor. 15:45). Jesus as the Word of the Father incarnated (John 1:14) can be seen in John as read from Jesus as the man raised according to the Spirit to be the Lord who imparts the very breath of God (John 20:22). Similarly, Jesus as conceived in Mary by the Spirit (Luke 1:35) can be seen as read from Jesus as raised to clothe the disciples with the Spirit of God (Luke 24:49). A significant aspect of Jesus' identity as Savior (and thus identifiable as Lord) is in the fact that he was raised to impart the Spirit. This is why it is only in the Spirit that we can truly recognize Jesus' lordship (1 Cor 12:13). It is only by the Spirit that we can confess Jesus as Lord, because it was from Jesus the risen Lord that the Spirit was bestowed as a living witness to that lordship. Here we can take Pannenberg's thesis that the deity of Christ was read historically from the event of the resurrection of Christ so as to place equal stress on the fact that it was read from Christ's resurrection as the one privileged to impart the divine Spirit on behalf of the Father.

The resurrection alone is not sufficient to lead the church to a confession of Christ's ontological unity with the Father. It is also in the goal of the resurrection, namely, in Jesus' becoming the one who imparts the Spirit of new

---

25. I am grateful to my Vanguard University colleague Jerry Camery-Hoggatt for planting the seed for this idea in my mind. He pointed out to me that the concept of God as both Father and breath are in the Old Testament but not God as Son.

life from the Father, which suggests this unity. Indeed, only God can impart the divine breath. St. Augustine said this best concerning Christ: "How then can he who gives the Spirit not be God? Indeed, how much must he who gives God be God! None of his disciples ever gave the Holy Spirit; they prayed that he might come upon those on whom they laid hands.... He received it as man, he poured it out as God" (De trinitatis 15.46). Implicitly, the church had to reject the adoptionistic heresy of the second century because a Spirit-inspired man who is not identifiable with God the Lord of salvation cannot impart the Spirit. The adoptionist Christ resides on our side of the Savior/saved relationship and, thus, cannot pass on his Spirit to others, cannot save, and cannot found a church. Jesus does not cross over from the saved to the Savior category unless he is not only the one who received but also the one who imparted the divine breath. Therefore, Jesus' anointing had to involve incarnation in order for him to be in resurrection the one who imparts the life of the Spirit to others.

The early rule of faith in the church had its source in early Christian baptismal formulas and confessions. Indeed, it was at Jesus' baptism that Christ is publicly and dramatically anointed as the one who will be the Son of God, the one anticipated as the Spirit Baptizer. The baptismal location of the rule of faith implicitly looks to the baptized Christ as the one who received the Spirit in order to bestow it. Without this memory at the root of Christian baptism, this baptism as an occasion for confessing the rule of faith would lose all significance. As Pannenberg noted, it is the presence of the Spirit in Jesus' baptism and designation as the Christ that kept the church from binitarianism.[26]

In a sense, the later Nicene confession of Jesus' ontological unity with the Father was tied historically (at least implicitly) to the church's observation that Jesus as the risen Lord breathed or imparted the very breath of God on the church, an activity designated by all four Gospels and by Acts as a baptism in the Spirit. Without the role of Jesus as the one who bestows the Spirit, his resurrection would have lost its eschatological goal and the relationship of Jesus to his heavenly Father would have lost its strongest clue.

We should, accordingly, not be surprised that Trinitarian orthodoxy should have first-century roots in Jesus' role as the risen Lord to baptize in the Spirit and to inaugurate the kingdom of God on behalf of the Father. The

---

26. Pannenberg, Systematic Theology, 1:268.

whole story of Jesus as anointed of the Spirit to be the Word of the Father sets up the climactic event of Christ's resurrection as a "life-giving spirit." We are not affirming here a docetic Christology, since Christ poured out the Spirit as the risen and glorified man for the renewal of creation. Spirit baptism implies a view of the kingdom of God as both a divine action and the renewal of creation in God.

All that we know about the triune life of God comes from the trajectory of this story of Jesus, from his conception by the Spirit in Mary's womb (as sent from the Father) to his rising again in order to bestow the Spirit and to inaugurate the kingdom of God decisively in power. The triune identity of God as an open life that bears suffering, redeems, and inaugurates the kingdom of God is read at least implicitly from the story of Jesus as the Baptizer in the Spirit. When Moltmann stated that Trinitarian theology is "baptismal" theology, he was saying more in my opinion than he perhaps intended to say.[27]

The foregoing implies for me that Spirit baptism can provide Pentecostals of all backgrounds globally with a way of contributing their unique emphasis on this powerful metaphor, especially in charismatic diversity and fullness, to a robust orthodox faith that involves other Christian voices as well. I refer here to an orthodox faith that is rooted in the will of the Father as Creator, centered in the Son as Spirit Baptizer and Inaugurator of the kingdom of God, and richly directed toward the life of the eschatological Spirit in perfecting creation as the final dwelling place of God. By resisting the *Geistvergessenheit* of the West,[28] such an orthodoxy would be implicitly oriented toward both "orthopathos" (right affections in spirituality and worship) and "orthodopraxis" (right living in holiness, vibrant witness, and participation in social justice). Since the setting for our common faith is not only the church but the reign of God in the world (the kingdom), our faith opens us up to the Spirit's witness outside the boundaries of the church as well.

It is obvious by now that no theology of Spirit baptism is complete without an exploration of its Trinitarian structure. Christ as the King and the Spirit as the kingdom begs for Trinitarian elaboration. I also think it would be productive to look at Trinitarian theology from the lens of Spirit baptism in relation to the coming kingdom. It is to this discussion that we now turn.

---

27. Moltmann, *The Trinity and the Kingdom*, 90.
28. That is, the fact that in the Western church, theologians have all but forgotten or abandoned the doctrine of the Holy Spirit.

SPIRIT BAPTISM AS A TRINITARIAN ACT

What is the Trinitarian structure of Spirit baptism? Specifically, how does the biblical connection between Spirit baptism and the kingdom of God help us to answer this question? Since Pentecostals do not place much of an accent on the Father or creation, being more oriented toward the eschatological work of new creation in Christ and the Spirit, they generally confront the Trinitarian framework for Spirit baptism through issues surrounding the relationship between Word and Spirit. In this context, all Pentecostals recognize that the Spirit is the agent by which we are incorporated into Christ and born anew. In search of a way to distinguish this Spirit indwelling from charismatic empowerment, some Pentecostals have made a distinction between the Spirit's baptizing us into Christ at regeneration (1 Cor. 12:13) and Christ's baptizing us in the Spirit at Spirit baptism as power among believers for witness (Acts 1:8).

This difference becomes metaphorical for how baptism in the Spirit reflects a fullness of spiritual experience allegedly not characteristic of prior existence "in Christ." One is reminded here of the medieval assumption that the mystics or ascetics experienced a greater fullness of the Spirit than ordinary Christians. Pentecostals, however, attached this greater fullness mainly to those caught up in Spirit's drive toward global mission. Though elitist assumptions have no place in the body of Christ, is there not an element of truth to this Pentecostal assumption? Do not Christians (Pentecostal or not) involved in charismatic ministry and mission in the world experience the Spirit in greater fullness than those who merely warm a bench on Sunday?

But the elitist assumptions of Pentecostal revivalism must still be addressed. Dale Bruner has noted that the difference between Spirit indwelling and baptism calls into question the sufficiency of Christ for the spiritual life.[29] Paul says that all spiritual blessings are in Christ (Eph. 1:3). There can thus be no stage of spiritual blessing "beyond" faith in Christ. Pentecostals can counter, however, that Christ is sufficient for the Christian life precisely because he is the one from whom and in whom we receive the Spirit (Gal. 3:1–5) and experience the Spirit in greater and greater fullness. There is thus no necessary contradiction between saying that Christ is all sufficient for the Christian life and maintaining that believers are to seek a greater "fullness" of the Spirit's working through us from and in Christ.

---

29. Dale Bruner, *The Theology of the Holy Spirit: The Pentecostal Experience and the New Testament Witness* (Grand Rapids: Eerdmans, 1973), 61ff.

One could argue that Pentecostals generally do not intend to seek for an encounter with the Spirit "beyond Christ," even though their language has given that impression with negative results (as I noted in a previous chapter). The challenge here, it seems to me, is to affirm that Christ is the starting point and ultimate goal of our life in the Spirit and that new encounters with the Spirit of Christ are possible within this eschatological framework. After all, the Spirit in eschatological freedom continues to break open new dimensions of the spiritual life that open up the Christ life for us in fresh and novel ways.

Many Pentecostals have sought to construe the relationship between Christ and the Spirit in redemption by distinguishing between the work of the Spirit in binding us to Christ and the work of Christ in baptizing us in the Spirit. The difficulty with this distinction is the implied misuse of the Trinitarian doctrine of appropriation. Appropriation involves the insight that persons of the Godhead have functions uniquely attributed to them. For example, of the Father is appropriated creation, of the Son redemption, and of the Spirit renewal of life. Of course, all three participate in every action in mutual working and every action involves the one God. Is it valid within an appropriation doctrine to say that the persons of the Godhead can be attached to stages in one's initiation into the Christ life, with the Spirit placing us in Christ and then Christ as a second step baptizing us into the Spirit? Biblically, it seems wise to attribute all of the blessings of the Christian life to Christ's impartation of the Spirit as the primary (and not secondary) act, which then provides the basis for the Spirit's drawing us to Christ and then, in Christ, drawing our lives into the flow of that living witness. Making Spirit baptism a more expansive category can in my view help Pentecostals construe the Trinitarian involvement of God in salvation in more biblical terms.

The issue of Spirit baptism also raised another issue for Pentecostals with regard to the Trinity. The Trinitarian structure of Spirit baptism was also granted urgency for Pentecostals early on through the Oneness controversy. Oneness Pentecostalism broke away from the Assemblies of God early in its history through its newfound conviction that baptism is in Jesus' name only and that Jesus is the full embodiment of the one Person of God (Col. 1:9). A modalistic understanding of the Trinity was affirmed in the process. The young Assemblies of God stood its ground in holding to the importance of the Trinitarian baptismal formula (but not without sympathy for the Jesus' name formula) and maintained a belief in the ontological Trinity.

In a sense, the entire Oneness controversy can be viewed as revolving around the issue of Spirit baptism. Though there was no uniform soteriology among the Oneness Pentecostals,[30] there was a common assumption that the fullness of God's presence dwelled in Christ and is channeled to believers through Spirit baptism. Trinitarian relations in God were denied because it was assumed among the Oneness that this Trinitarian doctrine confined the incarnation to only a third or a part of God, namely, a preincarnate "Son." As Frank J. Ewart complained about Trinitarian theory, "the sad part of their vain theory about the Deity is, that they make Jesus a separate individual in Spirit form from the Father—the SECOND Person—if you please." Ewart concludes that Christ is not the second, "He is the FIRST and the LAST- 'God Over All, blessed, forever, Amen.'"[31]

An incarnation of a subordinate or separate "Son" seemed to the Oneness from the beginning of the movement to undercut the theological foundation for assuming that the fullness of God dwelled in Jesus (Col. 1:9) and is available through Spirit baptism to the experience of believers. In other words, by confining God's involvement in history allegedly to a part of God or even to a subordinate "god" (the Son), God's presence through the Spirit to enact redemption in Christ and to infill believers is theologically undercut. Christ cannot function properly as the Spirit Baptizer to impart the Spirit in fullness if he is not the fullness of God incarnate.

In connecting Christ's deity with his role as the Spirit Baptizer, the Oneness intuited something essential to the church's orthodox faith. Though they denied Nicea, they did intuit something essential to what lay at its foundation. The fact that Spirit baptism would be implicitly central in the Oneness rejection of Trinitarian relations in God is a testimony to how important the doctrine has been to Pentecostal theology as well as Christian orthodoxy in general.

Beyond this insight, I am ambivalent about the Oneness protests. On the one hand, I do think, in agreement with David Reed, that the significance of Jesus' name to water and Spirit baptism needs more careful attention among

---

30. See Thomas Fudge, *Christianity without the Cross: A History of Salvation in Oneness Pentecostalism* (Parkland, FL: Universal, 2003).

31. Frank J. Ewart, *The Revelation of Jesus Christ* (St. Louis, MO: Pentecostal Publishing, n.d.), 4; reprinted in a facsimile collection entitled *Seven Jesus-Only Tracts, The Higher Christian Life: Sources for the Study of the Holiness, Pentecostal, and Keswick Movements*, ed. Donald W. Dayton (New York: Garland, 1985).

Trinitarian Pentecostals.[32] If we as Pentecostals believe that faithful prayers in Jesus' name bring with them the power of the Spirit, why not that baptismal act in which we identify with Christ in his death and resurrection? On the other hand, however, the Oneness Pentecostals failed to fully appreciate the fact that Jesus' name in Acts is a shorthand for the *Trinitarian* act of God in Christ by which the Father anointed the Son with the Spirit to bring about redemption (Acts 4:12; 10:38). The name of Jesus formula thus implies the Trinitarian formula of Matthew 28:19, making it impossible to collapse the latter into the former. Rather, the latter interprets the former as Trinitarian in nature.

However, in my view, the Oneness were especially mistaken in their understanding of classical Trinitarian theology as advocating only a "third" of God or a "subordinate god" as incarnated in Christ, which would be characteristic of polytheism and not classical Trinitarianism. Though the Son is the one incarnated (John 1:1–18), he subsists with the Father and the Spirit in the one divine nature, so that Trinitarians can also affirm the fullness of the divine presence through the incarnation of the Son in Christ. Yet, the Oneness saw more clearly than their Trinitarian counterparts within the Pentecostal movement that Christ's role as Bestower of the Spirit encompasses something that is essential and decisive to Christian identity. Christ's role as Bestower of the Spirit cannot be reduced to the experience of the *Charismageist* ("charismatic Spirit"), though the experience of the charismatic Spirit is certainly involved.

There is no question to my mind but that Pentecostals will be helped by a fuller consideration of the Trinitarian structure of Spirit baptism in the light of Christ's role as inaugurator of the kingdom of God. Allow me to raise two points in this regard and then to elaborate further on them.

First, it is important to stress that Spirit baptism accents the idea that the triune life of God is not closed but involved in the openness of self-giving love. Spirit baptism thus corresponds to the metaphor of outpouring (Acts 2:33; Rom. 5:5). The reign of God comes on us through an abundant outpouring of God's very Spirit on us to transform us and to direct our lives toward Christlike loyalties. From the Trinitarian fellowship of the Father and the Son, the Spirit is poured out to expand God's love and communion to creation. This outpouring prefigures the eschatological indwelling of God in all of creation. Indeed, "hope does not disappoint us, because God has poured out his

---

32. David Reed, "Oneness Pentecostalism: Problems and Possibilities for Pentecostal Theology," *Journal of Pentecostal Theology* 11 (1997): 81–83.

love into our hearts by the Holy Spirit, whom he has given us" (Rom. 5:5). Our participation in God through the Holy Spirit gives us the courage to continue believing in the final transformation of the entire creation into the very temple of God (Rev. 21:3).

Participation in God? Yes, my second point is that Spirit baptism also accents the unique idea that participation in God's redemptive will is a participation in God's presence. In being baptized in the Spirit, we are "baptized into God"! The life of the Spirit implies that God is both the Giver and the Gift of eternal life. God's will and gospel involve God's very presence given as the gift of life to enjoy and to live in relation to others. Spirit baptism supplies us with a lens through which to view this God and the divine will for creation. The view that this lens affords requires careful attention among those who are accustomed to viewing God from a distance as the sovereign King who imposes the divine kingdom on the world unilaterally. Spirit baptism implies a God who seeks to baptize the world through and into the divine presence in order to release powers of redemption, liberation, and hope toward the fashioning of the creation into the very dwelling place of God.

The Trinitarian structure of Spirit baptism thus has a two-way movement: from the Father through the Son in the Spirit, and then from the Spirit through the Son toward the Father. We thus pray and relate from God, in God, and to God (Rom. 11:36). Spirit baptism involves all three. The God of Spirit baptism surrounds us and fills us. This God is thus not "some distant and timelessly uninvolved deity," as Robert Jenson notes, but participates in the life of creation and draws creation into this divine participation. As Jenson notes further, "The particular God of the Scripture does not just stand over against us; he envelops us. And only by the full structure of the envelopment do we have this God."[33]

The goal is that Christ "fill all things" (Eph. 4:10 NRSV) and that God be "all in all" (1 Cor. 15:28). Herein lies the power of the metaphor of Spirit "baptism." The ultimate goal is that the creation becomes the temple of God's presence. This indwelling is the goal of the kingdom of God, as Moltmann states: "The kingdom of glory must be understood as the consummation of the Father's creation, as the universal establishment of the Son's liberation, and as the fulfillment of the Spirit's dwelling."[34]

---

33. Robert W. Jenson, *The Triune Identity* (Philadelphia: Fortress, 1982), 51.
34. Moltmann, *The Trinity and the Kingdom*, 212.

The first movement spans the story of Jesus from his conception in Mary's womb to Pentecost. The Trinitarian God emerges in the story of Jesus as the Christ, the man of the Spirit, who is constantly accountable to the Father as the source of all life. As Jenson states, "There is no way or need of getting to God past what happens to Jesus in time, so that the temporal structure of that event must be left as ultimate in God."[35] This insight has moved all of the great Trinitarian teachers of the Church. Pannenberg agrees, noting that the Trinity begins with "the way in which the Father, the Son, and the Spirit come on the scene and relate to one another in the event of revelation."[36] As noted above, Pannenberg shows that the involvement of the Spirit in the relationship between the Father and the Son in the story of Jesus prevented the early church from becoming binitarian.[37]

Central to the Trinitarian structure of the story of Jesus is the Father's loving bestowal of the Spirit lavishly ("without limit," John 3:34) on Jesus at his baptism as the sign of divine love and favor and to declare Christ's sonship (Matt. 3:17), an anointing that begins at Christ's conception (Luke 1:35), is found at his crucifixion (Heb. 9:14), and culminates in his resurrection (Rom. 1:4).

Central also is the constant return of the Son's devotion as the man of the Spirit to the Father. For example, led by the Spirit into the wilderness, the Son maintains devotion to the will of the Father in the midst of testing (Matt. 4:1–11). Jesus then offers himself on the cross in fulfillment of the Father's will "through the eternal Spirit" (Heb. 9:14). The Father responds by raising Jesus from the dead and declaring him the favored Son "through the Spirit of holiness" (Rom. 1:4). As Amos Yong has noted, the Spirit as the bond of love between the Father and the Son actually arises from the very fabric of the story of Jesus and is not an abstract and speculative notion.[38] As we will note, however, this notion of Spirit as the bond of love must be defined so as to enhance the sense of mutual dependence and reciprocity between the Spirit and both the Son and the Father so that the Spirit is not stripped of personhood.

What does the Trinitarian structure of the story of Jesus have to do with Spirit baptism? Spirit baptism basically describes the role of Jesus in pouring out the Spirit that comes from the Father in order to fulfill the kingdom of

35. Jenson, *The Triune Identity*, 26.
36. Pannenberg, *Systematic Theology*, 1:299.
37. Ibid., 1:268.
38. Amos Yong, *Spirit-Word-Community: Theological Hermeneutics in Trinitarian Perspective* (Burlington, VT: Ashgate, 2003), 49–81.

God. Jesus' role as Baptizer in the Spirit to fulfill the kingdom of God, however, arises from the life journey of Jesus as the Word of the Father anointed by the Spirit, a life that proceeds from his conception in Mary's womb, to his baptism and life ministry, and to his death and resurrection. As Karl Barth has noted, Jesus baptizes in the Spirit by opening his story up to history. Barth seeks to walk a fine line between a Christomonism that simply collapses history into the story of Jesus with the result that Pentecost and history are not viewed as avenues of revelation in their own right, and an anthropomonism that interprets Jesus from an anthropological ideal drawn from a preconceived anthropology or philosophy of history, thus collapsing Jesus and his story into some construal of human history. Barth sees Spirit baptism as the life "baptism" of Jesus from death to life becoming a force in history that leads all things toward eschatological fulfillment.[39]

The Father is not to be forgotten in our understanding of this redemptive drama. Ultimately behind the story of Jesus as the one who will baptize in the Spirit is the Father as the Creator. In creating all things by the divine Word and Breath (Gen. 1:1–2; John 1:1–3), the Father earmarks the creation as that which will be involved in the bond of love through the Spirit that exists between the Father and the Son. The creation is made for this divine Word and Breath and will remain unfulfilled until perfected by them. The creation is thus made through the Spirit by and for the favored Son (John 1:1–14; Col. 1:15–16).

The creation itself is already in a sense the "arena of God's glory." Though bound by sin and death, creation still lives from God's grace and shows forth this goodness (Acts 17:24–28). The tension between the goodness of creation as graced by God and its bondage to sin and death produces a "groaning" for the liberty to come, something with which the Spirit of God empathizes (Rom. 8:22–23). The work of Christ and the Spirit to redeem creation does not abandon the creation, it perfects and fulfills it. Spirit baptism answers the cry of creation for liberty. In the midst of this redemptive answer the Father does not act directly in the world but remains transcendent. Yet, the Father acts in the world through the Son and the Spirit as the "left and right hands of God."

To understand further what we have said thus far about the Trinitarian structure of Spirit baptism, we can draw from the interesting fact that Trinitarian theology has been related in recent discussion to the inauguration of

---

39. Karl Barth, *Church Dogmatics*, trans. Geoffrey W. Bromiley, Vol. 5, Pt. 4 (Edinburgh: T&T Clark, 1969), 19–20, 31.

the kingdom of God. This connection was forged by Karl Barth in the implicit relationship he made between the Trinity and the revelation of divine lordship over creation and salvation. Barth insightfully saw in the triune God an affirmation three times over of God as Lord of salvation. The Father exercises kingdom lordship as the Revealer. The Son exercises this lordship as the Revealed. The Spirit exercises this same lordship as "revealedness" or the power by which the revelation in Christ is entered into and grasped. God is thus Lord of salvation or Lord over the kingdom three times over, leaving no room for the creature to save itself or to exercise the lordship that belongs to God alone.[40]

Though not generally acknowledged, this differentiated understanding of divine lordship among Father, Son, and Spirit would have a profound influence on the recent relational Trinitarian theologies of Moltmann and Pannenberg. Moreover, Barth's focus on the exercise of divine lordship through *revelation* implies that the triune life of God is not closed or self-contained but dynamic and open to creation. As we have seen, such an insight is essential to Spirit baptism.

There can be little doubt that Barth's insight into the Trinitarian explanation of divine lordship is enormously important for our connection between the Trinity and the inauguration of the kingdom of God as a "Spirit baptism." But Moltmann wishes also to correct it. In an important study of the relationship between the kingdom of God and the Trinity, Moltmann suggests that the divine lordship at the heart of the drama of the kingdom of God in history is not that of a single subject who reigns supreme over the creation. He accuses Barth of applying this notion of lordship to the Trinity in the form of a threefold repetition of the one sovereign subject. This Barthian assumption is faulty in that it interprets the Trinity from the vantage point of a preconceived notion of divine lordship rather than allowing the actual Trinitarian involvement in the history of suffering and redemption to define divine lordship.[41]

The unity of the persons of the Trinity is not found is some abstract divine substance, nor in an absolute divine subject, since this would subordinate and even dissolve the differences among the divine persons. The persons in relation constitute both their differences and their unity. The ancient concept of

---

40. Barth, *Church Dogmatics*, Vol. 1, Pt. 1, 299ff.
41. Moltmann, *The Trinity and the Kingdom*, 92–95.

perichoresis ("mutual indwelling") is used to explain the divine life shared by Father, Son, and Spirit.[42] In this protest against Barth emerges the tension between a notion of the triune God as a single subject in threefold self-distinction and profoundly relational subjects or centers of consciousness in perichoretic unity. The lordship that arises from this latter notion is relational and governed by self-giving and suffering love. Pannenberg has leveled similar criticisms at Barth's Trinitarian theology from a perspective similar to Moltmann's.[43]

I think there are resources in Barth's theology for responding to Moltmann's concerns, although Moltmann deserves credit for taking the actual Trinitarian drama of the kingdom of God in history as the means of defining God and the liberating nature of divine lordship. Such a method of allowing redemptive history to define God for us rather than defining God *in abstracto* is Barthian to the core. In a sense, Moltmann has sought to correct Barth from Barth. Barth's earlier distinction between God as Revealer, Revealed, and Revealedness does assume a more linear understanding of God's self-disclosure as the Father sends the Son and then pours out the Spirit. Barth did later seek to arrive at a more interrelational understanding of God's Trinitarian life that noted an *analogia caritatis* (an analogy of love) between the triune God and the creation of humanity as relational beings.

Concerning the *imago Dei* in humanity, Barth later writes that humanity is the "copy and reflection" of a divine life that involves coexistence, cooperation, and even reciprocity.[44] Barth never sought to integrate this more interactive view of the three persons with his understanding of the one God in three modes of being. Moltmann's and Pannenberg's challenges make us wonder whether or not Barth's understanding of God as the divine Subject in threefold self-distinction (as modes of being) in the act of self-revelation is adequate to describe the personal interaction between the Father and the Son in the Spirit depicted in the drama of redemption.

Most significant to our discussion is the fact that both Moltmann and Pannenberg take the inauguration of the kingdom of God in history as the locus for arriving at a perichoretic understanding of the divine life. Moltmann accepts the Eastern notion of the monarchy of the Father as belonging

---

42. Ibid., 175.
43. Pannenberg, *Systematic Theology*, 1:296–97.
44. Barth, *Church Dogmatics*, Vol. 3, Pt. 1, 185.

uniquely to the Father, while the Son is viewed as generating from the Father and the Spirit as proceeding from the Father. He sides with the East in resisting a non-differentiated understanding of the procession of the Spirit from the Father and the Son. He also resists transferring the monarchy of the Father to the inner Trinitarian life of God in order to avoid a "monopatrism" that blurs the distinctions of the inter-Trinitarian relationships. Though he sees no need to speak explicitly of monarchy as indicative of the Father's unique role as the Unoriginate from whom the Son and the Spirit eternally proceed, he does regard this distinction of the Father as implicit in the nature of the inter-Trinitarian relationships.[45]

One can ask at this point whether or not Moltmann's positing monarchy as unique to the Father and the nature of the personal relations within God as distinguishable according to origin does not still posit some type of ontological inferiority of the Son and the Spirit to the Father. In fact, Pannenberg charges Moltmann with an attempt at holding on to one vision of the Godhead according to origin (implying an ontological inferiority of the Son and the Spirit that undercuts mutuality and reciprocity) and another according to perichoretic unity (implying mutual and reciprocal relation). Pannenberg wishes instead to see the monarchy of the Father as a shared and dependent reality that does not exist at some level other than the communion of persons in God. He notes that the monarchy of the Father is not the presupposition but rather the result of the common operation of the three persons. Indeed, "the monarchy of the Father is itself mediated by the Trinitarian relations," for the communion of the three persons finds its very content in the monarchy of the Father.[46]

Pannenberg notes that a construal of deity primarily and abstractly in terms of origin subordinates the Son and the Spirit to the Father and makes it extremely difficult to capture the kind of reciprocity and mutuality indicated in the story of the inauguration of the kingdom of God redemptively in the world. Pannenberg saw quite insightfully that the monarchy of the Father is related theologically to the inauguration of the kingdom of God in history. If the story of Jesus as the Spirit Baptizer involves a mutual participation of Father, Son, and Spirit to establish God's reign of life in the world, then the monarchy of the Father would seem to involve all three persons in commu-

---

45. Moltmann, *The Trinity and the Kingdom*, 188–89.
46. Pannenberg, *Systematic Theology*, 1:325.

nion and mutual working. It would seem to be a reality shared by all three persons in ways appropriate to each and mutually dependent on each.

It is precisely this kind of mutual dependence that Pannenberg sees in the story of the inauguration of the kingdom of God in the world. Pannenberg draws from Athanasius the insight that the Father is only the Father in relation to the Son. The Father's dependence on the Son for Fatherhood is the basis of the mutual reciprocity between them.[47] The Son and the Spirit's deity, therefore, is not only derived from the Father but conditions it.[48] The Father does not have monarchy apart from them but only in and through them.

According to the story of the inauguration of the kingdom of God through Christ, the Father hands over lordship to the Son so as to have it anew in him. Likewise, the Son delivers the kingdom back to the Father (1 Cor. 15:20–28).[49] Pannenberg notes that this handing back of the kingdom does not end the Son's lordship or share in the Father's monarchy but rather characterizes it. The Son's lordship is exercised precisely in humble and self-sacrificial devotion to the Father. The cross is thus essential to the Son's lordship as well as the resurrection. In handing the kingdom back to the Father, the Son's lordship is perfected and eternally established, for of his reign there will be no end (Luke 1:33).

Pannenberg assumes throughout his discussion that it is by the Spirit that the second movement of handing back the kingdom to the Father occurs, but the essential role of Spirit baptism in the Son's inauguration of the kingdom of God requires that this point receive further development. In line with Pannenberg's discussion, we can say that, in a sense, the Son commits his lordship to the Spirit, for the Lord is the Spirit (2 Cor. 3:17). The Spirit exercises lordship in living witness to the Son in fulfillment of the Father's will. The Spirit's lordship is realized in our submitting to the leading of the Spirit to confess Jesus as Lord (1 Cor. 12:1–3).

The Son is thus not Lord without the Spirit, just as the Son is not Lord without the Father. In other words, Jesus is Lord as the Spirit Baptizer and delivers the kingdom back to the Father as the Spirit-anointed man and, at the culmination of the kingdom of God, through the Spirit's indwelling and

---

47. Ibid., 311–12.
48. Ibid., 322.
49. Ibid.

renewing creation after the Son's image. The Spirit exercises lordship in witness to the Son as the Son exercises lordship by the Spirit in self-sacrificial devotion to the Father and as the firstfruits of the new creation. The Son and the Spirit share the monarchy of the Father in mutual dependence and working in a way that implies the Father's dependence on them as well.

Pannenberg's notion of the monarchy of the Father as mediated by the persons makes God as the Unoriginate Origin of self-giving love a perichoretic reality, as the persons draw from one another's fullness and pour out this fullness to involve creation—a superb definition of the Trinitarian structure of Spirit baptism. In Spirit baptism, the Son's devotion to the Father involves devotion to the world, for God the Father so loved the world (John 3:16). The Spirit's witness to the Son on behalf of the Father involves the transformation and indwelling of creation because God so loved the world and wills, without abandoning divine transcendence, to tabernacle with creation through the agency of the Son and the Spirit. In short, Spirit baptism in the context of the inauguration of the kingdom of God means that the Father's divine monarchy is not abstract but mediated by the Son and the Spirit in the redemption of the world. It is a mediated and mutually dependent divine life. It is characterized essentially by reciprocally and mutually dependent communion of divine love into which the creation is drawn through the overthrow of death as the reigning principle and the establishment of the reign of life through the divine transformation and indwelling of all things.

Significantly, Pannenberg rejects the filioque based on the unique nature of the Son's lordship as received from the Father and manifested in devotion to the Father. Yet, it may be said that the Spirit is involved in the return devotion of the Son to the Father as well as the Father's expressed love for the Son. The Spirit as the bond of love between the Father and the Son as well as between God and the world (Rom. 5:5) does not exclude the Spirit's reciprocity with the Father and the Son as a divine Person, for the monarchy of the Father and the Son is dependent on the Spirit to perfect its reign of life as outward moving "for others." Through the Spirit and the Son, the Father is the God for others. Through the Spirit, Jesus as the revelation of the Logos is the man for others. In the Spirit, the monarchy of the Father invites discernment and participation by creation, for the Spirit searches the deep things of God for us all (1 Cor. 2:10). Jesus' role as the Spirit Baptizer perfects the monarchy of God as an open, redemptive, and loving dynamic. The divine monarchy has communion at its core.

I do not wish to tie my theology too dogmatically to a particular version of the inner life of the triune God. Whether or not God is characterized as three distinct consciousnesses depends on how one defines "consciousness." There is some room to negotiate Barth's and Pannenberg's notions of the divine life in the inauguration of the kingdom of God through Spirit baptism. If, as I maintain, however, the establishment of divine lordship in history (the establishment of the kingdom of God) is defined biblically as a baptism in the Spirit, this lordship cannot be defined abstractly and certainly not by a solitary ego that acts unilaterally on the world.

Spirit baptism recalls the loving bestowal of the Spirit by the Father on Jesus and Jesus' anointed life as the faithful Son to the Father by way of response. It recalls God's Trinitarian openness to the world and the drama of how God would eventually pour the divine presence out in order to indwell all things through the role of the Son as the Spirit Baptizer. It involves God in human suffering as well as redemption and empowerment, and it empowers in order that others might empathize with those who suffer and seek to be channels of grace to them. The divine kingdom and lordship would not appear as alienating or oppressive but as liberating and redemptive, embracing or baptizing all things in the love of God. This much seems clear to me. In my view, if Moltmann and Pannenberg can enhance this vision for us, they will prove useful to our reflections.

I especially appreciate Pannenberg's and Moltmann's insight into God's vulnerability to be affected by the world. We can develop this understanding of God with the help of Michael Welker's view of God and humans as *empathetic subjects*. He criticizes the understanding of the goal of consciousness from Aristotle to Hegel as directed to self-knowledge and *self-reference*. Though Hegel advocated a complex notion of self-reference that involved community, "know thyself," the great injunction of the Delphic oracle, was still the ultimate goal and the all-encompassing context of personal fulfillment. Welker wishes, in the light of pneumatology, to understand the self as fulfilled not in self-reference but rather in empathy with others. One is personally fulfilled in empathy with others in the life of the Spirit. We groan with others and the entire creation for the liberation to come (Rom. 8:26).[50]

---

50. Michael Welker, "The Spirit in Philosophical and Theological Perspectives," lecture given at the International Consultation on the Work of the Holy Spirit (New York: Yale Univ. Club, Nov. 13–14, 2004).

Welker's understanding of the self has implications for our discussion of Spirit baptism. Shifting the ultimate goal of the self from self-reference to empathy in loving communion with others helps us to understand the Trinitarian involvement in Spirit baptism. Specifically, this insight may be taken from the Father's sending of the Son into solidarity with creation under the anointing of the Spirit. Christ's goal in the Spirit was to walk the path of the God-forsaken and oppressed and to come into solidarity with them through the Spirit on the cross (Heb. 9:14). As the sinners are "delivered over" to their sin (Rom. 1:24–28), so the Son is "delivered over" for their transgression but raised for their justification (4:25; 8:32).

Through the Jesus story, therefore, the plight and suffering of creation is brought into the redemptive presence of God, which, as Kazoh Kitamori has shown, was already implicit in God's grieving over faithless humanity in the Old Testament.[51] In Spirit baptism, God seeks to tabernacle with creation in empathy with the suffering creation and toward its final liberation. After all, the Spirit of Spirit baptism is the one who groans with the suffering creation for its eventual liberation through Christ. Spirit baptism reveals profoundly what is implied in the incarnation and the cross.

Through this Trinitarian empathy with the creation, Jesus becomes the Spirit Baptizer. Jesus' role as Spirit Baptizer thus involves Trinitarian empathy and suffering. As Jaroslav Pelikan explains, the church fathers struggled with the notion that God "suffers" in Christ, concluding at the fifth-century Council of Ephesus with the statement that the Logos "suffered in the flesh and was crucified in the flesh and tasted death in the flesh."[52] This development struck a blow to the Hellenistic tendency to regard God as impassive and static. In the twentieth century, the notion of the Logos's suffering in the flesh was expanded to involve a capacity within God, in part so as to protect God's immutability (the incarnation does not grant God a capacity not already inherent in God) and to account for God's grieving in the Old Testament over humanity's unfaithfulness. I regard as of seminal influence here Barth's rejection of Schleiermacher's understanding of sin as merely a lack of

---

51. Kazoh Kitamori, *Theology of the Pain of God* (Richmond, VA: John Knox, 1965).

52. Jaroslav Pelikan, *The Emergence of the Catholic Tradition, The Christian Tradition: A History of the Development of Doctrine* (Chicago: Univ. of Chicago Press, 1971), 1:261.

God-consciousness and not as a force that wounds the heart of God. Barth's criticism is worth quoting in full:

> As Schleiermacher sees it, God has no part in this matter, but stands inviolate above it. He merely sees to it that we become conscious of it, of his grace and therefore in contradistinction to our sin. In virtue of his holiness, he causes the discordance of our existence to become sin for us through conscience. God Himself has neither adjutant nor adversary. He is not assailed. He is neither offended, nor does he suffer.[53]

For Barth, the human condition is not confined to self-knowledge but actually affects a God who lovingly reaches out to the sinner and empathizes with those who suffer the effects of sin. Implied here is the divine capacity to empathize with the suffering creation to the point of entering into it and, through the lordship of loving communion, to liberate it unto the peace and joy of salvation. Kitamori and other theologians influenced by Barth, such as Eberhard Jüngel and Hans Urs Balthasar, noted that the participation of God in the suffering of Jesus has its roots in the divine capacity to grieve and to be adversely affected by human unfaithfulness and suffering in the Old Testament. This trend reached its most powerful expression in Moltmann's theology, which understands God's omnipotence as omnipotent love, namely, God's limitless capacity to suffer.

This Spirit baptismal metaphor is not the only one possible for describing God's redemptive act and the participation of creation in it, but it is one that accents the pneumatological substance and goal of that act. It shows us that Christology is inconceivable apart from pneumatology. In a Western theological heritage in which the Spirit is implicitly expected to play a subordinate role, such a turn to the pneumatological substance of God's redemptive act in Christ is a refreshing alternative.

Moreover, in a culture of death and terror, an accent on God as the presence of new life and hope through Christ, even in contexts in which the name of Jesus is not explicitly cherished or spoken, can also be an important expansion of the evangelical *kerygma* of conversion to Christ by faith. Pentecostal theologian Amos Yong helped me to see that a theological accent on the Spirit grants God's redemptive and empowering presence through Christ implicitly greater breadth than that which we acknowledge as present among those who

---

53. Barth, *Church Dogmatics*, Vol. 3, Pt. 3, 329.

consciously call upon the name of the Lord.[54] Geoffrey Wainwright similarly noted that addressing attention to the Spirit in the historic liturgy of the church "helped to keep open the possibility of recognizing that the divine Spirit may be present in worship on a plane wider than historic Christianity."[55]

This insight does not necessarily support a concession to an unqualified inclusivism, but it does imply that there is a mystery to the involvement of God through the grace of Christ in people's lives outside of the church that we leave to the eschatological freedom of God. The function of the Spirit Baptizer in the fulfillment of the kingdom of God has as its central locus the life of the church, but it is not confined to the church.

It is precisely eschatological freedom that constitutes the realm of the Spirit and the soteriological/missiological accent of Spirit baptism. But this eschatological freedom is not vague, lacking content and direction. It is determined and evaluated according to the specifics and implications of the redemptive story enacted in Christ. Christology is thus the area of free divine commitment that helps us to discern the eschatological freedom accented in pneumatology. Pneumatology is the divine freedom that channels the divine commitment revealed in Christ eschatologically into an increasingly diverse and expansive participation in the life-giving presence of God.

In a sense, Jesus of Nazareth can even be seen as the revelation of the "bond of love" between the loving Father and the eschatological freedom of the divine breath to fulfill the kingdom of God in history and in the eschatological future.[56] Jesus is the divine gift of love given by the Spirit to define the Spirit's future work throughout the cosmos. At the eternal source of both commitment and eschatological freedom is the Father, whose love is both eschatologically free in its faithfulness and faithful in its eschatological freedom.

In developing the Spirit's free and expansive furthering of the kingdom in the world, we will need to be specific about how to describe our participation in this work. It is important in this context to develop the significance of Spirit baptism for the various elements of life in the Spirit: justification, sanctifica-

---

54. See Amos Yong, *Beyond the Impasse: Toward a Pneumatological Theology of Religions* (Grand Rapids: Baker, 2003).

55. Geoffrey Wainwright, *Doxology: The Praise of God in Worship, Doctrine, and Life* (New York: Oxford Univ. Press, 1980), 106.

56. Note Jeremy Ive's insightful discussion of Robert Jenson's use of this concept, "Robert W. Jenson's Theology of History," in *Trinity, Time, and Church: A Response to Robert W. Jenson*, ed. Colin E. Gunton (Grand Rapids: Eerdmans, 2000), 153.

tion, and charismatic empowerment. Hendrikus Berkhof wisely isolated all three as elements of the baptism in the Spirit. He faulted the history of pneumatology in the West for focusing exclusively on justification and sanctification (Calvin's *duplex gratia*) to the neglect of the typically Pentecostal focus on the vocational or charismatic dimension of life in the Spirit.[57] More importantly, justification in particular has been developed in Protestant contexts in a way that neglected the work of the Spirit. In our development of the eschatological significance of Spirit baptism in ushering the kingdom of God, it is important to develop elements of life in the Spirit in a fully Trinitarian context. Other elements of life in the Spirit can be included, of course, but these three allow us to cover the major elements that have been most discussed in the history of pneumatology.

SPIRIT BAPTISM AND ELEMENTS OF LIFE IN THE KINGDOM

The Trinitarian structure of Spirit baptism has to do with the participation of creation by the Spirit in the redemptive act of the Son with the goal of participating in the bond of love between the Son and the Father. The ultimate goal is the fulfillment of the kingdom of God in righteousness as the dwelling place of God. Let us begin with the element of justification, which is that element of the Christian life most in need of a Trinitarian reinterpretation in the light of the connection between Spirit baptism and the kingdom of God discussed thus far. We will then proceed to sanctification and finally to charismatic empowerment. In the discussion of each element, we will rehearse what was said of the first Trinitarian movement, namely, the foundation in the story of Jesus as the man of the Spirit, but we will stress the second movement, namely, creation's participation by the Spirit in the bond of love between the Father and the Son.

Spirit-Baptized Justification

Justification in the light of Spirit baptism reveals the overlap between justification and sanctification as metaphors of the renewal of creation into the dwelling place of God. Article 15 of the *Joint Declaration on the Doctrine of Justification by Faith* (1999) insightfully called for a Trinitarian interpretation, even though, as I have noted elsewhere, the *Declaration* lacked a pneumatology

---

57. Hendrikus Berkhof, *Doctrine of the Holy Spirit* (Richmond, VA: John Knox, 1964), 85–90.

sufficient to the task.[58] Robert Jenson sought to provide such a Trinitarian framework by speaking of Paul's interest in the Father's self-justification (vindication) as Creator and the God of Israel (Rom. 1–2), the Son's work of justification on our behalf (the Protestant emphasis), and the Spirit's work in us to bring about righteousness unto new life (the Catholic stress).[59] As I have also noted elsewhere, it would indeed be interesting to explore how these three come together in the story of Jesus as the man of the Spirit and in the final new heavens and new earth in which righteousness will finally dwell.[60] In our effort to do this, we need to define the righteousness of justification as kingdom righteousness, the righteousness inspired by the Spirit in the work of Christ in fulfillment of the will of the Father.

Justification literally means to be "righteoused" by God. It is my conviction that *Spirit baptism* as the fulfillment of the "kingdom of God and its righteousness" provides us with a richer framework for understanding justification by faith than is possible within the narrow confines of a forensic notion of justification read from select Pauline texts.

I was first made aware of the connection between Spirit baptism and justification through a provocative paper written by D. Lyle Dabney, who drew from Romans 4:25 to note that the resurrection of Jesus by the Spirit of life justifies us. Interestingly, Dabney referred to justification as a "justification by the Spirit."[61] I decided to build on his essay to more fully develop justification from a pneumatological perspective. In my initial attempt at developing this topic, I drew from Ernst Käsemann's apocalyptic understanding of justification as a background for understanding how the righteousness of justification can be seen as an eschatological gift of new creation through the Spirit of God.[62] At the time, the concept of the righteousness of the kingdom

---

58. Frank D. Macchia, "Justification and the Spirit of Life: A Pentecostal Response to the Joint Declaration," in *Justification and the Future of the Ecumenical Movement: The Joint Declaration on the Doctrine of Justification*, ed. William G. Rusch (Collegeville, MN: Liturgical, 2003), 133–49.

59. Robert W. Jenson, "Justification as a Triune Event," *Modern Theology* 11 (1995): esp. 421.

60. Frank D. Macchia, "Justification through New Creation: The Holy Spirit and the Doctrine by which the Church Stands or Falls," *Theology Today* 58 (July 2001): 202–17.

61. D. Lyle Dabney, "'Justified by the Spirit': Soteriological Reflections on the Resurrection," *International Journal of Systematic Theology* 3 (March 2001): 46–68.

62. Macchia, "Justification through New Creation."

of God was not prominent in my discussion, even though it was implied in much of what I had to say.

In response to my published work on this topic, Jürgen Moltmann graciously sent me an intriguing essay in which he described his shift in evangelical identity from "justification to the kingdom of God."[63] His new evangelical identity had fundamentally to do with a shift of emphasis in the biblical canon from Paul to the teaching of the Gospels about the righteousness of the kingdom of God. For example, the category of "sinner" in the Gospels bore the implication of social outcast, which is not apparent in Paul's equally-important universalization of the category of sin in Romans 3:23. Furthermore, the righteousness that characterizes devotion to God in the Gospels is the life of the kingdom of God, which tends to be more explicitly social than Paul's more allegedly forensic teaching concerning our right standing before God. By shifting his fundamental allegiance from Paul to the Gospels, Moltmann shifted his evangelical identity from justification by faith to the radical implications of the kingdom of God dawning in the world for social renewal and the overall victory of life over death.

In response to Moltmann, I think it is possible to read Paul through the lens of an apocalyptic understanding of the gospel that is in basic continuity with the doctrine of the kingdom of God in the Gospels, as I think Ernst Käsemann and, more recently, Douglas Harink (among others) have implied.[64] In fact, Harink rightly notes that the apocalyptic context for justification preserves the theocentric focus of Paul on justification as a judgment and act of God, which is a better alternative than the anthropocentric tendencies of certain of the "new perspectives" on Paul.[65] Moltmann himself implied as much in what he wrote earlier about the Christological and eschatological nature of justification in the New Testament.[66]

With this qualification in mind, we may regard Moltmann's "shift" in evangelical identity as highly significant for our understanding of justification,

---

63. Jürgen Moltmann, "Was heisst heute 'evangelisch?' Von der Rechtfertigungslehre zur Reich-Gottes-Theologie," *Evangelische Theologie* 57 (1997): 41–46.

64. Ernst Käsemann, "The Righteousness of God in Paul," in *New Testament Questions of Today* (Philadelphia: Westminster, 1969), 168–82; Douglas Harink, *Paul among the Postliberals: Pauline Theology beyond Christendom and Modernity* (Grand Rapids: Baker, 2003), esp. 15–18.

65. Harink, *Paul among the Postliberals*, 17–18.

66. Moltmann, *The Spirit of Life*, 149.

except I will propose a shift in the meaning of justification in the light of the kingdom of God rather than a shift from justification to the kingdom of God. It is suggestive in this regard to take the order of the canon as significant to how we read the New Testament concerning justification as a gift of the Spirit. I regard as significant the canonical separation of Luke from Acts so that Luke could function as part of a Gospel corpus. Luke no longer functions in this canonical order as an isolated preparation for reading Acts but is now read instead as one voice in the larger set of voices in the Gospel corpus that sets the stage for the interpretation of the gospel in the remainder of the New Testament.

Even John can be understood as a nuancing of the Gospels' witness before the reader advances to Acts and to Romans. This insight grants the gospel of the kingdom presented in Luke greater depth and breadth in its own right as the basis for understanding its fulfillment in the pages of Acts and Romans. This is precisely the method I have used thus far in defining Spirit baptism, and it is the method I wish to use in defining justification in the context of the gift of the Spirit and the fulfillment of the righteousness that dawns with the coming of the kingdom of God.

This canonical shift to the Gospels (and to Acts) and to the reality of the kingdom of God as inaugurated by the Spirit Baptizer allows us to view the "righteousness" involved in justification more profoundly as a Hebraic notion than a Roman one, namely, as a liberating and redemptive concept that reorders life toward justice and mercy. As we noted already, the righteousness of the kingdom of God in the New Testament is a liberating concept that sets one on the path of loving God and neighbor with heart, soul, mind, and strength.

This righteousness comes from God like a mighty flood upon us in divine acts of liberation from the powers of darkness (Matt. 12:28). It changes us within so that like new wineskins, we can take in the new wine (9:17). We are so changed by it that we hunger and thirst for it daily above all else, even the essentials of life's physical sustenance, because we live daily by the simple trust in God's grace to provide all of our needs (6:33). It inspires devotion to the law of God as a living matter of the heart (Matt. 5). It begins with the recognition that we are sinners in constant need of God's mercy, who have no advantage before God over anyone else (Luke 18:9–14). It inspires a reordering of social relationships so that Roman centurions, tax collectors, women, and Pharisees are all expected to sup at the table of the Father's household together as those who share equally in the Father's inheritance (15:1–2, 11–

31). The righteousness of the kingdom is thus a precious pearl that one is willing to give all in possessing (Matt. 13:45–46). It is not confined to personal or even communal renewal but will one day bring the will of the Father to bear on the entire earth as it presently reigns in heaven (6:10), for even nations will fall under its judgment (25:32).

In the Old Testament as well, the righteousness of God is expected to run down as mighty streams from the mountain tops to the thirsty valleys below to inspire a life rich in true worship and devotion to justice and mercy (Amos 5:24). This renewed righteousness in the land starts with God's faithful acts of deliverance. Alister McGrath has argued that the Hebrew understanding of the righteousness of God is saving righteousness, namely, a righteousness that is revealed in God's redemptive acts among the people of God.[67] Similarly, Brevard Childs has maintained that righteousness in the Old Testament "consists, above all, in acts of the saving deeds of redemption" by which God maintains and protects the divine promise to fulfill the covenant obligations with Israel."[68] Righteousness in the Old Testament is consequently a right ordering of life by the power of God. It can even be called "new creation."[69] The sense of forensic judgment is not absent in the Old Testament. God declares in advance what God will do, and these words sustain people in faith, even in absence of sight. Thus, those who wait for the fulfillment of God's promises do not grow weary but will be renewed in strength, for the everlasting Lord tires not (Isa. 40:28–31).

This promised righteousness achieved by God as the righteous judge in the midst of redemptive deeds extends to the deliverance of the poor and downtrodden. It also reaches, according to Childs, to all of creation, to a "cosmic order" that spans law, wisdom, nature, and politics. The cosmic goal of righteousness suggests an eschatological dimension to justification. Childs notes that in the late postexilic and Hellenistic periods, "the eschatological

---

67. Alister McGrath, *Iustitia Dei: A History of the Christian Doctrine of Justification*, vol. 2, *From 1500 to the Present Day* (Cambridge: Cambridge Univ. Press, 1982), 33–34.

68. Brevard Childs, *Biblical Theology of the Old and New Testaments: Theological Reflection on the Christian Bible* (Minneapolis: Fortress, 1992), 488.

69. Hans Heinrich Schmid, "Rechtfertigung als Schöpfungsgeschehen: Notizen zur alttestamentlichen Vorgeschichte eines neutestamentlichen Themas," in *Rechtfertigung: Festschrift für Ernst Käsemann zum 70. Geburtstag*, ed. G. Friedrich et al. (Tübingen: Mohr, 1976), 406.

longing for the manifestation of God's righteous salvation increases in predominance."[70] By the time we reach the New Testament witness, justification is ultimately defined as the justice or righteousness that God's final act of redemption will create by the Spirit in the resurrection of the faithful and the transformation of creation.

This Old Testament and ancient Jewish understanding of justification was carried over into the New Testament. As Childs notes, "clearly the New Testament usage stands in the tradition in continuity with the Old Testament in emphasizing, not God's revenging justice but [God's] saving righteousness."[71] As we saw, this understanding of divine righteousness is prevalant in the Gospels in what they say about the righteousness of the kingdom of God.

Käsemann notes that the Old Testament and Jewish apocalyptic backgrounds inform Paul's reference to the saving righteousness of God as both a gift and the redemptive power by which is manifested God's eschatological saving activity toward creation.[72] According to Käsemann, Paul was convinced that justification would be achieved through Christ's death and resurrection, which set in motion an "eschatological hope of a cosmic restoration" that "has already appeared as a present reality to be grasped in faith."[73] In other words, the birth, life, death, and resurrection of Jesus through the Spirit of new life grants Christological direction to the eschatological fulfillment of justification. As eschatological, justification can be seen as God's saving righteousness achieved in fulfillment of his covenant obligations to creation through new creation.

To be more specific, justification as the "righteousing" of the kingdom of God inaugurated as a "Spirit baptism" can be understood in three dimensions.

- It consists first of the Father's favor expressed in the lavish bestowal of the Spirit on Jesus to declare him the Son of God. This is done in Jesus' conception by the Spirit (Luke 1:35), baptismal anointing (3:22), and resurrection from the dead (Rom. 1:4).
- Second, the righteousing of the kingdom of God consists of the Son's return devotion to the Father as the man of the Spirit and the incarnate

---

70. Childs, *Biblical Theology*, 488–99.
71. Ibid., 494.
72. Käsemann, "The Righteousness of God in Paul," 168–82.
73. Ernst Käsemann, "Justification and Salvation History in the Epistle to the Romans," in *Perspectives on Paul* (London: SCM, 1971; reprint, Mifflintown, PA: Sigler, 1996), 74–75.

Son of the Father, especially as this devotion climaxes in Jesus' obedient going to the cross. This historical drama of love between the Father and the Son in the Spirit is Christ's life "baptism" from mortality to immortality. Since this bond of love in the Spirit between the Father and the Son is not a closed circle but an open and redemptive one, Jesus' life baptism is opened to history and to creation through Jesus' role as the Baptizer in the Spirit. The divine favor is poured out from the filial relationship of the Son and the Father in liberating acts of deliverance that transform lives. Jesus thus opens up to creation the year of the Lord's favor in signs and wonders of healing and deliverance (Luke 4:18).

- Therefore, the inauguration of the righteousness of the kingdom of God consists of the creation's participation by the Spirit of Christ in the Father's favor through liberating signs of renewal. It consists also in an empowerment for a life lived in daily trust in God as well as in love for God and neighbor.

By refusing to ground justification in a timeless and abstract "absolute decree" (*decretum absolutum*), Karl Barth opened the door to an understanding of election that represents a divine decision worked out and revealed in the redemptive story of Jesus. In agreement with Barth, G. C. Berkouwer stated of the absolute decree that its timeless metaphysic "plants the kiss of death on eschatology, and on the way of salvation, and on the doctrine of justification as well."[74] In support of such an insight, Barth stated flatly, "there is no decretum absolutum." For Barth, God's election is the election of Jesus Christ. As the electing God and the elect person, Jesus represented the moment of reconciliation between God and humanity.[75]

This historical and dynamic understanding of election as played out in the story of Jesus begs for an active role for the Spirit. The Father's self-election as faithful covenant partner in the incarnation of the Word in Jesus involves the anointing of the Spirit (Luke 1:35). Jesus as the revelation of the electing God thus involves an incarnation mediated by the Spirit's anointing. Jesus as the elect man is also this by the Spirit. For it was by the Spirit that the Son is shown to be the chosen Son of God at his conception (1:35), at the Jordan

---

74. G. C. Berkouwer, *Faith and Justification* (Grand Rapids: Eerdmans, 1954), 156.

75. Barth, *Church Dogmatics*, Vol. 5, Pt. 2, 115.

(Matt. 3:16–17), in his faithful life (Luke 4:18), at his death (Heb. 9:14), and in his resurrection (Rom. 1:4). God's election of Jesus is fulfilled when he rises as the "life-giving spirit" (1 Cor. 15:45) or as the Spirit Baptizer. Election is a drama that is both Christological and pneumatological. Election is fulfilled in Jesus' role as Spirit baptizer.

Justification is thus brought about by Jesus as the man of the Spirit. In the Spirit, Christ was put to death for our trespasses but "raised for our justification" (Rom. 4:25). He was revealed in the flesh but "justified in the Spirit" (1 Tim. 3:15). As the incarnate Word of the Father anointed by the Spirit, Jesus inaugurates the righteousness of the kingdom of God as a liberating force in the world that will eventually make all things new for the glory of God. This is given not only in answer to the Father's loving will but also to the loving Spirit who groans with the suffering creation as advocate for its liberation and righteous reordering (Rom. 8:22–26).

In this regard, I am intrigued by Wilhelm Dantine's refusal to limit the Spirit's role in justification to the inward appropriation of justification by faith. He referred to the "forensic structure" of the Spirit's work in creation as advocate, intercessor, and witness.[76] To elaborate on Dantine's insight, we can refer to the Spirit's anointing of Jesus on behalf of the Father in order to answer the cry from creation with which the Spirit has been in solidarity as advocate and intercessor. In his redemptive work, the anointed Son answers the cry of the Spirit in solidarity with the groaning creation for the righteousness of the kingdom of God. One can view Spirit baptism as the outpouring of the Spirit by which this answer is given. Note in this light that the *locus classicus* of election, Ephesians 1:3–14, should begin with the point that we are "blessed ... with every spiritual blessing" in Christ (1:3) and close with the fact that in Christ as the beloved Son (1:5–6), we have received the down payment of our inheritance in the sealing and gift of the Spirit (1:13–14). This Spirit's outpouring is vital to God's election, the election of Jesus as the Baptizer in the Spirit.

Penultimately, the righteousness of the kingdom of God is received in the gift of the Spirit. Even justification is imparted "in the name of Jesus Christ and in the Holy Spirit" (1 Cor. 6:11). This righteousness is also received by faith, because the Spirit is received in the absence of sight as the down pay-

---

76. Wilhelm Dantine, *Justification of the Ungodly* (St. Louis: Concordia, 1968), 116–18.

ment of the redemption yet to come (Gal. 3:1–5). It is indeed interesting how Paul identifies justification by faith with the reception of the Spirit in Galatians. We are justified by faith and not the law (2:16), and we receive the Spirit by faith and not law (3:1–5). Just as Christ inaugurated the kingdom of God with signs and wonders of God's favor coming on the earth in righteousness (Matt. 12:28), so also Christians now receive the Spirit by faith with extraordinary signs of future new creation (Gal. 3:5; cf. 1 Cor. 2:4–5). Also, the blessing of Abraham is said in Galatians to be *both* justification (Gal. 3:8) *and* the gift of the Spirit on Jew and Gentile alike (3:14).

In the light of these associations, Ronald Fung has noted in his Galatians commentary that Paul seems to make justification and the gift of the Spirit the same reality.[77] What many might find astounding is Luther's early discovery of the same insight. We will quote Luther in full:

> Now is not the fact that faith is reckoned as righteousness a receiving of the Spirit? So either he [Paul] proves nothing or the reception of the Spirit and the fact that faith is reckoned as righteousness will be the *same thing*. And it is true; it is introduced in order that the divine imputation may not be regarded as amounting to nothing outside of God, as some think that the Apostle's word "grace" means a favorable disposition rather than a gift. For when God is favorable and when he imputes, the Spirit is really received, both the gift and the grace.[78]

Luther says here that the reception of the Spirit and the fact that faith is reckoned as righteousness will be the *same thing*! And he even notes that this makes justification a gift and not just a "divine disposition." Truly, Luther's insight here makes justification a pneumatological as well as a Christological reality. It is for Luther here a transformative gift as well as a reality rooted in God "apart from us."

Unfortunately, Luther did not develop this groundbreaking insight. The increasingly heavy emphasis in the later Luther and in Lutheran dogmatics on an abstract forensic justification based on a transfer of Christ's merits to believers neglected the Spirit's role in the inauguration and reception of kingdom righteousness. The vacuum caused by this neglect was filled by an abstract

---

77. Ronald Y. K. Fung, *The Epistle to the Galatians* (New International Commentary on the New Testament; Grand Rapids: Eerdmans, 1988), 136, 152.

78. Martin Luther, *Lectures on Galatians 1519*, in *Luther's Works*, ed. J. Pelikan (St. Louis: Concordia, 1963), 27:252.

declaration connected only to a medieval notion of a transference of Christ's merits. Justification loses connection with the full breadth of its concrete substance in the life of Jesus as the Spirit-anointed Inaugurator of the kingdom of God if it is defined essentially as an abstract declaration realized in a juridical transference of merits.

Moreover, there is also no biblical basis for speaking of a transfer of "merits" from Christ to us. Indeed, what gets reckoned to us in faith according to Paul is not Christ's merits but rather Christ's victory over sin and death. Read carefully with this thought in mind what Paul says about Abraham's persuasion concerning God's power to fulfill God's promises in Romans 4:21–25:

> ... persuaded fully that God had power to do what he had promised. This is why "it was credited to him as righteousness." The words "it was credited to him" were written not for him alone, but for us, to whom God will credit righteousness—for us who believe in him who raised Jesus our Lord from the dead. He was delivered over to death for our sins and was raised to life for our justification.

According to the above passage, what is the nature of the divine action that justifies us in our faith, a crediting of merits from Christ or a reckoning of Christ's victory over death in the resurrection "according to the Spirit of holiness" even as we live in the present era of death? I'll let the reader decide.

The law for Paul is accordingly fulfilled in the victory of life over death in Jesus and not by a transfer of abstract merits. The law cannot justify because the law cannot conquer death and give life. The law cannot impart the Spirit. It is weakened by the sinful flesh that holds one captive to death (Rom. 7:14–8:4). As Paul notes, "For what the law was powerless to do in that it was weakened by the sinful nature, God did by sending his own Son in the likeness of sinful [humanity] to be a sin offering" (Rom. 8:3; cf. Heb. 2:14). Justification is by faith because it is in faith in Christ that the Spirit is received, granting us access to the righteousness of the kingdom inaugurated by Jesus as the Spirit Baptizer. Since our participation through the Spirit in the love between the Father and the Son is eschatological, faith in the absence of sight also grants us access to the righteousness yet to be revealed in the new creation. For "by faith we eagerly await through the Spirit the righteousness for which we hope" (Gal. 5:5).

Thus, the urgent matter with regard to justification is not circumcision but rather "new creation" (Gal. 6:15). The righteousness of the kingdom of

God comes to contemporary experience through the liberating acts of the Spirit of God and not through outward forms of religion (cf. Rom 14:17). The essence of the law is thus fulfilled in a life reordered by the Spirit around God's love and the weighty matters of the law such as compassion, justice, and mercy, for "the only thing that counts is faith expressing itself through love" (Gal. 5:6; cf. Matt. 23:23).

Justified existence is thus pneumatic existence, Spirit-baptized existence. It allows us to participate in the "baptism" of Christ's birth, life, death, and resurrection, which is expansively opened to creation through Christ's role as the Spirit Baptizer and Inaugurator of the kingdom of God. It allows us to participate in the resurrection of the dead and the new heavens and new earth that will come when God indwells all things and all things bear the image of the Son. In the here and now, the righteousness of justification produces a life dedicated to the reign of God on earth, to the weighty matters of the law, to reconciled and reconciling communities of faith, and to the justice and mercy of God in the world.

Once the Trinitarian inauguration of justification as the "righteousing" of the kingdom of God is recognized, Luther's concept of faith as a union with, and participation in, Christ can play a vital role in our understanding of the transformative effects of justification. As Pentecostal theologian Veli-Matti Kärkkäinen has shown, faith causes one to participate in Christ, allowing us to discern overlap between justification and sanctification/*theosis*.[79] This is the great insight of the Finnish Lutherans. It is indeed interesting that a Pentecostal teacher of a generation ago, E. S. Williams, also sympathized with the connection between justification and *theosis* out of a desire to avoid using justification in the service of what we might term "cheap grace."[80]

The righteousness of Christ is alien to us because of our sin and weakness in the flesh (the Protestant emphasis), but it is experienced among us by faith within the realm of the Spirit of life (the Catholic accent). Both Protestant and Catholic impulses are thus taken up in this pneumatological understanding of justification. Both the righteousness of Christ and the life of the Spirit are

---

79. Veli-Matti Kärkkäinen, *One with God: Salvation as Deification and Justification* (Collegeville, MN: Liturgical, 2005). Note also Edmund Rybarczyk's significant comparison of Pentecostal and Eastern Orthodox soteriologies: *Beyond Salvation: Eastern Orthodoxy and Classical Pentecostalism on Becoming Like Christ* (Paternoster Theological Monographs; Waynesboro, GA: Authentic Media, 2004).

80. E. S. Williams, *Systematic Theology* (Springfield, MO: Gospel, 1953), 2:248.

the same, as the Gospels' witness concerning the life of the kingdom of God has shown us. The kingdom of God and its righteousness come to us through the liberating and renewing presence of the Spirit (Matt. 12:28; Rom. 14:17).

The question now becomes how justification through Spirit baptism overlaps with sanctification. Let us briefly explore this issue.

Spirit-Baptized Sanctification

Much of what was said of justification can be said of sanctification. In fact, as Peter Toon has shown, justification and sanctification are not stages of Christian initiation but rather overlapping metaphors of the entire Christian life. Justification implies that humanity has transgressed its covenant relationship with God and has become alienated from God. It describes how humanity is brought once again into covenant relation and favor with God. Sanctification implies the temple cult as its inspiration. Humanity is bound by sin and in need of separation from sin and consecration to God in order to bring God proper glory. The entire Christian life can be described from any one of these two overlapping metaphors.[81]

Toon's insights help us to call into question the logical distinction traditionally made in Protestant dogmatics between justification and sanctification. In this distinction, justification is said to be the objective side of our acceptance from God (*extra nos*, or "apart from us"), involving the righteousness of Christ "imputed" to us in faith. This justification through imputation then serves as a basis for sanctification as initiated by the Spirit subjectively (*in nobis*, or "in us"), involving our transformation toward the righteous life or Christ's very image. The element of truth in this distinction points to the fact that justification tends to focus on the eschatological judgment of God in "righteousing" us in Christ, while sanctification implies the divine act of consecrating us from sin and transforming us into a living temple of praise. There is perhaps to be distinguished an emphasis of the former on divine judgment from an emphasis in the latter on the divine work in the life of the believer.

We speak only of a distinction of emphasis, however, because of the obvious pneumatological and transformationist understanding of justification just noted from the Scriptures. I refer here especially to the Old Testament understanding of God's righteous judgments as divine acts of redemption and the development of this understanding in the Gospels' description of the righ-

---

81. Peter Toon, *Justification and Sanctification* (Wheaton, IL: Crossway, 1984).

teousness of the kingdom of God coming in upon us as the liberating divine breath to reorder life around God's active reign of life. Also misunderstood is the fact that sanctification in Scripture is just as "objectively" based in the grace of God revealed in Christ alone as is justification. Sanctification by grace through faith must play a role in our theology as well. Christ sanctified himself unto the Father in the truth of the Father so that by this same truth we might be set apart (John 17:17–18).

Paul, therefore, groups both sanctification and justification indiscriminately as in the "name of Jesus Christ and the Holy Spirit" (1 Cor. 6:11). Their difference is not to be determined along the lines of an "objective/subjective" paradigm for depicting the life of grace but rather in a distinction of emphasis as well as theological nuance and theme.

In fact, sanctification is based in Jesus' having been set apart and consecrated as the holy Son of God from his conception by the Spirit in Mary's womb (Luke 1:35). The prophets of old were set apart from their wombs as well in order to bear witness (Jer. 1:5). In Jesus' case, however, he was not set apart just to bear witness as a mere pointer to God but to impart life on behalf of God. John the Baptist was filled with the Spirit from the womb (Luke 1:41), but not to be the light but to point to the one who is the light, or not to give life but to point to the one who does give life, namely, Jesus as Baptizer in the Spirit (Luke 3:1–17; John 1:1–18; 3:22–30). Jesus thus bears witness to the Father as the one who grants abundant life to others in fulfillment of the Father's will (John 10:10; 11:25–26).

Jesus is thus the faithful witness to whom all other witnesses point (Rev. 1:5). His witness is of the first order because he bears witness to the light by being the light. Our witness is of another order: We point in the power of the Spirit to Jesus and hold onto him as the treasure in vessels of clay (2 Cor. 4:7). We are accordingly to receive the Spirit for our witness, while in his role as witness Jesus not only receives the Spirit at the Jordan but bestows the Spirit as the risen Lord (John 20:22). His witness has continuity with ours by the Spirit but is also qualitatively different from ours by the function of the very same Spirit. His anointing by the Spirit implied an ontological unity with the Father as the Word of the Father, who will also bestow the Spirit.

What specifically was the substance of Jesus' sanctification on our behalf? In Matthew 3:13–15, Jesus fulfills righteousness by identifying with the unrighteous in baptism. Keep in mind Pannenberg's insight that Christ exercises lordship through self-sacrificial obedience to the Father, which, we could add, is fulfilled in Christ's identification with sinners. John said that he should not be baptizing Jesus, implying that Jesus should not be counted among those repenting before God. But Jesus replied that such is needed "to fulfill righteousness." His holiness is thus not lived out by avoiding the sinners but by seeking them out as a redemptive presence (Luke 15). In fact, his holiness is lived out by expressing love for God and neighbor, the two being the sides of the same coin, since Jesus loves the neighbor in harmony with the Father's will and in devotion to the Father.

The Father expressed his pleasure in the Son when the Son went into the waters to identify with the sinners in baptism (Matt. 3:16–17). Those Pharisees who opposed Jesus understood the sanctifying effects to be mainly in the outward forms of religious devotion. Jesus accused them of being dead within and of neglecting the "weighty" matters of the law, such as mercy and justice (23:23, 27). Jesus came into conflict with these religious leaders who shuned sinners out of imagined devotion to the law of God. In this conflict, Jesus said that our devotion to the law must "exceed" that of the Pharisees who opposed him or else we cannot enter the presence of the kingdom being mediated through him (5:20).

To prove his point, in Luke 15:1–2, Jesus defiles himself according to the traditional interpretation of the ceremonial law in order to sup with sinners and to invite them all to the Father's banquet table. In 15:11–32, Jesus then reached out to the Pharisees who criticized him by imploring them as the proud "elder son" to join him at the Father's banquet in celebration of the return of the outcast younger son, who had squandered his inheritance. Only then would they understand the spirit of the law and the heart of their heavenly Father. Everything the Father has really belongs to them, if they would only look to see where it may be found.

Ultimately, it is found in the cross, where Jesus as the man of sorrows prays the prayer of the God-forsaken, "Why have you foresaken me?" In the resurrection of Jesus, the Father answers that the Son will not be abandoned to the grave (Acts 2:27). Since Jesus prayed his prayer in solidarity with the sinners, the Father's answer to him in resurrection is their answer too. Indeed, if the Spirit of the Father who raised Jesus from the dead dwells in us, so shall the Father raise our mortal bodies (Rom. 8:11). Jesus was delivered up for our transgressions but raised according to the Spirit of holiness for our justification (Rom. 1:4; 4:25).

There is ultimately no tension between Jesus as Inaugurator of the kingdom of God as the Spirit Baptizer and Jesus as the man of sorrows destined to die in solidarity with sinners. The former without the latter is triumphalistic, while the latter without the former is fatalistic. In holiness, Jesus inaugurates the kingdom of God in power in solidarity with the sinner and the outcast. The righteousness of the kingdom is lived out in mercy and justice toward those who are broken and cast down (Matt. 23:23). The Spirit of holiness that raised Jesus from the dead (Rom. 1:4) also empowered him on his path toward the cross (Heb. 9:14). The Spirit that Jesus pours out as the Spirit Baptizer makes us crucified with Christ living in newness of life in the power of the resurrection (Gal. 2:20). It empowers us to bear one another's burdens (Gal. 6:2) and so to yearn and strive with all those who suffer for the liberty of God's grace (Rom. 8:22).

Jesus remains devoted to his path as the sanctified Son no matter what. After Jesus' anointing at the Jordan, the Spirit led him into the wilderness where his consecration to the Father's will especially with regard to the path of suffering is severely tested by the devil. Jesus sanctified himself unto God by resisting the devil's temptation to live by bread alone (a "death by bread alone") rather than by the words of God, or to accept the kingdoms of the world rather than give his life for the inauguration of the kingdom of God. In the wilderness, Christ had a sanctification experience. When Peter later admonished him to forsake his words about the need to suffer and die for humanity, Jesus said to Satan to "get behind" him (Mark 10:33). Satan's temptation did not work in the wilderness, so it would not work later in the company of the disciples, even if the words were channeled unwittingly through the mouth of a close comrade.

As we noted, Jesus was obedient to the Father even unto a criminal's death on the cross (Phil. 2:8). He was "handed over," as sinners were, to God-forsakeness (Rom. 1:26–28; 4:25; 8:32) in order to justify them unto God's liberating righteousness through the Spirit of life (4:25). He was raised from the dead "according to the Spirit of holiness" (1:4) so that we might be sanctified from sin and consecrated unto God by the same Spirit (1 Peter 1:2). Indeed, we are washed, we are sanctified, we are justified "in the name of Jesus Christ and in the Spirit of our God" (1 Cor. 6:11).

Jesus prayed that his disciples be sanctified by the truth, which is God's Word (John 17:17). Jesus sanctified himself in devotion to the Father's Word so that the disciples may be sanctified (17:18). Like Jesus, the disciples were sanctified for faithfulness in the world and not for escape from the world (17:15–16). Their sanctification and consecration was unto a holy purpose that required their engagement with the world, not their avoidance of it. If Jesus fulfilled all righteousness by bearing the burdens of the sinners, how can we interpret kingdom sanctification as an avoidance of the sinners?

Jesus was depicted as Spirit Baptizer implicitly as the Sanctifier or as the One who would through the presence of the Spirit purge away all that resisted the reign of God (Matt 3:2, 12). At Pentecost, flames of fire resting on the disciples as they spoke in tongues indicated God's holy presence (Acts 2:3). The company of disciples speaking in tongues was being shaped into a holy temple of praise to God, consecrated for a holy task. The Jerusalem church, however, had a lesson to learn from the Spirit, called the "Holy" Spirit of God. What God has cleansed cannot be called profane (10:15). Translation: What God has washed for a holy purpose cannot be regarded as unclean because certain prescribed religious ceremonies remained unheeded. Christ is the perfect sacrifice that was empowered by the very breath of God to offer himself for the sins of the world (Heb. 9:14), and the Spirit he bestows makes that which receives it consecrated to God for a messianic task. Such matters are governed by God's truth and action and not by religion or those who manage it.

So, while Peter was yet preaching, before anything "religious" could be performed (including Christian baptism!), the Spirit visibly filled the Gentiles to overflowing so that they too could join the messianic mission as equal partners (Acts 10:44–46). The Jews present were astounded. The Gentiles too were being made into a sacred temple of praise to God by the Holy Spirit (10:46) so that they could be used effectively in the Lord's service. Peter later testified at the Jerusalem Council that the Gentiles had their hearts cleansed by faith and not law (15:9), for they repented unto life (10:18). The Spirit was the sign that the sanctifying powers of the Spirit had swept both Jew and Gentile alike into a reconciled and reconciling community consecrated to God as a temple of praise and empowered for service in the world. This sanctified church would represent a visible sign of God's final indwelling of all things made new and shaped into Christ's image—the final reign of God established through new creation (1 Cor. 15:20–28).

What, then, about the empowered life? To complete our discussion of the elements of life in the Spirit, we must discuss the issue of prophetic or charismatic empowerment.

Spirit-Baptized Witness

The broad pneumatological framework for the Pentecostal experience of Spirit baptism helps us to appreciate the richness of empowerment for witness. Empowerment for service is part of the inauguration of the kingdom of God in power to transform lives and to gift them for service in marvelous ways. Without this broad framework for Spirit baptism in the kingdom of God discussed above, empowerment for service can seem vacuous, as a raw energy for signs and wonders guided by little more than pragmatic considerations. For example, any separation of empowerment and the Spirit's sanctifying work is an abnormality that is sure to lead to the collapse of a person's ministry. The empowerment of the prophet always implied his or her being set apart and consecrated for a holy task.

Also, sanctification implies empowered witness. One is sanctified for a purpose. Jesus was separated in this way by the Spirit of God (Luke 1:35). Jesus is the supreme prophet from God who will create a community of prophets through the transference of the Spirit. Jesus thus breathed God's holy breath upon the disciples as a prelude to their being sent out into the world as living witnesses for God about the kingdom of God (John 20:22). Such is the symbol of Pentecost. Like Moses, who had the Spirit transferred from him to his assisting elders for a prophetic task (Num. 11), so Jesus transfers God's Spirit to his followers so that they may also function as prophets (Acts 2:17).

Yet, the sanctifying work of the Spirit needs to be released in life through powerful experiences of renewal and charismatic enrichment that propel us toward vibrant praise, healing reconciliations, enriched *koinonia*, and enhanced gifting for empowered service. Since the kingdom of God is a complex reality, empowerment for witness must have many dimensions to it, both individual and communal. The early Pentecostals noticed that empowered witness of the kingdom of God dawning in the world was accompanied by visible signs of God's righteous favor in the bodily and social realms that anticipated the final new creation of all things (Matt. 12:28). Sanctification as separation from sin and consecration implied an empowerment for vibrant witness in the world that bursts forth with signs of renewal. Luke favored the metaphor of being filled with the Spirit in order to describe how the church was empowered to speak inspired words and to follow Jesus in healing all those oppressed of the devil (Acts 4:29–31; 10:38). In this pneumatological and charismatic emphasis, Luke has become the theologian to the Pentecostals. This is the experience of Spirit baptism highlighted by the Pentecostals in the book of Acts and available to all those who embrace Jesus in faith as Lord and Savior. Let us develop more thoroughly this charismatic or vocational release of the Spirit in life.

It is important to note right off that in Acts the experience of Spirit baptism involves the proliferation of spiritual gifts, including what may be termed "signs and wonders." Miraculous signs and wonders were not incidental or nonessential to Jesus' ministry. Rather, these signs were at the very substance of his mission to inaugurate the reign of God in the world and to overthrow the reign of death, sin, and the devil. Such a victory is not reducible to the inner recesses of the religious or moral imagination but grants a foretaste of the renewal of creation in extraordinary signs of redemption, healing, and reconciliation. Only in a redemptive context can the religious imagination or the Christian moral life gain theological significance.

Such is the thrust of the biblical witness. The apostolic proclamation of Christ according to Luke consisted of a testimony to the fact that "God anointed Jesus of Nazareth with the Holy Spirit and power" so that Jesus "went around doing good and healing all who under the power of the devil" (Acts 10:38). Hebrews 2:14 adds that Jesus became flesh in order to taste death so that through his victory over death the reign of the devil might be broken and humanity freed from its grip. Gustaf Aulen rightly noted that this *Christus Victor* theme is the "classical" theory of the atonement prominent from the New Testament, through the writings of the Fathers, and up to the theology of Luther.[82] For Christ, "having disarmed the powers and authorities . . . made a public spectacle of them, triumphing over them by the cross" (Col. 2:15). As we noted above, God's kingdom climaxes with the final victory of life over death and of God's presence "all in all" to establish the reign of life throughout creation (1 Cor. 15:20–28).

Given the abundance of references to Jesus' miraculous deeds that follow in Mark and the other Gospels, Jesus as Spirit Baptizer and Inaugurator of the kingdom of God seems essentially tied in the Gospels to the signs and wonders of his ministry (Matt. 12:28). Catholic theologian Walter Kasper has written an enormously insightful treatment of the miracles of Jesus that is in basic harmony with what I have just noted. He points out that Mark reports the first miracles of Jesus immediately after his message of the approaching kingdom (Mark 1:15ff.). How do we explain this connection theologically?

---

82. Gustaf Aulen, *Christus Victor: A Historical Study of the Three Main Types of the Idea of the Atonement* (New York: Macmillan, 1969).

In explanation of the importance of Jesus' miracles to Jesus' inauguration of the kingdom of God, Kasper makes four important points. First, the miracles say something about the well-being or salvation wrought by the kingdom of God, namely, that it affects human beings as a whole. The kingdom of God has a physical and visible dimension. Second, the miracles are *signa prognostica* or signs of the coming new creation, "a taste of the future inaugurated by Christ." We may call them "the powers of the coming age" (Heb. 6:5). They are thus guarantees of our present hope for future liberation from death and decay (Rom 8:21). Third, it is precisely to this human hope that cries out from the depths that the miracles speak, not to our scientific or observational "recording intellect." This hope for that which is new in an unprecedented and unparalleled sense is essential to the human freedom to seek transcendence in the present moment. Fourth, miracles reveal that "the whole reality of the world has been taken into God's historical economy."[83]

As noted above, miracles are not interruptions into reality that suspend the course of nature but rather involve all of nature as graced to some extent already by God but, in wonderful signs of future renewal, transform nature further in unprecedented ways. The ordinary is not graceless, nor is it abandoned in the midst of extraordinary signs and wonders. It is taken up into the renewing presence of God so that it can function on another level and in a different sense than that which we can exhaustively, rationally explain. Miracles represent nature in the power of the Spirit reaching for a glimpse of its future renewal.

The key point that Kasper makes is that the extraordinary signs such as healing that characterized Jesus' prophetic or charismatic ministry were essential to the inauguration of the kingdom of God through him. We may, therefore, regard these signs as essential to Jesus' role as Redeemer and Baptizer in the Spirit. Pentecostals have long noted that the prevalence of extraordinary acts of the Spirit in the book of Acts were essential to the church's ongoing participation in the life of the Spirit transferred from the life of Jesus at Pentecost (Acts 3:7–8; 8:4–8; 11:28; 13:11–12; 14:8–13; 16:9, 18; 19:11–12; 21:8–12).

When Jesus is asked at the beginning of Acts about the kingdom of God, he answered that the disciples would witness with power (Acts 1:8). The final verse of Acts fittingly notes that the apostolic proclamation was of "the kingdom

---

83. Walter Kasper, *Jesus the Christ* (Mahwah, NJ: Paulist, 1976), 95–98.

of God" and "Jesus Christ." The signs that accompanied Jesus' inauguration of the kingdom accompanied the apostolic proclamation of the kingdom of Christ in between the first and the last chapters of Acts. Lest such an emphasis on the extraordinary signs of the Spirit be dismissed as an enthusiastic element in Luke, the same can be noted in Paul as well, as a sign that the life of the kingdom rests on the power of God and not on our own capacities (cf. 1 Cor. 2:4–5; Gal. 5:1–5).

The fact that Jesus revealed strength in weakness and suffering in solidarity with the sinners and outcasts does not in any way relativize or relegate as nonessential the miraculous signs of new life that characterized his Spirit-empowered ministry and that of his followers. Jesus magnified grace in signs and wonders as a sign of God's favor that reached out primarily to the poor and oppressed (Luke 4:18). We should add that the strength in weakness involved in the life in the Spirit is indeed often not obvious to the naked eye but is something to be discerned in faith. The fact that God's grace is sufficient for all things must be experienced in all things, including times of suffering and despair (2 Cor. 12). The kingdom is a seed or a treasure that is hidden and discovered in faith. But occasional signs of the future new creation confirm that the inner strength and hidden meaning of faith is reaching for a new creation that will become the final dwelling place of God.

There is a creative tension between the hidden meaning of faith and the visible signs by which faith reaches for the new creation to come. This tension should not be resolved through a reduction of faith to either hidden meanings or to visible triumphs over suffering. If the former, faith can become passive, glorifying suffering without any resistance or hope for visible healing in the here and now. If the latter, faith can become triumphalistic, with no capacity to comfort those who live unavoidably in a state of serious need or suffering. Faith in God involves both hidden strength and signs of renewal because it is ultimately in the God whose presence is sufficient in both situations of want and abundance (Phil. 4:12–13). In both inner triumph and outer signs of deliverance, God manifests freedom to transcend the present moment of suffering and to offer creation transcendence in Christ and the work of the Spirit.

The connection between extraordinary gifts of the Spirit and the inauguration of the kingdom of God points, according to Pentecostals, to the enduring significance of these gifts in the mainstream life of the church. These gifts are too deeply connected theologically to Jesus' inauguration of the kingdom of God and the early experience of the Spirit to be reduced to one type of gifting that can be disposed of in favor of other, more ordinary ones. The freedom of human hope to reach by the Spirit in extraordinary ways for the new creation to come cannot be limited by suspicions arbitrarily imposed by the church. We are not talking about unwise or unbridled enthusiasm, to a "rash" search for extraordinary gifts. Nor are we denying the fact that love is the greatest miracle that all extraordinary signs of the Spirit serve. But all true love occasionally participates in signs and wonders of renewal if it involves the God who makes all things new.

This fact means that churches in a given culture do not have the option of deciding that such extraordinary signs of renewal are totally irrelevant to its message. Neither should they on this basis comfortably dispense with them or confine them to the margins of church life. Individuals in such churches who might be gifted in extraordinary gifts of the Spirit can be shut out or marginalized in the process. In most cultures of the southern hemisphere where Christianity is gaining greatest strength, such an attitude toward extraordinary signs of the kingdom of God is regarded by many as unthinkable. This fact reveals that the traditional Western assumption concerning the "modern" waning of these gifts in the sovereign plan of God is culturally provincial and even presumptuous.

Of course, we are not to neglect any category of spiritual gift from the more ordinary to the extraordinary. As the international Pentecostal/Reformed dialogue from 1996–2000 noted, no single grid of New Testament gifts is to be imposed on the churches as all-encompassing.[84] The role of extraordinary gifts in signaling the inauguration of the kingdom of God in power is related to the church's contextual needs. Their occurrence will vary according to the challenges faced by the church. Their nature and frequency may vary according to time and context, but they should never be suppressed or ignored.

---

84. See statement 54 in "Word and Spirit, Church and World: The Final Report of the International Dialogue between the Representatives of the World Alliance of Reformed Churches and Some Classical Pentecostal Churches and Leaders, 1996–2000," *Pneuma* 23 (Spring 2001): 9–43. Similarly, the World Council of Churches consultation on the Charismatic movement notes: "In ecumenical encounters each confession realizes, in encountering the gifts of other confessions, the limitations and one-sidedness of its own gifts" (see *The Church Is Charismatic: The World Council of Churches and the Charismatic Renewal*, ed. Arnold Bittlinger [Geneva: World Council of Churches, 1982], 54).

Emil Brunner made a powerful case for embracing of these "paranormal" gifts in the body of Christ because of the depths of the human soul gripped by the Spirit of life.[85] The kingdom of God comes in power not only because of the depths to which the Spirit encounters us but also because of the expanse of the Spirit's freedom to confront us with the powers of the age to come. We speak in tongues, prophesy, heal the sick, and cast out devils. We not only proclaim the good news, we seek to be part of its eruption in our midst as a field of power and deliverance.

There is no question in my mind that Luke presents Spirit baptism as this kind of spiritual experience. Spirit baptism is power for witness, a power that reveals itself in bold witness and extraordinary gifts like inspired speech and bodily healing. The early church under persecution prayed, "Now, Lord, consider their threats and enable your servants to speak your word with great boldness. Stretch out your hand to heal and perform miraculous signs and wonders through the name of your holy servant Jesus" (Acts 4:29–30). In this prayer, the early church sought to continue the ministry of Jesus, which they proclaimed as descriptive of his redemptive work as the Spirit Baptizer. Peter proclaimed that "God anointed Jesus of Nazareth with the Holy Spirit and power, and . . . went around doing good and healing all who were under the power of the devil" (10:38). The early church saw its own reception of the Spirit as empowering it to continue in this messianic ministry. There is simply no compelling biblical reason not to assume the same about the church today.

I am not saying that a Christian whose life is not rich in miraculous occurrences is substandard. That would represent a ridiculous assumption. The sanctifying Spirit manifests itself in signs that are miraculous, but the deeper signs are acts of love. I am saying, however, that the Christian should remain open to an experience of the presence and power of the Spirit that transcends cultural expectations, including those of post-Enlightenment rationalism in the West. Luke's voice in the canon calls all Christians to an experience of Pentecost that is akin to a prophetic call felt deeply like Jeremiah's experience of fire in his bones.

For Pentecostals, such fire is typically released in speaking in tongues, prophetic speech, gifts of knowledge and wisdom, and healing the sick. Many

85. Emil Brunner, *Das Missverständnis der Kirche* (Zürich: Theologischer Verlag Zürich, 1988), 53ff.

of us realize that there are historical, cultural, and providential factors that have led us as a Christian movement to accent these particular gifts. I do not hold that all Christian families should become exactly like us. But I believe that we have been called to inspire global Christianity to a greater appreciation for them.

I realize that there are gifts cherished in the Bible that are not so obviously extraordinary in nature and that there is also caution expressed toward an excitement about extraordinary signs as an end in themselves (Matt. 16:4; 1 Cor. 13). Yet the apostolic testimony is that God has used such signs to remind us that we are saved by his power and not by human wisdom (1 Cor. 2:4–5) or works (Gal. 3:5). They have also been used to fulfill a hope that lies deeper in the human soul than that which rational thought can grasp (Rom. 8:26) and to aid in the foretaste of the new creation to come.

Moreover, we Pentecostals have been blessed by gifts that other traditions accent, such as the rich intellectual heritage cherished in the Reformed tradition. Hopefully, other Christian communions can be blessed by accents cultivated in our Christian family, so that members in those churches who happen to be gifted in these areas can feel cherished too and that all of the members can be blessed with a broader diversity of spiritual gifts. We have seen a development in this direction already and applaud its continuation.

In this increasing diversity of gifts among us all, we can all agree that the greatest release of the Spirit is in the form of divine love, to which all of these gifts point and from which they draw their strength as pointers to the power of the kingdom of God to transform lives. Even knowledge can "puff up" and be used as a weapon in the body of Christ if detached from its service to love (1 Cor. 8:1; cf. Eph. 4:15). Without the love of God enacted in Jesus, revealed in the cross, the gifts of the Spirit are reduced to nothing and the spirituality connected to them is reduced to a nebulous energy devoid of any real connection to human life under God's reign.

But the Pentecostal charismatic understanding of Spirit baptism has the following two valid points to make. First, Christian initiation must include a sense that the grace of God gifts Christians for ministry and mission. As the World Council of Churches Faith and Order paper, *The Nature and Purpose of the Church*, noted, water baptism is the "ordination service" of every Christian. It states further, "All baptized Christians must take seriously their potential to exercise gifts they receive from the Holy Spirit—never for their own sake alone but for the life and mission of the whole community."[86] There is no Christian initiation by faith and baptism in the full sense of the word without some sense of commissioning to service. Without this, initiation lacks something vital.

As Luke implies in Acts, the reception of the Spirit at Christian initiation should be regarded as preparation for self-giving to God in praise and to others in service. Many Pentecostals lessen the power of their focus on Spirit baptism by removing it completely from Christian initiation and identity and making it merely an enhancement of power supplemental to the life of grace. The ordination of every Christian as an inspired prophet cannot be reduced to a *super-additum* or a supplemental experience of grace that is not essential to Christian identity.

Second, Pentecostals note that Spirit baptism is not only a divine act and a creaturely participation in ways too deep for conscious awareness, it is also something consciously experienced. Though one cannot fix in advance what kind of experience this understanding of initiation will bring or when and how it will burst forth in the life of the believer, it is sure to manifest itself at some point through such avenues as inspired utterance, acts of love, and other signs of the Spirit's presence in power. Without this expectation, the church will tend not to experience them as much.

This is not to say that there is no distinction theologically between Christian initiation and an experience of Spirit baptism as a release of the Spirit for power in life. Interestingly, John Calvin distinguished between the Spirit of adoption and the "extraordinary graces of the Spirit . . . added as a culmination," as evidenced in texts like Acts 8.[87] Pentecostals have rightly seen that the Christian achieves a certain fullness in the experience of the Spirit through charismatic awareness, power, and ministry/mission. This insight is sorely needed by a church today that is still far too closed in upon itself and complacent about its Christian identity, about its "possession" of the Holy Spirit.

---

86. Statement 100, *The Nature and Purpose of the Church* (Faith and Order Paper No. 181; Geneva: World Council of Churches, 1998).

87. John Calvin, *Acts of the Apostles*, trans. J. W. Fraser and W. J. G. McDonald (Grand Rapids: Eerdmans, 1965), 236; quoted in Harold Hunter, H. Hunter, *Spirit Baptism: A Pentecostal Alternative* (Lanham, MD: Univ. Press of America, 1980), 164. Reformed theologian Henrikus Berkhof joins with Calvin in noting an experience of Spirit baptism in Acts that is profoundly charismatic and vocational; see his *Doctrine of the Holy Spirit* (Atlanta: John Knox, 1964), 89.

In reality, we do not possess the Spirit, the Spirit possesses us. Thus, we can only experience this life in God as we follow the Spirit's lead in giving glory to God and bearing witness of God's love to others. Seeking fresh power in the Spirit for this purpose must be the daily quest of the Christian if greater fullness of the life of the Spirit is to be substantially more than an empty confession. One cannot use a theology of Christian initiation to mute the valid reference to the power of Pentecost to be experienced in and through the church.

IN SUM

I will show my Pentecostal colors here and insist that, whatever else it is, Spirit baptism is a powerful experience received with or at a moment distinct from Christian initiation. This is not to say that the Pentecostal experience is unrelated to initiation and cannot serve to confirm it or bring greater fulfillment. But Christian initiation by grace through faith cannot be dependent on a certain experience or understanding of experience for its validity. God is not dependent on the adequacy of our experience or response of faith as judged according to precise biblical patterns in order to bind us to Christ by the power of the Spirit. Most Pentecostals acknowledge this. But Spirit baptism as an eschatological participation in the kingdom of God by faith involves Christian initiation *and* a release of the Spirit in life for power in witness. The broad theological framework of Spirit baptism as a divine act in inaugurating the kingdom of God involves theologically for Luke and the Pentecostals an experience of the Spirit in power for witness.

That Pentecostals ask the church to seek a definite experience of Spirit baptism as a renewal of faith and a prophetic anointing for service with or distinct in time from Christian initiation need not be interpreted as taking anything away from Christian initiation as that decisively initial point of identification with Christ as the one in whom all spiritual blessings may be found (Eph. 1:3). Rather, the experience of Spirit baptism cherished by Pentecostals brings to our awareness theological insights inherent in the meaning of initiation itself.

When a Pentecostal falls to her knees speaking in tongues in submission to God and to God's will for her life, her initial act of faith through confession and baptism can be viewed retrospectively in the light of that experience as her ordination service as a Spirit-baptized "minister" for God. Likewise, Christian initiation should be interpreted in the churches in a way that an expectation of conscious experiences of the Holy Spirit in power is cultivated.

The Pentecostal experience of Spirit baptism has theological implications for how we view Christian initiation as well as the lifelong walk of faith.

One enters Spirit-baptized existence at Christian initiation. But the experience of Spirit baptism connected to and following from initiation is meant to bring to conscious participation the justice of the kingdom, the growth in sanctifying grace, and the charismatic openness to bless others and to glorify God that begins in Christian initiation. These experiences are to be ongoing. We have been baptized in the Spirit, we are being baptized in the Spirit, and we will be baptized in the Spirit.

Christian initiation cannot exhaust the reality or even the theology of Spirit baptism, given the eschatological view of it developed above. Spirit baptism has decisive roots in Christian initiation, but it is also to be reaffirmed in the daily walk in the Spirit as well as in definite moments of Spirit-filling. Ultimately, it is realized in cosmic transformation. In the light of a theology of Spirit baptism as an eschatological dynamic (both now and not yet), we can affirm both the event of initiation and the ongoing experiences of the Spirit that characterize Spirit baptism as participation in Christ as the King and the Spirit as the kingdom.

Five

SIGNS OF GRACE IN A GRACELESS WORLD:
TOWARD A SPIRIT-BAPTIZED ECCLESIOLOGY

T HE CHURCH EXISTS IN THE OUTPOURING OF THE HOLY SPIRIT."[1] THIS statement from Ralph Del Colle causes us to question the assumption of many Pentecostals that Spirit baptism is merely an experience of power or renewal among individual Christians. Yet, interestingly, Pentecostals have also assumed an intimate connection between Spirit baptism and the interactive life of a charismatically enriched church within a great "rain" of the Spirit. With their individualistic understanding of Spirit baptism, they have lacked the conceptual framework in which to understand its connection to the church's communally-gifted life. The central thesis of this chapter is thus that *Spirit baptism gave rise to the global church and remains the very substance of the church's life in the Spirit, including its charismatic life and mission.*

Pentecostals require a more developed ecclesiology in the light of pneumatology. They have traditionally yearned for revival to come upon the "sleeping churches" but have lacked much of an appreciation for the even more seminal pneumatological constitution of the church. Fundamental here is Irenaeus' well-known statement that "where the Spirit of

---

1. Ralph Del Colle, "The Outpouring of the Holy Spirit: Implications for the Church and Ecumenism," in *The Holy Spirit, the Church, and Christian Unity: Proceedings of the Consultation Held at the Monastery of Bose, Italy, 14–20 October, 2002,* ed. D. Donnelly, A. Denaux, J. Famerée (Leuven: Leuven Univ. Press, 2005), 249.

God is, there is the church and all grace" (*Adversus Haereses* 3.24.1). Though the Spirit's work is vast and oriented first to the reign of God in the world, it is also centrally and uniquely ecclesial in nature. Helpful in this regard is Simon Chan's point that the Spirit present in and through the church is the "church-located, church-shaped Spirit," what we may call the *ecclesial Spirit*, who is active redemptively to make possible communion with God and one another.[2] The church thus has its being in the ecclesial Spirit, who is also the missionary Spirit. The Spirit in the *koinonia* and empowered mission of the church seeks to draw humanity into communion with God and to inspire a sighing for the day when all of creation becomes the temple of God's presence to the glory of God.

Thus, any discussion of Spirit baptism and the central role that it can play in a global Pentecostal theology necessitates a discussion of the church. Because of the importance of *koinonia* to the reign of God in the world, the church becomes the natural outcome of the Pentecostal outpouring of the Spirit in the world. Incorporated into Christ's filial relationship with the Father, the church is able to participate in Christ's spiritual fullness. Leslie Newbigin's insightful remark applies: "It is surely a fact of inexhaustible significance that what our Lord left behind Him was not a book nor a creed, nor a system of thought nor a rule of life, but a visible community."[3] The church is not incidental to Spirit baptism but is rather its integral outcome. Also, Spirit baptism is not a *super-additum* but is essential to the life of the church. As a relational dynamic, Spirit baptism not only empowers and renews the people of God, it has birthed the people of God as the sign of grace in an increasingly graceless world (to use a phrase I heard used more than once from my *Doktorvater*, Jan Lochman). We will thus explore the significance of the church to Spirit baptism by discussing first the role of *koinonia* in Spirit baptism.

SPIRIT BAPTISM AND KOINONIA

The Spirit is the Spirit of communion. Spirit baptism implies communion. This is why it leads to a shared love, a shared meal, a shared mission, and the proliferation/enhancement of an interactive charismatic life. Spirit baptism

---

2. Simon Chan, "Mother Church: Towards a Pentecostal Ecclesiology," *Pneuma* 22:2 (Fall 2000): 198.

3. Leslie Newbigin, *The Household of God: Lectures on the Nature of the Church* (London: SCM, repr. 1964), 27.

thus implies a relationship of unity between the Lord and the church that is not fundamentally one of identity but rather communion. Solidarity between Jesus or the Spirit and the church is then a quality of communion. This insight prevents the church from an overly realized eschatology that simply identifies the kingdom with the church or its hierarchy without an appropriate dialectic or eschatological reservation. There is implied a dynamic dialectic between the life of the Spirit and the church in its visible, historical existence that we will develop below. Communion implies participation by faith in God's love in the midst of weakness. The unity it offers is a gift but also a life and a mission to be pursued: "that all of them may be one, Father, just as you are in me and I am in you. May they also be in us so that the world may believe that you have sent me" (John 17:21).

It is difficult to overestimate the importance of the communion of saints to a theology of Spirit baptism and its impact in furthering the mission of God in the world. Interestingly, social historian Rodney Stark suggested the thesis that early Christianity spread rapidly and impacted its world effectively in the first few centuries of the Christian era (approximating a 40 percent growth rate per decade) *largely as a result of its quality of communal life.* Stark theorizes that the "basis for successful conversionist movements is growth through social networks, through a *structure of direct and intimate interpersonal attachments.*"[4]

Of course, the church as a *communio* is deeper in significance than a social network of personal attachments. But Stark is on the right path in pointing to the church's communal life as key to its effective missionary outreach. The church did not just proclaim the gospel, it *participated* in and *embodied* this gospel in its communal life and witness. We can say that the church offered a depth of communion and "graced" relationships based on charity and hope that made the gospel attractive to a population starved for community. Luke seems to have agreed, reporting that, as a result of Pentecost,

> They devoted themselves to the apostles' teaching and to the fellowship, to the breaking of bread, and to prayer. . . . All the believers were together and had everything in common. Selling their possessions and goods, they gave to anyone as he had need. Every day they continued to meet together in the temple courts. They broke bread in their

---

4. Rodney Stark, *The Rise of Christianity* (San Francisco: HarperSanFrancisco, 1996), 20 (emphasis his).

homes and ate together with glad and sincere hearts, praising God and enjoying the favor of all the people. *And the Lord added to their number daily those who were being saved.* (Acts 2:42, 44–47, italics added)

As is well known, there is globally a shift occurring today toward a "new Christendom" that has its greatest (though by no means exclusive) strength in the southern hemisphere and that tends to encourage charismatic, widely participatory, and missions-minded congregations. Multiple and extraordinary gifts among ordinary Christians such as prophecy, exorcism, and divine healing are emerging as far more relevant to the vibrancy of the missionary church globally than North American and European theologians laboring under the challenges of the Enlightenment could have ever imagined. The strength of this renewed Christendom is not in its sense of tradition or theological brilliance (as important as these are) but in a powerful experience of communal praise, liberation, and mission. This renewal tends toward an energized laity active in the realm of the Spirit in diverse and unique ways to build up the body of Christ and to function as witnesses for Christ to the world.

This new development in global Christianity of which Pentecostalism is a vital part is responding to an urgent need. Thomas Finger has noted rightly that "globalization continues modernity's dissolution of communal solidarities and relationships," separating "countless individuals from any sense of connectedness."[5] Christopher Lasch informs us further that even the family, traditionally a "haven" in the midst of a "heartless" world, is succumbing to the influences of an impersonal world governed by vast capitalist institutions. For example, parents urge children to respect their authority in return for services rendered, such as food, clothing, and shelter. Family members then seem to share little in common beyond the provision of these "services."[6]

Moreover, children are born into a socialization process that unjustly privileges one race, sex, social class, and so on over another, distorting their souls from the start and giving new meaning to the doctrine of "original sin." If there was ever a time in which the church needs to embody for the world a community of "graced relationships" in the God who bestows all grace abundantly and freely, it is now. Christ as the Spirit Baptizer offers hope, since in bestow-

---

5. Thomas N. Finger, *A Contemporary Anabaptist Theology* (Downers Grove, IL: InterVarsity Press, 2004), 157.

6. Christopher Lasch, *Haven in a Heartless World: The Family Besieged* (New York: Basic, 1975), 33–34.

ing the Spirit he imparts the *communio* of the divine life in all of its grace and healing power. He "bestowed gifts" to humanity so that he might fill the entire universe with his redemptive presence (Eph. 4:7–10). He fills with the Spirit to enhance communal life: "Be filled with the Spirit, speaking to one another in psalms and hymns and spiritual songs" (5:18–19 NASB). This may be a time for the distinctly Pentecostal focus on the charismatic Christ as the Spirit Baptizer to arise as a major theme in the ecumenical movement. But we need first to help Pentecostals develop the implicit connection that they make between Spirit baptism and the life and mission of the church.

Spirit baptism understood as a communal dynamic can help Pentecostals theologically integrate their concomitant emphases on Spirit baptism and the gifted church. Spirit baptism as a relational dynamic is essential to its role in birthing the church as a diversely charismatic body. It is indeed interesting that Spirit baptism is described by Luke in relational terms, as a divine "clothing" (Luke 24:49) or "infilling" (Acts 2:4) with the divine presence. It is not a "baptism" as something external to us but as something intimately participatory and interactive, involving God in us and we in God. The Spirit embraces us or fills us with the divine presence in order to sanctify us and empower us to be living witnesses to Christ as the Son of God and the Spirit Baptizer. When God surrounds and fills us with the divine presence, it is so that we can give of ourselves back to God in worship and witness. There is a relational dynamic at play in Spirit baptism: *God pours God's presence into us in order to receive it back along with the fullness of our renewed spirits in flaming tongues of praise and witness* (Acts 2:4). We are then to pour ourselves into one another: "speaking to one another in psalms and hymns and spiritual songs."

As Geoffrey Wainwright has noted, the classic notion of Trinitarian *perichoresis* involves the divine persons emptying themselves into each other in order to receive from each other's fullness.[7] As we saw in our previous chapter, the Father shares the divine reign with the Son in order to discover it anew in him. Likewise, the Spirit as the bond of love between the Father and the Son is poured out from the Father through the Son in order that the Son's giving of the kingdom back to the Father may involve the redeemed creation as the dwelling place of God. Wainwright thus says in the light of *perichoresis* that worship is "a participatory entrance into Christ's self-offering to the

---

7. Geoffrey Wainwright, *Doxology: The Praise of God in Worship, Doctrine, and Life* (New York: Oxford Univ. Press, 1980), 23.

Father and correlatively being filled with the divine life."[8] Spirit baptism has a relational structure that has communion at its essence, the communion of self-giving love.

The relational dynamic of Spirit baptism is not merely between us as individuals and God, it is also a shared reality among us in God. When Christ poured out the Spirit, he gave interactive gifts unto humanity so that they could build each other up in the love discovered in Christ (Eph 4:7–16; cf. Rom. 5:5). The Spirit is the "go-between God," so that starting with the third article of the Apostles' Creed, the Spirit-baptized church is constituted by the Spirit according to the substance and pattern of the Trinitarian life. Spirit baptism as a relational experience explains how Spirit baptism birthed the church and continues to renew and empower the church in its diverse and vibrant charismatic life. *Koinonia* at the very substance of Spirit baptism thus reveals how Spirit baptism offers us the link between the kingdom and the church.

Koinonia is an ancient category rediscovered among those interested in an ecumenical ecclesiology. As Lorelei Fuchs states, recent ecumenical reflection "situates the concept of communio/koinonia at the heart of imaging a church as a reflection of the Triune God."[9] This ecumenical focus on *koinonia* is significant, since there can be no radical disjunction between the kingdom and the church in the light of the Trinitarian structure of Spirit baptism. As we noted in our previous chapter, Jesus mediates the Spirit who proceeds from the Father. In mediating the Spirit, Jesus draws believers into the communion enjoyed between the Father and the Son and expands the circle of this love in the process so as to include the "other."

Baptized in the Spirit, the church seeks out the other as well in missionary outreach. The Spirit-baptized church mimics the Spirit-baptizing God. Jesus came on behalf of the Father to seek and to save the lost (Luke 15). Jesus bestows the Spirit so that we might in witness to Jesus seek the lost as well. Any assumption that the kingdom proclaimed by Jesus does not lead integrally to the church and its mission reveals a neglect of the biblical role of Jesus as the risen Lord to baptize in the Spirit.

---

8. Ibid.

9. Lorelei Fuchs, "The Holy Spirit and the Development of Communio/Koinonia Ecclesiology as a Fundamental Paradigm for Ecumenical Engagement," in *The Holy Spirit, the Church, and Christian Unity: Proceedings of the Consultation Held at the Monastery of Bose, Italy, 14–20 October, 2002,* ed. D. Donnelly, A. Denaux, J. Famerée (Leuven: Leuven Univ. Press, 2005), 160.

Spirit baptism as the link between the kingdom proclaimed by Jesus and the church is in fact at the heart of Luke's message. As we noted earlier, Acts 1 has the risen Christ introduce Spirit baptism in the context of the establishment of the kingdom (1:3–8). The question concerning the restoration of the kingdom is posed by the disciples as they are gathered in Jerusalem (1:6–7), the traditional location of the kingdom's fulfillment. Jesus' answer to the question implies that the details of the kingdom's fulfillment with regard to Israel are hidden in the Father's will. Revealed at the heart of Spirit baptism as the means by which the kingdom is fulfilled is the establishment of a community that will be defined as witnesses of Jesus as the one anointed of the Spirit to heal and deliver (1:8; 10:37–38).

The church participates in the liberating reign of God evident in Jesus' ministry through Spirit baptism. From a broader perspective we may say that the love and *koinonia* at the heart of the kingdom both constitute the church and are embodied and proclaimed through the church to the world by the baptism in the Spirit. In agreement with the Reformed-Catholic Final Report of 1977, we can affirm that Christ's gospel "gathers, protects, and maintains the *koinonia* of his disciples as a sign and beginning of his Kingdom."[10]

•Spirit baptism means that the *koinonia* of God is not closed but open to the world. As Moltmann notes, "God does not desire glory without his glorification through man and creation in the Spirit. God does not desire to find rest without the new creation of man and the world through the Spirit. God does not desire to be united with himself without the uniting of all things with him."[11] Spirit baptism implies a triune life that is motivated by love, not only as an internal dynamic but externally toward the other. Spirit baptism seeks the other for the other's sake, for liberation and communion.

But one might still ask, Why the church as the communion of saints and as the "sign and seal" of the kingdom? We might imagine that God in sovereign power could force the creation to conform to sanctifying grace. Such an action, however, would not be consistent with divine love. The reign of God

---

10. "The Presence of Christ in Church and World: Final Report of the Dialogue between the World Alliance of Reformed Churches and the Secretariat for Promoting Christian Unity, 1977," #75, in *Growth in Agreement: Reports and Agreed Statements of Ecumenical Conversations on a World Level*, ed. Harding Meyer and Lukas Vischer (New York: Paulist, 1984), 451.

11. Jürgen Moltmann, *The Church in the Power of the Spirit* (New York: Harper & Row, 1977), 63.

revealed in Christ is not overpowering but kenotic or self-giving. It does not force compliance but seeks to persuade. It is not overpowering but seeks to draw and to convict. It is not too obvious but inspires faith in the absence of sight. Most importantly, it does not dominate but draws the other into mutually-edifying fellowship.

Such a kingdom has thus involved in God's good pleasure the election of a people in Christ that can function as sign and seal of this kingdom, or that can "incarnate" it as the sanctified community and bear witness to it in power. Such a kingdom inspires a church to herald and to channel the grace of love in the midst of a world still oppressed by gracelessness, alienation, domination, and death. In weakness, this community will glory in God's grace and power. It will look to God and to the Lamb and proclaim that "salvation belongs to our God, who sits on the throne, and to the Lamb" (Rev 7:10). In weakness the church points to the kingdom as the mystery hidden but also disclosed in the church's living witness. In the power of the Spirit, the church will credit all that it is and will be to the baptism in the Spirit and not to its own resources.

This church will be a "kingdom of priests unto God" only as a result of redemptive grace and in service to God in the image of the crucified Lamb (Rev. 1:5–6). This church will conquer evil forces by the self-sacrificial blood of the Lamb in living witness to him (12:11), not by aggression or violence. It will participate by Spirit baptism in Christ's reign of self-giving love as revealed in the way of the cross. The reign committed to the Son in self-giving love by the Father and given back to the Father by the Son in self-sacrificial love is opened through Spirit baptism to the church that humbly accepts it as a "kingdom of priests" and prophets. The Spirit-baptized church "incarnates" this reign in living witness to the crucified Lord of glory. In the living *koinonia* of love in the Spirit, the church embodies and bears witness to the reign of God in the world.

It is important to note that Pentecostals would not typically formulate their ecclesiology through a concept of Trinitarian *koinonia*. Trinitarian *koinonia* is not generally a concept used in their teaching or preaching. As Miroslav Volf has noted more generally, "The idea of correspondence between church and Trinity has remained largely alien to the Free Church tradition."[12] Though *koinonia* is a New Testament concept, it is naturally not

---

12. Miroslav Volf, *After Our Likeness: The Church as the Image of the Trinity* (Grand Rapids: Eerdmans, 1998), 195.

explicitly used in the biblical text as a description of the inner life of God or of the church's participation in its self-disclosure in history. The Gospel of John implies a correspondence between our fellowship with Christ and Christ's fellowship with the Father (14:11, 20; 17:21), but the elaborate analogy (or participatory relationship) between the Trinitarian life of God and the fellowship of the church is a theological insight drawn from later Trinitarian theology.

This fact is not necessarily problematic in itself, since such participation is implied in the New Testament. But it serves to explain why Pentecostals, who tend to be biblicistic, have not come to emphasize it. This use of *koinonia* is not without its problems, however, as Volf has noted. Some have questioned the assumption that the transcendent mystery of the inner life of God can be used to explain the *koinonia* of the church.[13] In fact, both the difference and similarity between divine and human *koinonia* are related to a dynamic dialectic between the Spirit and the church. I think *koinonia* is thus useful to ecclesiology, but I wonder if there is not a tendency to discuss it in ecumenical contexts as an abstract concept rather than as a reality discovered from the bottom up from within the liberating story of Jesus and the diverse field of the Spirit's presence.

As noted above, *koinonia* is implicitly a *pneumatological* concept in Scripture. The church, after receiving the Spirit at Pentecost, enjoyed *koinonia* (Acts 2:42). Pentecostals do not start with a notion of God's inner life but rather, as the third article of the Apostles' Creed does, with the church as the realm of the Spirit (the forgiveness of sins and faith for life everlasting, as well as, we should add, multiple gifts of the Spirit). Pentecostals start with Spirit baptism, the story of God's actual self-giving in Christ as the Spirit Baptizer. The Pentecostals thus note concerning the nature of the church in the 1989 Final Report of the International Roman Catholic/Pentecostal Dialogue that the Catholics "stress the God-givenness of the *koinonia* and its trinitarian character," while Pentecostals "stress that the Holy Spirit convicts people of sin, bringing them through repentance and personal faith into fellowship with Christ and one another."[14]

Nevertheless, as we noted above, Spirit baptism has a Trinitarian structure.

---

13. Ibid., 198–99.

14. "Perspectives on Koinonia: Final Report of the International Roman Catholic/Pentecostal Dialogue (1985–1989)," 31, 32, *Pneuma* 12:1 (1990): 119.

It thus has *koinonia* at its essence. Though *koinonia* is explicitly a pneumatological concept in the New Testament, it implies a connection to Jesus' relationship with the Father, a relationship that is of ultimate significance for our understanding of God's very life as God (John 17:21). Thus, *koinonia* can still be a useful concept for Pentecostals. Interestingly, the Pentecostal team concluded in the same Catholic/Pentecostal Final Report mentioned above that "Pentecostals have been reminded of the importance of the communitarian dimension of the New Testament understanding of *koinonia*."[15] Since *koinonia* can be said to occur "in the Spirit" as the bond of love (both within God, between God and humanity, and within creation), this accent of the ecumenical movement is not necessarily in tension with Pentecostal worship and theology.

Volf has attempted to show that *koinonia* can enrich a free church ecclesiology by deepening its understanding of ecclesial communion. In fact, he characterized the basic intention of his book, *After Our Likeness: The Church as the Image of the Trinity*, as making "a contribution to the trinitarian reshaping of free church ecclesiology."[16] The church is not just an association of individual believers but a participation *in the Spirit* in the loving communion enjoyed within God's triune life. As the Faith and Order paper, *The Nature and Purpose of the Church*, confirms, "The Church is not the sum of individual believers in communion with God. It is not primarily a communion of believers with each other. It is a common partaking together in God's own life whose innermost being is communion."[17]

Perhaps the way forward for Pentecostals in response to this ecumenical focus on *koinonia* is to follow the advice of Walter Kasper by striving for "an ecclesiology devised under the influence of pneumatology according to the archetype of the Trinity."[18] The challenge for Pentecostals, of course, is in how Kasper's suggestion will relate Trinitarian with Oneness Pentecostals, who reject an ontological Trinity. If, as it seems agreeable to all Pentecostals, Jesus as the incarnation of God and the man of the Spirit communes with the

---

15. "Perspectives on Koinonia," 33 (p. 119).

16. Volf, *After Our Likeness*, 197.

17. *The Nature and Purpose of the Church: A Stage on the Way to a Common Statement*, Faith and Order Paper No. 181 (Geneva: WCC Faith and Order, 1998), #13, 10.

18. Walter Cardinal Kasper, "Present Day Problems in Ecumenical Theology," *Reflections* 6 (Spring 2003): 80.

heavenly Father, certainly an invocation of his name in baptism implies our entry in his image into the fellowship of love and devotion enjoyed between him and the Father. The Oneness will not want to regard this relationship between Jesus and the Father as transferable to the inner life of God. But that does not in my view necessarily omit the possibility that the communion between Jesus as the man of the Spirit and the Father in the story of Jesus cannot have significance for the Oneness understanding of the new life available in Spirit baptism.

Of course, Trinitarian Pentecostals will recognize the significance of *koinonia* as having absolute significance for our understanding of the essential life of God. As *The Nature and Purpose of the Church* proposes, *koinonia* helps us understand why the church is vital to God's redemptive plan: "Communion is the gift of God whereby God draws humanity into the orbit of the generous, divine, self-giving love which flows between the persons of the Trinity."[19] One can also maintain that the God of *koinonia* has "hard-wired" the creation for communion. *Koinonia* thus connects the church with humanity and creation itself, for there is a "natural bond between human beings and between humanity and creation which the new life of communion builds upon and transforms but never wholly replaces."[20] *Koinonia* is thus also an eschatological hope: "The final destiny of the Church is to be caught up in the intimate relation of Father, Son, and Holy Spirit to praise and to enjoy God forever."[21]

Koinonia grants Spirit baptism its relational dynamic and helps us to understand how the outpouring of the Spirit constitutes the church and involves the diversely-interactive charismatic structure of the church in the church's living witness to the kingdom. The Trinitarian and eschatological nature of Spirit baptism as it is portrayed in the Gospels gives us the theological foundation for understanding the role of *koinonia* in redemption. Since redemption by the liberating impact of the kingdom of the Father in and through the Son as the Spirit Baptizer involves *koinonia*, we cannot view the rise and life of the church as incidental or supplementary to redemption. It is Christ and not the church that saves us, but the church is the ordained sign and instrument of salvation in the world.

---

19. *The Nature and Purpose of the Church*, #54, 25.
20. Ibid., #60, 27.
21. Ibid., #59, 26.

When one is born again, one is born in the context of a family, the church. It is the family named by the Father (Eph. 3:14), in solidarity with the Son (Rom. 8:29), and born of the Spirit by the grace of God (John 1:12–13). It is a family that is elected by the Father, redeemed by the Son, and sanctified in the Spirit (1 Peter 1:2; Eph. 1:4–14). The new life of the Spirit allows us to "abide" in Christ and he in us as the Father abides in Christ and Christ in the Father (John 14:20; 17:21). The Father draws us to the Son by the agency of the Spirit (6:44) so that we can pray "Abba" to the heavenly Father in Christ (Rom. 8:15–16).

One day, we will be conformed to the image of the Son through resurrection, at which time our adoption will be complete (Rom. 8:23). This will lead to the new heavens and new earth as creation in conformity to the glorified Christ becomes the dwelling place of God (Rev. 21:1–4). Spirit baptism will have reached its climax in final judgment and purgation as a pouring out of the Spirit on "all flesh." The church then exhausts its purpose and is caught up in the more expansive new Jerusalem, the visible manifestation of the kingdom of God on earth. Notice how the bride of the Lamb morphs from the people of God clothed in righteousness (19:7–8) to the more expansive new Jerusalem that functions as a symbol of the new creation (21:1–4). Until then, the church as the Spirit-baptized communion of saints bears prophetic witness to redemption through Christ (Acts 2:17–21).

In the light of *koinonia*, Spirit baptism does not cause individuals when initiated into the church to become dissolved into a corporate *Geist* or spirit. *Koinonia* is a diverse and interactive communion that respects both the uniqueness of individuals as receiving a particular measure of grace for a particular gifting (Rom. 12:6) as well as the group dynamic of communion in the Spirit. For Paul, both individual and personal edification thus have their place along with the edification of the body (1 Cor. 14:4, 18).

Spirit baptism is a profoundly personal but not individualistic experience. The original band of Jewish disciples responds to Spirit baptism in their empowered witness by speaking forth tongues of the nations (Acts 2:4–11), symbolizing their reconciliation with people of other cultures and nations. Spirit baptism is also said to bring together male and female, young and old, bond and free (2:18–19). The Samaritans are filled with the Holy Spirit at the laying on of hands by representatives of the Jerusalem church (8:14–17). It happened to Paul as a personal experience but, interestingly, at the laying on of hands by a prophet at a time when the church as a whole was not yet ready to trust him (9:17). Communal reconciliation and communion were birthed with Spirit baptism even in Paul's personal experience of it across a gulf of hurt, fear, and suspicion.

Interestingly in this light, Paul's own use of the Spirit baptismal metaphor can be translated in this way: "In one Spirit we were all baptized into one body, whether Jews or Greeks, bond or free" (1 Cor. 12:13). The meaning according to Robertson and Plummer is as follows: "The Spirit is the element in (*en*) which the baptism takes place, and the one body is the end to (*eis*) which the act is directed."[22] Thayer also notes that the *eis* of 1 Cor. 12:13 indicates an "effect," namely, "we were all baptized in one Spirit with the effect of participating fully in one body."[23] Baptism in the Spirit is thus theologically prior to baptism in the body, for Spirit baptism is the all-expansive and transcendent incorporation into the kingdom of God that constitutes the body and in which the body participates for its life and mission. Yet, baptism in the Spirit is at the same time an initiation into a reconciled and reconciling communion of persons across cultural boundaries.

Baptism in the Spirit is baptism into an ecclesial dynamic, the ecclesial Spirit. By grace, the Spirit comes into empathy and solidarity with us so that we will in the Spirit do the same with one another and the world, especially among those who suffer. For Paul, the Spirit is affected by us and unites with us even in our most profound weakness and inner groaning for liberation (Rom. 8:26). In coming into solidarity with us, the Spirit furthers the witness of Jesus who came into solidarity with us by grace for our redemption. Jesus as the man for others is present in the Spirit as the Spirit for others, sanctifying and empowering a church as the church for others. This "presence for the other" is at the heart of a Spirit-baptized ecclesiology.

Paul then ties Spirit filling to communal life and sharing: "Be filled with the Spirit, speaking to one another in psalms and hymns and spiritual songs" (Eph. 5:18 NASB). Spirit baptism in the light of *koinonia* thus means that the

---

22. A. T. Robertson and Alfred Plummer, *A Critical and Exegetical Commentary on the First Epistle of St. Paul to the Corinthians*, 2nd ed. by Samuel Rolles Driver, Alfred Plummer, and Charles Augustus Briggs (International Critical Commentary; Edinburgh: T&T Clark, 1963), 272. I am grateful to Howard M. Ervin for this reference: *These Are Not Drunken as Ye Suppose* (Plainfield, NJ: Logos, 1968), 45.

23. J. H. Thayer, *A Greek-English Lexicon of the New Testament* (New York: American Book Co., 1889), 94. I am grateful to Howard M. Ervin for this reference: *These Are Not Drunken*, 45.

church in the power of the Spirit is not just a voluntary association of individual believers but rather a growing and empathetic fellowship that reconciles diverse peoples who can bear one another's burdens in the love of Christ. There is a group dynamic in the Spirit that must be nourished and cultivated through preaching, sacrament, and a variety of gifted expressions. Spirit baptism is experienced by individuals, not in isolation but as a preparation for *koinonia*. Spirit baptism is experienced by a church in communion but always in ways that respond to concrete individual needs and interactions. Prior to such experiences, however, Spirit baptism is also an event that constitutes the church. *Koinonia* implies a differentiated understanding of Spirit baptism as a diverse, relational, and polyphonic dynamic of constitution and renewal by the Spirit of Christ.

There is no spiritual fullness in alienation from koinonia. Fullness comes ultimately when "we all reach unity in the faith . . . attaining to the whole measure of the fullness of Christ" (Eph. 4:13). Spirit baptism thus conceived speaks to life in all of its concreteness, diversity, and charismatic richness. It speaks to a deep need within humanity and all of creation to be renewed through graced relation and fellowship. It is in this light that a brief exploration into a relational anthropology can help us understand better the creaturely life in the *creator Spiritus* that correlates with Spirit baptism as a doctrine of the renewal of communal life.

TOWARD A SPIRIT-BAPTIZED ANTHROPOLOGY

"In the beginning is the relation." These words, penned by the great Jewish philosopher Martin Buber in his classic *I and Thou*, represents an obvious play on words taken from the Genesis creation account.[24] Buber's meaning is clear: "relation" is not a human luxury or an addendum to human existence. There is something about relationships that is "ontological," or essential to human existence or that mode of being we call "human" and "creaturely." The longing for relation is innate, arising out of the interdependence of all of life that is apparent, for example, from the experience of the baby in the womb.[25] Spirit baptism as a bridge to communion assumes a relational anthropology.

Hence, the fact that relationship is fundamental to human existence and identity is not hard to understand. Child psychologists inform us that a child's

---

24. Martin Buber, *I and Thou* (New York: Charles Scribner's Sons, 1970), 78.
25. Ibid., 76–77.

life flourishes in bonding with significant others and gains identity in seeing this mirrored in the faces and attitudes of those with whom the child forms relationships. There is even a kind of bonding with another within the womb. That child is then born into a language and a social structure that shapes his or her way of perceiving the self and the world. The self is the self-in-relation, the self-in-community, for good and ill. As a person moves into an ever-more-complex network of human relationships, his or her sense of identity grows equally complex. One is a parent, a friend, a sibling, a neighbor, and so on—all labels we place on various kinds of relationships, which are fluid and constantly changing. A person moves in communities other than his or her own, creating a collision of worlds and a further expansion of one's sense of self.

One is constantly reminded that no person is an island. Relationships are not external to us but represent a complex field of life in which we define our very existence, whether we like it or not. We waffle between alienation and assimilation, both of which are signs of a fallen reality as well as that which distorts our souls or inner sense of self. This fallen reality is essentially relational, as are the symptoms of destruction and oppression that we feel in the midst of it. The yearning for grace as well as foretastes of it are also relational. We groan with the entire creation for liberty (Rom. 8:26). All of this will help us to understand the implicitly relational language of redemption in the Bible (Spirit baptism included) as well as the essential role of the communion of saints in occasioning this redemption.

What we have said thus far about how essential relationships are to human existence is not meant to promote the idea that there is no sense of self distinct from others. In fact, relationship implies a self that exists distinct (although ultimately inseparable) from others. Bonhoeffer said it best in his classic *Sanctorum Communio*: "One could . . . say that by recognizing a You, a being of alien consciousness, as separate and distinct from myself, I recognize myself as an 'I,' and so my self-consciousness awakens."[26] In fact, it is natural in our development both to take others in and to keep others at a distance. The boundaries of our existence have both barriers and bridges.[27]

---

26. Dietrich Bonhoeffer, *Sanctorum Communio: A Theological Study of the Sociology of the Church*, trans. Reinhard Krauss and Nancy Lukens (Minneapolis: Fortress, 1998), 71.

27. Miroslav Volf, *Exclusion and Embrace: A Theological Exploration of Identity, Otherness, and Reconciliation* (Nashville: Abingdon, 1996), 47.

The upshot of the dialectic of distinction and connection of the self-in-relation is that unity never necessitates uniformity or the dissolving of the distinct self. In fact, such would mean the destruction of the self, as would an alienation of the self from others. A healthy self is lived in a creative and constructive interplay of distinction and connection. Though the "I" only comes to know itself in relation to the "You," implying the essential role of relation in self-consciousness, the "I" and the "You" do not lose their distinction in an all-encompassing impersonal "spirit."[28] We never lose our capacity to discriminate to an extent in choosing or living within our relationships, nor is such discrimination necessarily prejudicial. In other words, the concept of relationship holds within it the two realities of interdependence of people for their sense of self (the essential role of relation in human life) and the distinct existence of a self in relation to others (a self that is not lost in a corporate ego or spirit without the capacity for a degree of freedom to relate wisely to others).

Let us explore this idea of the distinct existence of a self apart from others a bit further. If there is no such distinct self, there is no freedom. This is because the self that is not distinct from others becomes lost or bound within the expectations of others. For example, I live in a myriad of relationships that mediates my life to me. I am a husband, a father, a friend, a teacher, and the like. Yet, I engage in all of these relationships from a self-conscious center that I sometimes rediscover and nourish in solitude. Without this sense of self apart from others, I am wholly dependent on the acceptance of others to have any sense of identity. Such dependence can easily turn into an oppressive reality in which the significant others of my life can control me by threatening to withdraw their acceptance if I do not conform to their wishes. An oppressive manipulation of individuals can also happen by the state or by powerful social or cultural influences. Carl Jung wrote *The Undiscovered Self* as a stunning critique of the "mass mind" that seeks to dissolve the individual psyche into an oppressive corporate identity.[29] The fact that I "have a life" distinct from people and corporate forces grants me the free self from which I can give of myself unconditionally to others regardless of whether or not they reciprocate in kind.

---

28. Dietrich Bonhoeffer, *Sanctorum Communio*, 73.
29. G. C. Jung, *The Undiscovered Self*, trans. R. F. C. Hull (Boston: Little, Brown & Company, 1958).

But how do I gain this "life" or this center within that grants me the freedom I need to form relationships without being overwhelmed by alienation or assimilation? In the midst of relationships, one seeks to discover an inner core, an "autonomous self" who is free. But such autonomy is a modernist delusion that leads to alienation and oppression. What is really needed is a self in *solitude*. Solitude implies a safe space to develop the self without threats of abandonment or oppression. It assumes a supportive context, ideally one made possible by unconditional love and trust, something that could even be called "sacred." But where is such a context to be found?

Anthony Storr's *Solitude: A Return to the Self* grounds the search for such a trusting context for solitude in the child's early capacity in the context of trusting relationships to be *alone*. During a child's early development, the attachment figure becomes a part of the child's inner world as someone on whom the child can rely in the figure's *absence*.[30] In other words, the capacity to be alone is an essential aspect of a young child's healthy development in a trusting context. Storr concludes from this childhood experience that the "capacity to be alone thus becomes linked with self-discovery and self-realization; with becoming aware of one's deepest needs, feelings, and impulses."[31] Storr criticizes as one-sided the common assumption that maturity implies only the capacity to form healthy relationships. Storr considers the capacity to be alone as also a sign of emotional maturity. *Solitude both assumes, and is required for, the formation of trusting, gracious relationships.*

The capacity to resist alienation or assimilation into the mass mind is the capacity for solitude, which is the context in which a sense of self distinct from others is cultivated. Solitude as the context for self-realization thus becomes as essential to life as is time invested in cultivating relationships. Without solitude, one can be set adrift in one's identity among a myriad of relationships with all of their expectations and demands without the capacity to find in solitude a center of unconditional trust in which to cultivate a free and creative sense of self-realization. This solitude is the center from which one can give of oneself to others.

After all, there is no sense in talking about self-sacrifice if there is no self to sacrifice in the first place. Though Storr does not say this, we can add that

---

30. Anthony Storr, *Solitude: A Return to the Self* (New York: Free Press, 1988), 18–19.

31. Ibid., 21.

solitude in relation to God grants this center of unconditional trust a name and a narrative to support it. One cultivates a self-realization that is plugged into a constant source of grace and unconditional love.

We learn this about Jesus. His solitude with the Father formed a core from which Jesus gave of himself to others in resistance to their self-serving expectations. Carl Jung asked the right question in this regard: "Have I any religious experience and immediate relation to God, and hence that certainty which will keep me, as an individual, from dissolving in the crowd?"[32] Luke tells us through his depiction of Paul's sermon at Athens that we are all God's offspring, meaning that in God we all live and move and have our being (Acts 17:28). This means that from a theological perspective it is our birth from and into God that defines for us the foundational security in which to develop a healthy sense of self in solitude. In this capacity to trust God and to receive from God our calling and gifting for life, we discover who we are in relation to others.

Spirit baptism must be both an intensely personal and a communal experience. As a privileged sign of Spirit baptism, speaking in tongues shows itself to be this kind of experience, namely, an edification of the self before God (1 Cor. 14:3) *and* a communal experience in communion with multiple others (Acts 2:4ff.). It is this anchor in the fundamental relation in God that grants us the power to navigate our way through the waters of human communities with the rudder of our calling in Christ and our gifting in the Spirit. We also gain the sober mindedness to resist the thinking of the world and to not think of ourselves more highly than we ought (Rom. 12:1–3). Discovering ourselves in God, especially in solitude, grants us the sacred space for free self-giving in relation to others. We discover a justification in the Spirit by grace rather than by law or human culture. We are justified by the Spirit of God through our participation in Christ by faith. Spirit baptism thus frees us to give ourselves wisely and redemptively in love to others.

If we are relational beings, then both our spiritual sickness and the necessary healing involve a relational dynamic as well. Harry Stack Sullivan is known for his interpersonal theory of psychiatry in which relationships figure prominently in one's understanding of human brokenness and healing.[33]

---

32. Jung, *Undiscovered Self*, 33.
33. Harry Stack Sullivan, *The Interpersonal Theory of Psychiatry* (New York: Norton, 1968).

On a popular level, the well-known film *David and Lisa* dramatized for many how healing can occur in the context of relationships. David and Lisa, both patients at a mental health facility, end up receiving little help from their therapists. Ironically, they improve in the midst of finding each other and are able at the end of the film to embark on a path toward wholeness together.

That interpersonal healing and wholeness can occur outside of a conscious commitment to Christ is due to the existence of common grace in the world. All of life is graced, for in God the Creator all people "live and move and have their being" (Acts 17:28). Christ as the Spirit Baptizer fulfills this common grace redemptively so that it may flourish in communion with God and with others in the church. The Spirit will create analogues of such graced relationships in the world as a way of preparing the world for the mission of the Spirit-baptized church. Of course, we are wounded as well, since the church is an infirmary of the sick (Luther). We are a community of wounded healers.

We need to explore this process of interpersonal healing and redemption more specifically. Earlier, I mentioned that all relationships involve both discrimination and acceptance. In a sense, such a process is natural. It becomes problematic, however, when distinctive boundaries to one's existence turn into sinful exclusion. As Volf has taught us, the solution is in the redemptive will to embrace. The will to embrace that comes from the Spirit of God present in Christ seeks to create space for the other to be a part of oneself without either party experiencing alienation or assimilation.

Volf specifies that this grace is expressed in the *will* to embrace, since true embrace requires two or more who wish to connect in a way that does not oppress or exploit the other.[34] Volf speaks of the self remade in Christ's image, a "de-centered self" that submits to the lordship of Christ and wills to be changed so as to admit others in, without oppressing or destroying them. The Spirit of God is active in such a gracious transformation of persons in relation. Volf notes: "The Spirit enters into the citadel of the self, de-centers the self by fashioning it in the image of the self-giving Christ, and frees its will so it can resist the power of exclusion in the power of the Spirit of embrace."[35]

The Christian proposal of a de-centered self locates the trust for self-realization essential to solitude in a relationship with Christ in the Spirit. The

---

34. Volf, *Exclusion and Embrace*, 66.
35. Ibid., 91.

Spirit enables a lived confession of Christ as Lord. Solitude thus escapes a narcissistic preoccupation with personal identity by gaining its trusting support from an unconditional source of love and grace that affirms us in our unique calling but also urges us beyond ourselves toward the other. Solitude is then linked to communion through Spirit baptism. *The goal is not self-reference but dedication to God and prophetic empathy for others in the Spirit.* Empathy implies a common sharing of life, a capacity to feel something of the other's agonies and ecstasies, and an ability to bear one another's burdens. Through Spirit baptism, we avoid both alienation (a quest for solitude at the loss of communion) and assimilation (a quest for communion at the sacrifice of solitude).

Consequently, if healing is relational, so is our spiritual sickness. It is indeed interesting, as Walter Brueggemann shows us, that the Genesis narrative has the garden serpent engage Adam and Eve in a conversation about God that is meant to call God's motives into question. This is the very first conversation "about" rather than with God, and it is not positive in thrust. In fact, it is meant to exclude God or, in effect, to take place "behind God's back." In the light of Brueggemann's insights we can note that there was indeed a fundamental break in trust between humanity and God even before humanity's act of disobedience in eating the forbidden fruit.[36] Genuine solitude was lost as was genuine communion, because both are only possible in the context of a trusting relationship with God. These were replaced by alienation and oppression.

Noteworthy is the fact that the trust also seems broken between Adam and Eve as the consequence of their eating the fruit in disobedience by seeking knowledge outside of the will and direction of God. Although God intended for them to bear the divine image *together* through procreation and responsible lordship over creation (Gen. 1:27–28), Adam now decides to go it alone. Rather than having all things subordinate to him and Eve as they partner together in bearing the divine image, Eve is subordinated to him as he rules alone. Eve's desire will be for him, but all that she will receive is his domination over her (3:16). Their partnership is broken and she is humiliated through subordination.

Since Adam no longer trusts the woman, he must keep her in her place. This is the curse that Eve must bear as the oppressed and Adam as oppressor

---

36. Walter Brueggemann, *Genesis*, ed. James Luther Mays (Interpretation; Atlanta: John Knox, 1982), 97.

must bear in alienation from her and from the will of the Creator. Relationships in general are now a minefield of possible dangers involving potential exploitation and manipulation. The communities, languages, and social structures into which we are born condition our relationships and distort them from the start. Since relation is ontological to us as humans, the image of God is marred as a shared reality and its corruption becomes a social dynamic. We are born into sin and its oppression not only toward God but toward each other. Liberation from this curse is the promise of Spirit baptism. Spirit baptism replaces oppression with a just and loving communion. Spirit baptism has the church as its necessary and natural locus as we head toward the transformation of creation in which righteousness will dwell.

In his perfect self-giving to God and others, Jesus models the divine image for us. Though Jesus was conditioned by his setting, he resisted its evil and oppressive impact in order to be a redemptive force within it. He did not let his cultural environment or the expectations of others ultimately define him; only the will of the Father was his daily sustenance. In the wilderness temptation, Jesus affirms again and again his identity as the Son of God over against definitions of his self fashioned by the interests of the enemy. Had he accepted Satan's offers, the definitions of his being and mission received in the process would have enslaved and destroyed him. In his secure sense of self in communion with the Father distinct from the exploitive expectations of others, Jesus was able to pour himself out redemptively for others and to then mediate the Spirit of God for the redemption of others. His role as the Spirit Baptizer arose through his unshakable devotion to the Father, who bestowed the Spirit through him.

In a Christian context, we thus talk of dying to self, the self in bondage to sin and death, in order to awaken to a new sense of self-in-relation-to-God through Jesus Christ. This new sense of self in Christ does not abolish our former humanity but rather transforms and fulfills it. The unique self that cries out from infancy for relation and freedom is fulfilled in an intimate relationship to God through Jesus Christ. Paul summarizes the matter when he states that he was crucified with Christ, "I no longer live, but Christ lives in me. The life I live in the body, I live by faith in the Son of God, who loved me and gave himself for me" (Gal. 2:20). Crucifixion with Christ does not abolish the human self who cries out for relationship and freedom; this self lives on, fulfilled through participation in Jesus' filial relationship to God in the power of the Spirit.

This preservation and fulfillment of the unique self is why Spirit baptism does not dissolve the diversity of tongues or the diversity of giftings possible among a community of unique individuals. The gifted community that arises from the outpouring of the Spirit from Christ is a mutual and interactive communion in which "every supporting ligament" contributes to the building up of the church in love "as each part does its work" (Eph. 4:16). Spirit baptism enhances these uniquely functioning members and preserves them as they are swept up into the communion of the divine life. People who come to Christ are not abolished in their uniqueness and turned into a community of uniform zombies. "If the whole body were an eye, where would the sense of hearing be?" (1 Cor. 12:17). The Spirit is the one in the many. This Spirit brings people into the common life of the divine communion in a way that does not abolish their otherness but rather enhances and fulfills it. They are stripped of their self-centered tendencies and liberated to be all that they were meant to be in the midst of their uniqueness.

Important to note at this juncture are the implications in the bodily resurrection of Jesus for a holistic understanding of Spirit baptism as involving not just the "inner self," but also the entire realm of our bodily or incarnate life, including the network of relationships in which we live and flourish as individuals. The Gnostic movement in the early centuries of the church's history isolated redemption to the realm of the mind or "spirit" apart from the realm of flesh. The Hellenistic detachment of mind from body has plagued Christian theology ever since. The work of the Holy Spirit was thereby severely restricted to the realm of spiritual enlightenment. The physical and social realms of existence were removed from the work of Christ and the Spirit, nullifying the significance of Jesus' physical sufferings and death, his bodily resurrection by the Spirit of God unto new life, and the outpouring of the Spirit through his glorified existence upon all flesh. Consequently, the relational self fell out of view when it came to our understandings of the Spirit's work. It was easy to see the work of the church as a mere addendum to the life of the Spirit.

But the Gnostic gospel is not the gospel of the New Testament. The biblical gospel proclaims a God who enters our sin and death, including the broken and divided relationships that cry out for grace. The Spirit provides the way toward redemption and new life through the bodily resurrection of Jesus from the dead. There is no possibility within this message of Jesus' resurrection that the grace of God can be limited to an individual self before God.

Such a limitation would affect a realm of existence that is unreal and abstract, removed from life as it is actually incarnated and lived in flesh.

As Michael Welker has shown insightfully, the "all flesh" that is to be baptized in the Spirit in Acts 2 is relationally specific: young and old, male and female, rich and poor.[37] Barriers are crossed and reconciliation occurs in the communion of God through Spirit baptism. Murray Dempster appropriately notes further that there are significant breakthroughs in graced relationships wherever people are filled with the Spirit in Acts.[38] The poor are granted access to resources and reconciliation occurs between Jews and Samaritans, Paul and the Christians he persecuted, Jews and Gentiles, followers of John the Baptist and followers of Jesus, and so on, through Spirit-baptized existence. Spirit-baptized grace touches and affects our relationships and, viewed from another direction, can come to us through relationships. The coming of the Spirit through the laying on of hands is a fitting symbol of the relational dynamic of Spirit baptism.

The Spirit is the "go-between God" and, as such, baptizes people into a realm of relationships shaped by divine love. Spirit baptism inspires in part ecclesial existence, that is, existence within a network of graced relationships, as a way of giving us a foretaste of the redemption to come and of allowing us to be living witnesses to this redemption presently in the world. Since persons are relational beings, John Zizioulas notes that "the Church is not simply an institution. She is a 'mode of existence,' *a way of being*."[39] The life of the church is essential to our new life in Christ, because the new life involves renewed relationships. Spirit baptism does not just empower us for witness as some kind of naked energy applied to life from the outside. We are empowered by being changed and shaped into a person able to form and cultivate graced relationships with others in the image of God. The power for witness is the power of love at work among us. There is indeed an integral connection between Spirit baptism and the proliferation of spiritual gifts in the church.

In the light of the deep yearning for graced communion in the world, can we justifiably make Jesus alone the Spirit Baptizer who imparts the Spirit of communion? Would not our relational anthropology make Jesus just one

---

37. Michael Welker, *God the Spirit* (Minneapolis: Fortress, 1994), 148.

38. Murray W. Dempster, "The Church's Moral Witness: A Study of Glossolalia in Luke's Theology of Acts," *Paraclete* 23 (1989): 1–7.

39. John D. Zizioulas, *Being as Communion* (Crestwood, NY: St. Vladimir's Seminary Press, 1997), 15.

symbol among many others in human history for how humanity finds redemptive communion in fulfillment of the basic yearning of their souls? Furthermore, would it not be more presumptuous and even oppressive to assume that the church is uniquely elect among all of the communities of faith and/or goodwill in the world to be the central sign and instrument of Spirit-baptized life and communion? Pentecost is pluralist in nature, expressed in multiple tongues. But does this ecclesiological pluralism hint at a more radical religious pluralism that makes Christ only one avenue of the Spirit among others? Does the witness of the Spirit to the kingdom of God so relativize the church that the church can claim no elect calling to be the chief witnesses to Christ in the world? We will tackle these questions in the light of Spirit baptism next.

THE SPIRIT-BAPTIZED CHURCH: THE PLURALIST CHALLENGE

Those who take Spirit baptism and the symbol of Pentecost seriously as the point of departure for ecclesiology will be drawn from the start to the challenge of pluralism to the legitimacy of the church and its proclamation, especially its assumed integral relationship to the historical Jesus and the kingdom of God he proclaimed. After all, as we have seen already, Spirit baptism and Pentecost are all about plurality and diversity as well as the fulfillment in history of the kingdom of God proclaimed by Jesus. Many have taken the pluralism involved in the redemption of the kingdom as the context in which to reject the unique role of the church as *the* central sign and instrument of the kingdom in the world. How can Spirit baptism help us to counter this rejection?

As we approach the challenge of pluralism to the church, we will find ourselves haunted by Alfred Loisy's well-known statement that Jesus proclaimed the kingdom of God but what we got was the church.[40] Though Loisy's remark was not meant as a negative judgment on the church, it has certainly been used as such. There is nothing new about the assumption that Jesus' proclamation of the kingdom of God calls into question the church's elect calling in Christ. For example, Herman Ridderbos has noted in his study of the relationship between the kingdom and the church that the eschatological view of Jesus' understanding of the kingdom of God precluded any

---

40. Alfred Loisy, *L'evangile et l'église* (Paris: A. Picard, 1902), 111; quoted in Hans Küng, *The Church* (New York: Sheed & Ward, 1967), 43.

anticipation in Jesus' preaching of the future rise of the church, despite the implications of Matthew 16:17–19.[41]

It was also assumed that the rise of the church and its proclamation of Jesus as the divine Savior came as a substitute action in response to the failure of Jesus' expectation that the kingdom of God would soon come to pass. Jesus the proclaimer became the proclaimed, because the kingdom of God proclaimed by Jesus failed to materialize. The kingdom was then spiritualized and a Christ cult developed to grant us access to it.[42] Those who do not accept the church's account of his resurrection from the dead and of his commissioning the church to proclaim him to the nations are left with nothing more than the noble example of Jesus' courage to dream an impossible dream.

Especially on a popular level, however, this alleged discrepancy between the kingdom proclaimed by Jesus and the church has taken on the aura of a conspiracy on behalf of the early church to exalt Christ to divine status in order to gain political power in the world. This critique has been expressed recently with a particularly strong anti-Catholic bias. For example, *The Da Vinci Code* by Dan Brown offers us at a crucial point in the story a brief "lesson" in the political implications of Christological dogma. The role of Christ as Redeemer and the entire drama of Holy Week are said to be "stolen from the pagans" or from pagan redemption cults. The confession of Christ's deity at Nicea is then identified as the result of a "relatively close vote" in the controversial effort by leaders of the Catholic Church to form a "new Vatican power base." "Until *that* moment in history," the lesson continues, "Jesus was viewed by his followers as a mortal prophet . . . a great and powerful man, but a man nonetheless. A mortal."[43]

Of course, this lack of awareness of affirmations of Christ's deity prior to the fourth century and an understanding of the Council of Nicea as a power grab by the "Vatican" reveals little knowledge of the actual development of Christological dogma. We cannot deny that the church of the Constantinian

---

41. Hermann Ridderbos, *The Gospel of the Kingdom* (Philadelphia: Presbyterian & Reformed, 1976), 337. Oscar Cullmann rightly notes that *ekklesia* was a Jewish concept that foreshadowed the church but would have had relevance also to Jesus' historical context. There is thus no firm reason to doubt the text's historicity. *Peter, Disciple-Apostle-Martyr: A Historical and Theological Study*, trans. Floyd V. Filson (Philadelphia: Westminster, 1962), 194–95.

42. Ridderbos, *The Gospel of the Kingdom*, 337.

43. Dan Brown, *The Da Vinci Code* (New York: Doubleday, 2003), 232–33.

era was granted privilege and sought power. But this development requires more careful and accurate description and analysis than what is reflected in Brown's conspiracy theory.

Of course, we are not to dodge the critical issues surrounding the early development of Christology, especially as it relates to the awareness of the church concerning the relationship of Jesus to God. It is beyond the scope of my purpose here to discuss the myriad of issues surrounding the diverse development of Christology in the New Testament canon and beyond. I will pause to note that I. Howard Marshall has rightly called into question as lacking in evidence well-defined "evolutionary" developments from Palestinian Jewish Christianity to early Diaspora Jewish Christianity to pre-Pauline Gentile Christianity to post-Pauline developments.[44]

Most problematic in my view is the general assumption within this chronological sequence of an evolution within the early history of the church from a purely human to a divine/human Christ. This development from a low to a high Christology has been called into question not only by Marshall but also by scholars such as Richard Bauckham and C. F. D. Moule, who find an implied identification of Jesus with God to be so pervasive throughout the New Testament that it must go back as a widespread implication to the earliest proclamation of the church, even in some sense to Jesus himself.[45] Moule concludes:

> . . . the evidence, as I read it, suggests that Jesus was, *from the beginning,* such a one as appropriately to be described in the ways in which, sooner or later, he did come to be described in the New Testament period—for instance, as "Lord" and, even, in some sense, as "God." Whether such terms came in fact to be used early or late, my contention is that they are not evolved *away*, so to speak, from the original, but represent the development of true insights into the original.[46]

Considering that the crucifixion seems to have been motivated by the charge of blasphemy, some sense of Jesus' identification of himself with the

---

44. I. Howard Marshall, "Palestinian and Hellenistic Christianity: Some Critical Comments," *New Testament Studies* 19 (1973): 271–87. See also idem, "The Development of Christology in the Early Church," *Tyndale Bulletin* 18 (1967): 77–93.

45. Richard Bauckham, *God Crucified: Monotheism and Christology in the New Testament* (Grand Rapids: Eerdmans, 1999); C. F. D. Moule, *The Origin of Christology* (Cambridge: Cambridge Univ. Press, 1977), 1–46.

46. Moule, *Origin of Christology*, 4.

presence and reign of God must have been essential to his deeds and proclamation (including the cleansing of the temple) and his impact on his audiences. In other words, I agree with the great Oscar Cullmann that the "high"
Christological claims of the New Testament that led to the church's confessional statements concerning Jesus go back primarily to the "originality" of
Jesus himself and are not the mere products of Hellenistic religious culture.[47]

Indeed, though Jesus attributes all of his works to God the Father or to
God's Spirit, he is not in his person totally transparent in any of the New Testament accounts of his proclamation and deeds. It would be more accurate
to say that he assumed an identity between his words and deeds and God's in
a way that was unprecedented. The authority that Christ claimed for himself
as well as the New Testament assumption concerning Christ as the Savior or
the one who mediates the divine Spirit imply an identification with God.

As we noted in our last chapter, the basic assumption throughout the
New Testament that Jesus was raised from the dead as the one who imparts
or baptizes in the Spirit points more than anything else to Jesus' identification
with God. As noted earlier, Augustine recognized this connection in the New
Testament: "How then can he who gives the Spirit not be God? Indeed, how
much must he who gives God be God! None of his disciples ever gave the
Holy Spirit; they prayed that he might come upon those on whom they laid
hands. . . . He received it as man, he poured it out as God" (De Trinitatis
15.46). Given Paul's own testimony of an essential unity of faith or of kerygma
concerning Christ in the church from the beginning (1 Cor. 15:3–4; Gal. 2:6–
10; Eph. 4:5), the burden of proof shifts to those who wish to dispute that
claim. Efforts to do this with Q or one of the "lost Gospels" remain in my
view speculative and unconvincing.[48]

---

47. Oscar Cullmann, *Christology of the New Testament* (London: SCM, 1959), 5;
see Moule, *Origin of Christology*, 8.

48. Concerning Q and alternative Christianities in the formative period of the
Christian church, see Burton Mack, *The Lost Gospel: The Book of Q and Christian Ori-
gins* (San Francisco: HarperSanFrancisco, 1993), where he claims that the "remarkable
thing about the people of Q is that they were not Christians. They did not think of
Jesus as a messiah or the Christ. They did not take his teachings as an indictment of
Judaism. They did not regard his death as a divine, tragic, or saving event. And they
did not imagine that he had been raised from the dead to rule over a transformed world.
Instead, they thought of him as a teacher whose teachings made it possible to live with
verve in troubled times" (p. 4). Luke Timothy Johnson rightly notes that in positing an
early Q community that knows nothing of Jesus' atoning death, resurrection, or unique

Of course, especially unconvincing is Brown's conspiracy theory. But we must be quick to add that not so easy to refute is the kind of culture criticism toward the church that it represents. Many find the church and its dogma of the exclusively divine Christ narrow-minded, outdated, and domineering in all areas of life. Efforts to wed the church to the power of the state historically and hierarchical and juridical notions of the church only feed this perception. The pluralist challenge that has come to dominate these critiques has struck a chord in the hearts of many because of the failures of the church to manifest the liberty and justice of the kingdom of God proclaimed by Jesus. One can understand why many would disassociate the kingdom Jesus proclaimed from the church and simplistically connect Christ's exclusive deity to political domination and then associate democratic freedom with religious pluralism.

The problem is that in disassociating the church (especially its proclamation and dogma) from the kingdom Jesus proclaimed, one needs to disassociate Jesus himself from the kingdom he proclaimed in ways that make him replaceable by other, equally significant figures. It is my contention that the New Testament conviction concerning the role of the risen Christ as the one who imparts the new life of the Spirit makes such a loose connection between the person of Jesus and the kingdom he proclaimed impossible.

A significant representative of this effort to disassociate the kingdom from the church is John Hick. Hick notes that a new global consciousness has given rise to a rich awareness of the vast array of faiths and cultures that flourish around the world, making it increasingly difficult to cling to outmoded ideas of Christ's uniqueness as divine and the church's unique calling to be the sign and instrument of God's kingdom in the world. This new global awareness has allegedly "undermined the plausibility of the traditional Christian sense of supe-

---

relationship to God assumes that Q was the only document that informed the community or communities that preserved it. This is a massive assumption for which Mack offers no historical support. See Luke Timothy Johnson, *The Real Jesus: The Misguided Quest for the Historical Jesus and the Truth of the Traditional Gospels* (San Francisco: HarperSanFrancisco, 1997), 50–54. Mack's assumption even runs contrary to Paul's indication that his gospel was "of first importance" from the beginning (1 Cor. 15:3–4). Concerning the lost Gnostic gospels as indications of early competing Christianities, see Elaine Pagels, *Beyond Belief: The Secret Gospel of Thomas* (New York: Random, 2003). She too assumes with no firm historical evidence that there was a Gnostic Christian community at the time the Gospel of John was written that could have provided the context for the writing and preservation of the Gospel of Thomas, a Gnostic text that is generally dated to have been written late in the second century or even later.

riority and has thereby set a question mark against its theological core in the dogma of Jesus of Nazareth as God incarnate."[49] Hick claims that the dominical authority behind Jesus' alleged proclamation of himself as the divine Son of God come to redeem the world "has dissolved under historical scrutiny."[50]

Hick rejects James Dunn's insight that later affirmations of Christ's deity are implicit in Jesus' assumed unique role in inaugurating the kingdom,[51] since this Christological assumption seems for Hick "a long way from Jesus thinking that he was God."[52] Hick accepts the theory that "as the second coming failed to occur, Jesus was gradually elevated within the Gentile church to a divine status, and 'Christ' came to be equivalent in meaning to the pre-trinitarian 'Son of God' and eventually to the trinitarian 'God the Son.'"[53] Jesus the prophet who proclaimed the coming kingdom of God became himself the object of proclamation. Jesus' proclamation of the kingdom was replaced eventually by a dogmatic complex of incarnation-Trinity-atonement that secured Jesus' enduring significance for the church as well as the church's superiority in the world as the chief mediator of grace.

Who, then, is Jesus for Hick? His own description is telling. Hick follows E. P. Sanders in viewing Jesus as an anointed prophet proclaiming the coming Day of the Lord.[54] In a way reminiscent to an extent of nineteenth-century liberal theories of Jesus, Hick also finds that Jesus was deeply aware of God's presence as Father. In fact, Jesus' "extremely intense God-consciousness . . . sustained firm prophetic assurance and charismatic power."[55] Hick does find some value in an incarnational Christology, however, since it implies God's involvement in life, especially the life of Jesus. Jesus so "reflects the divine love" that one could conclude that he "incarnated" God in some metaphorical sense.[56] Of course, Hick finds it reasonable to assume other such metaphorical "incarnations" as well among figures in the history of religions.

---

49. John Hick, *The Metaphor of God Incarnate: Christology in a Pluralistic Age* (Louisville: Westminster John Knox, 1993), 9.
50. Ibid., 29.
51. Ibid., 31; see James Dunn, *Christology in the Making* (Philadelphia: Westminster, 1980), 60.
52. Hick, *The Metaphor of God Incarnate*, 32.
53. Ibid., 4–5.
54. Ibid., 5. See E. P. Sanders, *Jesus and Judaism* (Philadelphia: Westminster, 1985), esp. 156, 319.
55. Hick, *The Metaphor of God Incarnate*, 18.
56. Ibid., 9–12.

It would be interesting to begin by asking Hick how within the limits of his narrow understanding of Jesus' role as end-time prophet he would distinguish between Jesus and John the Baptist. After all, John was also an end-time prophet with an intense awareness of God's presence. Although Jesus presumably accented the Fatherhood and love of God far more than John did, certainly the Gospels are unanimous (not to mention Acts) that the difference between them is more profound than a variation of theological accent.

Prevalent in the New Testament (especially in John's own testimony) is the assumption that Jesus stands apart from John in being the Spirit Baptizer, or the one who will inaugurate the kingdom of God and impart new life to those who believe. John bears witness to the one who will come to give life, but he is not that one. Simply saying that Jesus is an end-time prophet intensely aware of God truncates the New Testament portrayal of Jesus and neglects the role of the risen Christ as the Spirit Baptizer. This omission is serious given the all-pervasive witness of the New Testament to Jesus' significance as the one who imparts the Spirit of the age to come in order to be the Savior of the world.

Indeed, as I have argued earlier, receiving the Spirit of new life from Jesus and by faith in him is the one assumption that runs throughout the New Testament portrayal of the gospel. The central question implied by the gospel is, "How did you receive the Spirit?" (cf. Gal. 3:2), and the answer is faith in Christ and not obedience to law. Or the related question is, "What leads to new creation?" (cf. 6:15). The eclipse of biblical pneumatology and the detachment of mind from matter in the West have shifted the question to what models or imitates for us the quality of human consciousness of God. This is Hick's question, but it is not the central question of the gospel. The fundamental issue in the gospel is redemptive, namely, how one attains to life in the Spirit. The answer nearly universally found in the New Testament is that Jesus is the Spirit Baptizer, the one through whom the Spirit is imparted.

In this light, it seems odd that Hick would use a modern description of Jesus' significance as centered on his "consciousness" of God when historically reconstructing Jesus' role as prophet of the kingdom of God, since such speculation is far more Greek than Jewish and is also at a considerable distance from the explicit concern of the New Testament. More credible even as a historical thesis is that Jesus uniquely connected himself to the Spirit of God associated within Jewish apocalypticism to end-time salvation (e.g., Joel 2:28). Jesus did not merely reflect or reveal intense God-consciousness; rather his originality was in his assumption that he imparted it along with the healing of life in the body by mediating the healing power of the Spirit of God to others: "If I drive out demons by the Spirit of God, the kingdom of God has come upon you" (Matt. 12:28).

Hick's focus on Jesus' religious consciousness is even more historically disconnected from the role of Jesus as the Jewish prophet than the Nicene affirmation of him as *homoousios* with the Father, which Hick finds to be a far cry from Jesus' actual self-understanding. That Jesus was aware of God, intensely or not, is not a unique prophetic assumption and is hardly original to any religious figure worthy of note. That Jesus can mediate the Spirit on behalf of God would have been far more striking and would also explain theologically for Hick and others why the church came to identify Jesus with God. The root of Nicea is Pentecost. Without Pentecost, Nicea is inexplicable, except as a consequence of Hellenistic religion or, even worse, a political power grab.

We also have good reason to question Hick's equally problematic treatment of Jesus' post-resurrection appearances. The affirmation of Jesus as the Spirit Baptizer requires his resurrection and glorification, since it is from Jesus' glorified humanity that he imparts the Spirit to inaugurate the kingdom as the new creation and final dwelling place of God. It is also the resurrection that essentially connects Jesus the Spirit Baptizer to the kingdom he proclaimed in a way that makes him irreplaceable and unique, something that Hick needs to deny to remain a religious pluralist. Hick thus speculates that Jesus' post-resurrection appearances were the result of mere mental states among those who claimed to have witnessed them, as "waking versions" of something analogous to near-death experiences.[57]

That such a phenomenon could be experienced by a number of people at various times and places to the point that it would have launched the Christian movement and thrown the New Testament documents into being is too fantastic in my view to take seriously and requires more faith than the belief in a bodily resurrection from the dead assumed by the apostles (e.g., Rom. 8:11). It is true, as Hick maintains, that martyrs in ancient Judaism could be said to have had an atoning impact on others, but such a martyr hardly qualified as the Messiah in Jewish thinking![58]

---

57. Ibid., 24.
58. Ibid., 23.

Similarly, Hick's point that the death of Jesus without a literal resurrection would not have cast his followers into despair or doomed the early Christian movement must also be questioned in the same light. True, John the Baptist's death did not mean the end of his movement (at least not in the short term).[59] But then again, there are no clear implications of messianic claims by John or later by any of his followers. It is the claim of Jesus' early followers that Jesus the crucified one is the Messiah expected by Israel that is truly remarkable and, in my view, unintelligible against the background of Jewish tradition without something unexpected to account for it, such as the resurrection, a point that Hick does not take seriously enough.

If Hick wants to interpret Jesus' post-resurrection appearances as a mental experience, he is free to do this. But in all honesty it must be conceded that such a view would have been the furthest thing from Paul's own theological assumption concerning the matter (or anyone else among the earliest followers of Jesus). Paul may have seen the risen Christ in a vision, but he was clear that the resurrection of Jesus involved Jesus' mortal body (Rom. 8:11). True, as Hick maintains, the earliest strata of the New Testament does not make reference to an empty tomb or to Jesus' visible/tangible resurrected body.[60] Paul even contrasts the "spiritual" body of the resurrection and the fleshly body of this life (1 Cor. 15:44). But the leap from these facts to the reduction of Jesus' post-resurrection appearances to a corporately-experienced mental state is great indeed.

Such a leap even runs contrary to all indications concerning early Christian belief about the nature of the resurrected body. Though Paul believed that the spiritual body of the resurrection transcends the earthly body (so that flesh and blood cannot account for the new birth or inherit it), it still involved the earthly body as its transformation (Rom. 8:11; 1 Cor. 15:51–54). Paul as an apocalyptic Jew saw Jesus' resurrection as involving a transformation of his mortal body. Paul saw the body as transformed to a higher, eschatological mode of "spiritual" existence.

Hick finds the development from Jesus as the prophet of the coming kingdom to Jesus as the incarnation of the divine Logos to be too great to digest because he has rejected the link between these mediated by the New Testament witness itself, namely, Jesus as raised from the dead by the Father

---

59. Ibid., 26.
60. Ibid., 23–24.

through the Spirit in order that, as the Lord of life and the glorified man, he would impart the divine Spirit for the renewal of creation. The basic problem is that Hick rejects the role of Jesus as the Spirit Baptizer. As we saw in our last chapter, Jesus' role as the Spirit Baptizer mediates between Jesus' role as the prophet of the kingdom of God and the later life and dogma of the church, especially the incarnation-Trinity-atonement complex that Hick regards as existing at a far cry from Jesus' kingdom consciousness. Such consciousness exists at a far cry from the later dogma of his identification with God for Hick only because the link between these in Jesus' role as the one raised from the dead to be the Spirit Baptizer has been neglected or eliminated.

Spirit baptism does not just help us to critique Hick's understanding of the tension between Jesus as the prophet of the kingdom of God and the rise of the church and its kerygma of Jesus as the divine Savior. It also gives us the resources for dealing with the connection that Hick assumes between this kerygma and the church's hierarchical authority and grab for power politically. Spirit baptism as described in the New Testament cannot be used to justify a reigning political or cultural ideology. The tongues of Pentecost (Acts 2) imply that the church constituted by the baptism in the Spirit is a church that involves a vast diversity of voices globally in the discernment of the truth of Christ. Pentecost centers on the risen Christ as the Imparter of new life, but it also inspires many tongues each from its own cultural background to convey the significance of Jesus for human salvation.

It is Christ the transcendent and living Person, not an ideology, that is the center of the multilingual witness of Pentecost. No single tongue can adequately bear witness to this center or have any absolute claim on its final meaning. The Spirit is the person in many persons or the one that draws the creation in all of its diversity and relationality to the renewal of life. Spirit baptism thus "incarnates" the presence of Christ in a body of believers that involves many different cultures and faith expressions. The implication of Pentecost is pluralistic and interactive, not hierarchical and domineering.

Luke even implies that global cultures (including religions) are not just accidents of history or tricks of Satan but are actually guided by divine providence as a legitimate groping after God and a real response to the divine presence in the world through the Spirit of God, for in God we live and move and have our very being (Acts 17:28). This living and moving and having being among humanity historically surely refers back to the migrations of peoples throughout the world among many diverse languages and cultures referred to in Luke's rendition of Paul's message in the previous two verses (17:26–27). In other words, Luke is assuming that one's culture is connected to one's very mode of being in the world, and he locates that mode of being in God as Creator and in the divine providence that graciously guides that mode of existence.

At Pentecost, the legitimate reaching for God implied in various cultures and religious expressions finds fulfillment in the grace of God revealed in the crucified and risen Christ as the one who imparts the Spirit in the latter days. Their differences and past histories are not dissolved but affirmed and granted a new loyalty and a new direction. In the process all idols are forsaken and the cultures are pruned. But the critical pruning is demanded of the church as well. Though the church is the central locus of the kingdom of God in the world, the church is also a loving fellow traveler with the world's religions while pointing them to the superiority of Christ. Spirit baptism can be developed so as to respond to Hick's critique of ecclesiastical superiority in the world but in a way that rejects his reduction of Jesus to simply one symbol of the sacred among others.

The issue of the superiority of the church, however, must still be taken to heart. There are more than enough examples of the church's abuse of power or cultural insensitivity over the centuries to fuel Hick's concerns. In this context, Spirit baptism must not be viewed triumphalistically without any sensitivity to issues of political power and influence. Spirit baptism must be seen as the impartation of the Spirit of the crucified Christ who has risen to grant life and liberty, especially in solidarity with those who suffer. As Moltmann wrote, "The transfiguration of Christ in the Spirit of glory must not be allowed to cast so dazzling a light that our eyes are blinded to his death in abandonment by God."[61]

Zinzendorf thus wrote that Jesus bestowed the Spirit from his wounds.[62] What a fitting image of the connection between the kingdom and Spirit of Christ and the self-giving of Christ in devotion to the Father and to the world on the cross. Indeed, it is "by the eternal Spirit" that Christ offered himself on the cross (see Heb. 9:14). The Spirit poured out from the risen and glorified

---

61. Moltmann, *The Church in the Power of the Spirit*, 37.

62. Nicholas Ludwig Count von Zinzendorf, *Ein und zwanzig Discurse über die Augsburgische Konfession, 1748, Der achte Discurs, Haupschriften*, Bd. VI (Hildesheim, 1963), 159ff, note esp. 160, 161, 163, 165, 166. Note my discussion of this in *Spirituality and Social Liberation: The Message of the Blumhardts in the Light of Wuerttemberg Pietism* (Metuchen, NJ: Scarecrow, 1993), 16.

Christ maintained the connection to the significance of the crucified Christ as well as to the self-sacrificial love at work there. The Spirit-baptized church lays claim to no inherent privilege except the privilege to bear witness to another, namely, the crucified and risen Christ and to live the crucified life in solidarity with the suffering and oppressed of the world.

I realize that this posture will not satisfy everyone offended by the exclusivist claims of salvation by Christ alone as the Spirit Baptizer. But we must keep in mind that no religious posture, not even John Hick's pluralist option, is totally immune from the charge of unjustified privilege. Atheists who find all talk of religious or transcendent sources of love to be nonsensical and oppressive will charge the religious pluralist with implying that the religious person is wiser or more consciously in touch with the essence of love than those who reject any notion of God. Some would be quick to maintain that what retards culture and politics is not just exclusivist claims concerning Christ but religion in general—any religion or notion of transcendence. The issue of superiority cannot be avoided for the person of faith, any religious faith, whether it focuses on "God" or the transcendent "reality." Hick must face it too with regard to his faith in a way analogous to the issue he raises for Christians. The person of faith in God can only be careful to interpret that faith in a way that draws attention to grace and not privilege.

Of course, whether or not Christian dogma draws the boundaries too narrowly must still be faced. Drawing the boundaries of the Spirit Baptizer to Christ alone is exclusivistic Christologically, but I believe with Jan Lochman that we deal here with an exclusivism *of Christ* "and not with the self-serving principle of sectarianism." It is an exclusivism of the one who is uniquely *inclusive* on the ecclesiological level, an "unconditional solidarity with others beyond all human gulfs and barriers."[63] The result will be that a clarity concerning the boundaries around Christ will produce a certain lack of clarity concerning the boundaries of the church. This is as far as we can go Christologically in response to Hick without stepping outside the proclamation of the gospel. There is simply no way of eliminating the risen Christ as *the* Spirit Baptizer from the gospel without affirming another gospel.

The Spirit's unique attachment to the crucified and risen Christ as the Spirit Baptizer and inaugurator of the kingdom of God means that the church

---

63. Jan M. Lochman, "Theology and Cultural Contexts," *Reflections* 2 (Spring 1999): 30.

is the church by the grace of God and must live in a way that lifts up Christ and not itself as the one who inaugurates and perfects the kingdom of God in the world. He is the author and perfecter of the faith because he conquered death with an indestructible life (Heb. 2:14–15; 7:16; 12:2). An accent on grace rather than privilege means that the church dare not simply identify itself with the kingdom of God in the world. The Spirit-baptized church as the sign of grace in the midst of the gracelessness in the world lives from the kingdom as its chief living witness.

Our defense of the special election of the church as the body of Christ to be the Spirit-baptized community cannot be taken to mean that we can posit an unqualified identification between the church and Christ, the Spirit, or the kingdom of God. The church is the natural result of the outpouring of the Spirit and the breaking in of the kingdom of God, but the church cannot simply be identified with the kingdom. Only *Christ's* witness is identical without qualification with the kingdom of God. Only in him is the Spirit given without measure. As Donald Baillie in his provocative attempt at a modern restatement of Christ's deity points out, only in Christ are the work of God and the work of humanity one work without discrepancy or paradox.[64]

Such is not the relationship between Christ and the church. In the communion of the church with Christ, there exists a critical dialectic of a "yes" and a "no" between them. It is in this dialectic that the church is the sign and instrument of renewal that is itself constantly under renewal. As Lochman notes, the Spirit is the "great dialectician" in relation to the church. In the following section, I would like to develop this theme more thoroughly.[65]

THE SPIRIT-BAPTIZED CHURCH: TOWARD A CRITICAL DIALECTIC

There are two extremes to avoid when comparing Christ or the kingdom and the church. The first extreme is a separation or a dualism. As we noted above,

---

64. Donald Baillie, *God Was in Christ* (New York: Charles Scribner's & Sons, 1948), 117–18; John Hick (*The Metaphor of God Incarnate*, 106–8) finds this formulation helpful, because it makes Christ's identification with God functional and not metaphysical. In my view, a functional identification with God implies a "metaphysical" unity, since to assume an unqualified identity without paradox or dialectic between God's words and actions and those of a mere human being is idolatrous.

65. Jan M. Lochman, "Kirche," in *Dogmatik im Dialog*, ed. F. Buri, H. Ott, and J. M. Lochman (Gütersloh: Gütersloher Verlagshaus Gerd Mohn, 1973), 1:135.

one cannot separate Christ from his body. Neither can one view the kingdom of God and the church as two entirely separate realms. The second, however, is an identification between Christ or his kingdom and the church. This identification results in an over-realized eschatology and the loss of a proper emphasis on the church under renewal as a humble servant to Christ. I will show my Barthian colors here and posit between these two extremes a dialectic in the role of the church as *witness or sign*, in which the church holds its treasure as vessels of clay.

In weakness, the church bears a broken or fallen witness in the Spirit. Spirit baptism is thus an indwelling and empowering of the Spirit that is not an unqualified possession of the church but possesses the church in constant waves of renewal. The church in communion with Christ faces a divine "no" with regard to its faithfulness, but also an all-embracing "yes" as sustained by the grace of God and the presence of the Spirit in all grace. As we will see, this dialectic is not static but dynamic and ever reaching more profoundly for eschatological fulfillment as we move closer from seeing through a glass dimly to seeing "face to face."

But first, let us unpack this dialectic by grounding it in the theological priority of Christ, the Spirit, and the kingdom to the church. When we use the phrase the "Spirit-baptized church," we are saying in effect that Spirit baptism is not something administered by the church but rather is itself that which administers the church. Spirit baptism is thus too limited if *merely* discussed as the spiritual side of water baptism or as individual regeneration or even as exclusively a personal empowerment for charismatic witness. I will not deny the significance of the church in its proclamation, its sacraments, and its empowered witness in occasioning the realization of Spirit baptism in people's lives, but Spirit baptism is what brought the church into being in the first place.

Hence, Spirit baptism as mediated through the risen Christ and fulfilled at his return on the "Day of the Lord" (Acts 2:17–21) cannot be reduced to what is theologically implied in individual regeneration, water baptism, or personal empowerment. Spirit baptism constitutes the church as *the church*, defining the very core of the church's essence but also transcending the church as it reaches for new creation. In being the church as the dwelling place of the Spirit/kingdom of Christ, the church is the consecrated and empowered witness to Christ and his kingdom in the world. It is at the vanguard of the transformation of creation into the dwelling place of God.

The Spirit and kingdom of God are thus prior to the church and determine its eschatological journey as a pilgrim people. As Lorelei Fuchs notes, "The Spirit forms the church as the continuing presence of Christ in the world, transforming it into the proleptic manifestation of God's eschatological reign."[66] More specifically, Christ's instituting the church as the Spirit Baptizer points to the divine commitment to Christ as the center of the church's charismatic, kerygmatic, and sacramental life as the chief means of renewal in the world. The pneumatological constitution of the church through Spirit baptism points to the divine presence in instituting the church and to the divine freedom and expansiveness that cause the church to reach for and signify the eschatological and global transformation of all things into the very dwelling place of God. On the way toward this fulfillment, the church signifies grace in the midst of an all-too graceless world.

The term "sign" is carefully chosen here as analogous to "witness." Both terms imply that the Spirit-baptized church participates in the inauguration and fulfillment of the kingdom of God in the world and can by grace be a living witness to it, embodying it and pointing to it. Spirit baptism essentially binds the church to Jesus and the kingdom he proclaimed. On the one hand, there can be no denial or displacement of the church as that body uniquely called to be the sign and instrument of the kingdom of God in the world. The dogma of the church cannot be rejected without rejecting essential elements of the truth of Christ. On the other hand, the church as sign and instrument of the kingdom of God in the world implies an eschatological reservation with regard to any kind of unqualified identification between the kingdom proclaimed by Christ and the church. The church proclaims a true word but not an exhaustive or final word.

There is no critical dialectic between Jesus and the Spirit. He is the king and the Spirit the kingdom. But, as noted above, there is such a dialectic between the Spirit/kingdom and the church. Thus, the church is not the final word but a penultimate witness to the word of the kingdom who is Christ. Hence, without denying the integral relationship of the kingdom and the church, we must add that there can be no unqualified identification of the church with the kingdom or Spirit of Christ. As Hans Küng has noted, "a church that identifies itself with the Spirit has no need to listen, to believe, to obey."[67] The church would only

---

66. Fuchs, "The Holy Spirit," 164–65.
67. Küng, *The Church*, 175.

have to listen to itself. Christ would then be viewed, according to Küng, as abdicating in favor of a church that has taken his place. Such a church, "for all its pose of humility is trying to be self-reliant, for all its modesty is trying to be autonomous. A knowing church has replaced a believing church, a possessing church has replaced a needy church, total authority has replaced obedience."[68] It is my view that such an identification between Christ and the church eliminates the needed critical relationship between the kingdom and the church, thus removing the ongoing need for the church to seek renewal or reformation and granting the church absolute and unquestioned authority.

Helpful also is Miroslav Volf's rejection of transferring the subjectivity of Christ to the church, forming a collective subject, a "total Christ." Volf speaks instead of a "juxtaposition" between Christ and the church that "precisely as such is constitutive of their unity." Volf draws from ecumenist Lukas Vischer to note that the biblical concept of unity is not an unqualified identity but rather a communion of one with the "other" that does not dissolve the difference between them. Jesus said of our unity with him that we will be in him as he is in us (John 14:20). Our oneness with Christ is through mutual indwelling and not sameness of identity.[69]

This is not meant to deny that Christ forms a real solidarity with his people (asking Paul "Why do you persecute *me?*" Acts 9:4). But he also asks the church not to lock him out but to invite him in to the table of fellowship (Rev. 3:20). Spirit baptism as a divine infilling implies a solidarity of love and communion, of a mutual indwelling that requires our faithful participation. Such must never be taken for granted but cultivated and lived. Such implies an eschatological reality of a "now" and a "not yet," for now we see through a glass darkly, then "face to face" (1 Cor. 13:12). Our oneness with Christ through Spirit baptism is dynamic and not static. It implies a dialectic of grace and fallenness, which is why we must constantly be renewed in it.

The concept of Spirit baptism can help us to negotiate this tension between a separation and an identification in the relationship of the kingdom to the church as well. Spirit baptism is a participatory metaphor that is dynamic, interactive, and eschatological, calling forth understandings of the church that avoid both its separation from, and unqualified identification with, the kingdom of Christ. A Christological determination of the church

---

68. Ibid., 239.
69. Volf, *After Our Likeness*, 141–44, 158.

alone tends toward a static understanding of the relationship of the kingdom to the church that results in either an intellectualistic rejection of a positive relationship or a rigidly dogmatic affirmation of an identification between them. A pneumatological construal of the relationship between the kingdom and the church grants us the dynamism and eschatological dialectics needed to negotiate the relationship more biblically.

However, a pneumatological constitution of the church alone runs the danger of alienating the church from the self-disclosure of God in Jesus of Nazareth, causing the church to lose its concrete identity and sense of direction. The gospel of Jesus Christ is the answer to such enthusiasm by anchoring the pneumatological constitution in the objective self-disclosure of God in Jesus. The eschatological Spirit at the essence of the kingdom then implies both the connection of the church with Christ as his body and the critical reservation needed to prevent the church's idolatrous identification with this divine self-giving in Christ so that the church can function as its effective sign and instrument in living witness. The church as a "pilgrim people" is thus "on the way" as a dynamic sign and instrument of renewal that is itself being renewed. As Ralph Del Colle wrote of the church existing in the outpouring of the Spirit, "the graces, energies, gifts, and powers of the Holy Spirit help constitute the church, beckoning it toward the Kingdom, establishing its *koinonia* or communion, and enabling its life and witness until fulfillment."[70]

These signs of grace in proclamation, sacrament, and the *charismata* have their origins and ongoing power from the God who baptizes in the Spirit or who gives of the triune life in order to inhabit the creation and to draw it into divine *koinonia*. This understanding of the church is regnocentric. Representative are the words of Jürgen Moltmann: "It is not the church that has a mission of salvation to fulfill to the world. It is the mission of the Son and the Spirit through the Father that includes the church, creating a church as it goes on its way."[71] Note as well Harvey Cox's point about the priority of the kingdom of God to the church:

A doctrine of the church is a secondary and derivative aspect of theology which comes after a discussion of God's action in calling man to cooperation in the bringing of the Kingdom. It comes after, not before, a clar-

---

70. Del Colle, "The Outpouring of the Holy Spirit," 250.
71. Moltmann, *The Church in the Power of the Spirit*, 64.

ification of the idea of the Kingdom and the appropriate responses to the Kingdom in a particular era.[72]

It is not the church that administers the Spirit but the Spirit in Spirit baptism from the Father through the Son that administers the church.

The priority of the kingdom of God can have a powerful role to play in a Pentecostal theology of the outpouring of the Spirit, as was shown in the message of the Blumhardts, father (Johann) and son (Christoph), nineteenth-century German Pietists. The Blumhardts developed a divine healing ministry against the background of a fervent desire for a latter-day outpouring of the Holy Spirit and a vision of global transformation. They placed their hopes fundamentally on the kingdom of God and looked to the church as its servant. This priority granted to the kingdom caused them to deal ambivalently with the church. The younger Blumhardt even "turned to the world" in his effort to find faithful servants of the Kingdom outside of the church.[73]

As became clear toward the end of his life, Christoph was against the church in order to be for it. He urged the church to "walk alongside the Kingdom of God, which is the great movement of God's reign in the world."[74] However, the kingdom is not to be wholly separate from the realm of the natural.[75] In 1910 Christoph wrote to Leonard Ragaz that "a movement of the Spirit of Christ proceeds through the times," presenting us with a kernel of truth that will push us ahead into that which is new.[76] In another context he wrote that the future is realized in the present at a point of "harmony" of the latter with the former.[77] Such perspectives are not far removed from the *kairos* event depicted in Paul Tillich's classic *The Socialist Decision*, a work he wrote under Blumhardt's influence.[78]

---

72. Harvey Cox, *The Secular City* (New York: Collier, repr. 1990), 108.

73. Note my book *Spirituality and Social Liberation*.

74. Christoph Blumhardt, *Ansprachen, Predigten, Reden, Briefe: 1865–1917*, ed. J. Harder, (Neukirchen-Nyun: Neukirchen Verlag, 1978), 3:70.

75. Ibid., 124.

76. Ibid., 61.

77. Ibid., 91.

78. Paul Tillich, *The Socialist Decision*, trans. F. Sherman (New York: Harper & Row, 1977). See Tillich's remarks in this regard: *A History of Christian Thought from Its Judaic and Hellenistic Origins to Existentialism*, ed. C. E. Braaten (New York: Harper & Row, 1967), 531–33.

Blumhardt's world piety did exercise a profound influence on Tillich and a generation of theologians "between the Wars." Tillich wrote that Blumhardt opened up early on for him a new vision of the relationship of the church to society "in an unheard of way" that focused on the world and not the church.[79] Eberhard Bethge noted that Blumhardt's world piety exercised a seminal influence on the thinking of Dietrich Bonhoeffer.[80] Harvey Cox wrote his *Secular City* in response to the world piety of Christoph Blumhardt and his followers, Herman Kutter and Leonard Ragaz.[81] Jürgen Moltmann worked under the same influence, noting that "Christoph Blumhardt, Kutter and Ragaz . . . took the practical step away from religion to the Kingdom of God, away from the church to the world, away from the concern for the individual to hope for the world."[82]

Most profound was the influence of Christoph Blumhardt on the theology of Karl Barth. Barth insightfully described Christoph's understanding of the dialectic of the kingdom as transcendent and free but also as a present reality in the context of human witness:

> The unique element, and I say it quite deliberately, the prophetic, in Blumhardt's message and mission consists in the way in which the hurrying and the waiting, the worldly and the divine, the present and the coming, again and again met, were united, supplemented one another, sought and found one another.[83]

For Barth, Blumhardt's critical dialectic inherent in the church's witness was dynamic and eschatological, felt and transcendent, present and yet future. The church lives from the kingdom in its inner life, continually "meeting" it as well in moments of Spirit filling and renewal. The Spirit abides in the church as its living "soul" (Augustine) but also sovereignly addresses and comes to the church in fresh power and winds of renewal.

The church is the central locus for the life of the Spirit or the life of the kingdom. As the great dialectician, however, the Spirit's presence in and

---

79. Tillich, *A History of Christian Thought*, 532.

80. See V. Eller, *Thy Kingdom Come: A Blumhardt Reader* (Grand Rapids: Eerdmans, 1980), xv.

81. Harvey Cox, *Religion in the Secular City* (New York: Simon & Schuster, 1984), 22.

82. Moltmann, *The Church in the Power of the Spirit*, 287.

83. Karl Barth, "Past and Future: Friedrich Naumann and Christoph Blumhardt," in *The Beginnings of Dialectic Theology*, ed. J. A. Robinson, trans. K. R. Crim (Richmond, VA: John Knox, 1968), 1:45.

through the church causes us to speak of the church of Jesus, of the Spirit, or of the kingdom with a certain reserve or "unrest."[84] As Küng notes similarly, "The reign of God cannot be identified with the people of God, the church, anymore than the saving act of God can be identified with man's reception of salvation."[85] Küng points out that "the New Testament message gives no basis at all for ideas about the development of the church which play down or even domesticate the idea of the reign of Christ."[86] Küng elaborates that "man's part is the way of readiness and openness, obedience and watchfulness, faith and repentance."[87]

Küng thus implies that the continuity between the kingdom and the church is achieved from the divine side as a gift of grace, God's very presence in Christ through the Spirit. I would say that as a "Spirit baptism," the divine presence is a divine act or event that has happened but is also ongoing and yet to be fulfilled. It is thus something that involves but also that transcends the church. Any current continuity with the kingdom from our side is striven for but never quite achieved through repentance, witness, and obedience.

An important component of understanding the role of the Spirit as the dialectician of the church is to view the church as both a pneumatological/eschatological reality and a fallen/historical reality. One of the major problems facing ecclesiological reflection since the dawn of critical historical consciousness in the era of the Enlightenment has been the dialectic of spirituality and historicity in judging the nature of the church. Since the Enlightenment, the church has been forced to consider the problems of its own historicity with unprecedented realism and intensity. The question that was implied in such critical self-reflection is how the church can be both a historical reality, with all of the ambiguities involved in such finitude, and yet a fellowship of the Spirit of God for the mission and the kingdom of God in the world. As Peter Hodgson and Robert C. Williams have pointed out, "The question is how the church can be both a divine gift and a human institution, both a spiritual and a historical reality, without confusing the dimensions of its being and without separating them."[88]

---

84. Moltmann, *The Church in the Power of the Spirit*, 3.
85. Küng, *The Church*, 74.
86. Ibid., 239.
87. Ibid.
88. Peter C. Hodgson and Robert C. Williams, "The Church," in *Christian Theology*, ed. P. C. Hodgson and R. H. King (Minneapolis: Fortress, 1982), 260ff.

The Reformation wrestled already with this problem and attempted to solve it through a distinction between the *ecclesia visibilis* (visible church) and the *ecclesia invisibilis* (invisible church). The visible church was subject to all of the limitations of the finite world, implying the ancient notion of the church as a *corpus per mixtum*. The real church determined through divine election and responsive to the Word of God was not visible because it was not simply identifiable with the visible, institutional church. This solution, however, was in danger of supporting a Platonic notion of the church usable as an escape from the scandal of the institutional church's divisions or other failures.

Pentecostals need to think about the general issue of the eschatological and historical realities of the Church's existence, since restorationism and primitivism make them vulnerable to an idealistic and implicitly timeless understanding of the ideal church empowered by the Spirit. Pentecostals tend to view themselves as striving toward the restoration of this ideal church of Pentecost. Their description of this ideal implies at times a reality removed from the fallenness and vicissitudes of historical existence. The Spirit comes in revival to lift us from the realm of human frailty and sin and to grant us something of the triumphant ideal once more.

A more realistic understanding of the primitive churches in all of their tensions and limitations might help Pentecostals view the living witness of the Church less triumphalistically. It might help them to recognize the voice of the Spirit more profoundly within the history of the church's witness and, today, among many different Christian communions. The visible realization of the unity of the church in history will not be viewed as a gift that merely comes "suddenly from heaven" but rather through a dialectical historical process involving humble and open ecumenical exchanges and genuine repentance and ability to change even the very structures of the church.

In general, I regard it important to avoid any implication of a dualism as well as a simple identification of the kingdom of God and the church in its visible, historical form. My use of the term *critical dialectic* reaches for an alternative between these two errors. Paul Tillich preferred the term *paradox*, informed no doubt by his Lutheran roots in the *simul justus et peccator* (simultaneously just and sinner). For example, Tillich noted that the paradoxical and ambiguous realization of the church's marks (unity, holiness, catholicity, apostolicity) signifies the church's historicity, subject to all of the finite limitations of any social institution. Tillich locates the relationship of eschatology and history in the paradox of human essence and existence, in which we *are* what we are as the church by God's grace *in spite of* what we are in the ambiguities and contradictions of actual existence. The essence of the church for Tillich does not leave us unchallenged in our existence but is our inner *telos*, effective in us in a struggle against our ambiguities.[89]

In another effort to avoid this dualism, Reformed theologian Jan Lochman noted that the notion of the *ecclesia invisibilis* (invisible church) can lead easily to an avoidance of the historical, institutional church in favor of a Platonic idea. He proposes that the *ecclesia invisibilis* be the faith, hope, and love of the community of the faithful that is inspired continuously by the Spirit of God right in the midst of ambiguous and historically conditioned visible churches. As noted above, Lochman referred to the Spirit as the "*great ecclesiological dialectician*," with the result that "the struggle for the true church takes place in its earthly, concrete congregation—but in constant protest of its actualized form in the direction of hope and change."[90]

The critical dialectic between the church and the kingdom helps us to avoid harmful dangers theologically, both to the left and to the right. But to avoid a merely abstract discussion of the church in dialectical relationship to the kingdom, it will be helpful to pause so as to look at some of the models of the church portrayed in the New Testament.

THE SPIRIT-BAPTIZED CHURCH: BIBLICAL MODELS

The fact is that there is no systematic statement about the church in the New Testament. The Spirit-baptized church has its core in a mystery, namely, the presence of the Spirit. As Christ is sent, so is the church. Hence, Spirit baptism is at the core of the church's mystery as the church of Christ. Any rational description of the church is bound to function as a weak and inadequate description of its soul and destiny. For that reason, the New Testament offers us models that symbolize powerfully what the church is in a way that defies any final description. We will explore here the church as the people of God, the body of Christ, and the temple of the Spirit.[91]

---

89. Paul Tillich, *Systematic Theology* (Chicago: Univ. of Chicago Press, 1963), 3:107–10, 138–40, 149–61, 162–82.

90. Lochman, "Kirche," 1:135.

91. I am following the choice of metaphors in the WCC Faith and Order Paper, *The Nature and Purpose of the Church*, #17–#25, 12–15.

People of God

Perhaps the classic biblical description of the church is the people of God. The church is the gathering and communion of God's people. The term *ekklesia* in the New Testament refers to the gathering together of the assembly of Christians by God. The fact that the church is the *ekklesia* of God (e.g., Acts 20:28; cf. Ps. 74:2) distinguishes this assembly from secular forms of *ekklesia*. As an *ekklesia*, the people of God form a visible community tied through Jesus to elect Israel.[92] The church is elect of the Father and has unity in the Father as well (Eph. 3:14–15; 1 Peter 1:2).

The church recognizes its connection with the elect people of God in the Old Testament, since there is only one olive tree created by God to be God's people (Rom. 11). Christ fulfills Israel's election and the mystery of God's plan for his people, causing the church to find its own election "in him" (Eph. 1:4). As the one who imparts new life, Christ exceeds elect Israel in fulfilling it. More specifically as this relates to Spirit baptism, Israel pointed in its elect witness to the coming of the renewal of life through the end-time Spirit, but it could not identify with it or impart it. As the ideal servant, Christ ideally embodied the kingdom of God. There was no critical dialectic or discrepancy between the kingdom of God or God's redemptive presence in the world and Jesus' person, deeds, and proclamation. Jesus as identifiable with God was qualified to bestow the Spirit hoped for by Israel. The Spirit Baptizer is thus superior to Israel in fulfilling its witness but also to the church as well, except the church lives from the fulfillment of the promise of the coming Spirit and points in its witness backward and forward to Christ, not just forward as did ancient Israel. The church can now live from Christ's spiritual fullness.

The difference between Israel and the church is thus found in Spirit baptism. Israel comes before the redemption of Christ and its inauguration/realization through Spirit baptism and prefigures this in its living witness as a renewed people (e.g., Ezek. 37). The church is caught up in the fulfillment of the Spirit's work through Christ and is grateful for what it learns from Israel's role in foreshadowing it. Though the church through Christ reaps the fruit of promises given to Israel and is nourished by their fulfillment, the church is not simply Israel's "replacement," since the witness

---

92. K. L. Schmidt, "ἐκκλησία," *Theological Dictionary of the New Testament*, ed. Gerhard Kittel, trans. Geoffrey W. Bromiley (Grand Rapids: Eerdmans, 1989), 3:505.

of every nation has enduring significance and Paul seems to imply that there is an "apocalyptic mystery" yet to be revealed through Israel's witness (Rom. 11:25–32).

In the context of the biblical canon, the church thus joins Old Testament witnesses in pointing to Christ as the elect of God. Hebrews fittingly involves faithful Israel with others faithful to God in the cloud of witnesses that point to Christ as the author and finisher of the faith (Heb. 12:1–3). Any church that thinks itself superior to Israel has placed itself in the position of Christ. Such idolatry cannot be tolerated. Thus, the church is also the *ekklesia* of the Christ as its Lord, for Christ is its foundation (1 Cor. 3:11). The church abides in Christ (John 14:4) and gathers in his name (Matt. 18:20).

As the people of God, the church is also the people of the Spirit, who was breathed upon the disciples by Christ after his resurrection (John 20:22; 1 Cor. 15:45) and was poured out on the post-Easter assembly in Jerusalem on the day of Pentecost after the ascension (Acts 2). The church is also empowered by the Spirit to proclaim the gospel and to bear witness to Christ in the world (Acts 1:8). This elect people depends on the intercessory ministry of Christ for its grace (Heb. 4), interceding also by the Spirit for a suffering world (Rom. 8:26). The church as a pilgrim people lives "between the times" from the down payment of the Spirit while awaiting in hope the fulfillment of the kingdom of God (Eph. 1:13–14).

Body of Christ

We turn next to the church as the body of Christ. We as the church are the people "baptized [in] one Spirit into one body—whether Jews or Greeks, slave or free—and we were all given the one Spirit to drink" (1 Cor. 12:13). According to this text, Spirit baptism not only formed the church as Christ's body, it initiates people into its life. Notice also that Spirit baptism involves a diversity of participants united as one. There is one Lord and one Spirit, not many lords and many spirits! Thus, there can only ultimately be one church. A local church body that is divided from other expressions of the body of Christ and that seeks to define itself without reference to the others is nothing less than a scandal.

For example, Paul knew that those who were divisive at Corinth were worldly by confusing apostolic leaders with cultural heroes, one of whom could be selected over the others for their preferred theological nuances and rhetorical skills (1 Cor. 1–3). There was even a "Christ" faction (1:12), which

Paul himself could not join, for he could not tolerate using Christ as a weapon to separate the others from the body and to splinter the church. In chapters 1–3, Paul admonishes these "carnal" believers to think spiritually. But to send these believers on their way was to Paul like amputating a limb. He thus struggles to hold the church at Corinth together as Christ's body and to convince everyone that the church must not lack any gift (1:7) while waiting for Christ's return. Everyone is needed in sustaining and building hope and love in the body.

The model of Christ's body implies both unity and diversity (1 Cor. 12). Everyone is uniquely gifted to be a channel of grace. There is a variety of gifts but the same God, the same Lord, and the same Spirit. If everyone is involved, the church will tend to be vastly diverse in function and interactive in nature. This point about mutual interaction of members in the body is the advantage of the body metaphor over the vine metaphor of John 15, which mainly stresses fellowship with Christ. Both the vine and the body metaphors symbolize the church's ongoing dependence on Christ for new life.

Spirit baptism thus implies an ongoing renewal, a continual drinking of the Spirit as a diverse body united as one (1 Cor. 12:13). We have been baptized in the Spirit, but we are in a real sense being baptized into this Spirit as we are renewed in a drinking from the Spirit of Christ. Similarly, John has the disciples abiding in Christ as the source of life (John 15). The advantage of the body metaphor, however, is the interactive and relational nature of this drinking of the Spirit from Christ. The Spirit-baptized body of Christ lives from diverse *koinonia*.

Incidentally, the body of Christ model is used in Ephesians 5:25–28 inseparably with the bride of Christ metaphor. Both in Ephesians 5 and Revelation 19, the church as the bride implies the church's ongoing faithfulness to the crucified Christ and to the self-sacrificial love symbolized in Christ's death. In the bride model, the relationship between the church and Christ is covenantal and not to be seen as simply a given. This covenantal theme qualifies the organic metaphor of the church as the body, the unity of which can be seen as a given. As Volf writes, "Only as the bride can the church be the body of Christ, and not vice versa."[93] Hans Küng adds that even the body of Christ image is not used by Paul in the context of christology, soteriology, or theoretical ecclesiology but rather as an admonition to *be* the body that we are

---

93. Volf, *After Our Likeness,* 143.

already by the Spirit of grace.[94] Spirit baptism implies a body that is being the body in constant renewal: "We were all given the one Spirit to drink."

Temple of the Spirit

The church as the temple of the Spirit is most explicitly connected to Spirit baptism among all of the models of the church. The church comes into being as a Spirit-baptized people filled with the very presence of God (Acts 2:4). Filled with the Holy Spirit, the church is a holy temple with Christ as its foundation (1 Cor 3:11): "Don't you know," Paul wrote to the Corinthians, "that you yourselves are God's temple and that God's Spirit lives in you?" (1 Cor. 3:16). Divisions in the church threaten to destroy that temple, God's holy dwelling place. Such is a serious matter, "for God's temple is sacred" (3:17).

The reference to this temple is obviously not to a physical structure, but to the people of God in its dependence on Christ as the wellspring of the Spirit. Spirit baptism is a symbol of dependence on Christ and ultimately the Father as the source of life in the Spirit. Indeed, the center of God's dwelling place is now Christ, in whom all the fullness of deity lives in bodily form (Col. 2:9). In Christ, the Spirit-baptized church draws from his fullness as his body, drinking together from the Spirit in him (1 Cor. 12:13). Led by the foundational witness of apostles and prophets (Eph. 2:20), we are "living stones" that are "being built into a spiritual house to be a holy priesthood, offering spiritual sacrifices acceptable to God through Jesus Christ" (1 Peter 2:5). Spirit baptism produces self-offering in the Spirit back to God. God's presence poured into us through Christ flows back from us to Christ and to the Father in praise and service.

The priesthood of all believers makes up the temple and the very sacrifices as well, since our chief sacrifice is ourselves as living sacrifices offered continuously to God in consecrated service (Rom. 12:1–2). We are crucified with Christ and the life that we live is the one given in self-sacrificial love by Christ for us (Gal. 2:20). In the church as the temple of the Spirit, the temple, the priesthood, and the sacrifices all become one in the living praise and witness of a Spirit-baptized people.

Notice that Peter refers to the Spirit-indwelt people as *being built* into a spiritual house" (1 Peter 2:5). The Spirit-baptized church is still under construction! We are still becoming the church as the temple of God's dwelling.

---

94. Küng, *The Church*, 227–28.

We are constantly in the process of being the Spirit-baptized people, constantly renewed as we drink continuously from the Spirit. We are constantly under renewal and expansion as we move toward eschatological fulfillment in the new creation of God. The goal is the pouring out of the Spirit on all flesh, all peoples of the world—indeed, the entire creation.

The Spirit-filled temple reaches in priestly ministry and prophetic witness for the four corners of the earth in order to foreshadow the coming new creation as the final dwelling place of God. The churches shine forth as temple lamps to illuminate to the world Christ as the Great High Priest (Rev. 1:12–13). Pentecost is fulfilled when Christ fills the whole universe with his presence (Eph. 4:10) so that God may be all in all (1 Cor. 15:28). At this time, the "dwelling of God is among men" (Rev. 21:3). The church as the temple of the Spirit becomes the harbinger of the sanctification of creation into the very image of Christ as God's dwelling place to the glory of God.

Until that time, the church groans in the Spirit with all of creation for the liberty to come (Rom. 8:26) and seeks to be a witness to the new life of the Spirit possible in Christ (Acts 1:8). The church is the temple for the sake of the world and for God's glory, and not primarily for its own sake. It is a temple that seeks to discern the presence of God within the realm of the profane and that prays and works for the renewal of creation and the realization of its destiny in God. The church is to be the sign of grace in an all-too graceless world.

The biblical models of the church raise issues vital to the church, such as its unity or holiness. It is fitting, therefore, at this juncture to discuss in the light of Spirit baptism the so-called marks of the church (*ecclesiae notae*).

THE MARKS OF THE SPIRIT-BAPTIZED CHURCH

The Nicene/Constantinopolitan Creed regards the church as "one, holy, catholic, and apostolic." Though more ancient in origin, these marks coalesced as the church came to affirm its solidarity against heresy as an empire-wide church. A century before the inclusion of the marks in the Nicene-Constantinopolitan Creed, the church had come out from centuries of persecution in which these marks were not experienced as abstract ideals but rather as witnesses to grace in an all-too graceless world. The unity, holiness, catholicity, and apostolicity of the church were like overlapping circles with a common core in the divine constitution of the church, but with elements of human participation that made these marks a visible witness to God's grace in the world. Behind the marks is a narrative of Jesus bestowing the Spirit to produce a community that is one, consecrated people under the guidance of the apostles and experiencing the richness of catholic grace. In the light of this narrative, one can say that the church has these marks as the Spirit-baptized church.

In the Constantinian era, however, the church formed a tendency to lay claim to these marks as avenues of power rather than as humble forms of witness to the crucified and risen Christ in the power of the Spirit. A pneumatological construal of the marks in the context of Spirit baptism calls the church back to the witness of Jesus as the Spirit Baptizer and of Pentecost as the church's participation in the life of the crucified Christ.[95] Our participation in the marks through Spirit-baptized witness means that the marks belong first to Christ and to the life of the Spirit that he graciously poured out. They belong to us only through the Spirit's presence and the sanctified, empowered witness that comes through Spirit baptism. I thus regard the following comment from Moltmann concerning the marks as seminal: "If the church acquires her existence from Christ's messianic mission and the eschatological gift of the Spirit, then her characteristics are messianic predicates at the same time."[96]

Since the marks are predicates of Christ and the presence of the Spirit, they are first predicates of the kingdom of God. The eschatological and transcendent marks of the church are hidden in the kingdom of God and yet to be revealed in the new creation. The church does not possess them in some unqualified sense. The church rather participates in them by faith as a gift of grace. The church is the first to say that at the same time the marks do not belong and do belong to the church, which is but another version of the dialectic of Spirit-baptized witness. The Spirit-baptized marks are revealed through the church in weakness, in obscurity.

Since these marks belong first to the Lord and the Spirit, they cannot be the exclusive claim of any one communion. Hans Küng has shown that apostolic succession belongs to all of the faithful: "The *whole* church, and hence every individual member, stands in the line of succession from the apostles."[97]

---

95. Amos Yong, *The Spirit Poured Out on All Flesh: Pentecostalism and the Possibility of Global Theology* (Grand Rapids: Baker, 2005), 233.

96. Moltmann, *The Church in the Power of the Spirit*, 339.

97. Küng, *The Church*, 433.

Building on this idea, Volf notes that the presence of Christ does not enter the church "through the narrow portals of church office but rather through the dynamic life of the whole church."[98]

Such was certainly the case at Pentecost. The Spirit descended on all of the faithful. Those called to be apostles were just as dependent on this event as the others. Spirit baptism is thus available to all flesh, "to all whom the Lord our God will call" (Acts 2:39). I take this to mean that the historic claim of apostolic succession cannot be used to anchor the marks of the church as centrally subsisting in one communion only, since these marks are polycentric, belonging to all communities who come to Christ to drink from his Spirit and to find help in time of need. The Spirit-baptized marks are broadly ecumenical in nature.

Since the Spirit-baptized marks of the church are broadly ecumenical, a Pentecostal response to these marks should be prefaced by the recognition of some variation in the tradition concerning the chief characteristics of the church that help one discern where the church is present. The marks in the Nicene/Constantinopolitan Creed were and are widely held but not emphasized everywhere the same. Other marks tended to eclipse them in some traditions. These classic marks tended to dominate ancient and sacramental traditions. Apostolicity and sacrament were dominant by the fourth century in the prevalent understanding of the church's unity, holiness, and catholicity.

Though these marks were affirmed by the Reformers, the Reformers tended to categorize the chief characteristics of the church mainly as the community shaped by and faithful to the promises of God given in the gospel of Christ. In the words of John Calvin, "wherever we see the word of God sincerely preached and heard, wherever we see the sacraments administered according to the institution of Christ, there we can't have any doubt that the church of God has some existence, since his promise cannot fail."[99] This latter phrase about the faithfulness of the promises is determinative to the rest of the statement. It is because the gospel cannot fail that the church will be the church as the locus of Christ's benefits as long as this gospel is faithfully proclaimed in preaching and sacrament.

---

98. Volf, *After Our Likeness*, 152.
99. John Calvin, *Institutes of the Christian Religion*, trans. Henry Beveridge (Grand Rapids: Eerdmans, repr. 1979), 2:289 (4.1.9).

Though not quite the same as the classic marks, these Reformation "marks" represent a renewed focus on the centrality of the gospel to the life of the church. The marks from the Nicene/Constantinopolitan Creed emphasize the unity of the church under the apostles and their successors, in the fullness of catholic life and grace. The Reformers' concerns stress instead the faithfulness of God's promises in preaching and sacrament and the need for the church to administer these in a way that is faithful to Christ. The nuances of difference here are significant and can broadly be categorized as the difference between a sacramental and a word-oriented ecclesiology. The former stresses the endurance of the apostolic office/gift and the continuity of tradition and catholic life; the latter, a recovery of a somewhat neglected core of that tradition and life in the centrality of the gospel to the being and life of the church.

To the Reformation marks can be added a discipleship ecclesiology. The Anabaptist (or radical Reformation) vision of the chief characteristics of the church stresses discipleship, fellowship, and the ethic of love and nonresistance.[100] The spotlight on discipleship brings with it concomitant accents on the discipline of the community, the life of the Spirit, and eschatological expectation. There is overlap here with the Reformed tradition's stress on discipline and order as well as the later Pentecostal emphasis on faithful living and eschatology. But the Anabaptist focus on discipleship is worth exploring, for it reflects an emphasis on life rather than proclamation or, put another way, on the witness to the gospel in both life and word.

Without necessarily denying the sacramental significance of baptism and Eucharist as divine actions, these sacraments become initial means by which the community acts out its faithfulness to Christ rather than, first and foremost, a word that comes to a passively receptive audience. Of course, proclamation is vital to the Anabaptist tradition also, but the stress on the Word of God lived out and on the credibility of the church's proclamation in a communal and individual life faithful to Christ is worth noting, especially in the light of current emphases on "orthopraxy," "enacting theology," and "practicing theology." I like Joy Ann McDougall's point that we "inhabit" doctrines and "perform" them in imaginative ways.[101] The "marks" of the true church

---

100. Finger, *A Contemporary Anabaptist Theology*, 48; see also Harold Bender, *The Anabaptist Vision* (Scottdale PA: Harold, 1944), 13.

101. Joy Ann McDougall, "Woman's Work: Feminist Theology for a New Generation," *Christian Century* (July 26, 2005), 20.

are still rooted in God's grace, but this grace is a mercy and a power experienced in the life of discipleship and not an abstract declaration.

The Pentecostals have tended to highlight a charismatic/missionary ecclesiology. Their fivefold gospel of regeneration, sanctification, Spirit baptism, healing, and eschatological expectation isolated by Donald Dayton as distinctive to Pentecostal theology can be seen as ecclesiological "marks" as well. The church for the early Pentecostals was the new creation in Christ consecrated unto God and baptized in power for gifted service, especially to empower the proclamation of a gospel that heralded healing and the imminent return of Christ. The focus is on a renewal of charismatic gifts and missionary power. The recovery of the promises of God in the gospel as central to the church is not neglected, but the purpose becomes a recovery of the kind of lived experience of the Spirit that the ancient church had. In a sense, the church was that body born again and faithful to minister according to those gifts bequeathed to the church by the charismatic Christ in the outpouring of the Spirit and to be fulfilled by Christ's soon return. The emphasis is on the charismatic and missionary church, faithful to Jesus' charismatic ministry.

All of the various accents have a place in a Spirit-baptized ecclesiology. The marks in the Nicene/Constantinopolitan Creed remind me that apostolicity has its original heritage in those commissioned by Christ to bear witness to him throughout the world and that there is a debt I owe to the historic churches for seeking to preserve the unity of the church under the guidance of those appointed to call us continuously back to the apostolic legacy and the richness of catholic life. The Reformation tradition can help us focus on the gospel as the enduring norm of the church's marks, and the Radical Reformation to discipleship as the locus in which the marks are lived out as "core practices of the church."[102]

Pentecostals can expand this core practice idea to accent the charismatic structure of the church as a missional force in the world. The unity and apostolicity of the church are required by its charismatic and missionary nature. The church is characterized as the community of end-time signs of renewal in the world and as those who proclaim the gospel with the signs of Christ's

---

102. As Reinhard Hütter described the classic marks: *Suffering Divine Things: Theology as Church Practice* (Grand Rapids: Eerdmans, 2000), 131–32; quoted in Yong, *The Spirit Poured Out*, 151.

charismatic ministry following. The implicit stress of the classic marks on the continuity of apostolic tradition in the one, sanctified church is qualified by the Pentecostal accent on the constant renewal of apostolic power and faithfulness among all the people of God through Spirit-filling, charismatic ministry, and fervent, eschatological hope. The classic marks are not replaced by these other "marks" but are qualified and read through these others as lenses.

The marks as eschatological gifts of the Spirit bestowed by Christ are also goals in which we are constantly to be renewed and toward which we strive. They are caught up in what Yves Congar called the "struggle for the Spirit" in the church.[103] They are also the means by which the church constantly turns to its center in Christ and its praise to the Father in ongoing reaffirmation and growth. They are realized eschatologically when the Spirit is ultimately poured out on all flesh and whosoever has called on the name of the Lord is saved (Acts 2:17–21). As Volf notes, "The all-encompassing framework for an appropriate understanding of the church is God's eschatological new creation," more specifically, "the mutual personal indwelling of the triune God and of his glorified people."[104]

Though the Spirit-baptized church at Pentecost foreshadowed imperfectly the global church of many nations in Acts 2, the symbolism indicates a generous outpouring of the Spirit "with all grace." The church is thus referred to as a local church (at Corinth, Ephesus, etc.) but also as a global, even universal, church that involves the living and the dead: the "whole family in heaven and on earth" (Eph. 3:15). Yet, the filling and richness of the Spirit were experienced also within a local gathering of the Jerusalem church in Acts 4. How can a local gathering experience the same "Spirit and all grace" as the global church?

Volf maintains that the eschatological gathering of God's people in the new creation has priority over both the local church and the visible network of churches throughout the world. The local church does not draw its realization of marks from a global communion as its local expression but rather from the eschatological fulfillment of the people of God in divine *koinonia*.[105] This priority of the eschatologically-fulfilled church means that the realization of the marks of the Spirit-baptized church does not assume a priority of the

---

103. Yves Congar, *I Believe in the Holy Spirit* (New York: Seabury, 1983), 2:57.
104. Volf, *After Our Likeness*, 128.
105. Ibid., 140–41.

local congregation over the church as a global body (as though the global body is a mere abstraction) or the priority of the global church over the local church (as though the local church is merely the local expression of the global body). *Both the local body and the global network of churches realize the marks from the same source, namely, the eschatological fulfillment of the people of God and the presence of the Spirit with all grace in the here and now.* This priority of the eschatological Spirit in determining the marks of the church explains why a local body can be filled with the Spirit with all grace.

Yet, divisions between churches do limit the ability of the local church to experience the eschatological Spirit in fullness. In my view, both the local congregation and the global network of churches realize the marks in ways analogous to each other in anticipation of the final gathering of the people of God under the ultimate baptism of all things in the Spirit of the risen and glorified Christ. I would only add that the global nature of the final eschatological gathering of the people of God (Rev. 7:9) means that the current global network of churches is not the church in some secondary sense, but rather falls as directly under the challenge of realizing the marks of the church of Christ as does the local congregation.

The fact that the global church is deeply fractured is a scandal that affects the capacity of the local church to experience the Spirit in all of the dimensions of grace possible in the here and now. Such divisions may be historically understandable, but they are theologically unjustifiable and spiritually damaging. One cannot postpone the challenge of the global unity of the church to the *eschaton* while the churches remain satisfied with mere ecumenical openness and cooperation. The ecumenical movement, which should be only a temporary means to unity, then becomes an end in itself, a means of avoiding the deepest challenges of visible unity.

Thus, the experience of fullness in the Spirit in the local church cannot be used to sidestep the urgency of global unity among God's people. As Küng points out, "While the individual church is *an* entire church it is not *the* entire church."[106] The global people of God are not yet visibly one, which calls its catholicity into question. Here is where the Reformation *ecclesia invisibilis* (invisible church) may be of help, not as an escape from the challenge of universal visible unity, but as a promise that a kind of spiritual unity does exist that strives toward visible expression.

---

106. Küng, *The Church*, 300.

Furthermore, Spirit baptism mandates that the entire laity participate in the marks, since Spirit baptism involves all of the faithful. There is no "aristocracy of the Spirit," as Jaroslav Pelikan has noted in commenting on the ecumenical significance of Montanism, missed by the church that reacted (somewhat understandably) against it.[107] The marks are characteristic of the whole church caught up in the life of the kingdom of God and seeking to be its chief sign and instrument. The marks of the church in the light of Spirit baptism involve empowered witness of the whole people of God (Acts 1:8). The marks cannot be held in secret as a mystery that is to remain hidden. They must become more and more visible in the community of the church. They must also be lived in discipleship and charismatic service. They must be there for the world and not just for the benefit of the church itself. They belong to the life of the kingdom first, and so they must be lived in struggle for the renewal of humanity and of the entire creation. In the light of these points, we can briefly discuss the classical marks themselves.

Unity

First, we can explore more thoroughly the unity of the church. Spirit baptism unifies the church around Christ and the Father, who sent both Christ and the Spirit to inaugurate the kingdom of God in the world. There is one God, one faith in Christ, and one Spirit (1 Cor. 12:4–6; Eph. 4:4–6). There is one baptism (Eph. 4:4). Divisions between churches that exclude each other imply more than one Spirit or one Christ or one Father, which is absurd. The mere assumption of such a division is scandalous. Using the Spirit or Christ or God as a weapon against others who genuinely profess Christ as Lord runs contrary to the ecumenical role of Spirit baptism: "For we were all baptized [in] one Spirit into one body—whether Jews or Greeks, slave or free—and we were all given the one Spirit to drink" (1 Cor. 12:13).

Divisions between churches that define themselves without reference to the others cannot be justified, no matter how understandable the divisions may have been historically. Notice what Barth has to say in this regard:

> There may be good grounds for the rise of these divisions. There may be serious obstacles to their removal. There may be many things which can be said by way of interpretation and mitigation. But this does not alter

---

107. Jaroslav Pelikan, *The Emergence of the Catholic Tradition*, Vol. 1, *The Christian Tradition* (Chicago: Univ. of Chicago Press, 1971), 107–8.

the fact that every division as such is a deep riddle, a scandal. And in the face of this scandal the whole of Christendom should be united in being able to think of it only with penitence, not with the penitence which each expects of the other, but with the penitence in which—whatever may be the cost—each is willing to precede the other.[108]

In the light of Spirit baptism, we can state that disunity in the body of Christ distorts the "pneumatic vitality" of the church, even threatening to destroy that which is essential to the church.[109]

Realizing visibly the unity we have in the Spirit, therefore, is no luxury but is an urgent task. This unity we seek to make visible, however, will also not try to quench the Spirit that is manifested in the increasing diversity of the churches. In a global context, it is important to note that Spirit baptism leads to a differentiated unity that opposes all uniformity. It is patterned according to the communion of persons in God. The unity of the church is thus "of the Spirit" in the "one Lord" and from the "one God and Father of all" (Eph. 4:3–6). This unity of diversely gifted members is also spoken of as by "the same Spirit," "the same Lord," and "the same God" who activates all of them (1 Cor. 12:4–6).

Jesus prayed that the company of disciples who would follow him be one, stating, "As you, Father, are in me and I am in you, may they also be in us, so that the world may believe that you have sent me" (John 17:21 NRSV). This unity is based in the *koinonia* of God and is thus diversely interactive, empathetic, and visible, or able to serve the church's witness to the gospel. It is also a goal worthy of intentional prayer and action. We have one faith (Eph. 4:5), and yet we are to grow toward the unity of this faith (4:13). The love of God exemplified by Christ and poured out in Spirit baptism (Rom. 5:5) contradicts a divisive spirit.

Speaking in tongues as a sign of Spirit baptism (Acts 2:4; 10:46) symbolizes this differentiated unity. This insight can speak to the global awareness of the issue of "otherness." As we noted above, "unity" in the New Testament does not refer to sameness of identity but rather a mutual participation of others in communion. Dale Irvin points out that such a notion of unity runs con-

---

108. Karl Barth, *Church Dogmatics*, Vol. 4, Pt. 1, trans. G. W. Bromiley (Edinburgh: T&T Clark, 1956), 675–76.

109. This is the major thesis of E. Rodner, *The End of the Church: A Pneumatology of Christian Division in the West* (Grand Rapids: Eerdmans, 1998), referenced by Del Colle, "The Outpouring of the Holy Spirit," 262.

trary to Western philosophical systems that have stressed uniformity or singularity of meaning. In particular, the "metaphysics of presence" can be construed so as to suppress forms of otherness by transmuting their alternative quality into the same. Similarly, some ecumenists have been tempted to view increasing diversification and difference within Christian traditions as threatening the work of the Spirit rather than as furthering it. They labor under an inadequate ecumenical hermeneutic.[110]

Irvin notes that ecumenical exchanges actually increase diversification because of the nature of language and dialogue as fostering a collision of worlds, creating both overlap and increasing diversity of responses. Inspired by the Russian thinker Mikhail Bahktin, Irvin argues that the "tension-filled unity and disunity of ecumenical discourse and experience are not indicative of the weakness but of the strength in the movement."[111] The result is that no single voice in the dialogue can unambiguously hold the truth. The ecumenical movement is a "polyphonic event that cannot be reduced to a single narrative" and is "alive still with multiple possibilities."[112]

Similarly, Michel de Certeau wrote of the vital "confrontations and comparisons" that arise in ecumenical exchanges that concern "functions that are necessarily distinct, 'charisms' to preserve, and tasks which are irreconcilable with each other."[113] Unity is a mutual communion that respects otherness and diversity, even creative tension. Oscar Cullmann thus described the churches as analogous to the Pauline *charismata*, each church preserving its own distinctive gifts as they engage other churches in interactive mutual challenge and edification.[114] In the words of Hans Küng, "unity not only presupposes the multiplicity of churches, but makes it flourish anew," for "no one has the right to set limits to God's vocations, to quench the Spirit, or to level out the member

---

110. Dale T. Irvin, "Towards a Hermeneutics of Difference at the Crossroads of Ecumenics," *Ecumenical Review* 47 (October 1995): 492.

111. Dale T. Irvin, *Hearing Many Voices: Dialogue and Diversity in the Ecumenical Movement* (Lanham, MD: Univ. Press of America, 1994), 11; note M. Bahktin, *The Dialogic Imagination: Four Essays*, ed. Michael Holquist (Austin TX: Univ. of Texas Press, 1981), esp. 269.

112. Irvin, *Hearing Many Voices*, 12.

113. Michel de Certeau, "Is There a Language of Unity?" in *Dogma and Pluralism*, ed. E. Schillebeeckx (New York: Herder & Herder, 1970), 85.

114. Oscar Cullmann, *Unity through Diversity: Its Foundation, and a Contribution to the Discussion Concerning the Possibilities of Its Actualization*, trans. M. Eugene Boring (Philadelphia: Fortress, 1988).

churches."[115] The communion of unity continually diversifies and raises new problems to be overcome by self-giving love and spiritual discernment.

More differentiated theological thinking is needed as we probe the issue of unity and division more deeply. Is unity always positive and a conflicting diversification among groups always negative? For example, is it not possible to have a unity that is really an oppressive uniformity, which disrespects otherness? Such a unity avoids conflict and diversification, stifling variety, freedom, and creativity. By contrast, is it not possible to have a conflicting diversification among groups of Christians that is divisive and harmfully alienating in nature? Otherness is on the minds of many in the church today who wish to discern the distinction between legitimate diversity and scandalous divisions or, on the other side of these two, legitimate unity and idolatrous uniformity. Such distinctions are not easy to make, thrusting one in the midst of ambiguity. Such ambiguity requires biblical guidance and careful theological reflection.

In the light of Luke's description of Spirit baptism in Acts 2, the images of Babel and Pentecost come to mind as symbolizing a simplified contrast in choices that tends to see diversification as confused and divisive and "unity" as valued at all cost. In the light of the tower of Babel narrative of Genesis 11, Babel symbolizes the confusion of peoples by God as they are scattered and divided from each other in judgment for the human folly of idolatry. Pentecost symbolizes the unification of peoples under Christ by the Spirit of God.

Such a simplified contrast is helpful as far as it goes but is ultimately not adequate for a theology of unity that fully respects otherness and the conflict-ridden, ever-expansive diversification of God's people. Communion is dynamic and alive, experienced in the tension of uniqueness and common life. Is Pentecost simply a gathering together of what Babel tore down and scattered abroad? Is Pentecost simply the reversal of Babel? Or is there not also a promise-fulfillment relationship between these two events that highlights the value of diversification and even constructive conflict in an understanding of unity that continues to embrace otherness?

In answering these questions, we should begin by accepting and understanding the contrast between Babel and Pentecost. As J. G. Davies has maintained, the Acts narrative of the tongues of Pentecost is based on the tower of Babel narrative in Genesis as its reversal. Luke's depiction of the tongues

---

115. Küng, *The Church*, 274.

of Pentecost is shaped in contrast to the confused tongues of Babel. At Babel, the tongues are confused, which is precisely the initial response of the audience at Pentecost, revealing a linguistic dependence between the two passages. At Babel, the one language is about to be disrupted, while at Pentecost, the many languages are understood in unison by the hearers. In the former, the people are dispersed in confusion, while in the latter they are sent forth in unity and clarity of truth. Whereas Babel scattered people abroad at variance from one another, Pentecost scatters people abroad to preach the gospel of reconciliation.[116] Though in our understanding of Acts 2 the contrast between Babel and Pentecost may be subtle and needs to be augmented by other connections to the Old Testament, there are good reasons to assume that a contrast with the Babel narrative was part of the scriptural background that informed and inspired Luke's Pentecost narrative.

Babel functions in Scripture as a negative symbol of human folly and divine judgment in contrast to the blessing of Pentecost. Instead of dispersing to fill the earth with the proliferation, enjoyment, and care of life as beings in the very image of God (Gen. 1:27–28), the humanity at Babel prefers security by homogeneity and centralization. The unity of their language is wielded toward a uniform and self-destructive end. They wish to build a city around a tower (or, better, a temple or ziggurat) that can touch the heavens and bring God in their grasp.

Central to this cause is for the residents of Babel to make a "name" for themselves. This is not the name that God gives to Abram or Jacob as a result of their reception by faith of the divine promise for history. The residents of Babel wish to create a name *for themselves*. Theirs is to be a name that they wish to impose on God so that their understanding of their own historical destiny can gain eternal and absolute significance. The use of their unified language toward this effort at absolutizing their social structures and sense of historical destiny is telling, for it implies that all human language has the potential of becoming the language of disobedience. Nietzsche could not have portrayed the deceptive power of language any more effectively than we find expressed in the tower of Babel story.

The folly of Babel lives on in history. In reflecting on Babel, Jose Miguez-Bonino recalls insightfully how conquering peoples in history commonly

---

116. J. G. Davies, "Pentecost and Glossolalia," *Journal of Theological Studies* 3 (1952): 228.

imposed their language on the conquered as a way of unifying them all under the vision of a people destined for greatness by a self-made divine sanction.[117] Is this not the negative side of Babel replayed down through the annals of history? Is this not the temptation that language as the means of socialization faces in every culture? Women and minorities are pressured by language to conform to an unquestioned and absolute understanding of self and destiny that is at least potentially oppressive and destructive to them. Genesis 11 is not primarily about the origin of diverse languages but rather the condemnation and defeat of the imperial arrogance and universal domination represented by the uniform unity of Babylon. If the church is to be the sign of grace in a graceless world, it must represent a countercultural community that socializes people in a language and relational network dominated by grace and communion.

However, *we must also proceed beyond the contrast to note a promise-fulfillment relationship between Babel and Pentecost.* The judgment at Babel in the confusion of tongues can lead to harmful fragmentation and divisiveness, but this was not the divine intention behind the confusion (*hominum confusione et Dei Providentia!*). The judgment was intended as grace, as a way of breaking the spell of idolatry and disobedience in their efforts at achieving an idolatrous unity. God desired to thrust humanity outward toward a diverse fulfillment of God's original intention of filling the earth. In his *Genesis* commentary, Walter Brueggemann thus opposes the typically "simplistic" understanding of the confusion and scattering of the people of Babel that views this as solely judgmental.[118] There is a dual edge to the scattering and diversification of the tongues that actually fulfills the divine plan for filling the earth (Gen. 1:27–28). Such is God's plan for the free proliferation and diversification of a life that harbors no idolatrous illusions and finds its true dignity in glorifying God.

Luke in Acts implicitly agrees with this positive understanding of the scattering of the peoples and the diversification of their tongues at Babel. First of all, the issue of the scattering of the peoples throughout the world is on Luke's mind in the writing of the Pentecost narrative. Luke depicts the audience at

---

117. Jose Miguez Bonino, "Genesis 11:1–9: A Latin American Perspective," in *Return to Babel: Global Perspectives on the Bible*, ed. John R. Levison and Priscilla Pope-Levison (Louisville: Westminster John Knox, 1999), 13.

118. Walter Brueggemann, *Genesis* (Interpretation; Atlanta: John Knox, 1982), 97.

the Pentecost event as consisting of Jews of the Diaspora who know something about the challenges of being scattered. But Luke knows that the scattering of peoples throughout the globe is not just important to Diaspora Jews. Such a theme allows Luke to reach back to a divine purpose that predates the Sinai covenant and has implications for all of humanity.

Interestingly, Luke describes Paul's address in Athens as having this issue of the global dispersion of peoples as its focus but in a way that holds broad implications for the Gentiles as well. In this address, Paul maintains in Acts 17:24–27 that God created the peoples of the world so that "they should inhabit the whole earth," precisely as it was stated of the human race in texts like Genesis 1:28 and 10:18 and fulfilled with both negative and positive possibilities at Babel in Genesis 11. God also providentially "determined the times set for them and the exact places where they should live" so they would seek and "perhaps find" God (Acts 17:27).

Most interesting is that Paul's address refers to the scattering of the peoples in the world in God's providence within the context of the futility involved in any effort to capture God through temples made with hands (Acts 17:24). Implied in 17:24–27 is a positive reading of the Babel narrative, or at least its message. In this Lukan reading, God dispersed the peoples throughout the earth so that they could find God again, but not in a way that functions as the divine sanction for their own self-serving achievements, for ultimately God does not need human-made religious temples or idols and can certainly never be confined to such human creations (17:24). Rather, the peoples of the world have been dispersed in a way that will help them to recognize God as the gift of life, breath, and being in the midst of their migrations and unique geographical and cultural settings. Reading Acts 17 in the light of Genesis 11 sets the stage for a more differentiated comparison between Babel and Pentecost.

The outpouring of the Spirit at Pentecost only reverses the *threat* that arose from the collapse of Babel and the diversified, even confused, dispersion of peoples but not their *promise*. The peoples that dispersed faced the threat of an enduring fragmentation but, as Acts 17 shows, God had other plans. The diverse tongues of Pentecost seem symbolic of the fact that Spirit baptism was the means by which this divine intention behind the scattering was to be fully realized among the peoples of the world who had been dispersed originally by the confusion of tongues. The confusion voiced initially at the miracle of tongues at Pentecost is connected to the same confusion that occurred when God broke the spell of that original effort at laying hold of God through an idol. But the scattering of Babel also held out a promise that humanity might rediscover a unity that does not dissolve but rather embraces the diversity of idioms, backgrounds, and stories that God willed to providentially release in history. This is the unity witnessed penultimately in the church.

The unity of Pentecost is thus not abstract and absolute but rather concrete and pluralistic. As noted above, the boundaries crossed are specific, namely, rich and poor, old and young, male and female (Acts 2:17ff.). The "all flesh" targeted eschatologically by Spirit baptism aims specifically at crossing such boundaries socially and culturally. The eschatological freedom of the Spirit bursts open human biases and oppressive structures. The unity of Pentecost aims to conquer injustice and hate with justice and compassion. It is not arrogant and self-serving but humble and obedient. It is respectful and tolerant of differences. It glorifies God rather than deifies the creature. It is free and not oppressive. In this unity, people will discover their true dignity as bearers of the divine image.

The unity of the church at Pentecost is expressed in a vast diversity of tongues "from every nation under heaven" (Acts 2:5). No language, culture, or journey of faith is neglected or devalued no matter how marginalized by more dominant or influential peoples. This is a unity that respects and fulfills the scattering and diversification of peoples from Babel. Otherness is not denied but embraced in this differentiated and complex unity of the church at Pentecost. This unity is not static but dynamic and eschatological in nature, ever increasing in its diversification but also participatory in its *koinonia*.

We must also keep in mind that the audience at Pentecost from every nation revolved around the experience of Diaspora Jews. The vast, global diversity of this company and their national tongues still needed to involve the Gentiles. This need to expand the diversified unity of Pentecost lies behind the significance of the fact that the Jewish-Christian company heard the Gentiles speak in tongues as well (Acts 10:46). It was one thing for Jews from around the world to speak in the tongues of the nations, but it was something else for them to do so in fellowship with Gentile brothers and sisters!

Expanding the unity of the church toward that kind of diversity implied creative conflict, as Acts 11–15 and Galatians 1–2 reveal. It was not easy for the Jewish church to break with tradition in entering the household of a Gentile and accepting them unconditionally as bearers of the eschatological Spirit.

The increased diversification of the one church involved conflict and an acceptance of otherness through a painful forsaking of cherished traditions. What will we need to forsake in our search for a diversified unity today, one that respects the otherness of the people who join with us in confessing the one faith and experiencing the one baptism? We must keep in mind that the goal of Spirit baptism is "all flesh" (i.e., all people) and, eventually, all of creation. Are we in our unity bearing witness to the final renewal and reconciliation of all things? If not, we damage our claim to be the Spirit-baptized church.

How do we proceed toward unity? For one thing, we need to respect and listen carefully to the marginalized voices in the churches and the broader society. Ecumenism is social and cultural as well as denominational. Spirit baptism is not aimed at "all spirit" but rather "all flesh," implying a reality that is not just spiritual but also physical and social. It cannot even be just ecclesiastical but also secular. "Flesh" reaches back to God's role as Creator and cannot be confined to the walls or even the reach of the church. Spirit baptism thus implicitly undercuts any effort to oppress or unjustly discriminate based on differences of gender, race, social class, or physical/mental capabilities. Spirit baptism intends to grace all of creation with the dignity of being accepted, called, and gifted of God.

Though the church cannot neglect its kerygmatic function in pointing explicitly to Jesus as the hope of the world, neither can it neglect the social implications of its loyalty to Christ and the witness of the Spirit. William Seymour and others in association with him were convinced that sanctification and Spirit baptism caused the church to bear witness to racial reconciliation before the world. For example, a certain T. Hezmalhalch wrote in William Seymour's paper, *The Apostolic Faith*, that a group of Native Americans pointed to "the white people and a colored brother" present with them to say that they were all "by the blood of Jesus Christ to be one great spiritual family." The author concluded, "Tell me, my brother, can you have a better understanding of the two works of grace and the baptism with the Holy Ghost?"[119]

This ecumenical openness includes female leadership that is waning in Pentecostal denominations. Pentecost means that both sons and daughters prophesy. Apostolic sensitivity to order (1 Cor. 14:34–35), cultural discretion

[handwritten margin note: This is so important and relative today]

---

119. T. Hezmalhalch, "Among the Indians at Needles, California," *The Apostolic Faith* (January 1907), 3.

(11:1–16), and the proper exercise of authority (1 Tim. 2:12) were contextual matters meaningful to ancient situations. Applying such guidance to our situations today requires sensitivity to the fact that narratives of women called to serve Christ as equal partners to men (e.g., Acts 2:17; Gal. 3:28) will affect us today in many different situations somewhat differently than was possible in the ancient world. We must heed what the Spirit is saying to the churches in our times and places. In Acts 15, the churches affirmed Gentiles as equal partners based on the obvious fact that the Spirit anointed and gifted them as well as the Jews. Why Pentecostals have in general not followed this contextual hermeneutic with regard to the obvious anointing of women in a limitless variety of roles today is impossible in my view to explain in a way that justifies it.[120]

Second, we must take the ecumenical journey forged among the churches today with utmost seriousness and not lightly by sitting on the sidelines making criticisms, usually with no direct experience of the ecumenism under scrutiny. Despite naïve and even triumphalistic understandings of unity among many early Pentecostals, Cecil M. Robeck has convincingly shown that Pentecostalism early on regarded Spirit baptism as implying the eventual visible unity of Christians everywhere.[121] That vision has waned as Pentecostalism sought the acceptance of the more ecumenically-reserved evangelical movement in deference to the charismatic movement among the mainline churches that urged Pentecostals toward a broader ecumenism.

Despite the stereotypical biases among some charismatics toward Pentecostalism, they implicitly called Pentecostals to a broader ecclesiastical solidarity and definition of "orthodoxy" than that which tended to be encouraged by the evangelicals. The effort of any church to limit the goal of unity to Pentecostal and explicitly evangelical churches in a way that neglects and criticizes the wider number of churches and individuals who work tirelessly toward this same end in loyalty to Jesus as "God and Savior" implies fear and lack of understanding, and it can appear at least from the outside as arrogant. This is

---

120. See John Christopher Thomas, "Women, Pentecostals, and the Bible: An Experiment in Pentecostal Hermeneutics," *Journal of Pentecostal Theology* 5 (October 1994): 41–56.

121. Cecil M. Robeck Jr., "The Assemblies of God and Ecumenical Cooperation: 1920–1965," in *Pentecostalism in Context: Essays in Honor of William W. Menzies*, ed. Wonsuk Ma and Robert P. Menzies (Sheffield: Sheffield Academic Press, 1997), 107–50.

not to deny that there are disturbing trends in the ecumenical movement, as there are more or less in any movement of Christians. But as Cecil M. Robeck has stated on more than one occasion, we have no right to criticize the ecumenical conversation taking place in a variety of contexts unless we are involved in the blood and sweat of laboring alongside it.

In the ecumenical task, the "all flesh" of Spirit baptism demands that we also respect the others we encounter outside of the Christian faith. Though I believe Christ to be the only Lord of all creation and salvation, I also regard him as more inclusive and expansive in significance through the witness of the Spirit than many of us wish to admit. As the Pentecostal theologian Amos Yong has taught us, there is significant "breathing room" in the eschatological Spirit's witness to Jesus in history for respecting the otherness of folks we meet outside the boundaries of the church.[122] The presence of the Spirit amongst these people is real, bearing implicit and unique witness to Jesus. We simply bring that witness to explicit expression, something we cannot hope to do with compassion, respect, and understanding if we have never sat at the table with them to discuss affections, beliefs, and practices. And those among them who do accept Jesus will develop a devotion and a theology that may not be expressed exactly as ours, though their witness will share the same essence. As Joy Ann McDougall has written, doctrines, though normative, "possess a certain fluidity that allows them to stretch across diverse lives and historical contexts and be embodied in culturally specific ways."[123]

What we are really talking about here is a unity that is willing to accept the dynamism, struggles, and expansive diversification needed to respect otherness and avoid uniformity. "If the whole body were an eye, where would the hearing be? If the whole body were hearing, where would the sense of smell be?" (1 Cor. 12:17 NASB). We are to come behind in no gift while waiting for Christ's return (1:7). We need all of the gifts that an increasingly diverse unity can grant the church as it seeks to discern God's will in the world.

This unity is not just to be local but global. The visible and global unity is not just something for the end of history, though it is fulfilled there. It is to be witnessed to, even if only weakly and fragmentarily, in the here and now.

---

122. See, e.g., Amos Yong, *Beyond the Impasse* (Grand Rapids: Baker, 2003).
123. McDougall, "Woman's Work," 21.

I refer here not to a world church but to a unity in diversity that respects diversity and independence but strives for visible forms of "full communion" in key areas of church life, such as confession, baptism and Eucharist, mission and worship. Spirit baptism and Pentecost must be read with the kind of complex and dynamic unity that will guide us in this journey with all of the agonies and ecstasies it involves until we all meet together as one in joyful praise before the throne of God.

Holiness

One of the major fears among Pentecostals in response to calls for Christian unity is the possibility of compromise with regard to truth or consecrated living. Since this concern is usually expressed most vigorously among those with little or no direct ecumenical experience outside of Pentecostal or evangelical families of churches, the fear tends to be based on ignorance. Yet the concern in general is sustained by a biblical principle. In the same chapter in which Jesus prayed for unity among his followers (John 17:21), a prayer that remains to this day unfulfilled, Jesus also prayed that his followers be sanctified in truth (17:17–19). This truth is fundamentally Jesus' faithful witness to the Father's love for the world. It is also the mission of the divine Son on behalf of the Father not to condemn the world but to save it from sin and death by bestowing the Spirit of life (cf 1:1–18; 3:16–21). Such truths stated in propositions are living symbols that we not only confess but also live in consecrated witness. There can be no communion or unity in the church in denial of such truths and the dedicated witness that they inspire.

The holiness of the church is dependent on Jesus' sanctification and our participation in it through consecration and empowered witness by the baptism in the Spirit (John 17:17–19). Spirit baptism in Luke assumes that the Gentiles were sanctified in the truth of the gospel by faith in Christ even as they remained ceremonially unclean in the eyes of many Jews (Acts 10; 15:9). They joined the ranks of the prophetic community set apart and empowered for a holy task, namely, to bear witness to the love of God in the world.

The holiness of the church is secured by the presence of the Spirit and all grace, thus transcending the personal holiness of its individual members. Even errant ministers can function at least for a time to impart the grace of God to others through prayer, proclamation, and other forms of gifted service. Though Paul's enemies preached the gospel out of "selfish ambition," Paul still rejoiced that the gospel was going forth to save many (Phil. 1:17–18).

Yet this holiness of the church in the presence of the Spirit and all grace cannot be taken for granted as unrelated to the actions of the church's individual members. Christ threatened to remove the lampstand of the church of Ephesus from its place if it did not repent (Rev. 2:5). The grace that makes us saints is costly, for, as Bonhoeffer stated eloquently, it cost God's very Son. The lack of love and works of love in a church among its members can grow in intensity to the point of calling that body's ecclesial status into question. During the Second World War, the *Deutsche Christen* faced this possibility. Such things are judged by Christ, although there are always people to whom God will grant the discernment to declare a warning. Faithfulness to the gospel in life is not just of the *bene esse* of the church but of its *esse*.

Spirit baptism is a mighty filling with the very presence of a holy God. It changes us in the process, for old wineskins cannot contain the new wine. It is baptism in the very love of God, for God's holiness is holy love, love that does not compromise with evil but transforms us in truth. "Love does not delight in evil but rejoices with the truth" (1 Cor. 13:6). Spirit baptism causes Christ to abide in us and we in him so that we are pruned to bear much fruit (John 15). Not all will bear the same fruit, but we bear one another's burdens so as to maximize our current fruit-bearing potential.

In the light of the universal outpouring of the Spirit, the category of "saint" is not just an elite title for a chosen few but belongs to the entire church by virtue of being "in Christ," for all of the elect redeemed in Christ are sanctified by the Spirit (1 Peter 1:1–2). The Spirit poured out at Pentecost with flaming tongues that symbolized God's holy presence belonged to the entire church by the grace of God. There are those who are still drinking milk and have attitudes more reflective of the world than the kingdom of God (1 Cor. 3:1–4). They are not radically at odds with the genuine life of faith. They do not destroy the church by their actions. They would not, if gaining a significant influence, call the church's identity as the bride of Christ into question. Yet they build with wood, hay, and stubble, rather than with enduring, precious stones (3:11–15). They must be admonished to grow in Christ so as to be transformed "from glory to glory" (2 Cor. 3:18) so that Christ be formed more manifestly in them (Gal. 4:19).

We must do this with patience and love, knowing that God's grace has been infinitely patient with us. We must not despise them because we may see tendencies in them that we despise in ourselves. Those who fall should be led compassionately to repentance and healing. Even though we meet such situations with godly sorrow, this should be expressed in solidarity with their godly sorrow as they repent. Our disappointment must never be turned into self-righteous anger or rejection. May God have mercy on us all.

Catholicity

Since unity as a quality of communion and holiness is secured by the presence of the Spirit "and all grace," we are led next to the richness and breadth of catholicity. Definitions of the term *catholic* are numerous and represent part of the ecumenical challenge facing the churches.[124] The term usually carries qualitative and quantitative implications. Qualitatively, the term can denote the fullness of grace, truth, or spiritual gifts. Quantitatively, catholicity refers to the church spread throughout the world. Spirit baptism on all flesh has the richness and breadth of catholicity implied within it.

Though catholicity is not part of the language of faith among Pentecostal churches, the substance of the term qualitatively understood would be defined among most Pentecostals in the context of an immediate experience of the Holy Spirit, a Spirit "filling" by which the believer feels possessed and overwhelmed by the presence of God. This immediate experience of Christ is not without "means of grace" but, in dialectical tension, comes to us as a kind of "mediated immediacy." The symbols are "broken" or "fallen," but they do occasion a genuine encounter with Christ through the Spirit. Such an experience moves one deeper than words can express but will ideally also involve prophetic insight from the Scriptures as well as a sense of personal calling/gifting, consecration, and love for others.

In Pentecostal settings, the Lord's Supper along with the preaching of the Word and congregational worship are meant to facilitate this experience of spiritual "fullness." David Martin notes, for example, that in Latin American Pentecostalism it is the entire worship service with music, song, dance, prayer, and testimony that creates the high voltage atmosphere in which one is filled with the Spirit.[125] We could add that within this charismatic atmosphere the Word of God comes forth most clearly and centrally in the preaching and the sacraments to inform, convey, and otherwise enhance this experience of the

---

124. Peter Staples, "Catholicity," *Dictionary of the Ecumenical Movement*, ed. Geoffrey Wainwright et al. (Grand Rapids: Eerdmans, 1991), 135.

125. Note David Martin's description of Latin American Pentecostalism: *Tongues of Fire: The Explosion of Protestantism in Latin America* (Oxford: Basil Blackwell, 1990), 163.

Spirit in "fullness." We will discuss below what implications this understanding of catholicity has on a possible Pentecostal understanding of word and sacrament in the light of Spirit baptism. Without denigrating the importance of preaching, the Word emerges in the context of Pentecostal worship in a way that is polycentric, through spiritual gifts, preaching, and sacraments. Volf thus refers to a polyphonic speaking of the Word of God to one another among all of the people of God.[126]

Early on, the term *catholic* also took on a quantitative dimension, as "the whole catholic church throughout the world" (*Martyrdom of Polycarp* 8.1). Cyril of Jerusalem combined the qualitative and the quantitative notions of catholicity by stating that the church catholic "is called catholic because it is spread throughout the world" and because it "teaches universally and completely all the doctrines," "subjects to right worship all humankind," and "possesses in itself every conceivable virtue, whether in deeds, words, or in spiritual gifts of every kind" (*Catechetical Lectures* 18.23). This language needs to be viewed appreciatively but also critically. On an appreciative note, there is no question but that the church's essence or center is in the presence of Jesus through the Spirit and that in Jesus is "every spiritual blessing in the heavenly places" (Eph. 1:3 NASB). On a critical note, talk of the church "possessing" all grace and virtue in "fullness" is problematic and can lead to assumptions that support a realized eschatology and an idolatrous identification of the church with Christ as the King or the Spirit as the kingdom.

We as the church are the church because of the presence of Christ and the kingdom allowing us to participate in, and bear witness to, the kingdom of God in the world. But this embodiment and witness are fallible and weak, eclipsed somewhat by our fallen existence. There is a discrepancy between our essence in the Spirit and our actual existence as the church. Furthermore, talk of spiritual "fullness," though having a certain rhetorical significance in pointing to the source of all fullness in Christ as the wellspring of the Spirit and the center of the church's life, needs to be qualified as experienced only in part and in weakness. It is not possessed; rather, it possesses us. We must constantly be renewed in it as an ongoing experience that reaches for ultimate fulfillment in the *eschaton*. This is why we are constantly "filled" as an ongoing dynamic in the church. If we possessed fullness already, there would be no need to constantly be filled as an ongoing experience of renewal.

---

126. Volf, *After Our Likeness*, 150, 224.

In the light of Pentecost, the rich variety of blessings offered by the church's catholicity is not only spiritual and denominational but also cultural. The tongues of Pentecost inspired by Spirit baptism were global and diverse, and all of this from a small gathering of Jewish Christians! What a sign of how the gift of catholicity transcends what the church can visibly manifest. But the church did not rest secure and complacently with the richness of its spiritual gift. It struggled to visibly manifest this catholicity historically, for in manifesting it they were able to participate more richly in its eschatological fullness. For the gathered people of God in the new creation will be from every nation, tribe, and tongue (Rev. 7:9). The journey of Acts takes us from Palestinian Jews, to Hellenistic Jews, to Samaritans, to Palestinian Gentiles, to Hellenistic Jews and Gentiles on Gentile soil. Catholicity expands in richness and variety. The Spirit is constantly "mediated" through a richer and richer prism of cultural and linguistic voices. Walter Kasper thus refers to catholicity as an "abundance of unity" among peoples, cultures, ministries, and roles.[127] Racism and other forms of unjust neglect or discrimination in the church is a cancer on its catholic soul.

The challenge of catholicity must also be confronted with relation to the variety of world communions. In particular, in speaking of catholicity as an eschatological reality yet to be fulfilled, we are confronted by the claim of the Catholic Church to be the *catholic* church. Can we speak about catholicity and ignore the one church that calls itself by this term? Hans Küng, for example, draws the obvious conclusion that in calling itself catholic, the Catholic Church is making a historical claim to be the mother church to which all other churches must refer in speaking of their origins and their catholicity.

Yet *Unitatis Redintegratio* 4 notes that the Catholic Church is itself weak in its witness to the kingdom:

> For although the Catholic Church has been endowed with all divinely revealed truth and with all means of grace, yet its members fail to live by them with all the fervor that they should, so that the radiance of the Church's image is less clear in the eyes of our separated brethren and of the world at large, and the growth of God's Kingdom is delayed.[128]

The fact that there are churches and faith communities divided from the mother church and experiencing valuable elements of catholicity also pre-

---

127. Kasper, "Present Day Problems in Ecumenical Theology," 17.
128. This is available at www.vatican.va/archive/hist_councils/ii_vatican_council/documents/vat-ii_decree_19641121_unitatis-redintegratio_en.html.

vents the Catholic Church from manifesting in history the richness of its grace throughout the world. Notice again *Unitatis Redintegratio* 4:

> The divisions among Christians prevent the Church from attaining the fullness of catholicity proper to her, in those of her sons who, though attached to her by baptism, are separated from full communion with her. Furthermore, the Church herself finds it more difficult to express in actual life her full catholicity in all her bearings.

However, catholicity still subsists centrally in the Catholic Church for Catholic ecclesiology: "The Lord entrusted all the blessings of the New Covenant to the apostolic college alone, of which Peter is the head, in order to establish the one body of Christ on earth to which all should be fully incorporated who belong in any way to the people of God" (*Unitatis Redintegratio* 4). Communions that are divided from the mother church lack catholicity to an extent because they lack unity in the church established by Christ. But such divisions affect the Catholic Church as well, since it is prevented from fully manifesting its catholicity in history without the unity with these divided churches.

We cannot discuss catholicity in avoidance of this Catholic claim. It must be taken seriously. We must ask whether or not we are guilty of gazing so intently on the pneumatological constitution and eschatological fulfillment of catholicity in the new creation that we are blind to the Christological institution of the church and its historic continuity as the visible body of the faithful. I believe that Küng is right that there is historical validity to the "mother church" idea. The Roman Catholic Church has a certain "parental" role in the family tree of the Christian church in the world. Simply seeking to rediscover the church of Pentecost in the latter rain of the Spirit in a way that ignores this history is unwarranted in my view. We cannot simply live in the biblical narrative as though hundreds of years of church tradition had not transpired. The family of God has a history that cannot be ignored. Children who have left their mother, even if for understandable reasons, and have spawned their own children should not now in concert with them despise their mother in favor of a future destiny conceived apart from her. There is a lifeline historically that leads us to view ourselves in relation to her and in appreciation for her, despite legitimate complaints that we might be able to recall against her (and she against us!).

Nevertheless, her claims in relation to us cannot simply be accepted uncritically. As adult children and grandchildren, we are responsible to decide for ourselves concerning the legitimacy of her claims on us. We will discuss the issue of apostolicity below. Suffice it to say here that the "mother" Catholic Church belongs herself to a heritage in the outpouring of the Spirit to which she is as accountable as any of us and on which she can, in my view, lay no privileged claim. We as her children and grandchildren respect her role in history in passing on to us a precious heritage in the form of witness. *But our reception of this witness draws us to the same source from which she has received it and must continue to receive it.* There are thus limits to how far one can stretch the metaphor of her maternal role in relation to us. From an eschatological perspective, we were born from above, from the Spirit, just as she was and is (John 1:12–13). The seed watered by the Spirit was the Word of God incarnate and proclaimed (1:1–13; 1 Peter 1:23). Hans Küng fittingly remarks, "It is the word which creates the church and constantly gathers it together again by arousing faith and obedience."[129]

In a sense, all Christian communions were born from Pentecost directly and not indirectly, for Pentecost and Spirit baptism are not simply a one-time event now channeled historically through the narrow portals of an apostolic office. Pentecost is now and the Spirit and the gospel of the kingdom are everywhere received in faith. Spirit baptism levels the ecclesiastical playing field when it comes to catholicity from the presence of the kingdom of God in power. Catholicity is consequently polycentric, subsisting within all of the world communions by virtue of the presence of the Spirit. Spirit baptism is an eschatological gift bound fundamentally to the gospel of the kingdom and accessible by the one faith shared among the entire people of God.

Since we are all constituted by the Spirit of promise, the eschatological fulfillment of the Spirit-baptized church in the new creation represents the catholic church in the full manifestation of its marks. No communion, even the most ancient historically, can make a privileged claim on that. As Hans Küng remarked concerning his church's special claim to catholicity, "The most international, the largest, the most varied, the oldest church can in fact become a stranger to itself, can become something different, can lose touch with its own innermost nature, can deviate from its true and original course."[130]

Such is especially true with regard to a young Pentecostal church or movement that lacks the depth of theological and liturgical heritage enjoyed within the

---

129. Küng, *The Church*, 375. Küng says the same of the Spirit as constantly creating the church as well (ibid., 175–76).

130. Ibid., 301–2.

Catholic Church. Catholicity is witnessed to historically through the transmission of a precious heritage. But catholicitiy is in essence an eschatological gift in which we participate by faith in Christ as the Spirit Baptizer. It cannot be taken for granted through privileged claims but must be constantly received anew in genuine faith. Though an ancient church tends to enjoy a certain advantage with regard to the possible richness and variety of its catholic life, catholicity is polycentric and eschatological. Its richness is not judged strictly in historical terms.

Apostolicity

If Pentecostalism is anything, it is "apostolic" by intention. Its original mission was dedicated to the "apostolic faith," and many Pentecostal churches around the world since then have raised the banner of "apostolic" quite high. The term has tended to serve a primitivistic and restorationist impulse, as a cry to return to the original experience of Spirit baptism in Acts and to the quality of life, mission, teaching, and practice of the earliest Christians who went forth from the Day of Pentecost. Of particular importance were the restoration of speaking in tongues, prophecy, and divine healing to the missionary church in the latter days. The missionary church was to reach the nations, all languages and tongues, with the message of Christ as Redeemer and Healer. Implied was that the mainline churches were less than fully apostolic because they to some extent neglected this early fervency and message.

Pentecostals searched further for "patterns" from Acts that legitimated their apostolic identity, such as tongues as evidence of being filled with the Spirit or the use of Jesus' name in baptism. Pentecostals tended to be biblicistic in nature. If something can be shown to have been advocated among the apostles, it was valid for today. If something can be shown as not advocated by the apostles, it was not considered mandatory today. If the apostles performed signs and wonders, the same is valid today. Historic tradition was submitted to the glaring light of what was detected in Acts. A valued aspect of creedal tradition was disposable, and the early Pentecostals did not flinch about requiring as universally binding on their churches doctrinal ideas heretofore unknown in the mainline churches.

This primitivistic and biblicistic hermeneutic was tested in the Trinitarian controversy of the Assemblies of God denomination not long after its founding. Oneness Pentecostals who emerged within the Assemblies of God argued that apostolicity must be used to radically prune the creedal tradition of the church, even to the point of rejecting the doctrine of the Trinity, since it cannot be shown to have been explicitly taught by the apostles. How ironic in the current ecumenical context that Nicea was largely rejected to preserve the church's apostolic identity! The Assemblies of God ended up affirming the Trinity and losing a third of their membership in the process, applying a hermeneutic that was not strictly biblicistic. One thing that all Pentecostals agreed upon, however, was that the whole church was apostolic in that it shared the original faith, experience, and mission of the earliest apostles and the churches they founded.

Indeed, the church is founded on Christ, for "no one can lay any foundation other than the one already laid, which is Jesus Christ" (1 Cor. 3:11). The church as a Spirit-filled temple of God is founded on Christ as the man and bestower of the Spirit. Yet upon this foundation there is a foundational ministry dependent on him, namely, the charisms of "apostles and prophets" who form part of an entire building raised up by Christ and indwelt by the Spirit (Eph. 2:20–22). The prophets require the apostles, who passed on the teaching of Christ through the Spirit to the church (Acts 2:42), a teaching that was inscripturated, was received among the people through the winds of the Spirit (2 Tim. 3:15–16), and was witnessed to through the guidance of the Spirit in creedal affirmations. The apostles also require the prophets, for the apostolic teaching and legacy must be contextually discerned and expressed over time by use of prophetic voices, for the church lives as much by the guidance of what the Spirit is saying to the churches (Rev. 1–3) as by the teaching of the apostles (Acts 2:42).

What about the ordained ministry of oversight in the church today? The threefold office of bishop, presbyter, and deacon emerged in the second century from a complex development in which these categories were fluid and interchangeable. There seems to have been no uniform "apostolic structure" founded by Christ and enduring universally in the church from the beginning. The commentary on ministry for the Faith and Order Report *Baptism, Eucharist, Ministry* states justifiably: "The actual forms of ordination and of the ordained ministry, however, have evolved in complex historical developments.... The churches, therefore, need to avoid attributing their particular forms of the ordained ministry directly to the will and institution of Jesus Christ."[131] The evi-

---

131. "Commentaries," 11, for *Baptism, Eucharist, Ministry: Report of the Faith and Order Commission, World Council of Churches, Lima, Peru 1982*, in *Growth in Agreement: Reports and Agreed Statements of Ecumenical Conversations on a World Level*, ed. Harding Meyer and Lukas Vischer (New York: Paulist, 1984), 499.

dence indicates that ministries of oversight in the church have always been fluid and contextually determined, as are all spiritual gifts. Such is especially apparent when one looks at the increasing diversity of church offices and ministries in the world today.

How one judges the apostolicity of the church with regard to the ministry of oversight will thus depend on the ecclesiology that one affirms. At the risk of oversimplification, I will note two major models to consider. One is hierarchical, stressing the dipolarity between those who have oversight in the church as representative of Christ and those who must faithfully receive their ministry and engage in appropriate lay ministries by way of response. The stress here with regard to apostolicity is first placed on the qualitatively distinct nature of gifts of oversight and the uniqueness of the apostolic office vis-à-vis the body of the faithful. The apostolicity of the entire church is not denied but is defined in a way that preserves the qualitatively unique nature of the church's apostolic structure. The office of the bishop mediating the presence of Christ through the sacraments is essential (*esse*) and not just beneficial (*bene esse*) to the church.

The other model grants priority to the metaphor of interactive *koinonia* by which all members of the church engage in mutual ministry of the Word of God as people of faith. Those gifted with oversight are defined in a way that is subordinate to the idea of the ministry of the entire people of God by virtue of their mutual faith. Those with oversight do not concentrate on mediating Christ to the church but rather protecting and guiding this prior polycentric emphasis on the mutual ministry of the whole body of the faithful. Ministries of oversight are usually seen then as equipping and guiding the gracious interaction and proliferation of gifted ministries and viewing themselves as among these gifts, not qualitatively but rather functionally distinct. The stress is on the corporately and mutually shared apostolicity of the entire church. The unique nature of ordained ministry is not denied, only defined so as to highlight their mutual accountability with the entire church, which is apostolic in its faith and mission. The office of the bishop is beneficial but not essential to the presence of Christ in constituting the church.

Both models aim at incorporating the other in some way into its own vision without fundamentally altering its own unique points of emphasis. Such is necessary, since both have at least some element of truth from the New Testament. For example, Acts highlights the ministries of the apostles. Yet Acts also stresses the corporate nature of ministry in the Spirit as "they were all filled with the Holy Spirit and spoke the word of God boldly" (Acts 4:31). Similarly, Hebrews 13:17 addresses the need of the faithful to submit to the ministry of the Word exercised by those who have oversight in the church. Yet, Ephesians 5:21 states that all members should submit to one another out of reverence for Christ, because all members grow up together, "speaking the truth in love" to one another (4:15). Indeed, from Christ the head "the whole body, joined and held together by every supporting ligament, grows and builds itself up in love, as each part does its work" (4:15–16). So, how do we negotiate this tension between ecclesiological models?

Of course, these models are not always held in pure form. There are Pentecostals, true to the restorationist logic, who believe firmly in the restoration of the apostolic office in the church today, disagreeing with many who view the ancient apostolic office as unique and not enduring in the church except in the form of the biblical canon and derivative forms of oversight accountable to Scripture for their validity. Such Pentecostals view this ministry as pneumatologically mediated directly from the risen Christ in obedience to his Word in the here and now without regard for that which may have been instituted historically by Christ and handed down through historical succession from there through an enduring apostolic church office or structure. There is even a movement afoot within the more free church wing of the charismatic movement that releases into the church world rogue apostles directly and independently appointed by the Spirit of Christ and in search of an ecclesiastical structure into which they could incorporate themselves! The fact that this strange practice has some precedent in the Pentecostal movement was dramatically portrayed for us in the movie *The Apostle*, starring Robert Duvall.

I do not hold to a succession from, or restoration of, the apostolic ministry that was originally and directly commissioned by the risen Christ. I hold rather to ministries of oversight gifted by the Spirit as analogous to the early apostolic ministry and in submission to the original apostolic witness and mission. Such ministries certainly arise from, and remain accountable to, the churches they serve! Those who serve in positions of oversight have as their responsibility the preservation and growth of the apostolic witness and mission throughout the entire church today through ongoing prophetic discernment, proclamation, and vision. Those in oversight today must "give an account" of their faithfulness in ministry (Heb. 13:17).

By way of general response to issues raised above, my conclusions stated earlier about the critical dialectic between Christ and the church will not allow me to accept a mere *transference* of power and authority from Christ to any human figure in the church, not even to the church as a whole. It is Christ and the Spirit that wields unquestioned authority, for Christ is the King and the Spirit is the kingdom. Infallibility is a characteristic of Christ alone. The authority of overseers and of the church is *delegated*, not transferred, and is therefore constantly exercised in weakness and humility and in a way account-able to the gospel of the kingdom for its legitimacy, for of the overseers of the church the New Testament states: "They keep watch over you as men who must give an account" (Heb. 13:17). It is through ongoing discernment in col-legial relationship among church leaders but also among the body of the faith-ful more generally as to whether or not the exercise of authority in the church is in harmony with the reign of Christ witnessed to in the gospel. The World Council of Churches Faith and Order Paper *The Nature and Purpose of the Church* notes correctly that the ministry of oversight in the church is exer-cised "communally, personally, and collegially."[132]

Concerning apostolic succession, Catholic theologian Michael Schmaus concludes that "it must be stated that nowhere in Scripture do we find any word of Christ instructing the apostles to appoint successors, or to pass on their mission in the form of the episcopal or priestly office."[133] Of course, Schmaus finds such an office and its succession *implied* in the witness of the New Testament. But not all voices from the Catholic Church have been so sure. Hans Küng wrote his classic *The Church* with no discussion of apostolic office or succession until the very end of his book. This discussion comes at the end of a lengthy argument for a view of the church as fundamentally charismatic and not juridical, with a functional and not qualitative difference assumed between ordained ministry and other ministries of the church. After a thorough examination of the biblical teaching concerning ecclesiastical office in the light of the charismatic structure of the church, Küng concludes that it remains an "urgent question as to whether, in this radical New Testament view of the church, there is room for any kind of ecclesiastical office."[134]

Küng in the end does not reject church office and the unique authority of oversight in serving the entire church shared by those who have this

---

132. *The Nature and Purpose of the Church* #94 (p. 47).
133. Michael Schmaus, *The Church: Its Origin and Structure. Dogma 4* (London: Sheed & Ward, 1972), 138.
134. Küng, *The Church*, 387.

charism. But he regards office as subordinate to the view of the church as a fellowship of believers who share and serve mutually the one faith in Christ, noting that "the church must be seen first and foremost as a fellowship of faith, and only in this light can ecclesiastical office be properly understood."[135] In other words, Küng does not dismiss the benefit of church office, but he defines the difference between it and other lay gifts as functional and views them all as ultimately part of the same working of the Spirit among the faithful. Küng thus concludes that, according to the New Testament, "there is no clear boundary between the permanent public ministries in the community and other charisms; the distinction between the two seems to be fluid."[136] Küng advocates a charismatic structure as descriptive of the church as a mutually edifying fellowship of the faith in the Spirit. More recently, Pentecostal theologian Veli-Matti Kärkkäinen has made use of this notion of the charismatic structure of the church in responding to various ecumenical issues.[137]

Many would maintain that Küng is faced with the problem of how to justify theologically the unique role granted those who have the function of oversight in the churches, as evidenced, for example, by a Paul who confronted the errant prophets at Corinth with a "command" from the Lord (1 Cor. 14:36–38), or the admonition of Hebrews 13:17 to the faithful to submit to those who have oversight in the church. Küng rightly does not deny that there is a difference between "free charisms" that might rise up on occasion to meet specific needs and the ordained ministry that exercises unique authority before the entire gifted congregation or network of congregations to help to guide and to nourish it/them.

Miroslav Volf as well, who holds much in common with Küng's view of the church, also recognizes some sense in which a functional "dipolar" relationship exists between the ordained minister and the congregation of the faithful as the ordained minister serves the church in preaching and sacrament. Like Küng, Volf desires, however, to qualify this dipolarity by locating it within (even subordinating it to) another vision of the church as a polycentric mutual and interactive ministry of many gifted members submitting to one another (Eph. 5:21) under Christ as the head from whom "the whole

---

135. Ibid., 363.
136. Ibid., 394; cf., 179–91.
137. Veli-Matti Kärkkäinen, "Pentecostalism and the Claim for Apostolicity: An Essay in Ecumenical Ecclesiology," *Ecumenical Review of Theology* 25 (2001): 323–36, esp. 333–34; see Yong, *The Spirit Poured* Out, 147–48.

body, joined and held together by every supporting ligament, grows and builds itself up in love, as each part does its work" (4:15–16).[138]

Even a distinction between enduring, especially ordained, ministries of oversight and "free charisms" needs to be qualified, since these free charisms tended to become established ministries as well, such as those of prophets and healers. I think Max Turner justifiably recognizes in the New Testament a spectrum of gifted ministry from established ministries to spontaneous gifts of the Spirit with no break but rather shades of difference within a fluid relationship between these shades. And these ministries of oversight in the New Testament function within the gifted congregation, not above it.[139] Even Hebrews 13:17 notes that those who have oversight "must give an account" for their ministries, meaning that their authority is not absolute but dependent on the Lord and responsible to those in fellowship with them. Spirit baptism means that there is no aristocracy of the Spirit in the church and, as Volf points out, the presence of Christ is not mediated to the church through the "narrow portals" of ordained ministry but rather polycentrically through many gifted ministries in the church interactively.[140]

Spirit baptism makes apostolicity a missionary characteristic and, therefore, a characteristic of the entire church. The term *apostle* refers to the quality of being sent. All gifted members within the *laos* or people of God are sent of God with a mission to fulfill in the baptism of the Spirit. All are laity and all are ministers. Though the apostles and others with ministries of oversight bear a special responsibility to lead, authority and leadership in the church are exercised through other gifts of discernment as well, so that Paul could exhort high-minded prophets to submit to the judgments of others who exercise discernment in the church (1 Cor. 14:29–32) and everyone submits to one another in reverence to Christ (Eph. 5:21). Küng thus notes rightly that the ordained clergy function in an authority "that is given to the whole church" by Jesus Christ.[141] In a sense the entire church is ordained or sent as apostolic so that it can "function with respect to the *ordaining of humanity* for fellowship with God in the consummation of his Kingdom."[142]

---

138. Volf, *After Our Likeness*, 231.

139. Max Turner, *The Holy Spirit and Spiritual Gifts in the New Testament and the Church Today* (Peabody, MA: Hendrickson, 1998), 439.

140. Volf, *After Our Likeness*, 152.

141. Küng, *The Church*, 389.

142. Ibid., 469.

In the light of the above discussion, we can view the apostolic office and the ordained ministry as a charism of the Spirit governed by the norm of the gospel and not qualitatively different from other gift bearers in the church, a point made by Veli-Matti Kärkkäinen.[143] The Pentecost narrative of Acts 2 grants valuable charismatic leadership to the apostles (2:42–43), a leadership confirmed by the rest of the book. The apostles are without a doubt the major players in the drama of Acts. Yet all believers receive the Spirit in Acts 2 directly and speak in tongues the mighty deeds of God (2:4).

Something similar was true in Acts 4. After the persecution of Peter and John, the entire community prays for courage. The result is that "they were *all* filled with the Holy Spirit and spoke the word of God boldly" (4:31). The apostles served on the vanguard of spiritually gifted congregations that served with them to proclaim God's Word in power with signs following. The entire church—indeed, all flesh, including those gifted to be apostles—are part of the Spirit-baptized church as a prophetic community (2:17–18). All are ministers of the word in the power of the Spirit.

The gift of apostleship along with other ministries thus serve to plant and water the seed of the Word so that it can bear fruit among the gifted congregation as all grow up to speak the Word to one another (Eph. 4:11–16; cf. 1 Cor. 3:5–15). For, "speaking the truth in love, we will in all things grow up into him who is the Head" (Eph 4:15). In this sense, the early Christians were not to idolize apostolic leaders as superheroes. The apostles belonged to the church as gifts to inspire and guide them as they grew to take their place as mature bearers of the Spirit and the Word themselves. The Corinthians were thus babes drinking milk in their idolizing the apostles instead of adult participants in the building of the church and its mission in the world (1 Cor. 3:1–15). "What, after all, is Apollos? And what is Paul? Only servants, through whom you came to believe," writes Paul (3:5). Such words were not a cloak of humility used to maintain a situation of apostles ruling over a passive, nonordained laity. Paul really meant that the apostles' role was principally in leading the recruitment and raising of faithful ministers of the Word of God within a Spirit-baptized, charismatic church.

Interestingly, Hans Küng urges looking as much to Paul for an example of apostolic leadership as to Peter, since Paul seems to place his own author-

---

143. Kärkkäinen, "Pentecostalism and the Claim for Apostolicity," 333–34.

ity on par with Peter's in Galatians 1 and 2. In responding to the churches, Paul hesitates to extend his powers of decision. In matters of church discipline he avoids authoritative decision (2 Cor. 8:8–10). In moral questions where a word from the Lord Jesus is not at stake, he prefers to grant freedom to the community to decide (1 Cor. 7:35). Even in cases where the needed action is clear, he does not offer a one-sided prescription but involves the community (1 Cor. 5). When exercising authority he usually urges but does not command compliance (4:14; 9:12, 18; 2 Cor. 13:10; 1 Thess. 2:7; 2 Thess. 3:9; Philem. 8–9). "Paul never confronts his communities as their Lord, nor even as their high priest. The apostle is not the lord, Christ is the Lord." He does not speak to them as children but as brothers and sisters, encouraging a meeting in which they can bless each other. He uses his authority to build up, not to subordinate.[144] We can say that it is the bestowal of the Spirit of "all grace" that guides their interactions, not the juridical authority of the rather graceless structures of the world.

Such humility did not prevent Paul from opposing errant prophets with a word from the Lord and an authority he did not expect to be challenged (1 Cor. 14:36–38). Yet Paul is equally clear that this authoritative word from the Lord was given in support of requiring errant prophets to submit to others in the church gifted with discernment so that "the spirits of the prophets are subject to the control of [other] prophets" (14:32). In other words, his harshest judgments were reserved for the high-minded, who threatened the powers of discernment active in the fellowship of the faithful. Likewise, tongue speakers have their sighs in the Spirit interpreted (14:27–28). All gifts are to be tested for their conformity to a love that "does not delight in evil but rejoices with the truth" (13:6). In other words, apostolic authority was that gift in the church given to encourage and protect a mutual submission and edification throughout the church that was faithful to the word of Christ. It was an authority accountable to the gospel and to the faithful body as well as a participant within it.

In the light of Spirit baptism as a charismatic event, the apostles were to lead the whole church not only in interpreting and proclaiming God's Word but also in ministering it with the power to heal and transform, thus overthrowing the reign of evil powers and bearing witness to the power of the kingdom of God to bring new life. The more recent research supports the

---

144. Küng, *The Church*, 473–74.

view that Jesus' commission of Peter and the other disciples to "bind" and "loose" most likely referred primarily to the passing on of Jesus' healing ministry, involving the binding of the devil and the loosing of people from evil's grip (Matt. 16:17–19; 18:18; cf. 12:28–29), a commission that applied to a wider circle of disciples and not only the twelve (Luke 10:17–18).[145] Binding and loosing undoubtedly involved forgiveness of sins as well as teaching truth to liberate people from the bondage of darkness.

The entire church participates in some of these apostolic gifts. Such was the case at Pentecost. Though signs and wonders did legitimate apostolic leadership (Acts 2:43), they were not confined to the apostles (cf. 8:6), for others were used to continue the ministry of Jesus to go "about doing good . . . healing all who were oppressed of the devil" (10:38 NRSV). Others taught and proclaimed the forgiveness of sins. This apostolic participation in Jesus' deliverance ministry forms the basis for the obvious proliferation of gifts of healing and miracles among ordinary Christians at Corinth who were not apostles (1 Cor. 14:9–10). As Küng maintains, apostolic succession includes multiple gifts of the Spirit and involves the entire church. The entire church hands down the apostolic mission not only to the faithful but externally to humanity in their invitation to faith. Küng thus wrote about the apostolic succession of the entire church.[146]

Jesus' commissioning of Peter in Matthew 16:17–19 deserves special attention in the light of our foregoing discussion. It is commonly assumed among Protestants, following Augustine, that the "rock" on which Christ would found his church is Peter's confession of Christ. But after a careful exegesis of this text, Oscar Cullmann concluded that the rock means Peter himself as an apostle of Jesus Christ. He holds, however, that the focus is on Peter's apostolic calling and ministry, something not confined to Peter but open to the other apostles (cf. 18:18). However, he also holds that Peter is to be "sure first among them" and "their representative in all things."[147]

I thus find value in the Petrine office of the Catholic Church as an implicit witness to the fact that Jesus commissioned apostles to serve the unity of the church around fellowship with Jesus in *koinonia* and mission. Peter symbol-

---

145. Richard H. Hiers, "'Binding' and 'Loosing': The Matthean Authorizations," *Journal of Biblical Literature* 104 (June 1985), 233–50.

146. Küng, *The Church*, 421.

147. Oscar Cullmann, *Peter*, 211. See also, Ridderbos, *The Gospel of the Kingdom*, 359–60, who draws a similar conclusion.

izes for me as a Pentecostal an apostle of deliverance in the church who preached the Pentecost gospel, helped to ground the Spirit-baptized church within major doctrinal teachings (Acts 2:42), performed the first recorded healing in Acts as he offered the poor man "such as he had" to give (3:1–10), whose very shadow "healed those tormented by evil spirits" (5:16), and who gave his life for Christ in martyrdom. Understood in this way, no one exercising oversight in the church in harmony with Peter's witness can seek to quench the Spirit among members of the church who recall Peter's ministry of healing and inspired proclamation.

As a Pentecostal, I am open to be inspired by the symbolic significance of the Petrine office as a pointer to the possibility that the church in all of its diversity and uniqueness might one day be one around Jesus as the Spirit Baptizer and as the one who commissioned disciples to further his witness. I think the more recent definitions of the Petrine office from *Ut Unum Sint* and beyond that highlight the service of love and unity have brought us all further in a constructive direction in discussing this important issue.

I think it goes without saying that I would not otherwise elevate Peter as the focal point of the global unity of the church as the Catholic Church has done, nor would I locate his role within an office that serves as a privileged possession of the Catholic Church (not even as first among equals). I certainly would not conclude that the bearer of this office has "full, supreme, and universal power over the church" (as does *Lumen Gentium* 22), even if this is meant to include some sense of shared authority in the church. Ironically, the Petrine office has come to symbolize the possible unity of the church, although it has also been the office that represents one of the greatest barriers to unity. Would that the grace of God actually use this barrier as a help in overcoming it! How this could be done is hidden in the mystery of God's will. But ecumenical reactions to Pope John Paul II's passing, especially on a popular level, lead me to believe that headway in this direction is possible.

We may safely conclude that the church is apostolic or sent to participate in the fellowship and mission of the Spirit of God in witness to Jesus in the world. Apostolicity is thus a mark of the church. As noted above, we can speak of an "apostolic succession" of the entire church, for all are ordained to forgive sins and serve as channels of grace to others. Küng makes it "a succession of apostolic faith and witness, service and life,"[148] as does the WCC Faith

---

148. Küng, *The Church*, 421.

and Order study *Baptism, Eucharist, Ministry*.[149] Küng writes further that "the whole church, and hence every individual member, stands in the line of succession from the apostles."[150] He would even involve an analogous "succession" of prophets, teachers, and other *charisms* as the church fulfills its apostolic function.[151] Through Spirit baptism, the deliverance ministry of Peter and the other apostles belongs to us all.

Catholic theologian David Stagaman wrote of various paradigm shifts in authority in the church under the influence of Vatican II and the ecumenical movement. We can list six:[152]

1. *Status to charism:* The shift of emphasis has turned from viewing church officials mainly in terms of their status to understanding them primarily in terms of their *charisms*.

2. *Obligation to persuasion:* Formerly authoritative acts tended to be viewed as impositions from above. There is a move toward understanding them as attempts to persuade both church members and the outside world of some value that will improve the corporate life of the church and even of the entire human community.

3. *Hierarchy to dialogue:* We are leaving behind a pyramid of authority in relation to a passive laity and are moving towards a dialogue model in which all Christians are granted some participation in the divine authority.

4. *Orthodoxy to orthopraxis:* We are leaving behind an exercise of authority aimed at provoking obedience viewed primarily as conformity within the community and are aiming toward an exercise of authority in worship/liturgy, the preaching of the Word, and individual and communal change towards liberation. We can also add here the rising emphasis on authority in the context of service and mission and the rise in sensitivity to the "charismatic structure" of the church as a context for the celebration of sacrament and Word.

5. *Institution to pilgrim people:* We are moving from a church seen as self-contained, almost completely visible unit that had practically all the

---

149. *Baptism, Eucharist, Ministry* 34 (pp. 490–91).
150. Küng, *The Church*, 433.
151. Ibid.
152. David J. Stagaman, *Authority in the Church* (Collegeville, MN: Liturgical, 1999), 3–4.

answers within its bosom, toward becoming a pilgrim people commissioned by its founder to discover authentic meaning through inser-
tion in and confrontation with the world.

6. *Essence to relationality:* We are moving in our view of the church's
authority from a fixed and permanent structure toward the church
viewed more as a relational stability in which lines of power are constantly in flux, though not haphazardly.

Even if one accounts for the forgivable level of optimism reflected in such
a list, one is still justified in assuming and seeking to build upon a growing
sensitivity among the churches to issues of community, selflessness, service,
and diversification in their understandings of apostolic authority within the
church and from the church as apostolic in the world.

"MARKS" OF PREACHING, SACRAMENTS, AND CHARISMATIC FULLNESS

The Pentecostal take on the marks of the church places a special focus on the
need for the sanctified and missionary church to proclaim healing to all the
nations in the power of the Spirit. The marks of Christ are Savior, Sanctifier,
Spirit Baptizer, Healer, and Coming King. Since the marks of the church are
also the marks of Christ, the fivefold gospel can be viewed as the Pentecostal
elaboration on the marks of the church. Even speaking in tongues powerfully
symbolized the global reach of this gospel of healing as well as the healing
power of the gospel. Through tongues we groan with the suffering creation for
the liberty to come.

Dorothea Soelle maintained rightly that suffering tends to cause one to
withdraw into silence.[153] While respecting that silence, the Pentecostal spotlight on tongues and healing implies a reaching out in power for the final healing to come in the Spirit-baptized new creation. Charismatic proliferation,
diversification, and fullness in the church not only enable and enhance the
ministry of the church to those in need, it *supports and enhances the experience of the Spirit through preaching and sacrament, for the divine presence is
mutual presence, presence in communion.*

The gifts of the Spirit (*charismata*) are not supernatural powers that are
channeled through people with no input from the people active in them. In the

---

153. Dorothea Soelle, *Leiden* (Stuttgart: Kreuz Verlag, 1973), ch.1.

words of David Lim, spiritual gifts are "incarnational."[154] We are gifted in relationship with God in a way that renews and enhances our natural talents, but also exceeds them. These gifts must be cultivated or "fanned into flame" through use and personal growth in interaction with others (2 Tim. 1:6). The end goal is a diverse witness to God's Word in relation to one another so as to build up the church in the love of God toward its head, who is Christ. The formative channels of grace in preaching and sacrament burst forth in multiple forms of witness in word and deed among many gifted members. The gifted church then shows forth signs of grace in an all-too graceless world. It models the loving *koinonia* of God to the world as the context in which his Word is proclaimed to the lost and the graceless structures and forms of life in the world are challenged.

As Michael Welker has shown us in his book *God the Spirit*, the gifts of the Spirit are *interactive and relational*.[155] Discernment guides prophecy, interpretation explains tongues, wisdom guides the proper use of knowledge, evangelism points those who are healed to the good news to which the healing bears witness, faith keeps scholarship loyal to the proclamation of the church and scholarship keeps faith open to critical questions, and so on. In spiritual gifts, church members interact in ways that are grace-filled and edifying. *Since spiritual gifts are relational and interactive, they serve to structure the church as a community of graced relationships that facilitate communion and show forth signs of grace to the world.*

As a result of Pentecost, the church was formed with a *charismatic structure*. This structure is fluid and relational, because spiritual gifts are graced ways of relating to each other that depend on the will of the Spirit at work among us and the contextual needs of the ministry of the Word of God (1 Cor. 12:11). Spiritual gifts signify and facilitate graced relationships. They expand our capacities to receive and further impart the grace that comes to us through preaching and sacrament. We can take this to mean that the *charismata* (spiritual gifts) represent the formation of edifying relationships in the church that inspire us in many different and unique ways to bear one another's burdens, affirm one another's dignity and worth before God, and build one another up in Christ. *Spiritual gifts open the church to God's grace and show forth signs of this grace in a graceless world.*

---

154. David Lim, *Spiritual Gifts: A Fresh Look* (Springfield, MO: Gospel, 1991), 187.

155. Michael Welker, *God the Spirit*, trans. John F. Hoffmeyer (Minneapolis: Augsburg Fortress, 1994), 268–70.

The *koinonia* of the church is thus experienced in multiple and interactive "individuations of grace"[156] or *charismata* (gifts of grace) bestowed by Christ on the church at Pentecost (Eph. 4:8). The outpouring of the Spirit on "all flesh" is not generic or abstract but concrete, diverse, and interactive, for "we have different gifts, according to the grace given us" (Rom. 12:6). Grace is uniquely received and shared according to each person's giftings. Grace is not generic. It is the Lord turning mercifully to us through the Spirit in the Word of God to transform us into unique vessels fit for the master's use. The Spirit is thus the divine presence in and through many persons. As the "go-between God," the outpoured Spirit proliferates grace diversely, inspiring interactive fellowship and edification as the church builds itself up in love.

The Spirit in the church seeks through fellowship to "fan into flame" the gifts functioning in and through one another (2 Tim. 1:6). Pastoral leadership needs to make this fanning into flame a top priority. Of course, flames require careful monitoring to make sure that they burn in the right directions. But quenching them is never an option. To the contrary, as John Koenig has stated, the church is to be a "gift-evoking fellowship."[157]

The flame itself must be seen as the flame of love (Rom. 5:5), for love is the greatest of all gifts. Not only is love the greatest gift, but it is the gift at the essence of all other gifts, for without love all other gifts become "nothing" or lose their substance. Speaking in tongues becomes clanging noises that hurt the ear, prophecy and faith lose their direction, and even martyrdom is harnessed to self-destructive ends (1 Cor 13:1–3). Without love, gifts are nothing. Without gifts, love becomes abstract, lacking its diversely interactive expressions, including its "signs and wonders."

The point here is that the Christological foundation of the church is not only to be found in church office, sacrament, and proclamation. Christ is also present in multiple gifts and signs of the Spirit in the fellowship of the church. Neglected to an extent in ecumenical documents on the nature of the church is the way in which the gifts of the Spirit proliferate and diversify Christ's presence through the church in the world. A juridical or sacramental understanding of the church that lacks an appreciation for the church's charismatic

---

156. Ernst Käsemann, *Commentary on Romans*, trans. and ed. Geoffrey Bromiley (Grand Rapids: Eerdmans, 1980), 344.

157. John Koenig, *Charismata: God's Gifts to God's People* (Philadelphia: Westminster, 1978), 123. He quotes Elizabeth O'Conner, *Eighth Day of Creation* (Waco, TX: Word, 1975), 8–9.

structure can seem overly institutional, abstract, hierarchical, and monolithic. Even the preaching of the church without the power and gifts of the Spirit can seem abstract and overly cerebral.

Placed within the framework of the charismatic structure of the church, the ordained ministry in relation to preaching and sacraments can be explained in ways that avoid the problems that accompany clericalism or an understanding of the church dominated by the clergy. The *koinonia* of the Spirit experienced in the interactive charismatic life of the church implies a mutually accountable and edifying ministry in the church involving all the people of God. We will conclude this chapter with a reflection on preaching and sacrament in relation to the charismatic structure of the church.

Preaching

It is difficult to overestimate the significance of preaching and Scripture in channeling God's grace to the church. The gospel of Jesus and the scriptural witness come to us through the very breath of God so that we may have the wisdom and the power to be saved through faith in Jesus Christ (2 Tim. 3:15–16). The Scriptures are inspired, though not in the sense of representing a static deposit of revealed truths that we can systematize into idols of ink and paper. The fundamentalistic tendency to view Scripture in this manner can cause the church to presume it has the final word on all of life's questions and challenges. Instead, as we interact with others on the Scriptures, we must learn to dialogue, to grow, or to change, not to pontificate. Following 2 Timothy 3:15–16, the Scriptures should be embraced as a living witness to Jesus Christ through the Spirit of God, inspiring ever-increasing faith in Jesus and granting us ongoing wisdom and power to serve one another and the world in Christ's name. As breathed by the Spirit, the Scriptures are a living guide or measure of our worship and witness, not a static deposit to master and control according to our own self-serving ends.

Because of the living breath of God, the gospel of the Scriptures bursts forth with signs of life in the charismatic structure of the church. Spiritual gifts then help to keep the apostolic Word of the Scriptures alive and relevant within the ongoing gracious and gifted interactions of God's people as they grow up into the full stature of Christ. Furthermore, spiritual gifts are always accountable to the living witness of the apostolic Word of the Scriptures, as Paul implies in his struggle with the pneumatically gifted members of the Corinthian congregation (1 Cor. 14:37). Within the charismatic structure of the church, the Spirit functions through the Scriptures as a living book of both freedom and order to guide our gracious interactions with one another and our mission in the world. In fact, the Scriptures themselves are a universally relevant and binding gift of the Spirit to the church in order to guide the particular and diverse charismatic structure of the church in its ongoing life, confession, and mission.

My approach to Scripture may be regarded by some as dangerously vague. Some may see in my description of Scripture a fluid and imprecise understanding of how the Scriptures speak to us. Are there not truths clearly revealed in Scripture on which we can rely? Certainly. As Karl Barth reminds us, the revelation of God is *verbal* as well as personal. Many evangelicals have misread Barth on this point. Barth did not deny that revelation through Scripture is verbal; he only denied that this verbal witness can be viewed as a static deposit to be mastered and placed at the disposal of our systems and ideologies. Notice what Barth wrote on this matter: "The personal character of God's Word means, not its deverbalizing, but the posing of an absolute barrier against reducing its wording to a human system."[158]

For Barth, God's placing divine revelation at our disposal in this way "would mean his allowing us to gain control over his Word, to fit it into our own designs, and thus to shut up ourselves against him to our own ruin."[159] Barth defends the sovereignty of God's Word by advocating a free text in the ongoing witness of the Spirit to Christ and not by making revelation nothing but a vague and subjective emotion. The confession that the Bible is the Word of God for Barth is thus not dependent on experience but on God's action in the Spirit. Barth wrote of this confession: "We do not accept it as a description of our experience of the Bible. We accept it as a description of God's action in the Bible, whatever may be the experiences we have or do not have in this connection."[160] One may thus speak of the "objectivity" of the Spirit's work in the text of Scripture. The text participates in Spirit baptism, and whether or not one hears its voice depends on whether or not one is open to the same Spirit. Let those who have ears to hear, hear what the Spirit is saying to the churches.

The Bible is verbally inspired and contains truths that we confess and live by. But this text and its truths are living and active, constantly channeling the

---

158. Barth, *Church Dogmatics*, Vol. I, Pt. 1, 139.
159. Ibid.
160. Ibid., 110.

power and wisdom of the Spirit to us by God's grace in diverse ways in the midst of gifted interactions among his people. Those ordained as leaders among us preach and teach the Word of God and administer the sacraments in a way that constantly places Christ and his biblical witness before us as the measure of our lives, especially our gifted interactions and ministries. Yet these leaders are also gifts among other gifted members of the congregation, despite their special functions as ministers among us, for "all things are yours, whether Paul, or Apollos, or Cephas" (1 Cor. 3:21). They are accountable to us and we are to them. Ultimately, the canonical witness through the Spirit inspires, empowers, and guides us all in our gifted praise and service.

The charismatic structure of the church also serves to expand the field of the grace that comes to us in the Word of God. Without this structure, preaching becomes an intellectualistic and abstract monologue rather than a living and life-transforming dialogue. In the Protestant focus on the Word of God, pneumatology has tended to be dominated by the exposition of the biblical text and the inward illumination of the text in the mind of the believer. This dominant emphasis on the *noetic* function of revelation has dogged Protestant theology from Calvin to Barth. Of course, the Reformers had a more expansive pneumatology than this. I refer here to a point of emphasis. More recently, theologians like Moltmann and Pannenberg have attempted to refer to the Spirit's work much more dominantly along the lines of a holistic and transformational "new creation" motif in an effort to transcend the limitations of focusing the work of the Spirit on the revelational and the noetic. A greater role for a diversity of *charismata* in our understanding of the ministry of the church to serve a multiplicity of needs will go far in enhancing this positive trend.

In addition, the Protestant emphasis on the realm of the noetic has tended to avoid or devalue the ecstatic and depth experiences of God in favor of the cognitive and the rational responses to the word, as Emil Brunner has shown us.[161] Gordon Fee has expressed the view of many Pentecostals when remarking that "contrary to the opinion of many, spiritual edification can take place in ways other than through the cortex of the brain."[162] More of an emphasis

---

161. Emil Brunner, *Das Misverständnis der Kirche* (Zürich: Theologischer Verlag, 1951), ch. 5.

162. Gordon Fee, *God's Empowering Presence: The Holy Spirit in the Letters of Paul* (Peabody, MA: Hendrickson, 1994), 129.

on the gifts of the Spirit among all the people of God will allow for a broader spectrum of gifted activity by involving the divine claim on the whole person, including the depths of the subconscious mind, the life of the body, and the disciplines of rational thinking.

Sacraments

We need to say something about the sacramental life of the church as well. As Calvin wrote, "Akin to the preaching of the gospel, we have another help to our faith in the sacraments."[163] The sacrament depends on the reception of the Word by faith for its efficacy.[164] The sacraments are not only an aid to faith but are the confirmation and further manifestation of the very Word of God that inspires faith. By the power of the Spirit, the gospel is further proclaimed with sacramental signs of baptism and Eucharist.

Reformed theologian G. C. Berkouwer finds the proclamation of the Word in preaching to be clearer than that which comes through the sacraments,[165] but Calvin would not agree: "The sacraments bring with them the clearest promises, and, when compared with the word, have this peculiarity that they represent promises to the life, as if painted in a picture."[166] The sacraments are efficacious as instruments of grace because they offer the promises of the gospel to the believer who receives them in faith, for, as Calvin notes further, "the Spirit performs what is promised."[167] The Spirit's performance involves our performance, which is the meaning of the sacrament. The sacraments thus "do not avail one iota without the energy of the Holy Spirit."[168]

Pentecostals have been ambivalent about ritual as a vehicle of the Spirit's work, even though, as Daniel Albrecht has shown us, their worship is more ritualized than they recognize.[169] The broader context for the Pentecostal

---

163. Calvin, *Institutes*, 491 (4.14.1).

164. Ibid., 494 (4.14.5).

165. In contrary response to G. van der Leeuw, who, according to Berkouwer, saw both the preached word and the sacraments as equal in their role in revealing God's Word; see G. C. Berkouwer, *The Sacraments* (Grand Rapids: Eerdmans, 1969), 45–55.

166. Calvin, *Institutes*, 491 (4.14.1).

167. Ibid., 495–96 (4.14.7).

168. Ibid., 497 (4.14.9).

169. Daniel E. Albrecht, *Rites of the Spirit: A Ritual Approach to Pentecostal/Charismatic Spirituality* (Sheffield: Sheffield Academic Press, 1999).

suspicion of ritual is the Enlightenment bias that "rituals are pagan, idolatrous, and popish."[170] But Tom Driver notes that there is a deep human longing for ritual that is often frustrated in our culture. He finds this longing rooted in the fact that ritual is a kind of performance that suggests "alternative worlds" and nourishes "imaginative visions" of God's goals for the world.[171] They are different from the routines of ordinary life even though they are drawn from them. The ritual sacraments thus point to the grace implied in all of life and also to God's desire to renew the creation into the very dwelling place of God. Driver states eloquently that "they move in a kind of liminal space, at the edge of, or in the cracks between, the mapped regions of what we like to call 'the real world.'"[172]

Geoffrey Wainwright also suggests that ritual is the "solemn way by which a community formulates its common mind on the meaning of life and world,"[173] except that for Christians this expression is meant to transform the present situation toward the fulfillment of that meaning, which is eschatological. This is because for Christians "meaning is in the making: life is oriented toward God's ultimate purpose, and history-making is the way to the attainment of that meaning for both individuals and humanity as a whole."[174] Through the sacraments, we "celebrate something that is humanly absurd, something literally unbelievable and beyond all worldly expectation," namely, the new heavens and new earth.[175] As the 1979 "Elucidation" of the Anglican-Catholic dialogue on the Eucharist affirmed, the Lord's Supper is the "food of the new creation," a "sacramental presence in which God uses realities of this world to convey the realities of the new creation."[176] The baptism in the Spirit is both the foundation and the goal of this expectation.

Let me address the issue of water baptism more specifically. A special relationship exists between water and Spirit baptism. The water rite of John

---

170. Tom F. Driver, *The Magic of Ritual: Our Need for Liberating Rites That Transform Our Lives and Our Communities* (San Francisco: HarperSanFrancisco, 1991), 9.

171. Ibid., 80–81.

172. Ibid., 81.

173. Wainwright, *Doxology*, 121.

174. Ibid.

175. Driver, *The Magic of Ritual*, 202.

176. "Elucidation," 6b, of the "Anglican-Roman Catholic Dialogue" (1979), in *Growth in Agreement: Reports and Agreed Statements of Ecumenical Conversations on a World Level*, ed. Harding Meyer and Lukas Vischer (New York: Paulist, 1984), 75.

the Baptist, which is not unrelated to the later rise of Christian water baptism, formed the original context for the Spirit baptismal metaphor, even if the contrast between them was the major emphasis (Luke 3:16–17; John 1:33; Acts 1:5). It has been my conviction that Spirit baptism as the eschatological gift of the Spirit transcends the water rite from which the metaphor was birthed by John. The difference between John the Baptist's rite and that which endured in Christian contexts is that John's baptism looked forward to Spirit baptism while Christian baptism lives from it and points to its fulfillment. Regeneration through faith in the gospel and the ritual performance of this conversion in baptism depend on the gift of the Spirit for their significance and power as a life-transforming experience.

Our experience of Spirit baptism may not be consciously felt most dramatically at the moment of conversion or water baptism. But when Spirit baptism is experienced, the experience cannot be defined apart from them. Yet neither is our experience of Spirit baptism confined to conversion and baptism, for it spills out from them into charismatic and missionary experiences that relate us to others in the church and to people in the world. Ultimately, Spirit baptism fulfills conversion and baptism to bring about the resurrection of the dead and the new creation.

Because Christ came into solidarity with us as the man of the Spirit in the baptismal waters, we can by the same Spirit come into solidarity with Christ in our baptism. Being buried with him in baptism (Rom. 6:3–4) means that our death is now defined in solidarity with his death. Just as his death was an act of the pouring out of a life through the eternal Spirit (Heb. 9:14) that was shown to be indestructible and victorious (7:16), so our death "with him" takes on the supreme act of an indestructible life poured out for God's kingdom as well. Likewise, to complete the performance, baptism causes us to rise up from the water in newness of life as Christ rose from the dead to fulfill the reign of God on earth. So we rise in baptism with Christ for the same purpose. Baptism thus also anticipates the resurrection from the dead "by the Spirit of holiness" (Rom. 1:4).

The purpose of this entire performance in baptism of our regeneration by faith in the gospel is to hear this word of the gospel again so that we can publicly perform our conversion to Christ and its fulfillment in resurrection. In performing it, we embrace its promise and confirm publicly the Spirit's claim on our lives, which is the claim of Christ's lordship. St. Basel thus describes baptism as a renewal of life: "The water receives our body as a tomb, and so becomes the image of death, while the Spirit pours in the life-giving power, renewing in souls which were dead in sins the life they first possessed."[177] I would not make the regenerated life through the indwelling Spirit absolutely dependent on the rite of water baptism, but I see regeneration as somehow fulfilled in the act of performing it in baptism in a way analogous to how a wedding ceremony confirms and fulfills a commitment between two hearts joined together in love. Someone can point to that baptismal act later, as Paul did in Romans 6:11, and say, "Count yourselves dead to sin but alive to God in Christ Jesus!"

It is difficult in this view of baptism to justify infant baptism. The case for it from the New Testament is weak at best. For example, references to a household being baptized may very well have referred to slaves and adult members of the clan.[178] The entire theology of baptism in the New Testament depends on the rite being a performance of our commitment to the crucified and risen Christ in faith and obedience. Though a ceremonial embrace of our children as laid claim to by God and the community of faith is certainly a meaningful act that is at least proleptically sacramental in nature, looking forward to the time when the child will respond favorably to the good news of Christ, calling this a "baptism" is problematic. Note what Wainwright says, that infant baptism threatens to do "violence to the relation between divine initiative and human response in the work of salvation" so that "baptism ceases to be a true embodiment of the gospel."[179] Baptism would then be in danger of becoming a divine embrace without the proper correlative response and performance by the one participating in the Spirit of new life through baptism. No faith of the church or parents can make up for the absence of conscious faith by the one being baptized.

This problem is made more intense by the many people baptized in the womb of a historic church (a reality not without value) but who have made no conscious faith response, something vital to the New Testament meaning

---

177. Quoted in Geoffrey Wainwright, "Veni, Sancti Spiritus: The Invocation of the Holy Spirit in the Liturgies of the Churches," in *The Holy Spirit, the Church, and Christian Unity: Proceedings of the Consultation Held at the Monastery of Bose, Italy, 14–20 October, 2002*, ed. D. Donnelly, A. Denaux, and J. Famerée (Leuven: Leuven Univ. Press, 2005), 305.

178. As Geoffrey Wainwright notes, *Christian Initiation* (Ecumenical Studies in History 10; Richmond, VA: John Knox, 1969), 44.

179. Ibid., 50.

of baptism. Moltmann adds that infant baptism has thus become the hand-maiden of "culture Christianity" or a national church that allows for a Christian identity of sorts to exist without a conscious commitment to Christ.[180] Wainwright will not go that far in his remarks, noting instead that the practice can have meaning in certain times and places in drawing people into the community of the faith who might not otherwise have any real exposure to the church or its gospel.[181] But Wainwright concludes: "I would hold that baptism upon profession of faith gives the best possibility of embodying the full range of the gospel truths of salvation."[182]

In the midst of this problem with the historic churches over infant baptism, we must be reminded that there is but "one baptism" (Eph. 4:5). This verse is an ecumenical challenge. Even if we may not agree with the baptismal form of infant baptism and its fulfillment in confirmation, is not that baptism within its liturgical framework an embrace of the Spirit of Christ? Even without confirmation, does not that baptism at least anticipate the life of the Spirit in that baby's life as it is taken up into the arms of a church that embraces Christ?

In a Pentecostal context, the controversy surrounds the baptismal formula. The Oneness Pentecostals will only accept baptism in the name of Jesus. By way of response to the Oneness Pentecostals, can we not assume that baptism in Jesus' name at least implies the role of Jesus as Savior in devotion to the Father in the power of the Spirit? What is Jesus' name without this Trinitarian and salvific life and work to give it meaning? Cannot Trinitarians recognize in baptism in Jesus' name an implicit reference to the Father, the Son, and the Spirit? And is not the baptismal candidate who is led to reach out to Jesus and confess him as Savior in the baptismal rite implicitly being baptized in Jesus' name, even if this name is not used as part of the baptismal formula?

The freedom and sovereignty of the Spirit in Spirit baptism means that the Spirit does not require slavish or perfect devotion to form or expression of faith in order to embrace a heart that reaches out to Jesus. The church does not administer Spirit baptism; rather, Spirit baptism administers the church, even in its weakness, including its inadequate forms. Not the precise expression of faith or the proper use of form but the Spirit is the reality that places

---

180. Moltmann, *The Church in the Power of the Spirit*, 229.
181. Wainwright, *Christian Initiation*, 55.
182. Ibid.

baptism within the realm of the life of the kingdom of God. "For the kingdom of God is not a matter of eating and drinking [i.e., ceremonial law], but of righteousness, peace and joy in the Holy Spirit" (Rom. 14:17). The Spirit is devoted first to the liberating love of the Father manifested in Jesus and not to the forms of ecclesiastical liturgy! Baptism provides a valuable link of unity and possible communion between the churches that we within our finite formulations of faith and ceremony might have difficulty accepting. So be it.

The greater ecumenical challenge lies in the Lord's Supper. Even though it is the *Lord's* Supper and table and the invitation to sup comes from him (Rev. 3:20), not all churches can find it possible to share it among all those who genuinely embrace Jesus as Lord. That table will one day involve all of the faithful at the marriage supper of the Lamb. The Spirit thus goes out from the Lord to invite all who genuinely confess Jesus as Lord to a proleptic sharing of the Lord's table in the here and now in anticipation of that day. In this invitation, the Spirit is not bound to any exclusive ecclesiastical claims on this table. Like baptism, there is but one table of the Lord. Everyone who shares it in genuine devotion to Jesus and his kingdom are valid participants.

With regard to the Lord's Supper, it is highly significant that the *anamnesis* of looking back to Jesus' death and resurrection as the inauguration of the kingdom in power should involve an *epiclesis* or invocation of the Spirit. The Christological link between the two is the fact that Jesus poured out his indestructible life in the Spirit on the cross and had it raised again by the Spirit of holiness in order to be the Spirit Baptizer. Without Jesus as the Spirit Baptizer, there is no clear link between the *anamnesis* and the *epiclesis*. In fact, the *anamnesis* is fulfilled in the *epiclesis* in the light of Jesus' resurrection from death to mediate the Spirit.

The *epiclesis* is thus at the heart of the meal. A lot of attention has been paid in the twentieth century in ecumenical discussion on the place given to the *epiclesis* or invocation of the Spirit in the Lord's Supper typical of the Eastern tradition.[183] The Liturgy of St. John Chrysostom states that the work of the Spirit in the Lord's Supper is for "fellowship with the Holy Spirit, for the fullness of the Kingdom."[184] But do we typically highlight this as an occasion for genuine Pentecostal experience? In reflecting on a typical eucharistic celebration, Tom Driver rightly observes that the Holy Spirit is invoked in the

---

183. Wainwright, "Veni, Sancti Spiritus," 318.
184. Quoted in ibid., 319.

liturgy, but typically "it does not linger over this. It does not wait for this to happen. Rather, it takes the petition for granted uttering it as a formula usually said in a ritual."[185] In such cases, "ritual rests content with its own form."[186] There is little opportunity for interaction or genuine experiences of renewal.

Most significant to a Pentecostal approach to the sacraments, Driver has studied the wide range of rituals globally and regrets that a wide gulf so often separates Christian liturgists and sacramental theologians from the advocates of Spirit possession. He regrets the relative loss in Christian understandings of the sacraments of an emphasis on becoming "filled with the immediate presence of the deity" as essential to the sacramental act.[187] He finds in the Pentecostal stress on a fresh Spirit infilling in worship as an example of a new definition of sacramental experience. Driver complains that the "experience of possession has been more or less banished, its place taken by an emphasis on symbolism."[188]

Signs as performances point in another direction, because through the agency of the Spirit they bring to realization that which they signify. After all, in the sacraments we participate in that which signifies the sanctification of creation to become the very dwelling place of God through the crucifixion and resurrection of the Spirit Baptizer. If this is so, how do we celebrate and perform the future effects of the outpouring of the Spirit without some experience of God possessing us to function as God's temple already in the here and now? I am not referring here to the tyranny of emotionalism, but I am calling for an expectation that God will visit us anew and possess us anew out of love as his own. As Simon Chan notes, the Pentecostal experience of being baptized or filled with the Spirit has a meaningful context in the sacraments.[189]

I know that the sacraments carry a promise of God's faithfulness regardless of my capacity to feel it during the service. I have come recently to cherish this promise in the worship service. I agree with William L. de Arteaga that greater attention to the promises of God realized in the Eucharist can

---

185. Driver, *The Magic of Ritual*, 197–98.
186. Ibid., 198.
187. Ibid., 208.
188. Ibid., 209.
189. Simon Chan rightly states that "Christ the truth is made present in the church by the action of the Spirit in the preaching of the Word and the sacrament" (*Pentecostal Theology and the Christian Spiritual Tradition* [Sheffield: Sheffield Academic Press, 2000], 107).

enrich religious revivals, granting them deeper spiritual experience and greater communal significance.[190] I also know that the experience of God in the sacrament is deeper than that which I may consciously feel or understand, for God is the one who is able to do "immeasurably more than we ask or imagine" (Eph. 3:20). The Spirit's involvement in the Lord's Supper transcends time but also human rationality and speech. Like art, these rituals bear more meanings than we know.

Richard Baer makes the interesting connection between the liturgy surrounding the sacraments and speaking in tongues in that both imply meanings too deep for words or rational reflection, even though both draw on the Scriptures for how we interpret them.[191] In the words of Harvey Cox, both tongues and ritual protest the "tyranny of words" in worship[192] and allow for the sacred to encounter us through a performance that emerges from deep within the soul. I have suggested elsewhere that tongues, the laying on of hands for healing, and foot washing have functioned in Pentecostal services in ways analogous to such in-depth sacramental experience.

Nevertheless, a more interactive liturgy during the Lord's Supper will encourage people to open up to deeper experiences of divine infilling than they might be prone to have if sitting in isolation on a pew. Keep in mind that Spirit infilling is ideally a charismatically interactive experience: "Be filled with the Spirit, speaking to one another through psalms, hymns, and spiritual songs" (Eph. 5:18–19 NASB). The diversity of spiritual gifts can play a valuable role in increasing the reception of all that the Lord's Supper has to offer. Clark Pinnock's insight is applicable here:

> As well as receiving the sacraments from the Spirit, we need to cultivate openness to the gifts of the Spirit. The Spirit is present beyond liturgy in a wider circle. There is a flowing that manifests itself as power to bear witness, heal the sick, prophesy, praise God enthusiastically, perform miracles and more. There is a liberty to celebrate, an ability to dream and see visions, a release of Easter life. There are impulses of power in the

190. William L. de Arteaga, *Forgotten Power: The Significance of the Lord's Supper in Revival* (Grand Rapids: Zondervan, 2002).

191. Richard Baer Jr., "Quaker Silence, Catholic Liturgy, and Pentecostal Glossolalia: Some Functional Similarities," in *Perspectives on the New Pentecostalism*, ed. R. P. Spittler (Grand Rapids: Baker, 1976), esp. 151.

192. Harvey Cox, *Fire from Heaven: The Rise of Pentecostal Spirituality and the Reshaping of Religion in the Twenty-First Century* (Boston: Addison-Wesley, 1995), 93.

move of the Spirit to transform and commission disciples to become instruments of the mission.[193]

The Pentecostal-Catholic 1976 Report affirms that "our Lord is present in the members of his body, manifesting himself in worship by means of a variety of charismatic expressions."[194] The eucharistic mode of God's presence, though special, is continuous with all other modes, according to the 1978 Report of the Catholic-Lutheran dialogue.[195]

These "modes of presence" are not only "continuous" but mutually interactive. Driver believes that the communal dimension of the sacramental act as an experience of the Spirit was somewhat eclipsed by the outmoded use of Aristotelian metaphysics to conceive of sacramental grace as a substance one can dispense or accumulate. He wishes to replace sacramental substances with the Spirit "invoked by the liminality of ritual performance."[196] We should shift the focus from the transformation of the elements to Christ's participation by the Spirit in the communal act and our communion with him and one another by means of the same Spirit.[197] After all, "genuine presence is mutual presence."[198] Sacramental presence is mutual presence, a *koinonia* in the Spirit in which Christ fills us with the Spirit and we give of ourselves in the Spirit to him. "Sacraments, like sacrifices, are acts that generate intense presence: Worshippers make themselves present to each other and to God, receiving in return the shock of God's presence among them."[199]

All of the marks are first marks of Jesus and of his Spirit in the realization of the kingdom of God on earth. They become marks of the church through Spirit baptism. Because Spirit baptism is not a once-and-for-all event but an

---

193. Clark Pinnock, *Flame of Love: A Theology of the Holy Spirit* (Downers Grove, IL: InterVarsity Press, 1996), 129.

194. "Final Report of the Dialogue between the Secretariat for Promoting Christian Unity of the Roman Catholic Church and Leaders of Some Pentecostal Churches and Participants in the Charismatic Movement within Protestant and Anglican Churches, 1976," 34, in *Growth in Agreement: Reports and Agreed Statements of Ecumenical Conversations on a World Level*, 428.

195. "The Eucharist: Final Report of the Joint Roman Catholic-Lutheran Commission, 1978," 16, in *Growth in Agreement: Reports and Agreed Statements of Ecumenical Conversations on a World Level*, 195.

196. Driver, *The Magic of Ritual*, 209.

197. Ibid., 210.

198. Ibid., 211.

199. Ibid.

ongoing, dynamic reality that is shared in *koinonia*, the marks are characteristics in which we must be constantly renewed and which we must reveal ever more clearly in the midst of weakness and ambiguity. They are held in faith and hope for a future manifestation. We struggle for them, not only locally but globally, not only now but in the future. It is part of our "struggle for the Spirit in the church." In the light of the marks, Spirit baptism constitutes the church as the body of Christ and remains a source of renewal not only for individual lives but for the life and witness of the entire church.

IN SUM

I believe that the baptism or outpouring of the Spirit can be the organizing principle for a Pentecostal ecclesiology that is responsive to distinctive accents of Pentecostalism as a global movement as well as to a broader ecumenical discussion. Accents such as regeneration, sanctification, Spirit filling, the coming kingdom of God in power, missions, and charismatic giftings (especially, but not exclusively, prophecy, speaking in tongues, and healing) can be drawn on to create a vision of the church as the central and unique sign of grace in an increasingly graceless world. In these latter days we need a fresh infilling of the Spirit to renew ourselves in the life and mission of Christ and his kingdom. If I have said anything in this chapter to inspire that hope in the readers, I would consider my task essentially fulfilled.

Six

BAPTIZED IN LOVE:
THE SPIRIT-BAPTIZED LIFE

T HE *CLOUD OF UNKNOWING* NOTES QUITE RIGHTLY THAT "BY LOVE CAN God be gotten and holden, by thought and understanding, never." Even when understanding fails, love keeps us close to the flame of the Spirit. This is the great value of the Pentecostal emphasis on speaking in tongues. Tongues are the language of love, not reason. Our understanding also gropes clumsily in our efforts to fathom the richness of the Spirit baptism metaphor in the New Testament. What we have been hinting at all along is that the outpouring of divine love upon us is the ultimate description of Pentecost: "God has poured out his love into our hearts by the Holy Spirit" (Rom. 5:5). This outpouring has its focus in Luke in the church's charismatic or missionary empowerment. But the boundaries of possible meanings for the metaphor in the light of the New Testament as a whole are broader.

As we noted at the conclusion of our first chapter, the unfinished business of Pentecostal theology is to cherish the charismatic empowerment and renewal of the church but also to situate this Pentecostal understanding of Spirit baptism within a broader pneumatological setting that accounts for *all* of the nuances of Spirit baptism throughout the New Testament. Luke's voice must be heard in all of its dimensions as a source of renewal for the churches, but other voices should be heard as well. The result is that Spirit baptism will be interpreted theologically most broadly against the background of the kingdom of God over which Christ is the King and within which the Spirit is the kingdom. Spirit baptism shows that the final end of this kingdom is to be viewed as the transformation of creation into the temple of God's dwelling, at which time the reign of death is overthrown by the reign of life so that God can be "all and in all" (1 Cor. 15:20–28).

The structure of Spirit baptism is thus Trinitarian, in which the divine lordship or monarchy of the Godhead is mediated through the Trinitarian relations. Christ is sent of the Father to defeat sin and death in order to impart the Spirit of life so that Christ's reign can become a historical and a cosmic reality. The kingdom is a reign of self-sacrificial love that comes to fulfillment through Christ and the Spirit, so that Christ's giving the kingdom back to the Father along with the renewed creation fulfills Christ's reign rather than ends it. It is through Spirit baptism that the creation is renewed and made to participate in the reign of Christ that is yielded back to the Father after death is finally defeated.

Christ as Spirit Baptizer is thus essential to his role as Savior and to the church's confession of him as Lord (identifiable with God). The Spirit who mediated the love between the Father and the Son is now poured out so as to draw humanity into the *koinonia* of God and to gift and empower the church to participate in the mission of God in the world. Spirit baptism is thus not only a *divine act* of drawing us into the grace of God to be broadly defined pneumatologically, it is also a *charismatic enrichment* to be had and renewed in fresh power among Christians. One's salvation or incorporation into the kingdom of God is certainly not dependent on experience, but that incorporation will inevitably call forth powerful forms of experience and participation. How is this Spirit baptism as a divine act and a charismatic experience to be defined ultimately?

If the Spirit is poured out from the Father who gave the Son and through the Son who freely gave himself, divine love must be at the essence of Spirit baptism. The Holy Spirit is the Spirit of holy love. What we have been hinting at all along is that Spirit baptism is a baptism into divine love. It is this aspect of the metaphor to which we must now turn to bring our discussion to completion. All of the debates surrounding the Pentecostal doctrine of Spirit baptism have tended to miss the fact that the doctrine of subsequence (Spirit baptism as separable from Christian initiation) has reached for the idea that Christians must rediscover their first love, but in even greater fervency than ever before. The flame of revival at its best is the flame of love rekindled and enhanced, for both God and the world.

Without divine love at the heart of Spirit baptism, the "power" to be gained through this renewal in the Spirit seems to be little more than raw energy without substance or direction, feeding little more than an emotional release. There is nothing more important to theological reflection on Spirit baptism than divine love. If Spirit baptism is ever to reconnect to sanctification and the fulfillment of the kingdom of God, it will do so with the help of Spirit baptism conceived as a participation in the love of God as Father, Son, and Holy Spirit. A discussion of the flames surrounding the event of Pentecost without a consideration of divine love would leave this entire effort wanting. Let us explore this point a bit further.

IMPORTANCE OF DIVINE LOVE

Love is God's supreme gift, for it transcends all emotion, conceptuality, and action only to inspire all three. It gives us life and that more abundantly. Love is not only God's supreme gift, it is at the very essence of God's nature as God. There is thus nothing greater than divine love (1 Cor. 13:13). Karl Barth's words are to the point: "The Christian life begins with love. It also ends with love."[1] Indeed, "there is also nothing beyond love. There is no higher or better being or doing in which we can leave it behind us."[2] Love is absolute to the nature of God. It is the essence of God and the substance of our participation in God.

This series of statements about the importance of divine love means one thing: Theological reflection on Spirit baptism as the organizing principle of a Pentecostal theology must ultimately conclude that the substance of the Christian life is God's love. As we noted earlier, Spirit baptism for a number of early Pentecostals was a baptism in divine love, an outpouring of love by the Spirit in our hearts (Rom. 5:5). Spirit baptism fulfills the heart of the law, which is love for God and neighbor that involves the whole person (Deut. 6:5; Matt. 22:36–40). The message of the prophets also is that God desires steadfast love rather than ceremonial sacrifice (Hos. 6:6). The Spirit poured out upon us in fulfillment of this message comes from the Father, "who so loved the world that he gave his one and only Son" (John 3:16), and through the Son, whose love surpasses knowledge (Eph. 3:18–19). The Spirit who is

---

1. Karl Barth, *Church Dogmatics*, trans. G. W. Bromiley, Vol. I, Pt. 2 (Edinburgh: T&T Clark, 1956, 1978), 371.
2. Ibid., 372.

poured out upon us is the very love of God extended to us (Rom. 5:5). The kingdom of God that creates the setting for Pentecost and the outpouring of the Spirit is the reign of divine love, for God "has rescued us from the dominion of darkness and brought us into the kingdom of the Son he loves" (Col. 1:13). Spirit baptism as the inauguration of the kingdom of God thus serves to integrate sanctification and charismatic gifting/empowerment. The two are distinct but inseparable dimensions of Spirit baptism.

The Trinitarian structure of Spirit baptism is the structure of the love mediated by the Spirit between the Father and the Son. The link between Spirit baptism and *koinonia* in the life of the believer and the church is forged by divine love, for we are "rooted and established in love" so that we may "comprehend with all the saints" and "grasp how wide, and long, and high and deep is the love of Christ" (Eph. 3:17–18). The integration of purity and power is facilitated by the Spirit's role in imparting God's love as a redemptive force in the world.

More broadly, eschatology is the drama of the victory of divine love over all that contradicts it in the world: "For I am convinced that neither death nor life, neither angels nor demons, neither the present nor the future, nor any powers, neither height nor depth, nor anything else in all creation, will be able to separate us from the love of God that is in Christ Jesus our Lord" (Rom. 8:38–39). All of the fractures that have plagued the Pentecostal theology of Spirit baptism can be healed ultimately by an understanding of love at the substance of life in the Spirit, love that fills us to overflowing as a purgative, empowering, eschatological gift of communion and new life.

All of our theological categories are abstractions without the love of God revealed in Christ and the outpouring of the Spirit. Within such an abstraction, Christianity becomes a religion rather than a lived-out relationship with God that grants new life and hope. Without the love of God revealed in Christ, we would not be certain as to why purity is so powerful or power so uncompromising in its devotion to Christ. We would not be certain as to why God's kingdom is liberating rather than dominating or how one is to understand the substance and direction of *koinonia*. We would not understand why justice requires mercy or why mercy cannot tolerate the oppression and indignity caused by injustice. Eschatology would become a formal chart of "end time" events rather than an ongoing event of living hope.

Without divine love, our categories become abstract and fall into a state of fragmentation. In a sense, theological reflection seeks to develop the logic of divine love and to speak about it with all of the spiritual reverence and devotion appropriate to the subject. For, as Luther noted, God's love is an "inconceivable fire, much greater than the fire which Moses saw in the bush, yea much greater than the fire of hell."[3] God's love is a holy flame that will one day transform the cosmos and make all things into the temple of his presence. The crowning chapter of this book must be about the nature of Spirit baptism as a baptism in the love of God. We must proceed, however, with what we mean by "love."

TOWARD A THEOLOGY OF LOVE

What is divine love? Emil Brunner rightly points to 1 John 4:8 that "God is love." He notes that "this is the most daring statement that has ever been made in human language."[4] This statement is daring because it speaks boldly and with certainty of the inner essence of God. Divine love is thus more than an attribute that God "has" and shares in common with creatures. Divine love is the very nature of God, so that if one abides in love, one abides in God (4:16). Methodologically, love as essential to God forbids us from arriving at a notion of love as an abstract concept and then applying it to God. Revelation or divine self-impartation becomes necessary to our understanding of divine love.[5] But even then we see through a glass dimly, because love as essential to God's self-giving is an eschatological gift. It is not seen clearly until it is experienced "face to face" with our Lord (1 Cor. 13:12).

Through Christ as the Spirit Baptizer, God imparts his divine self as all-embracing love and not just something about God. The benefit that God wills for the creature is not "something" but God's presence, "for this love is self-surrender, self-giving to the other, to whom love is directed."[6] God gave the Son so that we would have the eternal life of the divine Spirit (John 3:16). Brunner notes that the love proceeding from God "is the movement which goes-out-of-oneself, which stoops down to that which is below: it is the self-giving, the self-communication of God—and it is *this* which is His revelation."[7]

---

3. Martin Luther, *Pred. üb. Jn. 3:16–21*, 1532, E. A. 4, 124f. (quoted in Barth, ibid., 380).

4. Emil Brunner, *The Christian Doctrine of God*, vol. 1 of *Dogmatics* (Philadelphia: Westminster, 1949), 185.

5. Ibid.

6. Ibid., 186–87.

7. Ibid., 187.

Divine love is not an intellectual concept but an event: the event of the incarnation, the cross, the resurrection, and the outpouring of the Spirit on all flesh.

Like Barth, Brunner rightly criticizes the older effort to start one's theological reflection on God with abstract "metaphysical" attributes (such as omnipotence, omnipresence, etc.) and then proceed to "ethical" attributes such as love. God's love is not an attribute but God's very nature. There is no conception of God's attributes apart from it. Omnipotence is all-powerful love; omniscience is the personal knowing motivated by divine love, which is why it can have no limits in time or space; omnipresence is the all-present love of God to heal and direct (Ps. 139). Holiness is love as a purgative fire and a liberating right hand that does not yield to evil and oppression. It is divine love that drives divine self-impartation: "God's nature is the radiation of spiritual energy, an energy which is the will to impart Himself."[8] God is indeed "*actus purus*," but as self-giving love. Paul understood this well when referring to the outpouring of the Spirit as the outpouring of divine love (Rom. 5:5). God as the Spirit Baptizer is God as Self-giving Love.

God is thus not the speculative "self-sufficient Being of the Absolute of thought" but is rather the living God.[9] Brunner writes: "There is nothing in the Absolute which could move it to give itself and to seek *communion* with a being which is not absolute."[10] Such a perfect, self-sufficient God conceived apart from love "desires nothing outside Himself, hence He does not love." Such a God "can, of course, be *loved*, for the sake of His perfection, eternity, and blessedness, but He Himself cannot love."[11]

The God of love is the self-giving God or the Spirit Baptizer, the God who is personal and communicative as well as transcendent. The God of Jesus Christ self-imparts without reservation in incarnation, involving a wedding with flesh that will never be reversed. The God of Pentecost self-imparts in abundance and limitless expanse in witness to Christ, reaching out to all flesh in forces of liberation, reconciliation, and communion. What is self-imparted is divine love, a love that bears all things, including our sin, sorrow, and death. The God of Spirit baptism is the "crucified God." All-powerful divine love has a limitless capacity to suffer. This love cannot be overwhelmed or

---

8. Ibid., 192.
9. Ibid., 188.
10. Ibid., 187.
11. Ibid.

destroyed. It is sure to conquer all enemies until death, the final enemy, is defeated. Then God will be "all and in all" (1 Cor. 15:28).

Barth would essentially agree with these remarks, noting that we "cannot say anything higher or better of the 'inwardness of God' than that God is Father, Son, and Holy Spirit, and, therefore, that He is love in Himself."[12] Barth regards it important to add that God's love is free, meaning "without being forced to love us."[13] Since God as Trinity is perfect love and communion, God does not need to love us to be God. God loves freely out of grace and not necessity.

This concept of divine freedom is difficult to fathom and requires critical evaluation. On the positive side, Barth is trying to be faithful to texts that speak of God as the fullness of being who needs nothing but gives everything: "And he is not served by human hands, as if he needed anything, because he himself gives all men life and breath and everything else" (Acts 17:25). God's love is thus not motivated or conditioned by anything except God's free choice and good pleasure. The God of love critiques the God of religion. Yet, if God is not the self-sufficient Absolute of speculative Greek thought but rather the living God who is essentially self-giving love, how can divine freedom involve a freedom not to love? Jürgen Moltmann has made this criticism against Barth a major part of his theological project. Moltmann has noted that the divine freedom to love cannot involve a freedom not to love, since love is essential to God's nature.[14] God's freedom is to be understood *within* the context of divine self-giving and not *apart* from it.

Of course, Barth is not proposing that God has the freedom not to love, only that God as an intradivine communion of love is self-fulfilled and not in need of creating and loving *us*, not in need of creation or redemption for fulfillment. But Moltmann's protest understood on this level poses the question: Can God be God without being the God for the "other"? Can God be God without being the Creator and Redeemer? One wonders in the light of Barth's lofty statements about God as precisely the God revealed in Christ and at Pentecost if God can really be imagined at all apart from the loving self-giving that makes God who God is for us.

---

12. Barth, *Church Dogmatics*, Vol. I, Pt. 2, 377.

13. Ibid.

14. Jürgen Moltmann, *The Trinity and the Kingdom: The Doctrine of God* (San Francisco: Harper & Row, 1981), 52–56.

A God self-contained and self-sufficient who has never created or redeemed can hardly be God in the fullness of self-giving life that we understand God to possess. Can one drive such a wedge even theoretically between the divine *a se* and the divine *pro nobis* if overflowing, self-giving love is really essential to God? Does God have the freedom to choose not to be the Creator, Redeemer, and Spirit Baptizer? Would God really be overflowing love if it remained confined within the Godhead and did not create space for the "other"? Can God be anyone else but the God who breathed on the deep to give birth to life and who then breathed on us through Jesus the breath of new life?

Perhaps we are asking questions that ultimately cannot be answered. "Oh, the depth of the riches of the wisdom and knowledge of God! How unsearchable his judgments, and his paths beyond tracing out!" (Rom. 11:33). The point is that the God of Spirit baptism is the God who overflows with abundant life and who seeks to embrace the others with life-renewing love. The embrace does not oppress, force, smother, or annihilate the others but rather creates space for them in their unique otherness and fills them with life abundant so that they can be everything they were meant to be in all of their uniqueness. The tongues of humanity were not dissolved at Pentecost by the flaming tongues of God's holy presence (Acts 2:4). The diversity of human cultural self-expression was preserved in all of its uniqueness and differences but caught up into a shared praise, devotion, and witness. God's freedom in this outpouring of divine love is a freedom to overcome all resistance and barriers to reconcile a people into shared communion.

God's people are carried by Spirit baptism on the winds of God's holy breath to bear witness to Christ. They come to know that divine freedom as their own when they lay down their limited imaginations and are overtaken by God's missionary passion for the world. The self-giving God of Spirit baptism produces a self-giving people in mission. The God who seeks to save the lost produces a people who do the same. To love God is to be shaped by that love so as to share its affections and passions. Whether or not this divine freedom involves God in the possibility of being any other God but the God of Pentecost is a moot point. The only freedom of divine love actually displayed in Scripture is an eschatological freedom exercised in the passage of history toward a goal that ultimately transcends it toward the fulfillment of the kingdom of God.

The free *commitment* of divine love is expressed in the Word made flesh (John 1:14). God's love for the Son was expressed through the presence of the

Spirit at that moment when Jesus publicly showed solidarity with humanity at his baptism (Matt. 3:16–17). The Son returns devotion to the Father through the Spirit by fulfilling the Father's will to draw creation into the divine reign, the reign of divine love (Matt. 12:28; Luke 4:18). The cross in particular revealed God's unqualified sacrifice of suffering love, for "God proves his love for us in that while we were sinners Christ died for us" (Rom. 5:8 NRSV).

The outpoured Spirit then reveals the *freedom and expansive reach* of divine love. Faithful to Christ, the Spirit forms Christ in us (Gal. 4:19), in the many caught up in divine *koinonia*, "to the measure of the full stature of Christ" (Eph. 4:13 NRSV). Ultimately, all of creation is to be anointed by the Spirit as a temple of God's Holy Spirit in the very image of Christ. In the story of Jesus, the Spirit functioned as the bond of love between the Father and the Son. In a sense, the eschatological drama of Spirit baptism also implies that the Son is the bond of love between the electing Father and the expansive freedom of the Spirit's work in all of creation, so that all things spiritual proceed in a direction faithful to God's love revealed in Christ.

Since love is the greatest and is essential to God, we should explore a bit how it relates to faith and then hope.

FAITH AND LOVE

Divine love is "by grace through faith." Our love for God also involves trusting God for salvation. All love is based in trust. This statement sounds simple enough. Not so simple is the fact that the relationship of faith and love has raised a great deal of controversy in the West. The medieval tendency was to view love as that which perfects faith: "The movement of faith is not perfect unless it is quickened by charity, and so in the justification of the ungodly, a movement of charity is infused together with the movement of faith."[15] So writes Thomas Aquinas. We are justified by faith "formed by love." The result is that human love for God (*caritas*) played a role in justification, an assumption rejected by Martin Luther as implying works righteousness. God's acceptance of us must be based on Christ alone received by trusting in Christ alone to save us and not by the quality or expression of our love for God.

Anders Nygren argues that the biblical message of God's unconditional love confronts an established Platonic (Neoplatonic) notion of *eros* as a desire

---

15. Thomas Aquinas, *Treatise on Grace*, 113.4.

for self-fulfillment through ascent to the heavenly realm. *Eros* lays claim to what it has reached in its ascent. *Agape* (divine love) is the direct opposite of *eros*, for *agape* is an unconditional love that comes to us by grace alone: "Eros love ascends and seeks the satisfaction of its needs; Agape love descends in order to help and to give."[16]

Nygren claims that attempts at synthesis between *eros* and *agape* are never entirely successful. He faults Augustine for not seeing the radical contradiction between *eros* and *agape* and for thinking that *agape* merely corrects *eros* without fundamentally undermining it: "Augustine never sees that Christian *Agape* is the direct opposite of Neoplatonic *Eros*, and these two motifs agree no better than fire and water."[17] Rather than undermining and displacing *eros* as self-centered, Augustine has *agape* humbling *eros* and carrying it forward so that it can reach God.[18] Luther replaces *caritas* (*eros* corrected by *agape*) with God's *agape* flowing through us in Christ and by the Spirit. As we will note, I believe that Luther does see a place for *caritas* but one that functions consistent with faith in looking to Christ alone for favor with God.

Luther thus refuses to allow *caritas*, or the love arising in the believer as a *habitus*, to play a role in gaining favor with God. He cannot see faith as a "dead quality" in the soul that needs to be activated and completed by the infused virtue of love, since faith for Luther is not a metaphysical quality but a divine gift that involves a laying hold of Christ by grace alone. Luther wrote that the "fanatical spirits and sophists" "imagine that faith is a quality that clings to the heart apart from Christ. This is a dangerous error. Christ should be set forth in such a way that apart from Him you see nothing at all."[19] Faith for Luther is inconceivable apart from its living relation with Christ.

For Luther, faith is not the body and *caritas* the form. Faith is the body and Christ is the form. Luther wrote that faith "takes hold of Christ in such a way that Christ is the object of faith, or rather not the object but, so to speak, the One who is present in faith itself."[20] He also noted that faith "is the temple and Christ sits in the midst of it."[21] Thus, for Luther, faith is not adorned by

---

16. Anders Nygren, *Agape and Eros* (Philadelphia: Westminster, 1953), 469.
17. Ibid., 471–72.
18. Ibid., 472–75.
19. Martin Luther, "Lectures on Galatians (1535)," *Luther's Works*, ed. Jaroslav Pelikan (St. Louis: Concordia, 1963), 26:356.
20. Ibid., 129.
21. Ibid., 130.

love as a *habitus* but by Christ. Since faith is by nature a relationship to, and even participation in, the living person of Christ, Christ is seen as that which gives it its dynamism as a living faith. Christ functions for Luther in the place of *caritas*, a position Luther felt delivers us from self-righteousness or self-preoccupation, turning the believer's focus rather to Christ. Luther explains that faith "does not look at its love and say: 'What have I done? Where have I sinned? What have I deserved?' But it says: 'What has Christ done? What has he deserved?' Faith is adorned by Christ."[22] What is interesting about this quote is that Luther does not deny that faith "has" *caritas* for God, he merely refuses to look to this love as that which accounts for our acceptability from God. Rather, faith and its love look solely to Christ.

In point of fact, Luther did not intend to make faith "loveless," since, as Nygren and the recent Finnish Lutherans have noted, he did recognize the involvement of *divine* love (*agape*) in the rise of faith in the believer and Luther did see faith as a participation in Christ.[23] My own reading of Luther has led me to believe that he even saw faith as involving *caritas* as long as this is not viewed as a human virtue that somehow accounts for why I am acceptable to God. Faith clings rather to Christ as that which accounts for my acceptance by God.

But this clinging devoutly to Christ is a *caritas* of sorts, is it not? It certainly is, but not at the expense of its fundamental nature as a trusting solely on Christ for justification. In other words, for Luther, faith is not somehow activated by a human virtue, which then accounts for my justification. Faith is rather a living trust that clings devoutly (lovingly) to Christ alone for salvation. To make *caritas* itself the basis of God's acceptance of us is to base justification in part on obedience to the law, which Luther contrasts sharply with faith in the gospel. He notes that the law "can teach me that I should love God and my neighbor, and live in chastity, patience, etc.; but it is in no position to show me how to be delivered from sin, the devil, death, and hell." For this, Luther will listen only to the gospel, the crucified and risen Christ.[24]

In response to Luther, I am led to ask, Can we not see faith as inspired by *agape* and as involving a *caritas* that draws no attention to my virtue or

---

22. Ibid., 88–89.
23. Simo Peura, "What God Gives Man Receives: Luther on Salvation," in *Union with Christ: The New Finnish Lutheran Interpretation of Luther* (Grand Rapids: Eerdmans, 1998), 76–95.
24. Luther, "Lectures on Galatians (1535)," 91.

accomplishments but rather clings devoutly to Christ for that which makes me acceptable to God? I believe that Luther would have accepted this formulation. As proof, I have discovered a passage in Luther where he writes of his opponents that he would not be offended by their "faith formed by love" gloss if they would distinguish this faith from *false* faith rather than *unformed* faith.[25] In other words, Luther is willing to admit that faith involves *caritas* so long as it is not human virtue itself as a human quality that fulfills faith but rather Christ himself as alone the basis and object of trust.

Caritas functions at the essence of faith to look for fulfillment in Christ. Faith that lacks *caritas* is not *unformed* faith (which is ludicrous for Luther, since faith by nature is a clinging devoutly to Christ) but rather *false* faith. In other words, the focus of this human act of faith as inspired by the gospel remains on Christ as that which accounts for God's acceptance of me. Such an admission implies that Luther's "faith alone" that clings in trust and *caritas* to Christ alone may not have been much different from the medieval faith (as assent) formed by love, *depending on how this is construed*.

In point of fact, divine love does not base itself on human works or loveliness but rather on the grace and lovingkindness of God. The cross and Pentecost imply a divine love that bears the pain of human rejection and responds lavishly with a bestowal of love that is totally undeserved. God takes our place in Christ and takes the matter of life and death out of our hands.[26] God resolves this matter for us in Christ's canceling sin and conquering death. Through the risen Christ, God then bestows the Spirit upon us, which is the realm of divine favor, despite the fact that we were out of favor with God. It is in the realm of the Spirit that we are in the realm of Christ and can claim his favor with God as our own. It is in the realm of the Spirit that the divine love embraces us in Christ and reorients our lives around the one who loved us and gave himself for us (Gal. 2:20). How did we receive the Spirit as God's love poured into us—by works or by believing what we heard (3:5)?

Since God's love is love for the other, my love for God is credible only when I love the other as well. One who says he or she loves God but hates the other is a liar (1 John 4:20). Faith without love is dead and loses credibility. The Spirit links me not only to God but in God to the others whom God loves so much.

---

25. Ibid., 268–70.
26. Barth, *Church Dogmatics*, Vol. I, Pt. 2, 383.

It is in the realm of the Spirit that I participate in the *koinonia* of divine love with others and discover my unique gifting as a channel of grace to others. It is in the realm of the Spirit that I join my heart with the one who so loves the world and sent the divine Son to seek and to save the lost. It is on the winds of the Spirit that we are consecrated and called for a holy task and empowered to go forth as a vessel for the salvation of others, burning with the love of God for them. It is in the Spirit and the love of Christ that we confront injustice with a passion for the liberty and dignity of those who are oppressed as well as the transformation of those who benefit intentionally or blindly from that oppression. It is in the realm of the Spirit that I gain a foretaste of God's love in Christ and groan for the liberty and experience of it in fullness "face to face" one day, for "no eye has seen, nor ear heard, nor the human heart conceived, what God has prepared for those who love him" (1 Cor. 2:9 NRSV).

What about hope and love? It is to this topic that we now turn.

HOPE AND LOVE

Love gives one new life and causes one who is in despair to hope again. Love keeps one hoping and yearning for the beloved. Love keeps one open to the unexpected, to joys that take us by surprise and can even fill us with wonder. Divine love is eschatological and sustains a living hope for the future, calling forth dry bones from their graves and inspiring hope where there is despair. Paul wrote that we should love "understanding the present time. The hour has come for [us] to wake up from . . . slumber because our salvation is nearer now than when we first believed" (Rom. 13:11).

This "waking up" is another way of describing Spirit baptism in Pentecostal perspective. It has to do with God's love rising up within in fresh and renewed passion. It has to do with a fervent expectation for the return of the Beloved. One might look at Romans 13:11 and note that Paul was "mistaken" that "our salvation is nearer now than when we first believed." But this text asks us today why our love for Christ is so dim that we are not making the same mistake! The early Pentecostals yearned for Christ and were confident about his imminent return because of the awakening of their love for him in the Spirit. They were "mistaken" about the timing of Christ's return, but timing is not the issue. The issue is rather a yearning for Christ that made them certain Christ must be at the door.

The connection between Spirit baptism as a baptism in love and the fervency of Pentecostal eschatological expectation is seen in the dominant metaphor of Christ's coming as a bridegroom comes for his bride. The Pentecostal expectation of Christ's coming was expressed most typically in the cry, "the Bridegroom Cometh." As J. W. Hutchins wrote in Seymour's paper, *The Apostolic Faith*, "Awake! Awake! There is but time to dress and be ready for the cry will soon go forth, 'The Bridegroom Cometh.'"[27] Her cry was typical among Pentecostals, for the need of the church as the bride of the coming Bridegroom (Christ) to awaken and prepare for the coming of the Beloved was a common theme.[28] The bride must be found faithful at Christ's return, clothed in righteous deeds (Rev. 19:8). Though an element of fear, or at least sober-mindedness, was also induced at the prospect of the Bridegroom coming for a less than faithful bride, the element of love was present as well. Note C. H. Mason's testimony of his Spirit baptism:

> I surrendered perfectly to him and consented to him. He sang through me and took charge of me. It seemed I was standing at the cross and I heard him as he groaned, the dying groans of Jesus, and I groaned. It was not my voice but the voice of my beloved that I heard in me. He lifted me to my feet and then the light of heaven fell upon me and burst into me filling me. Then God took charge of my tongue and I went into preaching in tongues. I could not change my tongue. The glory of God filled the temple.[29]

According to Mason's testimony, God takes hold of us and "possesses" us in love. Though a greater sense of the dialectic between God's words and ours should be applied to such statements as Mason's above, we should also realize that his statement is more poetic than literal, more descriptive of an encounter with divine love than analytical. Mason's experience is analogous to a mystical encounter in which the distinction between us and God is not denied, only transcended momentarily by the Spirit as an illustration of God's solidarity with us in moments of need. In Pentecostal rhetoric, God takes possession of us, "fills us" with the divine presence again and again through the

---

27. J. W. Hutchins, "The Pentecostal Baptism Restored: The Promised Latter Rain Now Being Poured Out on God's Humble People," *The Apostolic Faith* (Los Angeles) (October 1906), 5.

28. See William J. Seymour, "Behold the Bridegroom Cometh," *The Apostolic Faith* (Los Angeles) (January 1907), 2.

29. C. H. Mason, "Tennessee Evangelist Witnesses," *The Apostolic Faith* (Los Angeles) (April 1907), 7.

renewing work of the Spirit. Spirit baptism is a kind of divine "embrace." Some Pentecostals have even referred to speaking in tongues as an infantile or playful speech in response to the loving Father or Christ as the Beloved embracing us in love.[30]

Gerald Sheppard thus calls Pentecostal experience "shamanistic" for its emphasis on Spirit-possession as a deeply felt experience, except in Pentecostal context this experience is appropriately understood as a prophetic empowerment for furthering the ministry of Jesus in the world.[31] If this experience is coupled with an equal stress on power encounters over the dark forces in personal healing, ecstatic tongues, and a sense of triumph in the Spirit over all that opposes the will of God, one can understand why Pentecostal Christianity and sibling movements have gained such a foothold in the Southern Hemisphere.

Spirit baptism is not mere empowerment for mission in Pentecostal interpretation, even though it definitely has this focus. If it were, there would be no way of accounting for the equally important Pentecostal stress on the greater intimacy with God and fervency in eschatological expectation that characterize Pentecostal testimonies of Spirit baptism. Spirit baptism is akin to a prophetic call that draws believers close to his heart in deeper love and empathy in order to help them catch a glimpse of the divine love for the world. It is this love that is at the substance of the power for mission. It accounts for the sense of wonder and enthusiasm that Pentecostals feel during moments of renewal in the Spirit.

Eschatology for Pentecostals is not just about "end times"—that is, the last chapter of a theological system—but is rather a fervent and living hope that pervades all of life, worship, and thought. In Moltmann's words, eschatology is "not just one element *of* Christianity, but it is the medium of Christian faith as such, the key in which everything else in it is set, the glow that suffuses everything here in the dawn of an expected new day."[32] The central

---

30. See Simon Chan, "The Language Game of Glossolalia, or Making Sense of Glossolalia," in *Pentecostalism in Context: Essays in Honor of William W. Menzies*, ed. Robert Menzies and Wonsuk Ma (Sheffield: Sheffield Academic Press, 1997), 80–95.

31. Gerald Sheppard, "Pentecostalism and the Hermeneutics of Dispensationalism: The Anatomy of an Uneasy Relationship," *Pneuma* 6:2 (Fall 1984): 32, n. 77.

32. Jürgen Moltmann, *Theology of Hope: On the Ground and the Implications of a Christian Eschatology* (London: SCM, 1967), 39, quoted in Walter Hollenweger, *The Pentecostals*, 2nd ed. (Peabody, MA: Hendrickson, 1988), 419.

role of Spirit baptism for Pentecostal theology is eschatological through and through. This is not to say that eschatology has maintained the brightness of its glow, especially among middle class Pentecostals who are becoming increasingly comfortable with this world and are no longer living in the light of Christ's coming, or that it is currently of equal importance everywhere in the world among Pentecostal groups. But eschatology is integral to the fabric of the Pentecostal message, to the Christian gospel in general, and it cannot be forsaken without losing something valuable to the faith.

There is an implicit connection between renewal in the Spirit, a fervent yearning for the return of Christ the Bridegroom, and eschatological hope. Emil Brunner is right: "We can trace in the history of Christendom something like a law, that the more vitally the hope in the Ekklesia, that is, the more powerfully life in the Spirit of God is present in it, the more urgent is its expectation of the Coming of Christ."[33] The reason for this "law" has to do with the fact that a rediscovery of one's first love can fuel and nourish a yearning for the coming of Christ and the fulfillment of Christ's kingdom on earth. Eschatological expectation of Christ's return tends to lift redemption beyond the individualistic confines of personal salvation or transport to heaven to the resurrection of the faithful and the new creation. We come to yearn for what God yearns for.

Part of the challenge facing the formation of Pentecostal hope has been the one-sided emphasis on the miraculous arrival of the kingdom at Christ's return from "beyond." Most Pentecostals historically have understood Christ's coming as "premillennial." Christ will come *before* his reign of peace for a thousand years (Rev. 20) because this reign is miraculously ushered in "from above" at his coming. Pentecostalism thus has a reputation for being otherworldly in its understanding of the eschatological fulfillment of the kingdom of God.

Donald Dayton has argued that the entire shift late in the nineteenth century within evangelicalism from a postmillennial to a premillennial eschatology involved a more basic shift from a gradual understanding of the inauguration of the kingdom of God in history through the mission of the church, which is the postmillennial vision, to a crisis-oriented understanding

---

33. Emil Brunner, *The Christian Doctrine of the Church, Faith, and Consummation*, Vol. 3 of *Dogmatics* (London: Lutterworth, 1962), 400; quoted in Donald Dayton, *Theological Roots of Pentecostalism* (Grand Rapids: Zondervan, 1987), 144. Dayton thanks J. Rodman Williams for bringing this quote to his attention.

of the in-breaking of the kingdom wholly from "above" at Christ's return, which is the premillennial vision. Pentecostalism was most influenced by this latter "otherworldly" emphasis.[34] Pentecostals not only expected the kingdom to be fulfilled miraculously at Christ's return, they also favored a current experience of the kingdom in power through the *extraordinary* gifts of the Spirit featured in the book of Acts and especially in 1 Corinthians 12–14. In Pentecostal experience, God breaks in "from beyond" to save, heal, empower, and create miraculous signs of the kingdom to come.

As Ernest Sandeen has shown, dispensationalism was the dominant form of eschatology in the rise of premillennialism late in the nineteenth century. This rise occurred through a series of prophecy conferences, which attracted broad attention among evangelicals and helped to give rise to American fundamentalism.[35] Gaining its impetus by John Nelson Darby and the Plymouth Brethren and popularized by the well-known Scofield Bible, dispensationalism advocated a series of dispensations throughout history that occasion God's different ways of dealing with humanity.

Essential to dispensationalism was a radical separation between Israel and the church and the different covenants established by God between them. The idea was that the church age is not the era of the Spirit promised in the Old Testament but occurs as a mere delay in the fulfillment of this era among Israel after Christ's return, during the millennial reign. This view grants the Spirit-empowered mission of the church in history no role to play in the fulfillment of the kingdom promised in the Old Testament. The Bible was fragmented into different compartments, with much of the Old Testament and the Gospels referring directly only to Israel.[36] There are a number of themes here that are inconsistent with Pentecostal theology, as we will note below.

More consistent with Pentecostal theology, dispensationalism encouraged a rather dismal view of the religious establishment in both Israel and the church. The dispensational prophecy chart at the front of A. B. Simpson's book *The Gospel of the Kingdom*, for example, reveals a clear distinction between the "formal" church and the faithful "little flock."[37] History in general was understood

---

34. Dayton, *Theological Roots*, 160–67.

35. Ernest R. Sandeen, "Toward a Historical Interpretation of the Origins of Fundamentalism," *Church History* 36:1 (March 1967): 70.

36. Ibid., 68–69.

37. A. B. Simpson, *The Gospel of the Kingdom* (New York: Christian Alliance, 1890).

as involved in a steady decline until God destroys all resistance, symbolized most profoundly by the Antichrist and his world government, at Christ's coming. In the midst of history's decline, the faithful little flock can only hope to be "raptured" out from the earth (1 Thess. 4:17) before the Antichrist comes to power and the seven years of "great tribulation" begins before Christ returns to earth with the saints to establish the millennial kingdom for the nation Israel. Until the rapture, the little flock can do little more than try through evangelism to save as many from the flames of wrath as possible.[38]

Books influenced by dispensationalism with titles like, *The Coming Crisis*,[39] *Armageddon*,[40] *The Beginning of the End*,[41] and *Racing toward Judgment*[42] seek as much to wake up complacent Christians as to convert sinners. In ways analogous to the preaching of hell to scare both the faithful and the sinner into passionate faith in Christ, the coming deluge of wrath on the earth is preached for much the same purpose. Just as one can die at any moment, Christ can come at any moment. The imminent horizon to eternity at the edge of which humanity stands is both individual (death) and corporate (second coming). The revivalist sees preaching the coming judgment in either case as the certain way of spreading the flame of commitment.[43]

Pentecostals do not universally hold to dispensationalism today (in its classical form; I realize it has changed somewhat more recently), but it still exercises a vast influence, especially on a popular level. There were a few impulses to dispensationalism that had great appeal to the early Pentecostals. The dismal view of the religious establishment and of the broader culture and the view of the church as the faithful flock fit well with Pentecostal sentiments. The use of apocalyptic images of coming doom to encourage revival was also integral to the Pentecostal passion. Finally, the overwhelming accent on the miraculous nature of the divine reign coming into the world was also appealing to the Pentecostal worldview.

With that said, I must also agree with Gerald T. Sheppard that there is an "uneasy relationship" between dispensationalism and Pentecostal escha-

---

38. Sandeen, "Toward a Historical Interpretation," 68–69.

39. Stanley Howard Frodsham, *The Coming Crisis and the Coming Christ* (Springfield, MO: Gospel, 1934).

40. Marilyn Hickey, *Armageddon* (Denver: Marilyn Hickey Ministries, 1994).

41. Tim LaHaye, *The Beginning of the End* (Wheaton, IL: Tyndale, 1991).

42. David Wilkerson, *Racing toward Judgment* (Old Tappan, NJ: Revell, 1976).

43. See LaHaye, *The Beginning of the End*, 5.

tology.[44] Pentecostals read the biblical text as a narrative that involves them directly through the work of the Holy Spirit. Each text transports one directly to the God of the kingdom, who reigns over all of history and is felt in the here and now. Compartmentalizing the relevance of the biblical text into historical periods moves contrary to the thrust of Pentecostal hermeneutics. In addition, Pentecostals see the age of the church as the era of the Spirit promised to Israel in the Old Testament (e.g., Joel 2:28). They do not see the church as a hiatus in between such promise and its fulfillment later in the millennium. Lastly, in tension with a pessimism toward established religious and social institutions is a remarkable optimism within Pentecostalism about what can happen among the faithful through faith and the latter-day outpouring of the Spirit. Rather than a beleaguered little flock waiting to be raptured away, the Pentecostal dreams of a great flood of the Spirit in the latter days to unite and to empower the church to do great things in the world. Their belief in a proliferation of apostolic signs and wonders amidst an empowered church also runs contrary to dispensationalist teaching.

I essentially agree with Sheppard's effort to distance Pentecostalism from dispensationalism. My reading of early Pentecostal literature shows a nondispensationalist openness to different understandings of end-time events, even a certain lack of interest in such questions.[45] One early Pentecostal author warned about end-time speculations: "Dear ones, do not puzzle yourselves by theorizing, but tarry in Jerusalem!"[46] Clearly, the Pentecostal priority with regard to eschatology was the empowerment of the Spirit for faithful life and mission rather than useless speculation about end-time doomsday scenarios. Sheppard argues persuasively that Pentecostalism accepted certain features of the end-time schema from the dispensationalists early on but did not swallow its larger hermeneutical implications until they attempted later to gain the acceptance of conservative evangelical churches.[47]

On the other hand, Pentecostal eschatology also embraces the body and physical life: "The time is coming when the Spirit will envelope us with His

---

44. See Sheppard, "Pentecostalism and the Hermeneutics of Dispensationalism."

45. See, e.g., Glen Menzies and Gordon L. Anderson, "D. W. Kerr and Eschatological Diversity in the Assemblies of God," *Paraclete* (Winter 1993), 8–16.

46. "The Apostolic Faith Movement" (author unknown), *The Apostolic Faith* (Los Angeles) (Sept 1906), 2.

47. Sheppard, "Pentecostalism and the Hermeneutics of Dispensationalism," 32–33, n. 76).

power, transform our bodies by His might, and transport us to glory."[48] What is interesting about this expression of hope by a Pentecostal leader is the attention paid to the final healing of the body. This emphasis is due no doubt to the well-known fact that the divine healing of the body is cherished globally among Pentecostal churches as vital to the blessings available in Christ. William Seymour refers more than once to divine healing as the "sanctification" of the body.[49] In Seymour's *The Apostolic Faith*, one author rightly links Jesus' resurrection and glorification with the healing of the body:

> If His flesh had seen corruption, then we could not have healing for the body nor look for another immortal body from heaven. So, dear beloved, we get healing for our body, soul, and spirit and an immortal body from heaven at His coming, through the perfect body of Jesus. Praise God![50]

Among Pentecostals, Christ is said to save us "fully" through the agency of the Spirit by sanctifying us, healing our bodies, delivering us from the oppression of sin, and coming again one day soon to raise us from the dead or to transform those of us who happen to be alive on earth so that this mortality may put on immortality.

This focus on the physical effects of salvation has social implications for how one understands the presence and power of the kingdom of God in our midst. Hollenweger accurately describes the common Pentecostal understanding of salvation through the lens of a Chilean Pentecostal testimony:

> He is now no longer at the mercy of uncertainty, hunger, unemployment, drunkenness, boredom and homelessness, because he has once again become part of a "family," because he has "brothers" and "sisters" who help him and give his life moral direction. . . . All of this he owes to the Saviour who has rolled away the burden of his sin, who has led him out of the prison of sin, indifference and hopelessness, and to the Holy Spirit, who has not just to be believed in, but who one can experience in all sorts of marvelous healings.[51]

---

48. Ralph M. Riggs, *The Spirit Himself* (Springfield, MO: Gospel, 1949), 188–89.

49. William J. Seymour, "The Precious Atonement," *The Apostolic Faith* (Los Angeles) (September 1906), 2.

50. "Virtue in the Perfect Body of Jesus," (author unknown) *The Apostolic Faith* (Los Angeles) (February/March 1907), 2.

51. Hollenweger, *The Pentecostals*, 316–17.

Pentecostals would agree with Moltmann that through the Spirit of life we "experience the abundant, full, healed, and redeemed life with all of our senses."[52] For Pentecostals, the eschatological experience of faith is not just a paradoxical affirmation of God's reign in the absence of eschatological verification in the here and now. Enduring faith is also an affirmation of tangible signs of renewal that vindicate faith already before the final vindication comes at Christ's return.

Pentecostals believe in miracles. These signs, such as divine healing, are sometimes extraordinary in nature, thus implying an explanation that points to Christ's saving grace. Of course, we cannot approach such signs naïvely in a way that overlooks their ambiguity, that seeks after them "rashly," or that accepts reports of miracles without an element of critical suspicion. Neither can we accept a "health and wealth" gospel that ignores the realities of unanswered prayer and the suffering of those in need. But Pentecostals also do not want to capitulate to suffering without resistance and faith in a God who can do the impossible through, or even beyond, natural means of healing available to us. They fully expect the mission of the church to be so blessed with such signs of healing and renewal that nonbelieving observers are provoked to ask the Pentecostal question, "What meaneth this?" (Acts 2:12).

Miroslav Volf thus notes a certain overlap between Pentecostal soteriology and the passion for social transformation within liberation theology, because both assume a certain "material" understanding of salvation.[53] Yet, as noted above, Pentecostalism tends also to see salvation as "otherworldly" or oriented toward the final eschatological fulfillment. Efforts at social liberation or reform tend to be viewed as less important than winning people to Christ in preparation for eternity. Lacking is a secular or providential understanding of divine grace in the midst of natural human efforts at healing. It seems that the otherworldliness that characterizes Pentecostal eschatology skews the inherent holism implied by the movement's healing doctrine.

Otherworldliness is typical of an "apocalyptic" eschatology, because apocalypticism gives up any hope for the life of the kingdom to emerge within history. The kingdom must break in miraculously from above to end history,

---

52. Jürgen Moltmann, "A Pentecostal Theology of Life," *Journal of Pentecostal Theology* 9 (October 1996): 4.

53. Miroslav Volf, "Materiality of Salvation: An Investigation into the Soteriologies of Liberation and Pentecostal Theologies," *Journal of Ecumenical Studies* 25 (Summer 1989): 447–67.

which is on a downward slope. "Prophetic" eschatology, on the other hand, is more oriented toward historical fulfillment of God's will in a way that involves human participation on a level more profound and more genuinely human than merely yielding by faith to supernatural interventions "from above." Having said this, we must also point out that apocalypticism has a valuable "critical function" to serve vis-à-vis any illusion that the kingdom of God can be a mere consequence of human actions or political agendas.[54] As Moltmann notes, the kingdom of God cannot "evolve" or emerge from human action any more than the resurrection of Christ evolved out from his crucifixion and death.[55] We are born from above in receiving the new life of the kingdom, not from the will of flesh and blood (John 1:13; 1 Cor. 15:50).

Furthermore, this apocalyptic focus on the ultimate horizon of the kingdom's fulfillment can have a sobering affect on our lives, directing our attention to that which is most important to life as a Christian. It can also give us an "eschatological boldness" to courageously resist oppressive forces in the world with full knowledge that the final triumph of God's kingdom is only a matter of time. The church can have the separation from the world through apocalypticism needed to center devotion in Christ and his kingdom.

Pentecostal eschatology has actually stressed the metaphor of the church as the bride of Christ. As we noted above, "the Bridegroom cometh" is the typically Pentecostal banner under which the church is called to faithfulness. The bride in Revelation is adorned in good works (Rev. 19:8). This metaphor of the church can help us to realize that our ecclesiality or essential nature as the church is not something we can simply take for granted but must renew in covenant faithfulness to God. Escapism is not the only response encouraged by an otherworldly eschatology among Pentecostals. The question, however, is, "How can Pentecostals integrate an otherworldly eschatology into a prophetic one so as to avoid succumbing to fundamentalist escapism and a one-sided otherworldliness?"

Pentecostal scholar Murray W. Dempster reaches for such an integration by viewing Pentecost as the link between Jesus' proclamation of the justice and mercy of the kingdom of God and the redemption proclaimed by the church. He notes, "When couched within the prophetic tradition, the escha-

---

54. Wolfhardt Pannenberg, "Constructive and Critical Functions of Christian Eschatology," *Harvard Theological Review* 76 (April 1984), 123–27.

55. Moltmann, *The Trinity and the Kingdom*, 28.

tological continuity between the 'already' and the 'not yet' kingdom implies that the apocalyptic act at the end of this age will not be one of total *annihilation* of the world but one of total *transformation* of the world."[56]

I reached for a similar integration through the message of the Blumhardts (father and son), nineteenth-century German Pietists, who wedded a divine healing doctrine with a vision of the kingdom of God coming to make all things new in the world, including human social life. They did not see the kingdom of God as either wholly from above or wholly as a result of human effort but as the new life that comes from our full participation in God's redemptive work through the Spirit.[57] Inspired in part by the Blumhardts, Moltmann uses the metaphor of "conversion" to indicate a kingdom that is inaugurated by God but which involves the full participation of the creature created by God.[58] Humanity in all of its capacities created by God is allowed to participate fully in the new life of the kingdom and its ultimate fulfillment when Christ returns.

Part of the difficulty in reaching for such integration is that Pentecostals stress the redemptive work of the Son and the Spirit to the near exclusion of the first article of the Creed, namely, God the Father, Creator of heaven and earth. In Pentecostal preaching, the redemptive and eschatological Spirit transforms creation in the direction of Christ's final triumph but not necessarily in fulfillment of the Spirit's presence in all of creation to reach for renewal. Pentecostals are thus not accustomed to detecting the presence of grace in all of life reaching for liberation and redemption through the Spirit of creation. Thus neglected is the insight that social transformation can be viewed as a legitimate sign of the redemption yet to come in Christ. Also neglected somewhat are gifts of the Spirit through natural talents that function as signs of grace in ways that bear witness to the fulfillment of life in Christ.

In the absence of a creation pneumatology, all that seems available to Pentecostals is a social action that is viewed as an extension of divine healing as a miraculous act of redemption in Christ. For example, Pentecostals in various

---

56. Murray W. Dempster, "Christian Social Concern in Pentecostal Perspective: Reformulating Pentecostal Eschatology," *Journal of Pentecostal Theology* 2 (April 1993): 62.

57. See my *Spirituality and Social Liberation: The Message of the Blumhardts in the Light of Wuerttemberg Pietism* (Metuchen, NJ: Scarecrow, 1991).

58. Jürgen Moltmann, *The Coming of God: Christian Eschatology* (Minneapolis: Fortress, 1996), 22–23.

places have diligently engaged in ministries to drug addicts and others who are destitute in order to bring them into the liberating power of Christ's redemptive work within the context of a loving Christian community. Of course, they have often had great success at this. In fact, Pentecostal communities in Latin America have been so successful as centers of hope and new opportunities for the poor that one Pentecostal scholar could quip that Pentecostals do not *have* a social policy for renewal, they *are* a social policy.[59]

But Pentecostals in general have been less attuned to the social structures and cultural realities that implicitly support poverty and racism. They have been less attuned to the sighs of the Spirit that yearn for these powers to be overthrown so that God's people might recognize more of the divine grace implicit in creation, a grace that is fulfilled, but by no means eclipsed, by redemption and healing through the gospel of Christ. In the meantime, the Pentecostal emphasis on the latter rain of the Spirit to bring redemption to the world will maintain its validity, even if this emphasis is somewhat one-sided.

SPIRIT BAPTISM AS LOVE'S "SECOND CONVERSION"

Spirit baptism as a charismatic renewal and an empowerment for witness tends to function for Pentecostals as a renewal in the experience and power of God's love in our lives so that the fires of hope and faithfulness might burn more brightly. Pentecostals view our experience of God's love in Spirit baptism in lavish terms. They liken it to becoming "God intoxicated." They like to quote the New Testament injunction not to be taken up with strong drink but rather filled with the Spirit (Eph. 5:18; cf. Acts 2:15). This revivalist "high voltage" experience of God can become shallow and fanatical if reduced to nothing more than an emotional release. Here is where sanctifying love as an eschatological gift can play a valuable role in providing a meaningful context for our understanding of religious ecstasy.

The term "ecstasy" refers literally to a state of being outside of or beyond oneself, as a form of "self-transcendence." Hans Urs Balthasar can thus write of an "ecstasy of service" as an "ascent to God being fully possessed by God for His purposes."[60] We do this in relation to God too when we groan with

---

59. A personal remark from Everett Wilson, cited in Douglas Petersen, *Not by Might nor by Power: A Pentecostal Theology of Social Concern in Latin America* (Irvine, CA: Regnum, 1996), 119.

60. Hans Urs Balthasar, *Prayer* (Fort Collins, CO: Ignatius, 1987), 64.

sighs too deep for words in glossolalic utterances. We engage in praise of God in ways that transcend our rational or linguistic abilities. The doctrine of subsequence (Spirit baptism as a charismatic experience subsequent to or distinct from regeneration) can function as a source of renewal in the church if interpreted in the context of an experience of the ecstasy of love as the power to self-transcend and to give abundantly of oneself to God and others.

Spirit baptism fills us with the love of God so that we transcend ourselves and cross boundaries. We find the power to transcend limitations through divine infilling to pour ourselves out for others. In transcending ourselves we are fulfilled, for we have been made for the love of God. God as a self-giving fountain of love poured out abundantly begins to shape us into something similar. Jesus pours out the Spirit so that the Spirit may pour forth in our empowered love for others. We become "Spirit-baptized personalities." Jesus thus says that believing in him will cause a spring of divine life to flow forth from us in abundance. From within those who drink from the Spirit "streams of living water will flow" (John 7:38). Spirit baptism as an experience of empowerment is not just renewed energy to do things for God. It is rather the power of self-transcending, self-giving love. It involves us entirely.

Those filled with the Spirit in Acts burst forth with tongues of praise (Acts 2:4), tongues that also became bridges of empowered ministry in Christ's love to others across linguistic and cultural boundaries. Tongues cannot be turned into a law that governs how Spirit baptism must be received without exception within the actions of a sovereign God. Tongues were the characteristic sign of Spirit baptism for Luke and can be for us, because they symbolize God's people giving of themselves abundantly in a way that transcends limitations and creaturely expectations. In tongues we groan for a liberty in the Spirit that is not yet fulfilled (Rom. 8:26). Russell Spittler is right when he wrote that tongues is "a broken speech for a broken body of Christ till perfection comes."[61] This statement, one of the most significant ever given by a Pentecostal scholar, falls like a bombshell on one-sidedly triumphalistic Pentecostal spiritualities. In this weak groaning of glossolalia, we already gain a foretaste of eschatological transcendence and bridge-crossing as we flow out from ourselves to others. Tongues symbolize this self-transcendence and bridge-crossing.

---

61. Russell P. Spittler, "Glossolalia," *Dictionary of Pentecostal and Charismatic Movements*, ed. S. M. Burgess and G. B. McGee (Grand Rapids: Zondervan, 1988), 341.

Other signs function this way too. In Ephesians 5:18–19, being filled with the Spirit causes us to address each other in psalms, hymns, and spiritual songs. Inspired speech of all types is "speaking the truth in love" (4:15). This empowered "self-transcendence" in ministry and mission begins when we are incorporated into the reconciling community of the church (1 Cor. 12:13) and continues as an actual experience of empowered self-transcendence as we are continuously filled with the Spirit.

I do not want us to lose our emphasis on the *experience* of the baptism in the Holy Spirit as something that Christians should expect in the life of faith at some point during or after their acceptance of Christ as Lord and as an ongoing experience of charismatic enrichment. The experience of the baptism in the Holy Spirit can be a renewal of faith, hope, and love as well as an enhancement of power for mission. It is an enhancement of our conversion to Christ but also a "second conversion" that turns us in Christ's love toward the world in prayer for its renewal and in our participation in God's mission. We groan in the Spirit with sighs too deep for words (glossolalic utterances) for the liberty of the Spirit to come, and we rejoice in signs of the new creation already among us through acts of love and signs of healing. "No eye has seen, no ear has heard, no mind has conceived what God has prepared for those who love him" (1 Cor. 2:9, quoting Isa. 64:4). The Pentecostals ask us to experience a foretaste of that glory in the here and now as a force for renewal in the Christian life and the life of the church. I think we should listen.

SCRIPTURE INDEX

GENESIS

1:1–2 119
1:27–28..............174, 215, 216
1:28......................................217
2:7.......................................109
3:16......................................174
10:18....................................217
11..............................216, 217

EXODUS

3:14..92
6:1–13....................................92
6:7..92
20:2–3....................................92

NUMBERS

11..145

DEUTERONOMY

6:5.......................................259

PSALMS

74:2.....................................200
139.......................................262

ISAIAH

30:27......................................99
30:28......................................99
40:28–31..............................133
61:1–3...........................93, 109
64:4......................................282

JEREMIAH

1:5.......................................141
4:4..98

EZEKIEL

20:2–3....................................92
36:25–27................................93
36:26............................98, 100
37................................88, 200

37:13–14a 93
39:10 48
39:29 93

HOSEA

6:6 259

JOEL

2:28 ....93, 109, 184, 275

AMOS

5:24 133

MATTHEW

3:1–12 ....59, 91
3:1–2 85
3:2–12 ....61, 90
3:2 144
3:8 93
3:11–17 85
3:12 144
3:13–15 141
3:16–17 ....136, 142, 265
3:17 118
3 ....86, 102
4:1–11 118
5 132
5:20 142
6:10 133
6:33 ....106, 132
9:17 132
12:28–29 238
12:28 ....48, 59, 86, 94, 97,
99, 105, 109, 132, 137,
140, 145, 146, 185, 265
13 97
13:31–32 97
13:45–46 133
16:4 151

16:17–19 ....179, 238
18:18 238
18:20 201
20:22–23 101
22:36–40 259
23:23 ....98, 106, 139, 142, 143
23:27 142
25:32 133
28:19 116

MARK

1:15ff 146
10:33 143
16:16 71

LUKE

1:33 123
1:35 ....110, 118, 134, 135,
141, 145
1:41 141
2 142
3:1–17 141
3:16–17 249
3:16 98
3:17 99
3:22 134
4:18 ....94, 96, 99, 106,
135, 136, 148, 265
7:18–19 99
10:17–18 238
12:49–50 101
15 ....142, 160
15:1–2 ....132–133, 142
15:11–32 142
15:11–31 132–133
18:9–14 132
24:49 ....14, 110, 159

JOHN

1:1–18.....................116, 141, 222
1:1–14..............................109, 119
1:1–13.......................................228
1:1–3..119
1:12–13.........................166, 228
1:13 ....95, 99, 109, 278
1:14 ....110, 264
1:33 249
3:1–8...88
3:5 ....71, 95, 99
3:16–21 222
3:16 ....109, 124, 259, 261
3:22–30 141
3:34 118
6:44 166
7:38 281
10:10 ....109, 141
11:25–26 ....109, 141
14:4 201
14:11 163
14:20 ....163, 166, 193
15 ....202, 223
17:4 104
17:15–16 144
17:17–19 222
17:17–18 141
17:17 143
17:18 143
17:20–23 107
17:21 ....157, 163, 164, 166,
                    212, 222
20:22 ....100, 109, 110, 141,
                    145, 201

ACTS

1 101
1:2–8............................58, 61, 90
1:3–8..............................15, 161
1:3–6...91

1:3 ....79, 85, 91, 100
1:5–8...............................107, 108
1:5 ....68, 249
1:6–7..161
1:6..85
1:8 ....14, 69, 75, 79, 93,
                    100, 101, 113, 147,
                    161, 201, 204, 211
2 ....102, 107, 177, 187,
                    201, 209, 214, 215
2:1–4...86
2:3 144
2:4ff. 172
2:4–11 166
2:4–5..100
2:4 ....75, 100, 101, 159, 203,
                    212, 236, 264, 281
2:5 218
2:10 124
2:12 ....76, 277
2:13 14
2:15 280
2:17ff.......................................218
2:17–21 .....58, 86, 101, 106, 166,
                    191, 209
2:17–18................................236
2:17 ....93, 145, 220
2:18–19 166
2:19–21 86
2:27 142
2:33 116
2:37–47 87
2:38 ....15, 72, 73, 95
2:39 ....64, 206
2:42–43 236
2:42 ....79, 163, 230, 239,
                    157–158
2:43 238
2:44–47 157–158

3:1–10 239
3:7–8 147
4:12 116
4:29–31 145
4:29–30 150
4:31 ....232, 236
5:16 239
5:32 93
8 ....68, 72, 152
8:4–8 147
8:6 238
8:14–17 166
9:4 193
9:17 167
10 222
10:15 144
10:18 144
10:37–38 161
10:38–39 100
10:38 ....76, 116, 145, 146,
150, 238
10:44–46 144
10:46 ....144, 212, 218
11–15 218
11:16–17 107
11:18 ....65, 68, 100, 103
11:28 147
13:11–12 147
14:8–13 147
15 ....107, 220
15:8–9 79
15:9 ....15, 100, 144, 222
16:9, 18 147
17 217
17:24–28 119
17:24–27 217
17:24 217
17:25 263
17:26–27 188
17:27 217

17:28 ....104, 172, 173, 187
19:5–6 73
19:11–12 147
20:28 200
21:8–12 147
22:16 71

ROMANS

1–2 130
1:4 ....46, 109, 118, 134, 136,
142, 143, 249
1:24–28 126
1:26–28 143
1:26–27 46,130
3:23 131
4:21–25 138
4:25 ....46, 126, 130, 136,
142, 143
5:5 ....15, 17, 18, 60, 63, 81,
116, 117, 124, 160, 212,
243, 257, 259, 260, 262
5:8 265
6:3–4 249
6:3 70
6:4 ....70, 73
6:11 250
7:14–8:4 138
8:3 138
8:11 ....142, 185, 186
8:14–25 103
8:15–16 166
8:18–25 ....102, 105
8:21 147
8:22–26 136
8:22–23 119
8:22 ....96, 143
8:23 166
8:26 ....49,125, 151, 167, 169,
201, 204, 281
8:29 166

8:32 ....126, 143
8:38–39 260
11 200
11:25–32 201
11:33 264
11:36 117
12:1–3 172
12:1–2 203
12:6 ....166, 243
13:11 269
14:17 ....91, 97, 109, 139,
 140, 252

1 CORINTHIANS

1–3 201
1:7 ....202, 221
1:12 201
2:4–5 ....96, 137, 148, 151
2:4 55
2:9 ....269, 282
2:10 124
3:1–15 236
3:1–4 223
3:5–15 236
3:5 236
3:11–15 223
3:11 ....201, 203, 230
3:16 203
3:17 203
3:21 246
4:14 237
4:20 55
5 237
6:11 ....136, 141, 143
7:35 237
8:1 151
9:12, 18 237
11:1–16 220
12–14 274
12 202

12:1–3 ....108, 123
12:4–6 ....211, 212
12:11 ....242, 243
12:13 ....15, 16, 57, 73, 87, 103,
 110, 113 167, 201, 202,
 203, 211, 282
12:17 ....176, 221
13 ....55, 151
13:1–3 243
13:6 ....223, 237
13:12 ....60, 193, 261
13:13 259
14:3 172
14:4 166
14:9–10 238
14:18 166
14:27–28 237
14:29–32 235
14:32 237
14:34–35 219
14:36–38 ....234, 237
14:37 244
15:3–4 181
15:20–28 ....123, 144, 146, 258
15:22–26 103
15:28 ....103, 117, 204, 263
15:42 95
15:44 186
15:45 ....100, 110, 136, 201
15:50 ....95, 278
15:51–54 186

2 CORINTHIANS

3:17 123
3:18 ....83, 223
4:7 141
5:14–15 60
8:8–10 237
12 148
13:10 237

GALATIANS

1	218, 237
1:6–9	108
2	218, 237
2:6–10	181
2:16	137
2:20	143, 175, 203, 268
3:1–5	108, 113, 137
3:2	108, 184
3:5	137, 151, 268
3:8	137
3:13–14	109
3:14	137
3:28	220
4:19	223, 265
5:1–5	148
5:5	96, 138
5:6	139
6:2	143
6:15	108, 138, 184

EPHESIANS

1:3–14	136
1:3	62, 87, 113, 136, 153, 225
1:4–14	166
1:4	200
1:5–6	136
1:12	87
1:13–14	48, 136, 201
2:20–22	230
2:20	203
3:14–15	200
3:14	166
3:15	209
3:17–18	260
3:18–19	259
3:20	254
4:3–6	212
4:4–6	211
4:4	211
4:5	73, 181, 212, 251
4:7–16	160
4:7–10	102, 159
4:8	243
4:10	117
4:11–16	236
4:13	168, 212, 265
4:15–16	232, 235
4:15	151, 232, 236, 282
4:16	176
5	202
5:18–19	159, 254, 282
5:18	14, 167, 280
5:21	232, 234, 235
5:25–28	202

PHILIPPIANS

1:17–18	222
2:8	143
4:12–13	148

COLOSSIANS

1:9	114, 115
1:13	260
1:15–16	104, 119
1:17	104
2:9	203
2:12	70, 73
2:15	146

1 THESSALONIANS

2:7	237
4:17	274

2 THESSALONIANS

3:9	237

1 TIMOTHY

2:12	220
3:15	136

2 TIMOTHY

1:6 242
3:15–16 ....230, 244

PHILEMON

8 237
9 237

HEBREWS

1:1–3 19
2:14–15 190
2:14 ....138, 146
4 201
6:5 ....48, 88, 96, 147
7:16 ....190, 249
9:14 ....118, 126, 136, 143,
                          144, 188, 249
12:1–3 201
12:2 190
13:17 ....232, 233, 234, 235

1 PETER

1:1–2 223
1:2 ....80, 143, 166, 200
1:23 228
2:5 203
3:21 71

1 JOHN

4:8 261
4:16 261
4:20 268

REVELATION

1–3 230
1:5–6 162
1:5 141
1:12–13 204
2:5 223
3:20 ....193, 252
7:9 ....210, 226
7:10 162
12:11 162
12:12 89
19 202
19:7–8 166
19:8 ....270, 278
19:13 46
20 272
21:1–5 106
21:1–4 166
21:3 ....103, 117, 204
21:5 ....94, 103

SUBJECT INDEX

anthropology, 168–78
baptism, 61, 64–65, 66–68, 70–
 75, 85–88, 98, 248–52
Christ
 anointed, 76, 85
 deity, 107–12
 Spirit baptizer, 85, 94, 100,
  107, 258
church, 17–18, 62–63, 155–256
 apostolicity, 229–41
 body of Christ, 201–3
 catholicity, 224–29
 dialectical witness, 190–99
 historical/eschatological, 197–
  99, 209–10
 holiness, 222–24
 Israel, 200–201
 koinonia, 157–68
 local/universal, 209–10
 marks, 204–56
 mission, 208, 271
 necessity of, 155–56
 people of God, 200–201

 preaching, 244–47
 temple of the Spirit, 203–4
 unity, 201–3, 211–22
 visible/invisible, 198–99
creation, 75, 96–97, 109, 119,
 168–78, 279–80
ecumenical, 25, 50, 206, 211–22,
 224–29, 251–52
 Anglican-Catholic, 248
 Catholic-Lutheran, 255
 Pentecostal-Reformed, 149, 161
 Pentecostal-Roman Catholic,
  163–64, 255
 World Council of Churches,
  149 fn.84, 151–52, 164–
  65, 199 fn.91, 230, 233,
  239–40
 See *pluralism*
eschatology, 38–49, 85–88, 91–
 107, 269–80
Father, God the, 119, 279–80
holiness, 222–24
justification, 129–40

kingdom of God, 91–107
law, 98, 104–5, 137–39
Lord's Supper, 251–56
love, 18, 40–41, 45–46, 55–56, 60,
  62–63, 81–82, 96, 149, 151,
  160, 223, 243, 257–82
  faith and love, 265–69
  hope and love, 269–80
  importance, 259–61
  theology of, 261–65
miracles, 96, 146–53
mission, 14, 87, 113, 128, 156, 158,
  160, 208, 264, 271
narrative theology, 49–56
Oneness Pentecostals, 20–22, 114,
  229–30, 251
Pentecostalism, diversity of, 33–38
pluralism, 178–90
preaching, 244–47
revivalism, 28–30
sacrament, 65, 71, 247–56
sanctification, 28–33, 40–41, 79–84,
  140–44
Scripture, 244–47
social concern, 219–21, 278–80
Spirit baptism
  centrality of, 20–28
  charismatic, 14, 17, 23, 26, 28, 29,
    57–60, 62, 75–85, 105, 145–
    53
  clothing, 14, 18, 110, 159

empowerment, 14, 69, 75–85,
  101, 145–53, 280
eschatological, 17–18, 38–49, 85–
  88, 91–107, 269–80
experiential, 14, 16
fluid, 14, 87
love, 18, 40–41, 55–56, 60, 81–
  82, 104–5
Luke, 15, 24, 26, 29, 57–60, 67,
  69, 87, 93, 153, 257
missiological, 14, 87, 113, 128,
  156, 158, 160, 208, 264, 271
Paul, 15, 29, 57–60, 67, 84, 87
sacramental, 62, 70–75
sanctification, 28–33, 40–41, 79–
  84, 86, 100, 140–44
soteriological, 15, 17–18, 57–60,
  62–72, 80, 84, 93, 103, 129–
  40
Trinitarian, 90–91, 113–29, 258,
  260
speaking in tongues, 35–37, 83, 212–
  18, 257, 271, 280–81
spiritual gifts, 77, 146–53, 202, 229–
  44
suffering, 56–57, 125–27, 188–89
theology
  narrative, 49–57
  systematic, 53–54
Trinity, 90–91, 113–29, 229–30,
  258, 260

AUTHOR INDEX

Albrecht, Daniel E., 247
Alvarez, Miquel, 21
Anderson, Allan, 21, 51
Anderson, Gordon, 77 fn.36, 275 fn.45
Aquinas, Thomas, 73, 265
Arteaga, William T. de, 253–54
Athanasius, 94
Augustine, 111, 181, 196, 238, 266
Aulen, Gustaf, 146

Badcock, Gary B., 55
Baer, Richard, 254
Bahktin, Mikhail, 213
Balthasar, Hans Urs, 127, 280
Barth, Karl, 49, 53, 65–67, 69–70, 119–121, 126–27, 135, 196, 211–12, 245–46, 259, 261 fn.3, 262–63, 268 fn.26
Basil, St., 249
Bauckham, Richard, 180
Bell, E. N., 81

Berkhof, Hendrikus, 65, 69, 129
Berkouwer, G. C., 62, 135, 247
Blaser, K., 105
Blumhardt, Johann and Christoph, 41–42, 45, 76, 195–96, 279
Bonhoeffer, Dietrich, 169, 170 fn.28, 196, 223
Bonino, Jose Miguez, 215–16
Brown, Dan, 179
Brueggemann, Walter, 174, 216
Bruner, Dale, 43, 113
Brunner, Emil, 55, 150, 246, 261–62, 272
Buber, Martin, 168

Calvin, John, 152, 206, 246, 247
Camery-Hoggatt, Jerry, 53, 110 fn.25
Certeau, Michael de, 213
Chan, Simon, 20–21, 23–24, 26, 52, 74–75, 156, 253
Cheung, Tak-Ming, 47
Chia, Anita, 82 fn.50

Childs, Brevard, 133, 134 fn.70
Cho, Youngmo, 58
Chrysostum, St. John, 252
Clifton, Jack Shane, 23
Congar, Yves, 209
Cosgrove, Charles, 108
Cox, Harvey, 25, 33, 44 fn.59, 53, 194, 196, 254
Cross, Terry, 24–25
Cullmann, Oscar, 25, 66, 93, 179 fn.41, 181, 213, 238
Cyril of Jerusalem, 225

Dabney, Lyle, 25, 48, 130
Dantine, Wilhelm, 136
Darby, John Nelson, 273
Davies, J. G., 214, 215 fn.116
Dayton, Donald W., 25, 31, 38–40, 208, 272
Del Colle, Ralph, 25, 155, 194, 212 fn.109
Dempster, Murray W., 33, 177, 278–79
Dieter, Melvin, 30 fn.27
Dionson, Narciso C., 47–48
Driver, Tom F., 248, 252–53, 255
Dunn, James, 29, 62, 67–70, 73, 90, 98 fn.13, 101
Durham, William, 28

Eller, Vernard, 196 fn.80
Ervin, H. M., 23, 62, 167 fn.22, 23,
Ewart, Frank, 82, 115

Faupel, D. William, 28 fn.20, 38–40
Fee, Gordon, 24, 246
Finger, Thomas, 158, 205 fn.100
Fletcher, John, 31
Flower, Joseph Roswell, 36–37
Frei, Hans, 52

Frodsham, Stanley, 82, 274 fn.39
Fuchs, Lorelei, 160, 192
Fudge, Thomas, 22, 115 fn.30
Fung, Ronald, 137

Gelpi, Donald L., 47–48, 75
Gregory of Nyssa, 89, 95
Grenz, Stanley, 104

Hagner, Donald, 86
Hanson, Paul, 92
Harink, Douglas, 131
Hart, Larry, 48 fn.69
Hayford, Jack, 37
Hezmalhalch, T., 219
Hick, John, 182–89
Hickey, Marilyn, 274 fn.40
Hiers, Richard H., 238 fn.145
Hocken, Peter, 46–47
Hodgson, Peter C., 197
Hollenweger, Walter J., 25, 27–28, 34, 49–51, 55–56, 271 fn.32, 276
Hunter, Harold, 23, 62
Hutchins, J. W., 270
Hütter, Reinhard, 208

Irenaeus, 155
Irvin, Dale T., 25, 212–13
Ives, Jeremy, 128 fn.56

Jacobsen, Douglas, 34
Jenson, Robert, 117–18, 128 fn.128, 130
Jung, G. C., 170, 172
Jüngel, Eberhard, 127

Kärkkäinen, Veli-Matti, 19, 24, 35 fn.38, 139, 234, 236
Käsemann, Ernst, 102, 131, 134

Kasper, Walter, 94, 146–47, 164, 226
Kelsey, Morton, 75
Kitamori, Kazoh, 126–27
Klaus, Byron D., 33
Koenig, John, 243
Küng, Hans, 192–93, 197, 202, 205, 210, 213, 228, 233–36, 237 fn.144, 238–40
Kutter, Hermann, 196

Ladd, George Eldon, 91, 92 fn.2, 97
LaHaye, Tim, 274 fn.41, 43
Land, Steven J., 23–24, 41–49
Lanne, Emmanuel, 61
Larbi, E. Kingsley, 82
Lasch, Christopher, 158
Lederle, Henry, 21, 35 fn.38, 37, 78 fn.39
Lee, Paul D., 35
Lee, Song-Whan, 21
Lim, David, 84, 242
Lindbeck, George, 53–54
Lloyd-Jones, Martyn, 78
Lochman, Jan M., 97, 156, 189–90, 199
Loisy, Alfred, 178
Luther, Martin, 137, 173, 261, 265–68

Macchia, Frank D., 42 fn.54, 130 fn.58, 60, 62, 188 fn.62
Marshall, I. Howard, 180
Martin, David, 224
Mason, C. H., 270
McDonnell, Kilian, 62, 72–73, 109
McDougall, Joy Ann, 207, 221
McGrath, Allister, 133
Menzies, Glen, 101 fn.16, 275 fn.45

Menzies, Robert, 15–16, 23–24, 26, 29, 57–59, 62, 76, 77 fn.38, 84
Moltmann, Jürgen, 49, 76–77, 95–96, 100, 101 fn.15, 104, 112, 117, 120–22, 125, 131, 161, 188, 194, 196, 197 fn.84, 205, 246, 251, 263, 271, 277–79
Montague, George, 62, 72–73
Moule, C. F. D., 180

Neve, Lloyd, 99
Newbigin, Leslie, 156
Niebuhr, H. Richard, 104
Nietzsche, Friedrich, 30, 215
Nolland, John, 86 fn.56
Nygren, Anders, 265–66

O'Conner, Elizabeth, 243 fn.157

Palma, Anthony, 77
Pannenberg, Wolfhart, 30, 97 fn.11, 109–11, 118, 121–25, 141, 246, 278
Pelikan, Jaroslav, 126, 211
Perdue, Leo, 53
Peterson, Douglas, 33, 280 fn.59
Pinnock, Clark, 25, 254–55
Plummer, Alfred, 167

Ragaz, Leonard, 195–96
Rahner, Karl, 65 fn.4,
Reed, David, 115, 116 fn.32
Ridderbos, Hermann, 178, 179 fn.42,
Robeck, Cecil M., 35 fn.40, 81 fn.43, 220–21
Robertson, A. T., 167
Rodner, E., 212 fn.109
Rybarczyk, Edmund, 24, 139 fn.79

Sandeen, Ernst, 273
Sanders, E. P.,183
Schleiermacher, Friedrich, 126–27
Schmaus, Michael, 233
Schmidt, Hans Heinrich, 133
Schmidt, K. L., 200 fn.92
Sepulveda, Juan, 24
Seymour, William, 35, 80–81, 83, 219, 270, 276
Sheppard, Gerald T., 52, 271, 274–75
Simpson, A. B., 273, 274 fn.38
Solivan, Samuel, 41–42
Soelle, Dorothea, 241
Spittler, Russell P., 24, 281
Stagaman, David, 240
Staples, Peter, 224 fn.124
Stark, Rodney, 157–58
Storr, Anthony, 171
Stronstad, Roger, 15–16, 23–24, 26, 29, 57–59, 62, 76, 79, 84
Sullivan, Francis, 74
Sullivan, Harry Stack, 172

Thayer, J. H., 167
Thomas, John Christopher, 220 fn.120
Tillich, Paul, 54, 195–96, 198–99
Toon, Peter, 140
Trotter, Will, 81, 82 fn.47

Tugwell, Simon, 83
Turner, Max, 235
Tyra, Gary, 104 fn.20

Van der Leeuw, G., 247 fn.165
Vischer, Lukas, 193
Volf, Miroslav, 25, 162, 164, 169 fn.27, 173, 193, 202, 206, 209, 225, 234–35, 277

Wacker, Grant, 30 fn.26, 32
Wainwright, Geoffrey, 54, 65 fn.3, 72 fn.25, 128, 159–60, 248, 250–51, 252 fn.183
Welker, Michael, 25, 32 fn.32, 126, 177, 242
Wesley, John, 30–31, 49
Wilkerson, David, 274 fn.42
Williams, E. S., 139
Williams, J. Rodman, 37
Williams, Robert C. 197
Wood, Laurence, 31

Yong, Amos, 24, 118, 127–28, 205 fn.95, 208 fn.102, 221
Yun, Koo Dong, 21, 24

Zinzendorf, Ludwig Count von, 188
Zizioulas, John D., 177

We want to hear from you. Please send your comments about this book to us in care of zreview@zondervan.com. Thank you.

ZONDERVAN™

GRAND RAPIDS, MICHIGAN 49530 USA

ZONDERVAN.COM/
AUTHORTRACKER

CPSIA information can be obtained at www.ICGtesting.com
Printed in the USA
LVOW07s2156291013

359062LV00003B/8/P